Unequal Freedom

Unequal Freedom

*How Race and Gender
Shaped American Citizenship
and Labor*

••

Evelyn Nakano Glenn

HARVARD UNIVERSITY PRESS
Cambridge, Massachusetts
London, England

Copyright © 2002 by the President and Fellows of Harvard College
All rights reserved
Printed in the United States of America

First Harvard University Press paperback edition, 2004

Library of Congress Cataloging-in-Publication Data

Glenn, Evelyn Nakano.
    Unequal freedom : how race and gender shaped American citizenship and
labor / Evelyn Nakano Glenn.
        p. cm.
    Includes bibliographical references and index.
    ISBN 0-674-00732-8 (cloth)
    ISBN 0-674-01372-7 (pbk.)
    1. Alien labor—United States—History.   2. Women alien labor—United
States—History.   3. Minorities—Employment—United States—History.
4. Citizenship—United States—History.   5. Immigrants—Economic
conditions—United States.   6. Immigrants—Social conditions—United
States.   I. Title: How race and gender shaped American citizenship and
labor.   II. Title.

HD8081 .A5 G57 2002
323.6′0973—dc21   2002020531

For my family
Gary, Sara, Antonia, and Patrick

Contents

Acknowledgments

The seeds of this book were planted many years ago, and since then roots and branches have been nourished by many friends and colleagues. An earlier article-length incarnation was read and given encouragement by Barbara Laslett, Ann Orloff, Sonya Rose, Joey Sprague, and members of the Women and Work Research Group: Chris Bose, Nancy Breen, Myra Ferree, Susan Lehrer, Fran Rothstein, Natalie Sokoloff, and Carole Turbin. For reading and providing wise advice on the manuscript, I am grateful to Al Camarillo, David Hernandez, Priya Kandaswamy, Elaine Kim, Waldo Martin, Fran Rothstein, Eileen Tamura, Carole Turbin, and Eric Yamamoto. The two anonymous readers for Harvard University Press as well as my editor, Kathleen McDermott, offered detailed feedback that pushed me to improve the book. I am also grateful to Myra Ferree, Beth Hess, and Judith Lorber for commissioning an article that led me to develop the conceptual framework described in Chapter 2. Michael Omi's thinking on racial formation and his support for my work have been very helpful as have been the writings of Elsa Barkley Brown on African American women in the South. Joyce Chinen informed me about the Romanzo Adams papers housed at the University of Hawaii–Manoa. Over the years she and Kiyoshi Ikeda made it possible for me to make several visits to Hawaii to do research and present my work to scholars familiar with the Hawaiian context.

I appreciated having opportunities to present papers related to this book at meetings of the American Sociological Association, the Society for the Study of Social Problems, and the Social Science History Association, at the University of California Council on Women's Programs conference on Feminist Futures, and at the Southern Conference on Women's History. I also received perceptive feedback from audiences and colleagues at colloquia at the Universities of Wisconsin, Michigan, California, Santa Cruz, and California, Berkeley; the Claremont Colleges; and the University of Bielefeld, Germany. The wonderful graduate students in the doctoral program in Comparative Ethnic Studies at Berkeley have pushed me to broaden my perspectives, particularly to delve more deeply into the burgeoning scholarship in Chicano/Latino studies. Students in two of my seminars actually asked me to assign them portions of the manuscript; their interest and enthusiasm buoyed my spirits.

A Humanities Research Fellowship from the University of California, Berkeley, gave me time to accomplish a great deal of research and writing during 1998–99. Several graduate students provided invaluable research assistance on this project: Rhacel Parrenas, Amalia Cabezas, and Wesley Ueunten. A Chancellor's Research Initiative Grant provided research funds for travel to libraries and archives.

Most of all I want to express love and gratitude to my life partner, Gary Glenn, who has read, critiqued, and proofread the entire manuscript several times over. He has been unfailingly enthusiastic and supportive. He has also helped me clarify my ideas and arguments. His passion for social justice has been a continuing source of inspiration.

Unequal Freedom

Introduction

AFTER MORE THAN two centuries of struggle to realize its professed principles of universal equality, the United States still faces continuing racial, gender, and class inequality. Inequality remains a source of great anguish and acrimony over its causes and deep conflict over what can and should be done to change it. In a society that proclaims freedom, individualism, and unlimited mobility, the persistence of rampant inequality along ascriptive lines of race and gender seems to be a contradiction. But is it?

In this book I examine two major structures through which unequal race and gender relations have been shaped and contested in the United States. *Citizenship* has been used to draw boundaries between those who are included as members of the community and entitled to respect, protection, and rights and those who are excluded and thus not entitled to recognition and rights. *Labor* places people in the economic order, affecting access to goods and services, level of autonomy, standard of living, and quality of life. Both have been constituted in ways that privilege white men and give them power over racialized minorities and women. Simultaneously, citizenship and labor have been arenas in which groups have contested their exclusion, oppression, and exploitation.

Citizenship and labor have been closely linked throughout American history. The founders of the nation set up a government based on prin-

1

ciples of control by independent (white male) producers who would participate in governance and enjoy freedom. Citizenship status (recognition as a full adult citizen) was tied to labor status (position as a free independent producer). Conversely, the lack of citizenship rights limited the ability of some groups to form unions, compete for jobs, and attain education and training for higher-level positions. Rhetorically, the concepts of liberal citizenship and free labor developed and evolved in tandem and in response to political, economic, and social transformations over the course of the nineteenth and early twentieth centuries. The two were brought together in the widely held ideal of the "worker citizen," which carried the twin attributes of whiteness and masculinity. Notions of which groups had the intellectual and emotional capacities to do conceptual work were similar to notions of which groups had the rational, self-governing capacity required for citizenship. Therefore, labor and citizenship are intertwined institutional arenas in which race and gender relations, meanings, and identities have been both constituted and contested.

To bring labor and citizenship into the same frame, one must look at practices at the local level. Labor markets are necessarily localized within a geographically limited area, roughly the distance a person can travel to work on a daily basis. Treating citizenship as localized is a departure from the way it usually has been viewed. We normally think of citizenship as being determined by the U.S. Constitution, federal and state statutes, and court rulings. However, even if these formal documents and rulings define boundaries and rights, they are often interpreted and enforced (or not enforced) by individual actors operating at the local level. In some cases the actors are state, county, or municipal officials, for example a welfare department social worker ruling on the eligibility of a black single mother for benefits. In other cases they are "private citizens," for example a movie theater owner deciding whether or not to allow Mexican Americans to sit on the main floor. It is these kinds of localized, often face-to-face practices that determine whether people have or don't have substantive as opposed to purely formal rights of citizens. When I say that individual actors interpret and enforce boundaries, I don't mean that they do so on the basis of their own idiosyncratic ideas; usually they are working within rules and social practices that are widely shared within the local community or region.[1]

The uncovering of these local rules and practices with respect to citizenship and labor is one of the aims of this book.

The period from Reconstruction through the Progressive Era, roughly 1870–1930, was one of considerable ferment in meanings of citizenship and labor and in race, gender, and class relations owing to the abolition of slavery, industrialization, urbanization, massive immigration from southern and eastern Europe, and imperialist expansion into Latin America, the Caribbean, and the Philippines. These upheavals led to social boundaries of all sorts being challenged and renegotiated. Ideologies and conceptions of race and sex difference also changed, as biological classification and evolutionary theory were harnessed to explain human variation and to rank groups hierarchically. Humankind was categorized into inferior and superior races, inferior and superior genders. Gender and race differences were interpreted similarly, so that skull size, physiognomy, hormones, and other physical attributes were seen as markers of distinct psychological and characterological traits of women and people of color. According to Nancy Stepan, through analogous thinking in science, "lower races represented the 'female' types of the human species and females the 'lower race' of gender."[2]

Within this historical period, I examine relations between dominant and subordinate groups in three regions: the South, the Southwest, and Hawaii. Each of these areas contained a substantial nonwhite population group: African Americans in the South, Mexican Americans in the Southwest, and Asian Americans in Hawaii. This regional approach enables me to make certain comparative statements about how U.S. citizenship and labor systems affected these three groups and how the groups struggled against exclusion and oppression. The three regions are also comparable in the roles they played in building the national economy. They supplied agricultural products and raw materials to more industrialized regions of the country, and these basic industries employed large masses of immigrant and racialized labor. All three regions developed coercive labor systems that relied on racialized structures of control, and in all three, struggles over labor and citizenship rights were dominant issues that shaped relations among white and nonwhite groups.

The past two decades have witnessed the emergence of a significant

body of literature based on meticulous primary research that documents the experiences of blacks in various cities and states in the South
during Reconstruction and the Jim Crow era, and of Mexicans in the
Southwest and Japanese in Hawaii during approximately the same period. Much of this research has focused on women or gender, and many
scholars have sought to uncover activism, community building, and
other forms of agency on the part of people of color. Now that the literature has reached a critical mass, the time is ripe for synthesis that allows us to draw a larger picture than is possible with localized studies,
to capture variability as well as overall trends, and to refine our theories
of race and gender inequality.

The issue of gender is integral to all aspects of my approach. Although many recent regional histories of race relations, labor histories,
and studies of citizenship have "included gender," they have usually
done so by having a separate chapter on women. Many other books discuss groups in global terms, for example whites and blacks, without
specifying that "whites" really refers to white men and "blacks" really
refers to black men, or that "women" really refers to "white women."
In this book, because I have had to rely on sources such as government
agency reports and secondary accounts in which gender is not specified, it has not always been possible to avoid this distortion. Nonetheless, I have tried to be as specific as possible in talking about, for example, Anglo men, Anglo women, Mexican men, and Mexican women.

This book is organized as follows: The first three chapters set out a
historical and conceptual framework for each of the major nodes of this
study, race and gender, citizenship, and labor. In Chapter 1 I offer a
conceptual approach that brings race and gender into a common analytic frame so they can be studied together. In Chapter 2 I examine the
roots of American citizenship as a white masculine domain that excluded women and racialized "others." In Chapter 3 I trace the rise of
industrial capitalism and the shift from small farming and independent
artisanry to concentrated property and a wage labor system over the
course of the nineteenth century, a history that was closely intertwined
with that of citizenship. Chapters 4, 5, and 6 are the three regional case
studies. Although each region has unique aspects that are brought out
in detail, the chapters are organized around certain common topics so
as to facilitate comparisons across the regions. In the final chapter I
draw connections between national policies and local practices and

compare practices among the three regions. I also identify points of slippage between national and local and within the local that create opportunities for maneuvering and negotiation, and thus for significant agency on the part of both dominant and subordinate groups.

OF ALL WEALTHY countries in the world, the United States is the only one to have substantially relied, for its economic development, on the labor of peoples from all three nonwhite areas of the globe: Africa, Latin America, and Asia. Thus a central feature of the U.S. economy has been its reliance on racialized and gendered systems of control, including coercion. Racialization in the labor market has been buttressed by a system of citizenship designed to reinforce the control of employers and to constrain the mobility of workers. Although I do not, for the most part, explicitly draw parallels between the historical development of race and gender inequality and present-day conditions, I believe that many of the deep tensions within our contemporary society can be traced directly to the period covered in this book. I hope that my comparative analysis of the three regions—and the three major racialized groups—will shed light on the historical development of the inequality that is so evident in twenty-first-century America.

· 1 ·

Integrating Race
and Gender

To EXAMINE HOW labor and citizenship constitute—and are constituted by—race and gender, we must conceptualize race and gender as interacting, interlocking structures and then consider how they are incorporated into and shaped by various social institutions.[1] Thus the first challenge is to bring race and gender within the same analytic plane.

In the past, gender and race have constituted separate fields of scholarly inquiry. By studying each in isolation, however, these fields have marginalized major segments of the communities they claimed to represent. In studies of "race," men of color stood as the universal racial subject, while in studies of "gender," white women were positioned as the universal gendered subject. Women of color were left out of both narratives, rendered invisible both as racial and as gendered subjects.[2]

In the 1980s women of color began to address their omission through detailed historical and ethnographic studies of African American, Latina, and Asian American women in relation to work, family, and community.[3] These scholars not only uncovered overlooked dimensions of experience, they also exposed the flaws in theorizing from a narrow social base. For example, explanations of gender inequality based on middle-class white women's experience focused on women's encapsulation in the domestic sphere and economic dependence on men. These concepts by and large did not apply to black women, who historically had to work outside the home.

6

Initial attempts to bring race into the same frame as gender treated the two as independent axes. The bracketing of gender was in some sense deliberate because one concern of early feminism was to uncover commonalities that could unite women politically. However, if we begin with gender separated out, we have to "add" race in order to account for the situation of women of color. This leads to an additive model in which women of color are described as suffering from "double" jeopardy (or "triple" oppression if class is included). Women scholars of color expressed dissatisfaction with this model. African American, Latina, Asian American, and Native American women, they said, did not experience race and gender as separate or additive, but as simultaneous and linked. They offered concepts such as "intersectionality," "multiple consciousness," "interlocking systems of oppression," and "racialized gender" to express this simultaneity.[4] Yet, despite increased recognition of the interconnectedness of gender and race, race remained undertheorized. In the absence of a "theory" of race comparable to a "theory" of gender, a comprehensive theory of both has proven elusive. Especially needed is a theory that neither subordinates race and gender to some broader (presumably more primary) set of relations such as class nor substantially flattens the complexity of these concepts.[5] Building on the valuable work of such scholars as Tessie Liu, Evelyn Brooks Higginbotham, Amy Kaminsky, and Ann Stoler, I argue that a synthesis of social constructionist streams within critical race and feminist studies offers a framework for integrated analysis.[6] Social constructionism provides a common vocabulary and set of concepts with which to look at how gender and race are mutually constituted—that is, at the ways in which gender is racialized and race is gendered.

Gender

Social constructionist theory has had somewhat different trajectories with respect to gender and to race. In both fields social constructionism arose as an alternative to biological and essentialist conceptions that rendered gender and race static and ahistorical, but it achieved centrality earlier and has been elaborated in greater detail in feminist scholarship on women and gender than in race studies. This is so even though—or perhaps because—gender seems to be rooted more firmly than race in biology: in bodies, reproduction, and sexuality. Indeed, *away from sex* [handwritten annotation in left margin]

feminist scholars adopted the term "gender" precisely to free our thinking from the constrictions of naturalness and biological inevitability attached to the concept of sex. In the mid-1970s Gayle Rubin proposed the term "sex-gender system" to capture the idea of societal arrangements by which biological sexuality was transformed into socially significant gender.[7]

Since then, gender has emerged as the closest thing we have to a unifying concept in feminist studies, cutting across the various disciplines and theoretical schools that make up the field. Many feminist historians and sociologists use gender as an analytic concept to refer to socially created meanings, relationships, and identities organized around reproductive differences.[8] Others focus on gender as a social status and organizing principle of social institutions detached from and going far beyond reproductive differences,[9] and still others focus on gender as a product of everyday social practice.[10] The concept of gender thus provides an overarching framework from which to view historical, cultural, and situational variability in definitions of womanhood and manhood, in meanings of masculinity and femininity, in relationships between men and women, and in their relative power and political status. If one accepts gender as variable, then one must acknowledge that it is never fixed but is continually constituted and reconstituted.

By loosening the connection to the body, the notion of socially constructed gender freed us from thinking of sex/gender as solely, or even primarily, a characteristic of individuals. By examining gender as a constitutive feature and organizing principle of collectivities, social institutions, historical processes, and social practices, feminist scholars have shown that major areas of life, including sexuality, family, education, economy, and state, are shot through with conflicting interests and hierarchies of power and privilege along gender lines. As an organizing principle, gender involves both cultural meanings and material relations. That is, gender is constituted simultaneously through deployment of gendered rhetoric, symbols, and images and through allocation of resources along gender lines. Thus an adequate account of any particular phenomenon from the perspective of gender requires looking at both representation and material arrangements. For example, understanding the persistent gender gap in wages involves analyzing cultural evaluations of gendered work, such as caring, and gendered meanings of concepts, such as "skill," as well as divisions of labor in the home, occupational segregation, and labor market stratification. ex *material +* *cultural meanings*

Recent theoretical work is moving toward imploding the distinction between sex and gender. The distinction assumes the prior existence of "something real" out of which social relationships and cultural meanings are elaborated. Poststructuralist feminist critics have problematized the distinction by pointing out that sex and sexual meanings are themselves culturally constructed. The sociologist Judith Lorber carefully unpacks three concepts and shows that they are all socially constructed: biological sex, which refers to either genetic or morphological characteristics; sexuality, which refers to desire and orientation; and gender, which refers to social status and identity. One result of this kind of work is to undermine categoricalism, the idea that there are "really" two sexes or two genders or two sexual orientations. At present, the conceptual distinctions among sex, sexuality, and gender are still being debated, and new work on the body is revealing the intertwining and complexity of these concepts.[11]

Race

Scholars have been slower to abandon the idea of race as rooted in biological markers, even though they recognize that social attitudes and arrangements, not biology, maintain white dominance. As Barbara Fields points out, historians were reluctant to accept the conclusion, reached by biologists by early in the twentieth century, that race did not correspond to any biological referent and that racial categories were so arbitrary as to be meaningless. Race was exposed as a social creation—a fiction that divided and categorized individuals by phenotypic markers, such as skin color, which supposedly signified underlying differences. Nonetheless, as Peggy Pascoe notes, historians continued well into the 1980s to study "races" as immutable categories, to speak of race as a force in history, and to view racism as a psychological product rather than as a product of social history. Pascoe suggests that the lack of a separate term, like "gender," to refer to "socially significant race" may have retarded full recognition of race as a social construct. In sociology, liberal scholarship took the form of studying "race relations"—that is, examining relations among groups that were already constituted as distinct entities. Quantitative researchers treated race as a preexisting "fact" of social life, an independent variable to be correlated with or regressed against other variables. How categories such as black and white were historically created and maintained was not investigated.[12]

Only in the late 1980s did historians and social scientists begin to systematically study variation and change in the drawing of racial categories and boundaries. The greatest attention has been paid to the construction of blackness. In an influential pair of essays, Fields examined shifts in the definition and concept of blackness over the course of slavery, Reconstruction, and the Jim Crow era. Slaveowners created the category "black" from disparate African groups, and then maintained the category by incorporating growing numbers of those of "mixed" parentage. Concerned with maximizing the number of slaves, slaveowners settled on the principle that a child's status followed that of the mother, in violation of the customary patriarchal principle of inheritance. Exploring the "one-drop rule" for defining blackness in the United States, James Davis shows it to be peculiar in light of the wide variation among Latin American, Caribbean, and North American societies in the status of people of mixed ancestry. Competing understandings of racial categories may even coexist in the same society. In Louisiana, Virginia Dominguez found that the "Creole" designation was claimed both by people of mixed black-white ancestry (to distinguish themselves from darker "blacks") and by white descendants of original French settlers (to distinguish themselves from later Anglo immigrants). By the 1970s, however, white "Creoles" had ceded the label to the mixed population and relabeled themselves as "French."[13]

Whiteness has also been problematized. Historians have looked at the shift from an emphasis on "Anglo-Saxon" identity to a more inclusive "white" identity and the assimilation into the white category of groups that had been considered separate races, such as the Irish, Jews, and Italians.[14] These groups achieved "whiteness" through a combination of external circumstances and their own agency. State and social policies organized along a black-white binary required individuals and groups to be placed in one category or the other. Individuals and groups also actively claimed whiteness in order to attain the rights and privileges enjoyed by already established white Americans. Because of the association of whiteness with full legal rights, scholars in the field of critical legal studies have scrutinized the concept of whiteness in the law. Cheryl Harris, for example, argues that courts have protected racial privilege by interpreting whiteness as property, including the right to exclude others deemed to be nonwhite.[15]

Only a few scholars have looked beyond the black-white binary that dominates conceptions of race. Yen Espiritu examined the forging of a pan–Asian American identity in the late 1960s when Chinese, Japanese, and Filipino student activists came together to organize in "third world" solidarity with African American and Latino students. Activists asserted both essentialist grounds (similarities in culture and appearance) and instrumental grounds (a common history of discrimination and stereotyping) as the basis for the new identity. Yet scholars have pointed to tensions and divisions among Asian American groups along ethnic, class, generational, and political lines, for example between longer-settled Japanese and Chinese and more recently arrived Filipinos, South Asians, and Southeast Asians. Also, Aihwa Ong argues that among new Asian immigrants, rich and poor groups are being differentially "racialized" within the black-white binary in the United States: Well-educated professional and managerial Chinese immigrants are "whitened" and assimilated into the American middle class, while poor Khmer, dependent on welfare, are "blackened."[16]

Many of these studies on shifting racial categories and meanings have been influenced by the pathbreaking theoretical work of the sociologists Michael Omi and Howard Winant. Their model of racial formation is rooted in neomarxist conceptions of class formation, but they specifically position themselves against existing models that subsume race under some presumably broader category such as class or nation. They assert that in the United States "race is a fundamental axis of social organization," not an epiphenomenon of some other category. At the same time, they see race not as fixed but as "an unstable and 'decentered' complex of social meaning constantly being transformed by political struggle." The terrain on which struggle is waged has varied historically. Just as social constructionism arose as an alternative to biologism or essentialism in the twentieth century, the concept of biological race arose in the eighteenth and nineteenth centuries to replace religious paradigms for viewing differences between Europeans (Christians) and "others" (non-Christians) encountered in the age of conquest. With the waning of religious belief in a god-given social order, race differences and the superiority of white Europeans to "others" came to be justified and legitimated by "science." Omi and Winant note that the "invocation of scientific criteria to demonstrate the natural basis of racial hierarchy was both a logical consequence of the rise of [scientific] knowledge and an attempt to provide a subtle and more nuanced account of human complexity in the new 'enlightened' age."[17]

After World War II, liberal politics emphasized equality under the law and an assumption of sameness in daily encounters. In the 1960s and 1970s identity politics among civil rights activists emphasized differences but valorized them with such ideas as Black Power and "La Raza." The 1980s and 1990s saw a questioning of the essentialism and solidity of racial and sex/gender categories and a focus on structural concepts of racial and patriarchal social orders. Paralleling the structural approach to gender, Omi and Winant assert that race is a central organizing principle of social institutions, focusing especially on the "racial state" as an arena for creating, maintaining, and contesting racial boundaries and meanings. Their concept of the racial state is akin to feminist conceptions of the state as patriarchal.[18]

An Integrated Framework

There are important points of congruence between the concept of racial formation and the concept of socially constructed gender. These convergences point the way toward a framework in which race and gender are defined as mutually constituted systems of relationships— including norms, symbols, and practices—organized around perceived differences. This definition focuses attention on the processes by which racialization and engendering occur, rather than on characteristics of fixed race or gender categories. These processes take place at multiple levels, including

> *representation*—the deployment of symbols, language, and images to express and convey race/gender meanings;
> *micro-interaction*—the application of race/gender norms, etiquette, and spatial rules to orchestrate interaction within and across race/gender boundaries; and
> *social structure*—rules regulating the allocation of power and resources along race/gender lines.

Within this integrated framework, race and gender share three key features as analytic concepts: (1) they are relational concepts whose construction involves (2) representation and material relations and (3) in which power is a constitutive element. Each of these features is important in terms of building a framework that both analyzes inequality and incorporates a politics of change.

Relationality

By relational I mean that race and gender categories (such as black/ white, woman/man) are positioned and therefore gain meaning in relation to each other. According to post-structural analysis, meaning within Western epistemology is constructed in terms of dichotomous oppositions or contrasts. Oppositional categories require suppressing variability within each category and exaggerating differences between categories. Moreover, since the dichotomy is imposed over a complex "reality," it is inherently unstable. Stability is achieved by making the dichotomy hierarchical, that is, by according one term primacy over the other. In race and gender dichotomies, the dominant category is rendered "normal" and therefore "transparent" while the other is the variant and therefore "problematic." Thus white appears to be race-less[19] and man appears to be genderless. The opposition also disguises the extent to which the categories are actually interdependent.

One can accept the notion of meaning being constructed through contrast without assuming that such contrasts take the form of fixed dichotomies. In the United States "white" has been primarily constructed against "black," but it has also been positioned in relation to various "others." For example, the category "Anglo" in the Southwest, which is constructed in contrast to "Mexican," and the category "haole" in Hawaii, which is constructed in contrast to both Native Hawaiians and Asian plantation workers, are not identical in meaning to the category "white" in the South and the Northeast. Similarly, the meaning of dominant masculinity has varied as it has been contrasted to historically and regionally differing subordinate masculinities and femininities.

The concept of relationality is important for several reasons. First, as in the above examples, it helps problematize the dominant categories of whiteness and masculinity, which depend on contrast. The importance of contrast is illustrated by the formation of "linked identities" in the cases of housewives and their domestic employees, reformers and the targets of reform, and colonizers and colonized peoples.[20] In each of these cases the dominant group's self-identity (for example, as moral, rational, and benevolent) depends on casting complementary qualities (such as immoral, irrational, and needy) onto the subordinate "other."

Second, relationality helps point out the ways in which "differences" among groups are systematically related. Too often "difference" is understood simply as experiential diversity, as in some versions of multi-culturalism.[21] The concept of relationality suggests that the lives of different groups are interconnected, even without face-to-face relations. Thus, for example, a white person in America enjoys privileges and a higher standard of living by virtue of the subordination and lower standard of living of people of color, even if that particular white person is not exploiting or taking advantage of a person of color.

Third, relationality helps address the critique that social constructionism, by rejecting the fixity of categories, fosters the postmodern notion that race and gender categories and meanings are free-floating and can mean anything we want them to mean. Viewing race and gender categories and meanings as relational partly addresses this critique by providing "anchor" points—though these points are not static.

Representation and Material Relations

The social construction of race and gender is a matter of both material relations and cultural representation. This point is important because a social constructionist approach, which eschews biology and essentialism, could be interpreted as concerned solely with language and images. This is particularly tempting in the case of race, where it can be argued that there is no objective referent. Indeed, Barbara Fields has argued that race is a category without content, unrooted in material reality; race is pure ideology, a lens through which people view and make sense of their experiences.[22] However, Fields seems to be conflating biology and material reality. It is one thing to say that race and gender are not biological givens, but quite another to say that they exist only in the realm of representation or signification. Race and gender are organizing principles of social institutions. Social arrangements, such as labor market segmentation, residential segregation, and stratification of government benefits along race and gender lines, produce and reproduce real-life differences that cannot be understood purely in representational terms.

Conversely, other theorists view meaning systems as epiphenomena and maintain that race and gender inequality can be understood through structural analysis alone. But historical evidence suggests that a materialist approach alone is not sufficient either. As historians of working-class formation have pointed out, one cannot make a direct connection between concrete material conditions and specific forms of consciousness, identity, and political activity. Rather, race, gender, and class consciousness draw on the available rhetoric of race, gender, and class. In nineteenth-century England skilled male artisans threatened by industrialization were able to organize and articulate their class rights by drawing on available concepts of manhood: the dignity of skilled labor and family headship. Symbols of masculinity were thus constitutive of class identity. Their counterparts in the United States drew on symbols of race, claiming rights on the basis of their status as "free" labor, in contrast to black slaves, Chinese contract workers, and other figures symbolizing "unfree labor."[23] Class formation in the United States was then and continues to be infused with racial as well as gender meanings.

In the contemporary United States, the paucity of culturally available class discourse seems to play a role in damping down class consciousness. Lillian Rubin found that white working-class men and women whose incomes were stagnating or declining were strikingly silent about class. Instead they drew on a long tradition of racial rhetoric, blaming immigrants and blacks, not corporations or capitalists, for their economic anxieties. By constructing immigrants and blacks as unworthy beneficiaries of welfare and affirmative action, they articulated their own identities as whites, rather than as members of an economic class.[24]

constructed by defining "other" in race terms.

The preceding examples suggest a dialogical relation between material conditions and cultural representation. The language of race, gender, and class formation draws on historical legacy but also grows out of political struggle. Omi and Winant's concept of rearticulation—the investment of already present ideas and knowledge with new meanings—is relevant here. For example, the black civil rights and women's liberation movements in the 1960s and 1970s drew on existing symbols and language about human rights, but combined them in new ways and gave them new meanings ("the personal is political," "Black Power") that fostered mass political organizing.

Power

The organization and signification of power are central to the constructionist framework, despite the frequent charge that this approach elides issues of power and inequality. For Joan Scott, gender is a primary way of signifying relations of power; for R. W. Connell, gender is constituted by power, labor, and cathexis. Power and politics are also integral to Omi and Winant's definitions of race and racism, when they describe race as constantly being transformed by political struggle and racism as aimed at creating and maintaining structures of domination based on essentialist conceptions of race.[25]

The concept of power as constitutive of race and gender draws on an expanded notion of politics coming from several sources. One is the feminist movement, where activists and scholars have exposed the power and domination, conflict and struggle that saturate areas of social life thought to be private or personal: sexuality, family, love, dress, art. Another is Antonio Gramsci's concept of hegemony, the taken-for-granted practices and assumptions that make domination seem natural and inevitable to both the dominant and the subordinate. Social relations outside the realm of formal politics—art, literature, ritual, custom, and everyday interaction—establish and reinforce power; for this reason, oppositional struggle also takes place outside the realm of formal politics, in forms such as artistic and cultural production. A third is Michel Foucault's work on sexuality and scientific knowledge. Power in these loci is often not recognized because it is exercised not through formal domination but through disciplinary complexes and modes of knowledge.[26]

In all of these formulations, power is seen as simultaneously pervasive and dispersed in social relations of all kinds, not just those conventionally thought of as political. This point is particularly relevant to race and gender, where power is lodged in taken-for-granted assumptions and practices, takes forms that do not involve force or threat of force, and occurs in dispersed locations. Thus contesting race and gender hierarchies may involve challenging everyday assumptions and

practices, take forms that do not involve direct confrontation, and occur in locations not considered political.

THE FRAMEWORK I have laid out makes race and gender amenable to
historical analysis so that they can be seen as mutually constitutive. If
race and gender are socially constructed, they must arise at specific moments under particular circumstances and will change as these circumstances change. One can examine how gender and race differences
arise, change over time, and vary across social and geographic locations
and institutional domains. Race and gender are not predetermined but
are the product of men's and women's actions in specific historical con-
texts. To understand race and gender we must examine not only how
dominant groups and institutions attempt to impose particular meanings but also how subordinate groups contest dominant conceptions
and construct alternative meanings.

·2·

Citizenship: Universalism and Exclusion

CITIZENSHIP HAS BEEN a principal institutional formation within which race and gender relations, meanings, and identities have been constituted in the United States. Since the earliest days of the nation, the idea of whiteness has been closely tied to notions of independence and self-control necessary for republican government. This conception of whiteness developed in concert with the conquest and colonization of non-Western societies by Europeans. Imagining non-European "others" as dependent and lacking the capacity for self-governance helped the Europeans rationalize the takeover of their lands, resources, and labor. In North America the extermination and forced removal of Indians and the enslavement of blacks by European settlers therefore seemed justified.[1] This formulation was transferred to other racialized groups, such as the Chinese, Japanese, and Filipinos, who were brought to the United States in the late nineteenth and early twentieth centuries as low-wage laborers but denied the right to become naturalized citizens.

It was not just whiteness but masculine whiteness that was being constructed in discourse on citizenship. Indeed, the association of republican citizenship with masculinity had even more ancient roots than its link with race. As the American colonists struggled to articulate their cause in the struggle for independence from England they harked back to classical associations of patriotism and public virtue with masculinity. As Rogers Smith noted: "American republicans identified citizenship with material self-reliance, participation in public life, and martial virtue. The very words 'public' and 'virtue' derived from Latin terms signifying manhood."[2] The equation of masculinity with activity in the public domain of the economy, politics, and the military was drawn in explicit contrast to the equation of femininity with the activities of daily maintenance carried out in the private domestic sphere. Those immured in the domestic sphere—women, children, servants, and other dependents—were not considered full members of the political community. Given these discourses it is perhaps not surprising that until the late nineteenth century full citizenship—legal adulthood, suffrage, and participation in governance—was restricted to "free white males."

Citizenship, Equality, and Inequality

At its most general level, citizenship refers to full membership in the community in which one lives. Membership in turn implies certain rights in and reciprocal duties toward the community.[3] In his account of the growth of citizenship in Britain, T. H. Marshall distinguished among civil, political, and social rights. Civil citizenship consisted of "the rights necessary for individual freedom—liberty of the person, freedom of speech, thought, and faith, the right to own property and to conclude valid contracts, and the right to justice"; political citizenship meant "the right to participate in the exercise of political power, as a member of a body invested with political authority, or as an elector of the members of such a body"; and social citizenship was composed of "the whole range from the right to a modicum of economic welfare and security to the right to share to the full in the social heritage and to live the life of a civilized being according to the standards prevailing in the society." This third type was necessary to transform formal rights into substantive ones; only with adequate economic and social resources would individuals be able to exercise civil and political rights.[4]

The modern Western notion of citizenship emerged out of the political and intellectual revolutions of the seventeenth and eighteenth centuries, which overthrew the old dynastic orders. While the traditional dynastic realms were populated by *subjects*, the new nation states were seen as consisting of *citizens*. The earlier concept of society organized as a hierarchy of status, expressed by differential legal and customary rights among subjects, was replaced by the idea of a political order established through social contract among citizens. Social contract implied free and equal status for those party to it. Citizenship came to be conceived as a universal status: that is, all who are included in the status supposedly had identical rights and duties, irrespective of their individual characteristics.[5] Equality of citizenship did not, of course, rule out economic and other forms of inequality. Moreover, equality among citizens existed alongside inequality of others living within the polity who were defined as noncitizens.

The citizen and noncitizen were not just different; they were interdependent constructions. Rhetorically, the "citizen" was defined and therefore gained meaning through its contrast with the oppositional concept of the "noncitizen" (the alien, the slave, the woman), who lacked standing because she or he did not have the qualities needed to exercise citizenship. Materially, the autonomy and freedom of the citizen were made possible by labor (often involuntary) of nonautonomous wives, slaves, children, servants, and employees.

Because citizenship has been a major nexus in the creation and maintenance of equality and inequality, it has been the site of contestation over who is included in the status and what rights and responsibilities are associated with the status. Stuart Hall and David Held have described the history of citizenship as one of successive attempts (presumably led by those who have profited from its restriction) to limit citizenship to certain groups—men, whites, property owners—and to define rights narrowly.[6] The other side of the history is one of struggles by those excluded—women, nonwhites, wage workers—to be included and to expand rights into new areas.

American citizenship is characterized by two conceptual dichotomies that have permeated discourse on citizenship since the beginning: public-private and independent-dependent. These dichotomies have been central elements in the conception of the "ideal citizen" since classical times. In the Aristotelian tradition, citizens, free from their individual, concrete, material interests, came together to make decisions on behalf of the general welfare. This formula depended on strict separation of *polis* from *oikos*—the private, material realm of people and things. In the Roman/Gaian tradition, the citizen was one who was free to act by law, to ask and expect the law's protection. Citizenship meant membership in a community of shared or common law; thus to be a citizen of Rome was to be a person entitled to rights and protection of Roman law. In contrast to the Aristotelian ideal of leaving the world of things behind, the Roman formulation made the capacity to act on things the central attribute of citizens. Possession of property was evidence of this capacity. Although the concept of citizen differed in the Greek and Roman formulations, in both traditions independence was a necessary condition for exercising citizenship; independence was established by family headship, ownership of property, and control over wives, slaves, and other dependents. Also in both traditions the public realm of citizenship was defined by bracketing household, domesticity, and "civil society" as outside the domain of equality and rights.[7]

The public-private and independent-dependent dichotomies were also central in the writings of Locke, Rousseau, and other Enlightenment philosophers who shaped American political thought. Feminist theorists such as Carol Pateman, Iris Marion Young, and Susan Okin have traced the exclusion of women from Anglo-American concepts of citizenship to these canonical writings. They have concluded that the "universal citizen" defined in these writings is in fact male. Pateman notes that in the liberal tradition the public and the private are constructed in opposition: the public is the realm of citizenship, rights, and generality, while sexuality, feeling, and specificity—and women—are relegated to the private. Citizenship was essentially defined in opposition to womanhood. Uday Mehta argues that in Locke's account, though rationality was potentially reachable by all, it required extensive social inscription; those viewed as naturally irrational, less civilized, uneducated, or otherwise inadequately socially inscribed were unable to exercise reasoned choice. Thus the notion of natural hierarchy was inherent in Lockean liberalism.[8]

The colonial experience and the subsequent war to establish an independent nation heightened Americans' preoccupation with independence. Independence, always a core element of republican citizenship, took on additional weight and meaning as advocates of separation sought to justify breaking from England. They did so through a new rhetoric that constructed a fundamental opposition between independence and dependence, associating independence with liberty and dependence with slavery.

In the seventeenth- and eighteenth-century British context, dependence did not have uniformly negative connotations. All men and women occupied a dependent position as subjects of the crown. Dependence was viewed not as involuntary subjugation but as a reciprocal relationship involving a web of obligations in which rights and duties flowed in both directions. Independence was thought of primarily in economic terms, a condition made possible by ownership of property, which kept one from having to work for or under someone else. Independence in this sense was an exceptional rather than a usual state. Thus dependence was not race and gender specific.[9]

The meanings of independence and dependence were transformed as American revolutionaries sought to replace the concept of subjectship with that of voluntary citizenship. Subjectship was rooted in one's relationship to the monarch, which was akin to the relation between child and parent. British citizenship was therefore viewed as natural and immutable, as expressed in the common designation "freeborn Englishman." Voluntary citizenship in contrast was viewed as consensual and mutable. Consent required independence, not only in terms of having property, but also in terms of personal freedom.[10]

Revolutionary-era debates over loyalty and suffrage reveal considerable anxiety about dependence. Historians such as David Roediger, Winthrop Jordan, and Judith Shklar have connected the fear of dependence to the proximity of chattel slavery. Slavery was often used metaphorically in revolutionary rhetoric to describe the colonists' subordination to the British Parliament, but the existence of actual slaves made the matter seem more urgent. Independence was what distinguished American colonists from despised slaves and protected them from the possibility of "white enslavement." Economic independence and political freedom were linked in the minds of republican artisans. The imposition of duties by the British Parliament was nothing less than the confiscation of property necessary to "Man's Preservation," deprivation of which would reduce Americans to a state of feudal dependence or slavery.[11]

Simultaneously, Linda Kerber notes, the political founders manifested an anxiety about the stability of their new construction, which "led them, in emphasizing its reasonableness, its solidity, its link to classical models, also to emphasize its manliness and to equate unreliability, unpredictability, and lust with effeminacy. Women's weakness became a rhetorical foil for republican manliness." Rogers Smith also notes the connection that republicans made between masculinity and civic virtue and their rhetorical linking of effeminacy with the "ultimate republican evils of corruption and ignorance. It was hard for them to conceive that women might have the qualities that public-spirited, virtuous republican citizenship demanded."[12]

Dependence, previously accepted as a status shared by many, came to be viewed as incompatible with white masculinity. Increasingly, independence became race and gender specific: all white men were independent and all women and blacks were dependent. Women's dependence became the rationale for excluding them from full citizenship. As dependents, they had no separate interests that needed to be represented in the polity; their interests were assumed to be identical to those of their husbands. At the same time, the definition of women as categorically dependent made it possible to define men as categorically independent. When the United States was established, all but one of the state constitutions denied suffrage to property-owning white women, who as *femmes soles* had been allowed to vote in many colonial jurisdictions. The example of New Jersey, the lone state to enfranchise property-owning women, confirms the shift in the meaning of independence. New Jersey's 1776 constitution granted suffrage to all inhabitants with fifty pounds of proclamation money, a qualification that allowed *femmes soles* (whether black or white) who had this much money to vote, as apparently some did.[13] However, in response to widespread "abuses"—voting by men and women who did not hold property—the legislature redefined the dependency status in 1807 to exempt all white men, while classifying all white women as dependent. Joan Gunderson notes that "ironically the legislature enfranchised two economically dependent groups of males who also voted fraudulently, adult sons living at home and propertyless males. Redefining dependency as a sex-specific trait transformed dependent males into independent voters, while subsuming single women, who were in every practical sense independent, into a category of dependency."[14] *problematic*

Universalism and Exclusion

While no definition of citizenship precludes exclusion on the basis of ascriptive or achieved status, what makes the U.S. case notable is its philosophical grounding in the doctrine of natural rights and principles of equality. American citizenship has been defined, by those who have it and therefore speak for all citizens, as universal and inclusive (the so-called American Creed), yet it has been highly exclusionary in practice. While republican rhetoric declared that individuals have inherent human rights that transcend specific attributes, whole categories of people were excluded from citizenship and denied fundamental civil, political, and social rights. The major groups left out by the nation's founders were the poor, women, slaves, and Native Americans.

The first three of these groups were deemed to lack the independence needed to exercise free choice and the moral and intellectual qualities needed to practice civic virtue. Paupers were disqualified because their neediness rendered them unable to know and act for the common good. Women of all strata were presumed to be members of a dependent class. Under the common law doctrine of coverture, a married woman's legal identity was subsumed by her husband's. She could not bring suit in a court of law, make contracts, own property, or pursue independent occupations. Enslaved blacks occupied the status of commodity or property. As chattel, they did not have any independent legal identity and could not own property, even their own persons. Native American peoples were considered uncivilized and as members of separate nations and thus external to the U.S. polity. Exclusion of racialized minorities was made national policy by the Naturalization Act of 1790, which limited the right to become naturalized citizens to "free white persons."[15]

A standard historical view has been that liberal egalitarianism eventually prevailed, and that "defects" in the American Creed were gradually repaired over the course of the nineteenth and twentieth centuries as formal civil and political rights were extended to each of the excluded groups. However, a closer examination of historical changes shows that the course of American citizenship has been jagged at best. Liberalizing changes occurred rarely and usually only in the context of major social crises. Three periods in which major upheavals occurred were the years of the American Revolution and Confederation, the Civil War and Reconstruction, and the post–World War II civil rights era of the 1950s and 1960s. These times of expanding egalitarianism typically were followed by periods of regression during which hard-won gains were rolled back and new exclusions put in place—the current post–civil rights period being an obvious instance.

There are numerous examples of the tortuous paths that various groups have trod. For some four decades after the Revolution, free blacks were considered citizens and could vote in many states, even in parts of the South. By the late 1850s most free blacks were barred by their states from voting and they were ruled by the Supreme Court not to be citizens. Blacks regained citizenship and large numbers gained suffrage in the 1870s, but these rights were once again lost by the early 1900s. Not until the 1960s did significant numbers of African Americans in the South regain the franchise.

Native Americans had more recognition of their independence in the 1780s than was later the case. For several decades they were still accorded recognition as separate quasi-sovereign nations with whom matters of land and trade were to be regulated by treaty with the United States government. By the 1850s, after years of encroachment and taking of native lands and finally forced removal from "civilized" areas, Native Americans were reduced to the status of "domestic dependent nations" and were declared wards of the federal government. After the Civil War, recognition of Native American nationhood, including communal land rights, was phased out, without however giving Native Americans citizenship rights. Native Americans were specifically excluded from birthright citizenship in the Fourteenth Amendment while continuing to be denied the right to become naturalized on the basis of race under the 1790 Naturalization Act. This double exclusion was not redressed until Congress passed the Indian Citizenship Act in 1924.[16]

With regard to the nation to which a woman owed her citizenship, before 1855, women had citizenship independent of their husbands. After that, an alien woman marrying an American citizen was automatically naturalized, regardless of her preferences. Between 1907 and 1922 an American woman who married an alien automatically lost her U.S. citizenship. In 1922 Congress passed the Cable Act, which allowed native-born women to retain their citizenship provided the alien spouse was racially qualified to be naturalized.[17]

Race-based barriers to immigration were a relatively late development. Before the 1882 Chinese Exclusion Act there were no race or ethnic barriers to immigration, nor before 1924 any nationality-based quotas. Moreover, although the 1790 Naturalization Act was used to bar Japanese and Chinese immigrants from being naturalized from the 1880s on, not until the 1910s did states, courts, and Congress invent a new category, "aliens ineligible for citizenship." This category of noncitizens was subject to special restrictions not placed on other noncitizens. Eleven states passed so-called Alien Land Acts prohibiting "aliens ineligible for citizenship" from owning land. At the federal level, the above-mentioned Cable Act of 1922 provided that any woman citizen who married an "alien ineligible for citizenship" ceased to be a citizen.[18]

In stressing the continuity of exclusion, I am not asserting that racism and sexism are eternal and unchanging forces. Rather, my intent is to point out the nonlinear, dialectical character of change in race and gender boundaries of citizenship over time. Race and gender have continuously been organizing principles of American citizenship; concomitantly, race and gender have been primary axes for contesting boundaries and rights. There have been shifts, however, in the way boundaries have been drawn and contested.

Struggles for Civil and Political Citizenship

During the nineteenth century, organized movements sought civil and political citizenship for previously excluded groups—propertyless white men, African American men, and women. At stake in these struggles was not only who was included but also what being included meant. Proponents for white workingmen, blacks, and women not only sought inclusion within the realm of freedom and equality; they also articulated new meanings for these terms. In some instances, as in the case of propertyless white men, proponents harnessed race-gender ideologies to distance themselves from other excluded groups and to buttress restrictions on rights of those groups. In other instances, as in the case of blacks, proponents articulated more capacious definitions that expanded the meanings of freedom and equality for all.

The most concerted and sustained collective struggles in the nineteenth and early twentieth centuries occurred over suffrage, which had not been included as an essential element in the founders' definitions of citizenship. Civil citizenship—equality before the law, freedom of contract, and protection of person and property—was considered fundamental and natural. Political citizenship—the vote—was seen as a privilege reserved for those who were qualified to exercise it. Thus jurists, legislators, and political philosophers agreed that (white) women were moral and virtuous citizens, but that their citizenship did not entail suffrage. Those excluded from the vote, however, increasingly came to view it as essential to full personhood and its lack as a mark of inferiority. As Shklar points out, those denied suffrage felt "dishonored, not just powerless."[19] The vociferousness of their statements forcefully demonstrated that, in a nation grounded on principles of universal freedom, suffrage meant more than having the ballot. The vote signified full membership in a collective national identity.

reason for change

Working-Class White Men

Nothing in liberal democratic theory ruled out denying the vote to individuals who lacked education, property, or other qualifications. American political leaders in the eighteenth century apparently agreed with Blackstone that property qualifications were necessary in order to "exclude people of so mean a situation as to be esteemed to have no will of their own." Thomas Jefferson concurred, reasoning that ownership of property conferred the independence required of a "responsible and virtuous electorate." A significant proportion of white men initially were excluded from the electorate because they held no property.[20]

The argument for universal manhood suffrage appeared to be a radical departure from the Jeffersonian ideal of a polity made up of landowning yeomen farmers. Yet despite this, in contrast to the slow progress in England (where agitation for extension of the franchise began around the same time but did not succeed until the mid-twentieth century), universal suffrage for white men was quickly achieved in the United States. Of eight new states admitted between 1796 and 1821, five were admitted with full adult white male suffrage and three with taxpaying qualifications. Existing states with real property requirements moved first to taxpaying or other more easily met qualifications and then to universal suffrage. By the middle of the nineteenth century, all existing states had repealed property qualifications for white men, and all new states entered the union with guaranteed votes for white men regardless of property ownership.[21]

Even with the end of property requirements, independence remained a key ideological concept anchoring citizenship. However, the meaning of independence was transformed to be consistent with prop-

*transformed
as connected*

ertyless white manhood. Two sorts of rhetorical revisions occurred.
The first was to depict all wage-earning white men as potential, if not
actual, property owners. American political leaders from the time of
Franklin to that of Lincoln subscribed to the notion that wage work
was a temporary, not permanent condition. In Lincoln's vision, expressed to agricultural groups and then to a national audience, the ideal
was a "prudent, penniless beginner in the world," who worked for
wages "awhile," then, thanks to education and self-discipline, became
his own boss. What was radical about America, according to the historian George Fredrickson, was not its willingness to enfranchise the
working classes but rather its expansive belief that virtually all white
men could rise into the propertied and entrepreneurial classes. The
rapid expansion of the economy and the opening up of "vacant land" in
the West made mass mobility plausible. Seen in this light, mass enfran-
chisement in the Jacksonian era did not signal a triumph of radical
democratic principles; rather, it was largely a product of specific American conditions.[22]

"*american
dream*"

Although the dream of eventual property ownership as a route to independence persisted, a second ideological development transformed
the meanings of property and independence to make them more consistent with wage work. As wage work became more common, new notions arose of property as residing in ownership of one's labor and
therefore of independence as based on productivity and mastery of
skills. By the third decade of the nineteenth century, the growth of industrial capital and the spread of urbanization were eroding the position of small farmers, self-employed artisans, and craftsmen and increasing the proportion of men reliant on wage labor. In a society in
which the small producer was viewed as the backbone of a democratic
polity and masculinity was equated with independence, the transition
to wage labor created a crisis for white male identity.

In the 1820s and 1830s a new working-class rhetoric emerged that
valorized wage labor and denied that it compromised the worker's freedom and independence. Workers increasingly rejected the connotations of servility or dependence in the traditional terminology of "masters" and "servants." As the meaning of "master" shifted from "master
craftsman" to "master of men," workers substituted the Dutch term
"boss" to refer to their employers. The dependence inherent in wage
work was transmuted into "independence" by being contrasted with

slavery and indentured servitude. The voluntary nature of "free labor" *new perceptio* was stressed in opposition to the involuntary nature of various forms of unfree labor.[23]

This transmutation ultimately aided capitalists by redirecting the hostility of white workers toward blacks and other people of color, by masking the subordination of wage work with an illusion of freedom, and more broadly by legitimating the wage labor system and the wage contract. Yet wage-earning men were not simply passive recipients of capitalist ideology. White working-class men, through labor organizations, actively helped create and elaborate the new ideology of independence. They constructed their identities as whites and as citizens around the concept of themselves as "free, productive, independent" workers in opposition to the concept of people of color as "unfree, unproductive, dependent" labor. In the short run at least, they gained some material advantage and psychic wages.[24]

White workingmen's notion of "independence" was gendered as well as racialized. Scholars such as Nancy Fraser and Linda Gordon and Sonya Rose identify this theme running through wage-earning men's claims for manhood and full citizenship in the nineteenth-century United States and England. Artisanal men staked their claims on their positions as fathers and heads of household as well as on their independence through honorable labor and membership in a skilled trade.[25] *fam wage*

In short, white working-class men's claim of independence (and therefore of full rights of citizenship) was built on the subordination of people of color and women. White working-class men mapped various forms of dependence that were not considered congruent with white male status onto blacks and women. In William Forbath's words, "White men often defined their identity as citizens in terms of not being black and not women."[26] The articulation of new and more derogatory definitions of dependence as moral and psychological in nature drew tighter and more explicit race-gender boundaries around citizenship. Race and gender thus displaced class as the primary axes of exclusion.[27]

This raises the question of why arguments for universal manhood suffrage took the form of denying the rights of blacks and women. The debate over suffrage that took place at the Virginia Constitutional Convention in 1829–30 is instructive in this regard. Judith Shklar finds that the most common plea made by disfranchised white men was that without the vote they were slaves. In the words of one western Virginian, "As long as you hold political domination over me, I am a slave." Opponents of universal manhood suffrage quickly went on the offensive, taunting proponents with the "reminder that if the vote was a natural right, then women and blacks should vote. The former were as good if not better than men, and the latter, though certainly inferior were men by nature." Together the two would outnumber white men, a specter that was clearly unacceptable. Grounds needed to be found that would justify "universal" suffrage for white men only. The answer, predictably, was that "'nature' made women so weak as to require male protection, and blacks so stunted that slavery was their true condition." Thus one of the "conditions" for the acceptance of universal manhood suffrage was to make gender and race explicit criteria for suffrage.[28]

This is not to say that race and gender had been irrelevant up to this time. To the contrary, prior to the nineteenth century women and blacks in the North were not considered members of the political community and did not, for the most part, vote. However, their exclusion was based largely on custom, not on statute or constitutional provision. Only at the end of the colonial period and in the early years of the republic did states begin to establish constitutional and legal bars against Native Americans, blacks, and women voting. Still, many northern states and even some southern states did not have legal bars to black suffrage in the first two decades of the nineteenth century. The constitutions of New Hampshire, Vermont, Connecticut, Rhode Island, New York, Massachusetts, and Pennsylvania did not specifically mention "white" as a qualification for voting. The 1776 Pennsylvania Constitution, for example, referred to adult male "freemen," while Vermont extended the franchise to all adult males who could take the "Freeman's Oath." Perhaps more surprising is that North Carolina, Maryland, Kentucky, and Tennessee permitted propertied blacks to vote until the mid-1830s.[29]

However, as state laws were revised to democratize the franchise for white men, they simultaneously became more restrictive with regard to race. From 1819, when Maine was admitted to the Union, until the end of the Civil War all new states guaranteed suffrage to white men irrespective of property and denied the vote to blacks. Legislatures in several states lacking such provisions in their original constitutions passed restrictive legislation.

The link between expansion of suffrage for white men and political exclusion of black men can be clearly seen in successive changes in suffrage provisions in New York and Pennsylvania, the states with the largest black populations in the North. Prior to the 1820s New York allowed black men to vote, subject to the same property requirements as white men. In 1821 the New York Constitutional Convention removed property requirements for white male voters by allowing taxpaying and military service to serve as qualifications, but set a requirement of $250 freehold for blacks. Five years later New York instituted universal suffrage for white men while retaining the $250 requirement for black voters. An English observer who visited New York in 1832 remarked: "To be worth two hundred and fifty dollars is not a trifle for a man doomed to toil in the lowest stations; few Negroes are in consequence competent to vote. They are in fact very little better than slaves, although called free." Then in 1846 New York revoked black suffrage altogether. Pennsylvania began with a relatively expansive suffrage provision in its Constitution of 1776, which enfranchised adult male "freemen" who were taxpayers. By the 1830s Pennsylvania was home to a substantial number of accomplished and educated blacks; nonetheless, in 1837 the electorate overwhelmingly approved revision of its constitution revoking black suffrage. By 1854 only six states with relatively small free black populations allowed black men to vote on the same terms as white men, and 94 percent of northern blacks lived in states that restricted black suffrage.[30]

As the example of New York shows, while blacks had to prove their independence, white men's independence was assumed. Despite the rhetoric, workingmen's independence was largely illusory. Notwithstanding the discourse of male breadwinning, few men actually earned a family wage. Nonetheless, the illusion was useful to the workings of capitalism. It gave to each individual man the "power to engage as an independent unit in the economic struggle (of a competitive market economy) and made it possible to deny him social protection on the ground that he was equipped with the means to protect himself." Nancy Fraser and Linda Gordon have pointed out that in the United States the concept of civil citizenship, encompassing individual liberties and rights, was richly elaborated, while the concept of social citizenship, the idea that citizens are entitled to a modicum of security and a decent standard of living, was largely absent.[31]

This failure to incorporate notions of economic equality or economic justice hobbled substantive equality of citizenship. Economic insecurity and lack of access to legal and other services made it difficult for working-class men to exercise their civil and political citizenship. Without adequate material or cultural means, workers theoretically had the right to bring suit and to hold political office, but practically they could not exercise either right. There is a further irony. The argument against any right to a modicum of support from the state was and continues to be framed in terms of the responsibility of citizens to be independent, that is, to work and earn, rather than to rely on the state.[32]

Blacks

The course of black struggle for citizenship starkly illustrates the persistence of exclusion and inequality. As has been noted in the case of suffrage, blacks actually lost ground in the nineteenth century. More generally, blacks, especially free blacks, had fewer explicit restrictions on their rights at the beginning of the century than by mid-century. Indeed, there was a brief period after the Revolution when some blacks were able to realize in a small way the status and rights of citizens. Blacks themselves had seized the initiative during the Revolution, taking advantage of the upheaval to escape bondage. Some joined British forces while others simply went into hiding. In response, many states, including those in the South, recruited both free blacks and slaves into their regiments, later offering freedom to the latter.[33]

Requirements for private manumission were liberalized in the upper South, resulting in a sizable growth in the free black population. New state constitutions written in the Revolutionary period in the North and in some states in the upper South allowed free black men who could meet general property qualifications to vote. The libertarian climate of the times also gave rise to renewed antislavery agitation, especially among Quakers in Philadelphia and religious societies in New England. By 1800 constitutional provisions, abolitionist statutes, and judicial decrees had ended slavery in most of the North, though it lingered in New Jersey until the 1830s. Abolitionist forces also won antislavery provisions in the Northwest Ordinance of 1787, ensuring a slavery-free zone running from the northeast coast to the northwest borders. In sum, though far from enjoying equality, for the first quarter-century after the Revolution free blacks were conceded to be citizens of a sort, and in many states could vote on the same terms as whites.[34]

Their status deteriorated rapidly after that period in tandem with rising sentiment for universal suffrage for white men. Blacks came to be regarded, not simply as noncitizens, but as anti-citizens. In the 1820s a British visitor reported that blacks were viewed "as 'enemies,' rather than members of the social compact." On those grounds, they were driven from Independence Day parades as "defilers" of the body politic and routed from their homes by patriot groups. It seemed their very powerlessness constituted a threat because they could be manipulated by the rich against the interests of white freemen.[35]

At the national level, a seminal event was the controversy over the admission of Missouri as a slave state. The resulting Compromise of 1820 prohibited slavery west of the Mississippi River and north of latitude 36°30' except in the new state of Missouri. The proposed compromise was threatened by a clause in Missouri's draft constitution that prohibited entry of free blacks and mulattos into the territory. As this clause violated one of the most fundamental privileges and immunities of citizenship, much of the ensuing debate in Congress focused on whether free blacks were citizens or not. Defenders of black citizenship cited free status at birth and birth on American soil as conferring citizenship, while opponents referred to the 1790 Naturalization Act as proof that Americans had never considered blacks to be citizens. In the end Congress evaded the issue by inserting a proviso that nothing in the document authorized passage of any laws that excluded citizens from privileges and immunities of the U.S. Constitution. When Missouri subsequently barred the entry of free blacks, Congress did nothing, thus acquiescing to the view that free blacks were not citizens. Citizenship status of free blacks was left to local and state discretion. Subsequently, as racist state laws proliferated, neither Congress nor the federal courts defended black citizenship.[36]

In the South, fear of slave rebellion was fed not only by Gabriel's insurrection in Virginia (1800), Santo's insurrection also in Virginia (1802), and Denmark Vesey's conspiracy in South Carolina (1822) but by growth in the free black population, which doubled between 1820 and 1860 to 260,000. The presence of emancipated blacks was viewed as a potent spur to slave rebellion. Accordingly, slaveowners moved to disallow manumission or at least to make it more difficult. Bondsmen and bondswomen were barred from hiring themselves out to earn money to purchase their freedom. Southern legislatures passed laws prohibiting free blacks from entering their states or requiring them to post sizable bonds. Most states instituted registration systems to keep track of free blacks; North Carolina required free blacks to wear shoulder patches signifying their status. Some states passed laws forbidding free blacks from assembling and allowing local officials to arrest them for vagrancy and put them to forced labor. Free blacks lost rights to vote, to obtain a jury trial, to testify in court, and to retain counsel. The loss of legal protections was especially dire as criminal codes imposed brutal penalties on blacks and courts applied common law doctrines to punish blacks for insolence and other offenses not specifically defined by statute. Blacks were also denied the most fundamental right of citizens, to pursue an occupation of their own choosing; they were refused commercial licenses and shut out of certain trades. And they were barred from public institutions such as libraries and schools.[37]

Although blacks in the North constituted only about 1 percent of the region's population, northern whites grew anxious about the black presence and took measures to prevent in-migration. Four new "free states," Illinois, Indiana, Iowa, and Oregon, passed laws barring entry of blacks into their territories. Though not systematically enforced, the laws could be used to harass blacks. Overall, free blacks retained more formal procedural protections in the North, but they came under increasingly stringent restrictions. At the beginning of the nineteenth century color lines in employment had ensured that blacks remained in menial positions performing unskilled labor or personal service, but their hold on even these positions became more tenuous by mid-century as European immigrants flooded into these jobs. In the matter of voting, no northern state had restricted voting on the basis of race in 1800, but by the late 1850s only five states, all in New England and containing a mere 6 percent of the northern black population, allowed black men to vote on the same terms as whites. In most northern states African Americans were denied access to public schools, excluded from public accommodations and places of amusement, and prohibited from serving on juries and in state militias. By 1860, Leon Litwack notes, "they were often educated in segregated schools, punished in segregated prisons, nursed in segregated hospitals, and buried in segregated cemeteries."[38]

As white southerners girded up in defense of slavery and their property rights in slaves, they become more aggressive in challenging the emancipation of blacks who migrated to the North. Under pressure from southern members, Congress strengthened laws to enable slaveowners to recapture escaped slaves. Under the Fugitive Slave Act of 1850, any claimant with an affidavit of ownership could go before a federal commissioner to take possession of a black person. The law provided no provisions for a jury trial, judicial hearing, or any other legal safeguard. With the force of federal law behind them, slaveowners became relentless in the pursuit of their property, appearing themselves or sending slavecatchers to retake blacks and re-enslave them. When blacks and antislavery plaintiffs mounted legal challenges, the federal courts tried to evade issues of free black citizenship by deciding cases on the basis of whether white owners bringing slaves into free states were relocating permanently or temporarily.[39]

The increased threat of re-enslavement heightened tension in northern black communities. Some 20,000 blacks fled to Canada. Others organized to thwart slaveowners' attempts to recapture slaves. Black and white abolitionists in New York City and Boston defied the law by rescuing and hiding fugitives. In one sensational case in Boston, a vigilante committee kidnapped a fugitive from a courtroom while a trial was in recess and sent him to Canada. Armed rescuers of slaves sometimes resorted to violence, which outraged southern defenders of slavery. Frederick Douglass, who had long adhered to principles of nonviolence, came to endorse the use of force when dealing with slavecatchers. Noting that blacks had long been stereotyped as passive and meek, he declared, "Every slavehunter who meets a bloody death in his infernal business, is an argument in favor of the manhood of our race." Widespread resistance by blacks and white radicals, supported by a sympathetic public, made the Fugitive Slave Law increasingly difficult, if not impossible, to enforce.[40]

Others sought to have the principles of universal citizenship affirmed through the courts. Blacks who had left slave states and were recognized as citizens in their new states sought to assert their free status. As state and federal courts wrestled with the issue, a few courts in the North held that birthright citizenship included blacks. Other courts, especially in the South, cited the 1790 Naturalization Act and other documents and rulings as evidence that the nation had not originally consented to black citizenship. According to this line of reasoning, all free black children born in the United States were descended from noncitizens and thus, on the basis of the legal doctrine of *jus sanguinis* (which states that a child's citizenship is determined by its parents' citizenship), were not citizens.[41]

The Supreme Court conspicuously avoided making an explicit ruling on the national citizenship of blacks. Finally in 1857, in the case of Dred Scott, who petitioned for freedom on the basis of his residence in a free state, the Supreme Court for the first time ruled that blacks never had been and therefore never could be citizens. The majority found that blacks, even if emancipated, did not compose a part of "the people"—the political community—brought into existence by the Constitution. In the court's interpretation, blacks "are not included, and were not intended to be included, under the word 'citizens' in the Constitution, and can therefore claim none of the rights and privileges which that instrument provides for and secures to citizens of the United States." In Chief Justice Taney's infamous formulation, Negroes were "so far inferior that they had no rights which the white man was bound to respect." Moreover, the Court ruled, although states could naturalize their own residents, they had no power to secure them the rights and immunities of United States citizens.[42]

The Dred Scott ruling remained the law of the land until directly negated by post–Civil War constitutional amendments: the Thirteenth Amendment banned involuntary servitude, and the Fourteenth Amendment defined all persons born within the jurisdiction of the United States as both national and state citizens. The Fourteenth Amendment also prohibited the states from abridging a citizen's privileges and immunities; depriving any person of life, liberty, or property without due process; or denying individuals equal protection of the laws. The Fifteenth Amendment prohibited federal or state governments from placing racial restrictions on the franchise. Of these the Fourteenth Amendment was most significant in that it inserted into the Constitution the principle of equality before the law and also created the rights of national citizenship and a new role for the federal government as guarantor of citizens' rights. These principles had first been enunciated in the federal Civil Rights Act of 1866. According to Eric

Foner, one purpose of the Fourteenth Amendment was to fix the Act's provisions into the Constitution so that they would not be vulnerable to shifting political winds.[43]

The expansion of black citizenship in the South during Reconstruction and the imposition of and resistance to new repressive regimes that denied black citizenship are major subjects of Chapter 4. Here I will focus only on developments at the federal level and in the North that form the larger context for the legal, political, and social changes associated with Reconstruction, the Gilded Age, and the Progressive Era that affected black citizenship.

Reconstruction was highly significant for the 200,000 or so African Americans residing in the North as patterns of segregation and discrimination were challenged and partially dismantled. Between 1865 and 1885 fourteen states passed civil rights laws that banned discrimination in public accommodations. Five states with anti-miscegenation statutes repealed them in the 1880s. Reforms were undertaken to enfranchise blacks and they were sometimes elected to office by predominantly white constituencies. Allan Spear asserts that blacks probably had more genuine political influence during Reconstruction than at any time before or after until the second civil rights revolution of the mid-twentieth century. Public schools in many states were integrated. Although the color line in employment remained firm, some blacks did succeed in businesses and professions, drawing on a white as well as a black clientele.[44]

The end of federal Reconstruction, the waning of commitment to black civil rights by the Republican Party (which had been the primary force behind Reconstruction and civil rights legislation), and worsening economic conditions all contributed to a rise in nativism and white racism. These forces gave rise to movements to draw firmer racial lines in all areas of life. For example, prior to the 1890s black residences were interspersed within white neighborhoods. After 1890, however, blacks were increasingly confined within concentrated neighborhoods, which evolved into ghettos. Residential segregation was a deliberate product of white political activity. White-controlled municipalities passed ordinances creating racial zones. When these laws were found to be unconstitutional, whites formed neighborhood associations and turned to "private" arrangements such as economic boycotts, violence, and restrictive covenants. These restrictions deprived blacks of a central element of liberal citizenship, namely property rights. The lack of access to property prevented them from acquiring the main form of wealth enjoyed by white Americans. Blacks were also deprived of political citizenship through racial gerrymandering of districts and exclusion from party machines that controlled big-city politics. Civil rights laws passed during the Reconstruction era were nullified by lack of enforcement by local officials and by economic retribution against blacks who dared to protest violations of the laws.[45]

The edifice of second-class citizenship was buttressed by the federal courts, which over the next three-quarters of a century erected a legal scaffolding for de jure segregation in the South and de facto segregation in the North. The courts reconciled the apparently inclusionary provisions of the Fourteenth Amendment with the deprivation of black rights by states, public institutions, and individuals in two major ways. First, they distinguished between citizenship in the United States and citizenship in a state and disclaimed federal responsibility for affirmatively protecting citizens' rights. Contrary to the intent of the Amendment, they subordinated national citizenship to state citizenship and limited constitutional protections by ceding to the states the right to regulate civil rights and voting requirements. Second, they carved out a vast area of "private" and "social" actions not subject to intervention by the states or the national government.

This dual strategy was used by the Supreme Court in 1883 to nullify the Civil Rights Act of 1875, which prohibited discrimination in public accommodations and conveyances. The majority ruled that Congress was not invested with the power to legislate upon matters that were within the domain of state legislation or to create codes regulating "private" rights. In essence the court expanded the boundaries of the private and social realm to encompass employment situations, housing, hotels, theaters, restaurants, recreational facilities, and public conveyances.[46] Further elaboration of the private realm was made in the landmark 1896 *Plessy v. Ferguson* case, in which the Court ruled that segregated facilities did not constitute a violation of the Fourteenth Amendment's requirement of "legal-political" equality. The majority opinion stated that "social" inequality, which segregation was designed to maintain, was not covered by the Amendment. As for state-level laws against discrimination, courts rarely enforced them, on the grounds that enforcement would impose unjust restrictions on individual rights to control or manage private property. The right to exclude was considered essential to property rights. Thus the Supreme Court sanctioned local governments' power to enforce "private" exclusion agreements, such as restrictive covenants, which were widely used in the urban North to prevent the sale of property to "nonwhites."[47]

The executive and congressional branches of the federal government also began to enforce second-class status for blacks. Prior to 1912 black employees of the federal government worked alongside whites, ate in the same lunchrooms, used the same bathrooms, and occasionally held supervisory positions over whites. The administration of Woodrow Wilson instituted segregation of blacks in the civil service, the military, and the prison system. In contrast to the 1870s when congressional support for the Fourteenth Amendment was seen as asserting the new doctrine of national citizenship and the role of the national government in protecting civil rights, Congress in the early twentieth century reverted to the doctrine of States' Rights and left it to local authorities to determine the rights of citizens. From 1912 until the second civil rights revolution of the 1960s, the Congress mandated and the executive branch implemented programs that denied equal access to blacks in the area of housing (FHA), old-age and employment insurance (Social Security), relief programs, and even in the National Parks, which assigned black visitors to segregated facilities.[48]

Many northern black leaders disputed the concept of Separate but Equal and voiced their understanding of segregation as inequality of citizenship. In 1914 the New Englander William Monroe Trotter protested segregation in the federal government by noting that, despite protestations to the contrary, "such placement of employees means a charge by the government of physical indecency or infection, or of being a lower order of beings, or a subjection to the prejudices of other citizens, which constitutes inferiority of status." At the local level, blacks continually challenged the stripping of their rights in quiet as well as more vociferous ways. Allan Spear notes that the post-Reconstruction period was one of great ferment in African American thought and of growth in organizing and institution building, but such institutions were hampered by lack of access to capital and political patronage.[49]

The communities blacks built sheltered them to some extent from white scrutiny, but they could not escape the injustices and restrictions imposed by white society. While they were forced to accommodate to some restrictions, they reacted strongly against others which directly affected their daily lives and prospects. Seeing education as the key to economic and political mobility, blacks were particularly militant about the denial of adequate schooling for black children. During the antebellum period, blacks in the North had sought integrated education "by petitioning the public authorities, conducting litigation in the courts and working to secure anti-discrimination legislation."[50] After the Civil War blacks organized to secure legislation in most northern states barring segregated public schools. August Meier and Elliott Rudwick observe that blacks also engaged sporadically in nonviolent direct action in the form of sit-ins and boycotts to protest Jim Crow schools. However, with the influx of black migrants to northern and border cities during World War I, numerous school boards promoted policies resulting in increased racial segregation, which black opposition did not succeed in countering.[51]

Struggles over black citizenship had ramifications for other groups deemed to be "nonwhite," such as Chinese, Japanese, and Mexicans. Policies and formulas adopted by white Americans to constrain black citizenship were often applied to these other groups, who were also subject to segregation, denial of suffrage, and restricted mobility. For example, federal court decisions that affirmed the rights of states and localities to institute and enforce race-based restrictions on suffrage, access to pubic accommodations, and eligibility for state services generally began with issues of black rights and then were extended to cover other racialized groups. However, such factors as relative sizes and class composition of local populations, distinct regional economies, and different histories of incorporations led to group- and region-specific histories of citizenship.

White Women

Revolutionary-era American rhetoricians justified overturning the old hierarchical order on the basis of natural rights and equality of all. Yet the same men who claimed the right to overthrow their lords assumed the continuing exclusion of women from political participation. According to Linda Kerber, American revolutionaries resolved this contradiction by refashioning the doctrine of baron and feme, which defined men as masters over their wives' persons and property, to make it consistent with republicanism. Women's traditional labor for their husbands and families was recast as the duties of "republican motherhood." As republican mothers, women were thought to play a critical but entirely different political role from that of men. They served the republic not by taking up arms, voting, or holding office but "by their refusal to countenance lovers who were not devoted to the service of the state," and by raising "sons who were educated for civic virtue and for responsible citizenship" and "self-reliant daughters who, in turn, would raise republican sons." Lawrence Friedman argues that the most fundamental quality of the "True American Woman" was her malleability, "which made it possible for men to demand assertive daring when national or personal exigencies required. The retiring goddess of the hearth . . . could rear a Spartan family to promote an assertive and masculine nation. She might even step beyond the hearth."[52]

The concept of republican motherhood helped assert women's moral worth and valorize their contributions to the republic. Simultaneously, however, it helped keep women consigned to the domestic sphere. Republican motherhood was thus an equivocal concept that could be used to argue either for or against women's participation in the political realm. Kerber notes that in the nineteenth century republican motherhood was frequently deployed by middle-class women to "claim a role of expanded scope, to claim powers of the mind that most men denied women had, and to claim convictions and resolution of which most men thought women incapable."[53]

The early decades of the nineteenth century saw further polarization of the public-private dichotomy and further separation between men's and women's spheres. In the 1830s Tocqueville was struck by the degree to which men's and women's roles and functions were separated; he attributed part of American prosperity to this separation. Rapid social change and mobility were accompanied by a variety of social ills, which came to be associated with industrialism and urbanization. The public realm could no longer be seen as the domain of virtue. The private sphere came to be viewed as morally superior, and women as mistresses of the hearth, its guardians. The elevation of the domestic sphere did not promote women's independence; rather it underlined the importance of coverture—the fiction of merged interests—to maintain family harmony. Still, the emphasis on women's roles as moral guardians and nurturers of future citizens did give them a measure of worth. It also justified the expansion of schooling so as to educate them to play this crucial role.[54]

White women also made some gains in the area of civil citizenship, including expanded parental, property, and divorce rights. Starting in 1839 states began passing Married Women's Property laws, which allowed women to retain rights over property they brought into marriage. According to some legal historians the laws were passed not out of conviction that women were equal but as a response to increases in family separation and market transactions in a mobile and expanding society. Women's title to family property needed to be clarified so as to facilitate transactions of property in cases where men deserted wives and children to migrate to the West. The laws were more often invoked by couples to shelter their assets from outside creditors than by women to protect their individual rights. Such reforms were viewed as necessary to protect dependent women and were not intended to promote women's independence within marriage. Husbands continued to have the right to control and manage their wives' property, including collecting fees and rents. Also, until late in the nineteenth century, earnings and property obtained during marriage still belonged to the husband. In ruling after ruling involving women's property rights, courts cited the necessity of women's dependence to maintaining the patriarchal family, the cornerstone of American values. Nonetheless, Married Women's Property laws were important insofar as they established the principle that (white) women could own property; by implication, unlike black slaves, they were not themselves property.[55]

Paralleling the separation of male and female spheres in the family was the development of distinct spheres for political activity. While partisan electoral politics increasingly absorbed men's energies, an active core of women worked to influence government and the community through social service and reform organizations. According to Ellen DuBois, middle-class women's experience in social reform politics, particularly in the abolitionist movement, combined with their "growing awareness of their common conditions and grievances," contributed to the development of a women's rights movement. "Borrowing from antislavery ideology, they articulated a vision of equality and independence for women, and borrowing from antislavery methods, they spread their radical ideas widely to challenge other people to imagine a new set of sexual relations." Many pioneers in women's rights, including the Grimké sisters, Elizabeth Cady Stanton, Susan B. Anthony, Lucretia Mott, and Lucy Stone began their activism in the cause of abolition. With encouragement from William Lloyd Garrison and other male abolitionists, women formed more than one hundred female anti-slavery societies between 1833 and 1838.[56]

Women's involvement in such a public issue occasioned criticism from some quarters. When attacked by Congregationalist ministers in Massachusetts for their public involvement, the Grimké sisters of South Carolina began speaking and writing in defense of women's rights based on Enlightenment principles and their interpretations of the Bible. And when male abolitionists refused to support women's rights and to combine feminist and antislavery causes, Stanton and Mott organized the famous meeting in Seneca Falls, New York, in 1848 that launched the first women's rights movement. The organizers issued a Declaration of Sentiment that proclaimed that women were free citizens, entitled to equal rights to teach and speak, to "the sacred right of the elective franchise," and to "equal participation with men in the various trades, professions, and commerce."[57]

Franchisement became the cornerstone (and the most controversial issue) of the movement, but some leaders, such as Stanton, championed broader changes including egalitarian marriage, property reforms, and equal roles in marriage. Other prominent thinkers, such as Catharine Beecher, defended domesticity and motherhood as women's special province and the source of their moral power and saw suffragists and other feminists as threats to women's place. These differences formed at least one fault line within the women's movement between so-called liberal egalitarian and social feminist arguments for women's citizenship. Over the next sixty years the latter came to dominate, as arguments based on women's domestic roles and superior morality proved more acceptable and effective.[58]

The struggle for women's rights was eclipsed during the Civil War by the overriding issue of black rights. When the Reconstruction Amendments were passed, some women's rights advocates were angered that the Fourteenth Amendment specifically referred to males in most of its provisions and that the Fifteenth did not include sex along with race, color, and previous condition of servitude in the guarantee of political rights. Controversy over the lack of Republican and male abolitionist support for combining female and black suffrage through an Equal Rights Association led to a split among women's rights activists, who formed two separate organizations in 1868–1869. The more conservative American Women's Suffrage Association remained allied with the Republican Party, and, accordingly, acceded to giving black rights precedence at the national level. The AWSA concentrated its efforts at the state level and advanced the domestic feminist argument that feminine virtue made women good voters. The more radical National Women's Suffrage Association led by Anthony and Stanton opposed deferring women's suffrage, emphasized change at the national level, and challenged traditional familial arrangements that subordinated women. Eventually the NWSA (which merged with AWSA in 1890) focused on winning a separate suffrage amendment for women.[59]

In the meantime, however, the NWSA pursued a strategy of interpreting the Reconstruction Amendments inclusively and claiming that they established national citizenship rights that included women. The Fourteenth Amendment held particular promise. The first section, which recognized birthright citizenship and stipulated that citizenship entitled a person to all the rights in the Constitution and the Bill of Rights, was written in gender-neutral language, referring only to "citizens" and "any person." Thus some women's rights advocates argued that its three main clauses guaranteeing privileges and immunities, due process, and equal protection of the law applied equally to women. Courts quickly rebuffed the claims; initially they did so by ruling that the Amendment addressed only race.[60]

In higher court rulings, however, as in cases challenging state restrictions on black rights, justices whittled away at national citizenship by differentiating between national and state citizenship and reserving to individual states the right to define categories of people and to restrict rights accordingly. One major test case involved a woman's right to pursue an occupation, which might be assumed to be a fundamental right of national citizenship. In a precedent-setting case, *Bradwell v. Illinois*, 1873, the U.S. Supreme Court upheld the right of Illinois to bar women from practicing law, rejecting the well-qualified Myra Bradwell's claim that the Illinois Bar Association's refusal to license her to practice law deprived her of privileges and immunities of citizens under the U.S. Constitution. The majority opinion written by Justice Miller concluded that the right to practice law was not a privilege or immunity of national citizenship, but only of state citizenship. Thus states could confer the privilege as they wished. While the majority opinion firmly centered on states' rights, a concurring opinion signed by three justices went much further in curtailing rights solely on the basis of gender, stating in part:

> The harmony, not to say identity, of interests and views, which belong, or should belong, to the family institution is repugnant to the idea of a woman adopting a distinct and independent career from that of her husband . . . It is true that many women are unmarried and not affected by any of the duties, complications, and incapacities arising out of the married state, but these are exceptions to the general rule. The paramount destiny and mission of women are to fulfill the noble and benign offices of wife and mother. This is the law of the Creator, and the rules of civil society must be adapted to the general constitution of things, and cannot be based upon exceptional cases.[61]

A second major test of the applicability of the Fourteenth Amendment to women involved suffrage, as hundreds of women around the country tested the law by trying to register or vote. The most prominent among the women was Susan B. Anthony, who was arrested for voting illegally; however, the judge settled the case by directing a jury verdict so that it could not be appealed. Thus the precedent-setting case became that of Virginia Minor, president of Missouri's women's suffrage movement, who appealed her arrest for voting though she was ineligible by state law to do so. In *Minor v. Happersat*, which reached the U.S. Supreme Court in 1875, the Court agreed that women were citizens, but that political participation was not an essential right of citizenship: "The Constitution does not confer the right to vote on any one."[62]

After the loss of the voting cases in 1875, the NWSA focused its efforts on trying to pass a constitutional amendment guaranteeing the franchise for women. Anthony's friend the California Senator A. A. Sargent introduced the Anthony Amendment in 1878. The proposed amendment was submitted to almost every Congress thereafter, failing year after year. State-based efforts to introduce and pass referenda to achieve suffrage were only marginally more successful. Of some four hundred referenda efforts, only two succeeded, both in the West, in Colorado (1893) and Idaho (1896); additionally, two new states were admitted with women's suffrage, Wyoming (1890) and Utah (1896).[63]

Although the NWSA and AWSA continued their efforts, their combined membership declined to only 13,000, leading them to merge in 1890. After 1875 leadership for women's rights shifted to other organizations. The largest of these was the Women's Christian Temperance Union, which under Frances Willard grew to 135,000 members in thousands of locals by 1895. Although focused on temperance, the WCTU championed women's suffrage and a variety of other reforms. Willard allied the WCTU with the Knights of Labor, formed units for youth and colored women, and had special departments to work with Native Americans, immigrants, and working women. But with the rise of nativism in the 1890s the WCTU and Willard herself became more exclusionary. By 1897 Willard was testifying before Congress on behalf of immigration restrictions to stem the flow of "the scum of the Old World." With Willard's death the organization became even more nativist and racist.[64]

Many other organizations were also involved in advocating for women's suffrage and more broadly for equal civil and political citizenship. The National Federation of Afro-American Women, formed in 1895, worked for the vote for all women; its white counterpart, the General Federation of Women's Clubs, excluded blacks and refused to endorse women's suffrage until 1914. In the late 1900s rural farm women and urban working-class women also began to get involved in political movements. The Grange was the first national organization to extend membership equally to women, who became active in efforts to assist farm families. In 1885 the Grange upheld the principle of equality of the sexes and urged suffrage and equal citizenship for women. The Knights of Labor organized women's assemblies.[65]

In the meantime, Gilded Age courts continued to issue decisions that cited coverture to circumscribe women's property rights. During this period justices ruled that women could purchase land only with their husband's consent; that they lacked power of attorney; that they could not legally settle on federal lands; and that they could not testify against their husbands whatever violence their husbands had done to them.[66]

Women's rights advocacy became even more closely tied with

nativist and racist thinking in the Progressive era. This period saw
the rise of scientific racism, which melded evolutionary theory, testing
and measurement, and genetics to elaborate on purported race and
ethnic differences. Eugenic thinking was congenial to Progressives,
who sought to reform society to be more orderly and efficient along
scientific lines. Upper-middle-class women such as Florence Kelley,
Jane Addams, Julia Lathrop, and Sophonisba Breckenridge deployed
civic maternalism to claim active roles in social reform. They founded
settlement houses to help women affected by the ills of urbanization
and industrialization and also founded organizations such as the National Consumer's League and the Women's Trade Union League to
improve the sweatshop conditions and long hours many working
women were forced to endure. Although these reformers spoke of
women's domestic responsibilities and gender differences in conventional ways, unlike conservatives they supported government regulation of the economy, especially to protect women and children. Strate-
gically, arguments based on women's dependence and special needs
proved the most effective in garnering support for protective legislation and wage and hour laws for women.[67]

Although some strains of universalistic egalitarianism could still be
heard in the Progressive Era, the dominant thread was a rhetoric of difference that stressed women's need for protection to realize their special mission. Progressive-era women's support for suffrage was often
premised on the notion that women's role as domestic housekeepers
uniquely qualified them to clean up and reform politics. This approach
made the suffrage movement less able to forge alliances with working women, new immigrants, and blacks. Moreover, the leadership in
women's rights organizations had become less broad-based, with fewer
housewives and more professionals, writers, and women with substantial means. Many of these women were antagonistic toward the increasing numbers of immigrants. Indeed, many leading suffragists so-
licited support by arguing that native-born white women would help
defend the nation against contamination by freed blacks, Chinese, and
southern European immigrants, and would support literacy and other
qualifications that would restrict voting by these groups. The NWSA
board in 1903 issued a statement allowing their southern affiliates to
bar black women from membership by recognizing a state association's
"right to arrange its own affairs in accordance with its own ideas and in

harmony with the customs of its own sections." These racial appeals undoubtedly helped attract support for suffrage in the South, but they also ensured a continuing divergence of interest between white women and women of color. This divergence mirrored the gap in the valuation of women's worthiness between those considered mothers of future citizens and those who produced only dependents.[68]

Passage of the Nineteenth Amendment in 1920, more than forty-two years after its first introduction, was a long-delayed victory for women's political citizenship. Still it did little to alter the common law and myriad statutes that circumscribed women's civil citizenship by assuming women's dependence and husbands' prerogatives over wives' labor and income. Women had to challenge laws that denied them equal civil status and full adult personhood in a piecemeal fashion. Consequently, change came slowly and painfully. In the absence of laws specifying otherwise, courts continued to hold that women were subordinate to their fathers and husbands and that men held property rights over the labor of daughters and wives. A 1904 Supreme Court ruling held that husbands had "personal and exclusive" right of sexual intercourse with their wives, a right upon which "the whole social order rests." Women still could not bring suit against their husbands for assault and battery, nor could they have citizenship in a different state than that in which their husbands held citizenship unless a court found that it was necessary for their protection. Women's supposed domestic obligations also continued to trump their obligations as citizens. Thus as late as 1965 only twenty-one states made women eligible for jury duty on the same basis as men. The others either excluded women or granted special exemptions based on their domestic responsibilities.[69]

Explaining Exclusion

Until recently many American historians and social scientists viewed ascriptive exclusions from citizenship as deviations from otherwise dominant professed principles of universal equality. Some saw the exclusions as carry-overs of outmoded feudal ideas about natural hierarchies; others viewed them as stemming from the self-interest of white male patriarchs and property owners; still others viewed exclusions as the product of jealousy, selfishness, or other irrational impulses.

Rogers Smith traces the belief that liberal egalitarianism was the dominant principle of American political thought to Alexis de

Tocqueville, who, writing in the 1830s, stressed the uniqueness of American democracy. As a European, Tocqueville was struck most by the revolutionaries' rejection of aristocratic privilege, which he attributed to American liberal egalitarianism. Tocqueville also spent most of his time reflecting on the political activities of a small segment of American society, namely middle- and upper-class white men. He only briefly considered the situation of blacks and Native Americans and brought women into the picture only when describing social, not political life. Tocqueville and those who followed took gender and race hierarchies for granted or relegated them to the margins, so that inequality was not seen as central to the American political system.[70]

Over a hundred years later the Swedish sociologist Gunnar Myrdal focused on the subordination of African Americans as a central "dilemma" in American society. He nonetheless subscribed to the Tocquevillian notion of an overarching American Creed—a belief in universal equality. Myrdal interpreted the widespread racial segregation and discrimination against blacks as therefore contradictory to Americans' professed beliefs. The challenge that he posed to (white) Americans was whether they would live up to their highest ideals by accepting blacks as equal citizens. Speaking from the perspective of the early 1940s, a period of democratic ferment, Myrdal concluded that "not since reconstruction has there been more reason to anticipate fundamental changes in American race relations, change which will involve a development toward the American ideals."[71]

In this respect, Myrdal was more optimistic than the vast majority of American social scientists at mid-century. As James McKee has pointed out, prior to the 1960s civil rights revolution even the most liberal scholars assumed that any progress would come at a glacial pace. Locked into an assimilationist framework, many sociologists and social anthropologists viewed blacks as a "folk" people who would have to go through a long process of education and acculturation to become integrated into American society. In this view full citizenship for blacks would occur only when white Americans were ready to accept blacks as equals, a process that would take many generations. These scholars discounted the possibility of black agency, overlooking evidence of black discontent and political activism. Race-relations "experts" were taken by surprise by the civil rights revolution of the 1950s and 1960s; in fact their accumulated wisdom suggested its impossibility.[72]

More critical perspectives on liberalism and liberal concepts of citizenship have been offered by Marxist and feminist writers. Marx himself was somewhat equivocal about the relationship between liberal democracy and capitalist rule. On the one hand, he saw the universalistic elements of democracy as incompatible with class divisions in capitalist society. On the other hand, his general claims about the liberal state were to the effect that it was a means for organizing and reproducing class rule. According to Anthony Giddens, Marx preserved the primacy of class by treating democratic rights as "narrow and partial." Workers in a liberal democratic regime might be allowed to participate in democratic elections every few years, but they lacked any real power to control their own lives or to affect the distribution of material resources. Thus such rights as they had were largely hollow. Liberal citizenship not only failed to address material inequality, it actually helped justify and perpetuate it. By sanctifying private property rights, liberalism reinforced the power of those who monopolized productive property. In this view liberal egalitarianism helped mask class inequality by creating an illusion of equality. Thus liberal universalism was both logical and functional for a capitalist system. Under liberal hegemony, political debate and contestation took place only within the narrow limits of liberal orthodoxy.[73]

As previously noted, some feminist theorists have also been critical of liberal citizenship, arguing that exclusion of women is inherent in liberal assumptions. Some have pointed out that the rights-bearing subject in liberalism is a discrete and disembodied individual who can act according to abstract principles. Women are viewed as held in thrall by bodily demands (pregnancy and childbirth). As the ultimate embodied subjects, they cannot be accommodated within the liberal concept of citizen. Still, despite their criticism of particular liberal writings, many feminist critics have acknowledged that classic liberal contract theory, which is premised on natural rights, has the potential for challenging all forms of hierarchical authority; moreover, because liberal rights doctrine has been the most effective rhetorical device for subordinated groups to claim rights, many feminists, including critical race theorists such as Angela Harris, have emphasized the importance of retaining a commitment to universalistic principles such as truth, justice, and objectivity even while recognizing their insufficiency.[74]

Some important writers have concluded that race and gender exclusion is indeed a central and continuing theme in American citizenship, but argue that it stems from distinctly nonliberal roots. Benjamin Ringer argued in 1983 that exclusion of racial minorities has been an inherent feature of the U.S. political system from its inception. American citizenship was the product of its origins in a white settler society. The founders set up a dual legal and political system based on colonial and colonialist principles. The "people's domain" consisted of those included in the national community, among whom "universalistic, egalitarian, achievement-oriented, and democratic norms and values were to be ideals." Existing alongside the people's domain was a second level of those excluded from the national community, who, on the basis of colonialist principles, were "treated as conquered subjects or property."[75]

More recently, Rogers Smith has documented the history of exclusion of women, blacks, and Native Americans from citizenship. Smith hypothesizes that U.S. concepts of citizenship have been shaped by multiple ideological strands, some of which are consensual and egalitarian and some of which are ascriptive and inegalitarian. He identifies three major strands in American political thought: liberalism (which emphasizes limited government, personal freedom, and protection of individual rights); republicanism (which emphasizes self-government, political participation, civic virtue, and regulation of the economy to ensure the public good); and ascriptive Americanism (which emphasizes the notion of Americans as a special people endowed with superior moral and intellectual traits associated with certain ascriptive traits such as race, religion, gender, and sexual orientation). Smith argues that all three strands have been used in different combinations by political leaders to achieve their dual goals of creating a sense of peoplehood in their followers and persuading them of the rightness of their vision and the need for their leadership. In his view liberalism and republicanism have been effective in creating a sense of progress, prosperity, and personal freedom, but not in convincing people that "we" are a special people. For this task, ascriptive Americanism has been effective in that it has offered civic myths about our specialness as a people.[76]

Ringer's and Smith's works are important because of their view that ascriptive exclusion and stratification are central and not peripheral to the story of American citizenship. I build on these works, but my focus and approach differ in at least two major ways. First, both Ringer and Smith concentrate on the national level and on formal definitions and doctrines as decreed in official documents, laws, and court decisions. Second, their analyses center on debates and arguments among key political actors (political leaders, reformers, judges, lawyers). Because of this focus, although they consider conflict, they look primarily at discursive conflict among competing members of the elite, rather than at "hidden transcripts" of resistance by excluded groups.[77]

In my view, very important parts of the story of American citizenship are thereby overlooked. Citizenship is not just a matter of formal legal status; it is a matter of belonging, including recognition by other members of the community. Formal law and legal rulings create a structure that legitimates the granting or denial of recognition. However, the maintenance of boundaries relies on "enforcement" not only by designated officials but also by so-called members of the public. In the South, for example, segregation of public conveyances was enforced not only by white drivers and conductors but also by white passengers, who imposed sanctions on blacks whom they perceived as violating boundaries. Contrarily, men and women may act on the basis of alternative schemas of race, gender, and citizenship that differ from those in formal law or policy. For example, in the Southwest, in an era when full citizenship rested on white racial status, Mexicans were designated as "white" by the U.S. government, but many Anglos did not recognize the official "whiteness" of Mexicans and often refused to consider them "Americans" entitled to political and civil rights. As a result, Mexicans were often denied entry to public facilities designated for "whites only" and were disbelieved as to their American citizenship status when they attempted to exercise their political rights.

Similarly, challenges to exclusion have not only been made through formal legislative and legal channels. Certainly such challenges have been a significant element in the history of American citizenship, and one that has only recently been documented in the case of certain groups, such as Asian Americans and immigrant minorities.[78] Still, because excluded groups by definition have often lacked resources and access to courts and other formal venues to mount such challenges, much of their opposition has taken place in informal or "disguised" ways and in informal sites. These less formal types of contestation have been even more neglected by scholars of citizenship than formal challenges. The regional case studies in this book highlight these everyday forms of contestation and struggle as well as legal and formal political challenges. For example, as will be shown in Chapter 4, blacks challenged segregation of public conveyances not only by bringing legal suits and organizing boycotts but also by frequent instances of "spontaneously" refusing to "move to the back of the streetcar." Citizenship is constituted through a process that involves not only beliefs and activities of various elements of the elite but also those of ordinary people, including those denied recognition and rights.

In the regional case studies I focus on how the boundaries and meanings of citizenship are reinforced, enacted, and contested in ways related to race and gender at the local level and in everyday interaction. This focus clarifies the distinction between formal and substantive citizenship, and it avoids an overly monolithic view of oppression by revealing the variability and unevenness in the race-gender boundaries of citizenship.

Formal citizenship is that embodied in law and policy, while substantive citizenship is the actual ability to exercise rights of citizenship. Substantive citizenship involves two issues. One has to do with a capacity to exercise rights to which one is formally entitled. T. H. Marshall made this point when he argued that social citizenship—the right to a modicum of economic security, education, and other resources—was necessary to realize one's civil and political rights. For example, the right to bring suit in court (a civil right) is only possible if individuals have access to legal representation.[79] The second issue has to do with enforcement or lack of enforcement of formal citizenship rights by the national, state, or local government or by members of the public. Racialized and gendered citizenship is created when theoretically universal citizenship rights are differentially enforced. For example, universal suffrage may be guaranteed by the Constitution, but historically the right to vote has been differentially protected. Even today, blacks are disproportionately disfranchised by the lack of enforcement of equal access to the ballot.

With regard to this second issue, comparing the experiences of blacks in the South, Mexicans in the Southwest, and Japanese in Hawaii reveals similarities and differences in the ways national laws and policies regarding citizenship were interpreted at the local level and in day-to-day relations. Within each region, we can also view variability in the enforcement of boundaries of inclusion/exclusion and changes over time in the drawing of these boundaries. In this way we can begin to untangle the processes by which historically and regionally specific citizenship has shaped and been shaped by historically and regionally specific race-gender formations.

Different groups may also be excluded from different facets of citizenship. Several aspects of citizenship should be differentiated. At the most general level is the notion of citizenship simply as belonging—membership in the community, sometimes defined as the nation. Within this meaning, however, there are several sub-meanings, including the notion of *standing* (being recognized as a full adult capable of exercising choice and assuming responsibilities); the notion of *nationality* (being identified as part of a people who constitute a nation, whether corresponding to the boundaries of a nation state or not); and the notion of *allegiance* (being a loyal member of the community). A given category of people may be excluded from one of these meanings of citizenship but included in other meanings.

A second set of distinctions has to do with different kinds of rights that go with belonging. The most widely used model is T. H. Marshall's tripartite model of civil, political, and social citizenship. Those who have applied Marshall's model to the United States have argued that there is unevenness among the three facets: while civil and political citizenship emerged early and were highly elaborated, social citizenship emerged late and was weakly developed. They see social citizenship as having emerged only in the 1920s and developed more fully as a response to the Great Depression in the New Deal era with the creation of Social Security, unemployment insurance, and other social safety nets. According to these scholars, social citizenship remained weak in the United States compared with that in England and other western European nations. In the period that I am covering, 1870–1930, civil and political citizenship, along with standing, nationality, and allegiance, were the main facets of citizenship that were being elaborated and contested. An additional facet that I will touch on is one that recent scholars have called cultural citizenship. Cultural citizenship refers to the right to maintain cultures and languages differing from the dominant ones without losing civil or political rights or membership in the national community.[80] The term "cultural citizenship" was not in use during the period covered in this book. However, Mexican Americans in the Southwest and Japanese in Hawaii were insisting on schooling in their own languages and were retaining interest in political developments in their countries of origin while simultaneously declaring their allegiance to the United States and claiming civil and political rights. It appears therefore that they were beginning to formulate a concept of citizenship that included cultural rights.

FOR NONWHITE people and women, citizenship has always been a malleable structure, molded by the efforts of dominant groups seeking to enforce their own definitions of citizenship and its boundaries, and by the efforts of subordinated groups to contest these definitions and boundaries. Thus the meaning of citizenship has evolved over time, has varied by place, and has differed for different people. It is out of struggles at the local level that regionally and historically specific formal and substantive citizenship has emerged.

To understand how citizenship has been shaped by race and gender and in turn how it has helped create and maintain race and gender inequality, we have to study citizenship, not in isolation, but in relation to race-gender formation in other institutions in the society—the family, schools, political parties, and the labor market. Of these institutions the one most closely entwined with the formation of American citizenship has been the labor system, to which we now turn.

·3·

Labor:
Freedom and Coercion

BOTH RACE AND GENDER have been incorporated as fundamental organizing axes of the labor system in the United States, and in turn the labor system has been organized in ways that create and re-create race-gender categories and relationships. This was true both in the early republic and during the antebellum period, when the economy was still primarily agrarian and characterized by small producers, and after the Civil War and at the turn of the century, when the economy was being transformed by industrialization and monopoly capital.

The democratizing movement for political equality among white men in the early nineteenth century led to a shift in the meaning of economic independence, which had long been defined in terms of property ownership. White male independence came to be anchored in the notion of "free labor." For free labor to emerge as a supposed source of independence, it had to be distinguished from "unfree labor." Thus there was a gradual differentiation in which statuses between freedom and slavery, such as indentured servitude and master-servant relations, were eliminated for native white men while continuing for blacks and other people of color (and sometimes immigrants). The category of unfree labor thus became racialized as nonwhite at the same time that free labor was racialized as white. What did not change was the assumption that independent manhood entailed control of and ownership of wives' and children's labor. This meant that women were excluded from the category of free labor and therefore from economic independence. The status of free labor proved precarious, however, threatened on one side by growing capitalist industrialization, which was displacing the small-producer economy, and on the other side by the existence and spread of racial slavery.

The Civil War removed one of the threats: slavery, as well as indenture and peonage, was formally abolished, rendering all men free laborers in a system regulated by the legal doctrine of "liberty of contract." It did not remove the other threat, industrial capitalism, which in fact mushroomed after the Civil War. The central question is why and how in the new capitalist industrial labor system, in which, according to the operative myth, race and gender ought to have been irrelevant, they instead became central organizing features. Part of the answer lies in the continuation of older common law traditions. Women continued to be excluded from "free labor" protections because the common law marriage contract obligated wives to provide labor for their husbands. The Elizabethan-era obligation of the poor to work was revived in expanded vagrancy laws which subjected the poor, but especially those of color, to forced labor.

The other part of the answer lies in the changes brought about by capitalism itself. First, capitalist industrialization reorganized production and reproduction, removing much production from the home and drawing men into the labor force to work for wages and leaving reproduction to be carried out as unpaid work by women at the household level. This led to a greater separation and demarcation of home and work, to differential valuation of men's and women's work, and to a secondary disadvantaged position for women in the labor market.[1] Second, capitalist industrialization was characterized by cyclical crises, new class formations, and heightened conflicts between capital and labor, between capitalists in different sectors, and between different segments of workers. The main conflict was between capital and labor, as workers resisted the new disciplinary regimes, deskilling, and relentless downward pressure on wages. These conflicts often took the form of competition between male and female or white and nonwhite workers, as capitalists sought to drive down wages by hiring cheaper and more docile workers—those with less political leverage. Simultaneously, higher-priced workers used whatever leverage they had to keep cheaper workers out of desirable jobs and industries. Complex patterns of labor market segmentation and segregation can be seen as an unstable compromise that ultimately benefited capital by fragmenting workers into smaller interest groups and hampered coalitions across race, gender, skill, nativity, and other lines. Capitalist industrialization both incorporated existing race/gender hierarchies and reformulated and rearticulated race/gender relationships.

Despite the abolition of slavery and bonded labor, coercion persisted in the labor system. Certain regions and industries that disproportionately employed labor of color adopted debt peonage and other restrictions on their mobility. The denial of full citizenship to people of color and their subjection to coercion in the labor market were thus mutually created.

Antebellum Labor

The concept of labor, particularly free labor, has held a pivotal position in the definition of white manhood since the early republic. This was perhaps inevitable given the existence of chattel slavery in a nation founded on principles of freedom. Just as the United States developed a duality in the structure of citizenship, it also developed duality in the labor system: free labor for whites and unfree labor for blacks and other subordinated minorities, such as Native Americans, Mexicans, and Asians. The demarcation between free and unfree labor evolved over time, and the line was drawn differently in different periods.

Labor and Independence in the Early Republic

According to Eric Foner the dignity of labor was a central tenet of American culture from the very beginning. This characteristic reflected the early settlers' Calvinist beliefs, a central element of which was the conviction that each man had a calling or occupation to which he was divinely appointed. Success in one's calling was a way of serving God on earth. Labor was thus transmuted into a religious value, a Christian duty. More was involved than simply the "Protestant Ethic," however. Grafted onto the belief in the sacredness of work was a vision of the United States as a dynamic growing society, in which individuals could improve their lot through hard work. Striving was important not just for personal advancement but also for societal progress. Patriotic

Americans believed that the nation was destined to advance because its people were hardworking and public spirited. It was precisely these qualities that distinguished Americans from Indians, who had failed to husband resources and subdue nature, and from Europeans, whose advancement was stunted by an unproductive aristocracy.[2]

According to Judith Shklar, "the sheer novelty of the notion of the dignity of labor in general and as an essential element of citizenship, can scarcely be exaggerated." In the European tradition, Shklar notes, it was almost universally believed that physical labor was defiling. Ancient philosophers had "regarded productive and commercial work as so degrading that it made a man unfit for citizenship." Shklar argues that these attitudes continued in European society for centuries, institutionalized in the division of society into three strata: "those who pray, those who fight and"—the lowest stratum—"those who labor."[3]

To early-nineteenth-century European visitors, Americans appeared to have an inordinate desire for improvement and an overweening confidence in being able to achieve success. Tocqueville commented that "the first thing that strikes one in the United States is the innumerable crowd of those striving to escape from their original social conditions." To Tocqueville and other contemporary observers, the desire for advancement lent American life an aspect of almost frenetic activity and motion as Americans moved from place to place and from occupation to occupation. The spirit was apparent in the steady stream of settlers who abandoned eastern homes to seek fortunes in the West. Those who migrated were not the destitute but rather middle-class farmers who sold their land or left their fathers' homesteads.[4]

The objective of all this activity seems to have been less to acquire great wealth than to attain economic independence. Tocqueville noted not only Americans' addiction to work and love of money but also their desire for self-sufficiency. Historians by and large agree that Americans subscribed wholeheartedly to the republican concept of freedom as entailing ownership of productive property so as not to have to depend on another for one's livelihood. Under the prevailing conditions of open land and an expanding economy in the early nineteenth century, most white American men had a reasonable chance of realizing their aspirations for economic independence. Nine out of ten Americans lived on the land. With the exception of the wealthy and the growing merchant class in urban areas, households still grew much of their own food, manufactured cloth and other goods, and bartered produce for other necessities. In these semi-subsistence households, men did field work and made and maintained work implements, while women engaged in manufacture: processing and preserving food, weaving cloth, and making soap and candles and other goods. In this context the meaning of "labor" was broader than it later became. What Andrew Jackson called "the producing classes" encompassed all those involved in the production of goods—farmers, planters, laborers, mechanics, and small businessmen. Only those who profited from the work of others or whose occupations were financial or promotional, such as speculators, bankers, and lawyers, were excluded from the category of producers. At the other end of the scale and also excluded were those who also labored but were "dependent"—slaves. In Jackson's view the great middle stratum of producers formed the backbone of American democracy, and their independence needed to be preserved against the threats posed by nonproductive classes both above and below.[5]

The democratization of the ideal of economic independence involved ideological and material breaks with the past. As Robert Steinfeld has documented, labor arrangements in colonial America had mirrored English practices, which subjected workers to substantial control by employers. In the traditional master-servant system, minors were apprenticed to master craftsmen to learn a trade, eventually rising to journeymen. Apprentices and journeymen worked alongside the master, lived in his household, and took meals with his family, blurring boundaries between personal and work relations. Seventeenth- and eighteenth-century legal statutes regulating master-servant relations granted masters considerable authority to discipline servants and compel performance. They also defined the master's reciprocal obligation to provide protection and shelter, even if a servant became unable to work because of illness or injury.[6]

Another common type of unfree labor carried over from England was indentured servitude. In the labor-short colonial economy, indentured immigrants were a major source of workers. In one classic type of indenture, men and women desiring to immigrate signed contracts (before or after being transported) to serve for a specified period of time, typically four to seven years, in exchange for passage, a living, and the promise of "freedom dues" at the end of the contract. Bernard Bailyn has calculated that in the years 1773–1776 nearly 50 percent of

English and Scottish immigrants arrived as indentured servants or re-demptioners (who had to work to pay off debt for passage). Indenture was not limited to the unskilled: four out of five immigrating artisans in most highly skilled crafts arrived under indenture, only a slightly lower proportion than those in lower-skilled trades. The practice of importing indentured workers did not cease with the Revolution. Large numbers continued to be imported as late as 1819, and the prac-tice did not disappear until the 1830s.[7]

In the seventeenth and eighteenth centuries the work activities of white indentured servants and black slaves were often interchangeable, and there was considerable social intermingling among these groups. The major distinction, and a momentous one, was that indentured la-bor was not bound for life. Like apprentices, journeymen, and unin-dentured servants, indentured servants were dependent, but their de-pendence was considered temporary. After a period of service, they could expect to go out on their own, establish their own shops and farms, and become independent craftsmen or farmers. This was in marked contrast to chattel slavery, which involved involuntary, lifelong servitude and was a status limited to blacks. Thus from the beginning black racial status was closely linked to the most extreme form of un-free labor. Yet for over a century there existed a variety of labor ar-rangements aside from slavery that were far from free: apprenticeship, imprisonment for debt, tenant farming, hiring out of convicts, and im-pressment of sailors. Because there was a continuum between extreme independence and extreme dependence, we can speak of gradations of freedom-unfreedom among white men.[8]

Constructions of free and unfree and independent and dependent became more clearly polarized and racialized in the early decades of the Republic. Revolutionary-era rhetoric had spread egalitarian and liber-tarian ideas that called into question hierarchical labor arrangements among free men. Forms of relative unfreedom that white men had commonly experienced during at least some periods in their lives came to be seen as inconsistent with white male adulthood. As noted in Chapter 2, workers increasingly rejected the connotations of servility or dependence in the traditional terminology of "masters" and "ser-vants." European visitors were struck by what they considered the "ar-rogance" or "folly" of American workers, who were not loath to per-form any task put to them, but vociferously rejected the appellation of servant. The preferred terms were "help," "hired help," or sometimes hired man, woman, or girl. Such attitudes were not limited to American men. A European caller at a New England home in 1807 reported the following dialogue with a "maid servant" who opened the door: "Is your master at home? . . . I have no master . . . Don't you live here? . . . I *stay* here . . . And who are you then? . . . Why I am Mr. ———'s help. I'd have you to know, *man*, that I am no *sarvant*; none but *negers* are *sarvan*ts." Certain kinds of tasks had become so clearly racialized as black that they were considered too "servile" and degrading for whites. James Flint, who visited the United States from Britain in 1818–1820, noted that poor whites in Border States shunned certain types of labor which were associated with blacks, such as shoeblacking and carrying water.[9]

In a democratizing move to erase distinctions among them, laborers, journeymen, and artificers proudly assumed the title of "mechanic," which had earlier referred to less-skilled workers. Together they formed their own organizations, separate from craft associations headed by master craftsmen. By the 1790s and early 1800s journeyman societies in a number of crafts were engaged in struggles over wages and terms of employment, even taking part in strikes. As journeymen began to be prosecuted for criminal "conspiracy," their lawyers made clear that their clients no longer accepted what they considered the "slavish subordination" of traditional relations of employment. In an 1806 case involving Philadelphia cordwainers, their attorney Walter Franklin declared that the journeymen "conceived that every man being the sole owner, and master of his own goods and labour, had the right to affix the price of them; leaving to those who are to employ or purchase the right to accept or reject as they might think."[10]

Here was a clear statement of the emerging definition of independence, not as rooted in ownership of land or other productive resources, but as resting on ownership of one's own labor. Journeymen, along with domestic servants and laborers, were articulating a vision of workers as political equals with employers—as citizens entitled to self-government within the work relationship. Already, however, the logic of an emerging industrial economy was defining work as a market relation, not a political one. The court agreed with prosecutors that the journeymen were attempting to set up an illegitimate "private government" outside the democratically elected one. It declared the "combine" a criminal conspiracy: in a free market, employer and worker would have to meet each other as individuals negotiating the wage bargain according to the impersonal laws of supply and demand.[11]

The shift in language and meanings toward a market model had parallels in changing employment practices. Traditional arrangements such as living with the employer, taking meals at the employer's table, and working for long periods for a single family declined. Courts increasingly refused to enforce traditional rights of employers to chastise workers or to compel performance. By the same token courts also relieved employers of the obligation to take care of sick or injured employees.[12]

By 1800 northern state statutes and court decisions had largely eliminated indentured servitude for native adult men and women, limiting it to immigrants and minors. By the second decade of the nineteenth century slavery had been abolished in the northeast and middle states, and prohibition of all indenture followed not long after. Prior to 1820 many courts had viewed indenture as "voluntary" and therefore enforceable as long as it had been willingly entered into. After 1821, owing to various court decisions, "involuntary servitude" was deemed to exist as soon as a worker wanted to leave and was prevented from doing so.[13]

The doctrine of liberty of contract did not, however, alter the common law interpretation of the relationship between employer and employee. Once in the employment relationship, the worker was bound by the common law of masters and servants. Workers were required to obey their employers' directions as to how the work was done. Employers could withhold payment until the end of the term of contract. Max Weber later described the great power this formulation gave to employers: "The formal right of a worker to enter into any contract whatsoever with any employer whatsoever" means that "the more powerful party in the market, i.e. normally the employer, has the possibility to set the terms, to offer the job 'take it or leave it,' and, given the normally pressing economic need of the worker, to impose his terms upon him."[14]

Labor spokesmen disputed the law's notion of freedom and pointed out ways in which the power of wealth made a mockery of choice. A New England organization of workingmen called the region's mills monuments to "cupidity and avarice" that would crush the independence of "American freemen." A factory worker involved in the National Trades Union, the first national body of unionists, formed in 1834, charged that the factory system was "subversive of liberty—calculated to change the character of a people from . . . bold and free, to enervated, dependent, and slavish."[15]

Workingmen sought to reassert the traditional rights of artisans and artificers to work according to their own rhythms and to set their own hours. In their view employers should not be allowed to stretch out the workday to twelve or fourteen hours. Invoking the republican ideal, unionists said that worker citizens needed time for self-education and political discussion. During the 1820s and 1830s workers coalesced around drives for a ten-hour day. Workingmen's parties were active in several states in the late 1820s. These parties asked for what became standard demands for labor unions: an end to imprisonment for debt, mandatory militia duty, and the prison labor system, as well as reform of the legal system, more equitable tax laws, and mechanics' lien laws for first right to employers' payrolls. Workingmen's parties died out in the 1830s, but within a few years falling wage rates and worsening conditions for journeymen and factory workers during a time of price inflation sparked renewed trade union organizing. Strikes were mounted throughout the Northeast in 1836 to renew demands for a ten-hour day. In that year women textile workers in Philadelphia, Paterson, and various parts of New England participated in strikes that resulted in a compromise settlement for an eleven-hour day. Factory women marched through the streets of Lowell, Massachusetts, singing, "Oh I cannot be a slave, I will not be a slave." According to Bruce Laurie, this was one of the first references to "wage slavery," a term that became a battle cry of northern workers by the time of the Civil War and that continued to be invoked in the Gilded Age.[16]

Antebellum Northern Free Labor Ideology

By the 1850s "free labor" clearly became the basis of a sectional ideology, as the newly formed Republican Party enlisted northern citizens under its banner. The ideal of free labor drew together disparate antislavery elements: abolitionists morally opposed to slavery because it violated fundamental principles of freedom, equality, and justice; Republicans opposed to slavery because it threatened free labor and the

wage labor system of the North; and Jacksonian Democrats antagonistic to slavery because its existence weakened the position of white
workers.[17]

Northern free labor ideology drew on both major strains of American political thought, republicanism and liberalism. The republican
strain, inherited from the Revolutionary era, held that freedom required ownership of productive property. This strain can be traced
through Jefferson's ideal of the United States as a nation of yeomen
farmers; Jackson's championing of the "producing classes"; and Lincoln's depiction of the average northern "workingman" as an artisan,
farmer, or small entrepreneur who worked for himself, "taking the
whole product to [himself]." The second strain, derived from classical
liberal political economy, defined workers' freedom as residing in their
ownership of their labor. Adam Smith had described "the property that
everyman has in his own labor" as "the original foundation of all property." In this formula workers were "free" to the extent that they were
not tied by any legal bonds to particular tasks or masters. This strain
ran through the claims of journeymen in the 1790s asserting their right
to negotiate the terms of their employment on the grounds that they
were the owners and masters of their own labor. It can also be traced
through nineteenth-century arguments of propertyless white men for
the right to the franchise on the grounds that they were free, productive, and independent workers.[18]

Though seemingly contradictory, the two strains were often intertwined in the thinking of northern Republicans. Foner points out that
for Lincoln and for Horace Greeley (the editor of the influential *New
York Tribune*), the lifelong wage worker was in many ways as unfree as a
slave in the South. However, their assumption was that wage labor was
only a temporary condition for the northern worker. In the words of
Lincoln, "the man who labored for another last year, this year labors
for himself, and next year he will have others labor for him." Even as
Lincoln spoke of wage work as a way station on the road to eventual independence, economic changes were under way that would mean that a
large portion of the labor force could expect to remain lifelong employees. David Montgomery estimates that by 1870, 67 percent of pro-
ductively engaged individuals were employed by others rather than being independent.[19]

The abolitionist critique of slavery was framed primarily in moral terms, but it also included condemnation of slavery's violation of free labor principles. Convinced of the unique evils of slavery, abolitionists rejected the claim that the conditions of northern workers constituted "wage slavery." They etched a sharp line between the illegitimate coercion of slavery and the freedom of wage labor. According to Eric Foner, by drawing this dichotomy abolitionists helped popularize the notion that autonomy derived not from owning productive property but from property in one's self and the ability to sell one's labor. In William Forbath's words, the abolitionist critique affirmed that "a free society was compatible with a dependent class of workers. Put baldly, abolitionism implied that only chattel slavery created unfreedom while the harsh new dependencies and disciplines of proletarianization did not." Still, abolitionists went beyond advocating labor freedom: many supported economic independence for workers and called for equality before the law, universal citizenship, and color-blind treatment.[20]

Most northern Republicans, including Lincoln, opposed slavery on narrower grounds. Contrasting northern economic progress with southern stagnation, Republican proponents of free labor held that the free labor system was the source of dynamism in the North, while the system of slavery had stunted development in the South. Not only was slave labor less productive and less efficient; reliance on slave labor promoted laziness, undermined democracy, and corrupted the morals of slaveowners. Living on the "unrewarded work of others," the aristocracy of the South "ruled tyrannically over a subject population." Slavery, in the words of one critic, bred "pride, indolence, luxury, and licentiousness" among white southerners.[21]

In the 1850s antislavery forces coalesced around opposition to the extension of slavery into western territories. Touting economic development in the West as necessary to advance the nation's prosperity, northern Republicans began emphasizing the deleterious effects of slavery not only on economic growth but also on the status of white labor. If slavery expanded into the West, they argued, northern white workers would effectively be barred from entry because of the stigma attached to labor. Conversely, banning slavery would secure the western territories for white labor. This appeal harnessed antiblack sentiments to the antislavery cause and elicited support even from those who were not principled abolitionists. Free Soilers and Jacksonian Democrats joined in opposing the extension of slavery on the grounds that slavery brought labor into contempt. One speaker declared, "Because bondage degrades, cramps and degenerates man, labor shares the same disgrace because it is part of the slave." Antislavery convictions of white workers, small businessmen, and small farmers were thus fueled by self-interest and hostility to blacks rather than by sympathy toward slaves or concern with their plight.[22]

Thus by the 1850s Republican free labor ideology viewed work as a market relation, not a political one, and this represented a shift from Revolutionary-era republicanism that had portrayed work as the production by free citizens of useful goods for the benefit of the community. The new framework viewed work as the sale of labor power at a price determined by impersonal laws of supply and demand. In this framework, as the legal historian Arthur McEvoy notes, "the political aspects of the employment relation—control over the work itself, duties of care and obedience between workers and employers, and so on—were subordinated to the contractual relation and thus disappeared from view."[23]

As in the case of suffrage, those excluded from earning in the labor market were the most ardent in expressing its value. Frederick Douglass rejoiced at his first paying job in New Bedford, Massachusetts, after escaping from the South: "The thought, 'I can work! I can work for living: I am not afraid of work; I have no Master Hugh to rob me of my earnings'—placed me in a state of Independence." Nineteenth-century feminists also recognized the problem of women being forced to be economically dependent. Some activists understood women's unpaid labor for the family as real work that contributed to family resources and called for joint property laws on that basis. Other feminists saw earning in the labor market as the way for women to achieve independence and called for recognition of women's right to earn on their own.[24]

Republican free labor ideology did not go unchallenged. According to some labor leaders, the terms that workers accepted were not freely chosen. Northern labor spokesmen drew on the language of slavery to describe the plight of wage workers. In doing so, they sometimes claimed not just that the workers' situation was akin to that of slaves in the South but that it was actually worse. Northern workers, they said, were more productive and worked longer hours, so more profit was extracted from them. Some leaders even alleged that because slaves were valuable as property, owners at least took care not to overwork them, whereas white workers enjoyed no such protection and could be worked to death.[25]

Exclusions

Mid-nineteenth-century free labor doctrine, though stated in universalistic terms, applied only to those considered "sui juris," that is, legally entitled to participate in the market. Race was one basis for exclusion from contract. While black slavery was the main point of contrast with "free white labor" in the North, other nonwhite racial groups were associated with unfree labor in the newer (and therefore peripheral) regions of the West. Forms of servitude considered unacceptable for white manhood were considered fitting for Native Americans, Asians, Mexicans, and other racialized minorities.

In the Southwest and the West, Indians could be legally bound to indentured servitude amounting to slavery long after indenture had been eliminated for whites in the East and the Midwest. Despite the dominance of free labor ideology in California, the state legislature passed an Indenture Act in 1850, which allowed any citizen to take custody of an Indian child and place him or her under apprenticeship in exchange for providing clothing and other modest necessities. The vagrancy portion of the law let law enforcement officers arrest Indians for a wide variety of offenses, from loitering to drunkenness, and hire them out to the highest bidder. The act was amended in 1860 to make it easier for white petitioners to take custody and bind Indian minors and to regularize periods of indenture, extending "apprenticeships" up to age thirty for Indian men and twenty-five for Indian women. Although the law also specified monetary fines for failure to clothe or feed indentured Indians or for subjecting them to inhumane treatment, conviction was virtually ruled out by another section that stated that "in no case shall a white man be convicted on the testimony of an Indian or Indians." One scholar estimates that upward of 10,000 children and adults, or 10 percent of the California Native American population, may have been enslaved under the terms of the act, which was not repealed until 1863.[26]

The territorial legislatures in Utah and New Mexico also adopted measures regulating contracts between masters and servants that were used to bind Indians. In 1851 the New Mexico legislature passed a bill reviving Mexican decrees authorizing peonage. Under the law servants could not leave their masters' service while in debt to them. In 1859 the legislature amended the law to prevent any interference with masters' rights to correct their servants. Legalized peonage continued in New Mexico until 1867 when the U.S. Congress passed a federal antipeonage act barring voluntary and involuntary servitude in all U.S. states and territories.[27]

In California, railroads, mining, and other industries imported thousands of indentured Chinese workers in the 1850s. Still, free labor ideology and antislavery sentiment were sufficiently strong that, despite lobbying by employers, California courts refused to enforce contracts in cases of workers who escaped. Employers then turned to the credit ticket system, in which labor importers advanced money to pay for transportation. Although bound by debt, Chinese laborers could repay the loans by working on jobs of their own choice. The construction of Chinese as unfree labor remained firmly fixed, however. Anti-Chinese labor leaders continually railed against "coolie labor" as undercutting the position of "free white labor."[28]

THE OTHER MAJOR EXEMPTION from antebellum free labor principles was women of all classes. Though industrialization was starting to remove manufacturing from the household, a great deal of production still took place at the household level. Family-owned small businesses, farms, and shops relied on unpaid labor from all family members, including wives and children under the control of the male head. The specific work activities of men and women differed by class, urban-rural residence, and race/ethnicity, but, generally speaking, both men and women were involved in production.

Men were responsible for field work, artisanal production, and, increasingly, outside wage work, and women were in charge of manufacturing many goods used by the household and assisted husbands in workshops or businesses. Wives of skilled and semiskilled urban workers contributed to family income by taking in boarders and performing "outwork" such as hand loom weaving, hat making, shoe binding, and sewing, which employers distributed to married women to do as piecework in their homes. Outside of industrial centers, married women still did spinning, weaving, milking, foraging, and gardening, and made

I worked regardless of race

butter and cheese. Among freed blacks, men were less likely to find steady employment, and wives more frequently worked outside the homes, but black women too earned much of their income at home by taking in boarders or doing washing, ironing, and sewing.[29]

Women in all classes had primary responsibility for social reproduction—cooking, cleaning, childcare, shopping, and other labor that maintained people on a daily basis and intergenerationally. Middleclass women might have household servants to assist them, but in some ways their maintenance work was more complex because of the rising standards of domestic comfort. In any case, women performed reproductive labor alongside their productive activities, and men had some responsibility for reproductive labor, such as disciplining and training sons. Thus there was a clear gender division of labor, but men and women were economically interdependent: the labor of both was needed to provide for the family.[30]

The decision to marry was increasingly recognized as a freely chosen contractual action, but after marriage the old common law doctrine of coverture came into play. The wife's legal identity was subsumed under the husband's, and both parties had to abide by terms of the marriage "bargain." These terms included wives' duty to provide labor and husbands' ownership of the fruits of that labor. Under the doctrine of marital service, courts throughout the nineteenth century refused to recognize income-earning work wives did in family businesses, in keeping boarders, or in industrial homework as entitling them to payment or a share of family property. The principle of men's ownership of women's and children's labor also can be seen in the practice of contracting with male heads for the whole family's labor, still common up to the 1840s in New England shoe mills.[31]

In some ways women's labor became less visible with the advance of capitalist industrialization. The growing capitalist sector was characterized by separation between workplace and place of residence and between the activities of producing goods and those of social reproduction. Reproductive activities remained lodged in the home and were assigned to women and thus became "women's work." "Men's work" in the meantime, increasingly took place in the public labor market. The ideological split between the public world of the market and politics and the private world of the household became more sharply delineated. The market and politics came to be viewed as ruled by competition and desire for individual gain, while the household and the family were viewed as realms where altruism and mutual care reigned. Historians have suggested that men thrown into this new harsh world needed the idea of a domestic haven where they could find succor and support. Women, as maintainers of the home, were cast into the idealized role of domestic angels who provided respite and comfort to wage workers.[32]

The reality was that daily maintenance required a great deal of difficult and often physically taxing labor. In an evolving economic system in which value and independence were measured by earning, unpaid productive and reproductive labor did not count as real work. Courts would not even recognize private agreements in which a wife gained a share of a husband's estate on the basis of her services. Reva Siegel has documented the efforts of some antebellum feminists to win joint property rights for married women in recognition of the contribution women made to the accumulation of assets through their labor. Such recognition would have undermined men's property rights in women's labor, and male legislators and judges rejected this reform out of hand. Nonetheless, other social forces, including growing numbers of single women and deserted wives of men moving west, led to reforms that advanced married women's capacity to act independently. Many states passed acts that gave women rights to property they brought into a marriage; several states passed earnings statutes that recognized employed women's separate earnings as belonging to them.[33]

Capitalist Industrialization and Stratified Labor

Post–Civil War constitutional amendments and other federal legislation ended not only chattel slavery but also all forms of indenture. As noted previously, the U.S. Congress passed an antipeonage act in 1867 banning voluntary as well as involuntary servitude in all states and territories. Thenceforth all Americans, regardless of race or prior condition of servitude, were legally "free labor." Simultaneously, however, the rise of a new capitalist industrial order meant that "free labor" would be subjected to novel forms of control and discipline.

The Civil War was followed by a period of unprecedented economic growth, a manufacturing boom fueled by coal, iron, and steam. The building of the transcontinental railroad and the spread of branch railroad lines tied the nation together, opened up new areas for commercial farming, and made possible a national market for manufactured goods. The voracious appetite for capital by the great trunk railroads facilitated the consolidation of the nation's financial market in Wall Street. The process of economic concentration saw the rise of giant corporations in major industries such as steel, oil, agricultural machinery, sugar refining, and meatpacking.[34] Although artisanal production continued in major cities, the factory system was coming to dominate much of industrial production. With mechanization and the breakdown of work processes into separate steps, industrialists could substitute semiskilled for skilled labor. More and more jobs thus required only minimal skills. Many semiskilled jobs were filled by displaced artisans and laborers from rural areas and from Europe.[35] Corporations introduced new management strategies (rational planning and bureaucratic hierarchy) and new forms of organization (vertical integration to encompass supply of materials, production, and marketing) to escape the uncertainties of market forces and to break the power of worker associations.[36]

In a sense, capitalist industrialization and the abolition of slavery transformed both northern independent producers and chattel slaves into "hirelings." Theoretically, impersonal capital should not have cared about the race or gender of the hireling: on the grounds of maximum efficiency, all individuals having the capacity to do a job should have been considered interchangeable units of labor. Yet the capitalist labor market that emerged was fundamentally organized by race and gender. Alexander Saxton stated this puzzle with respect to race: "As labor power assumed its characteristically capitalist form of commodity, economic theory might have predicted that racial characteristics would lose their relevance in the labor market. On the contrary, they dominated the labor market. From what socioeconomic nutriments, in the era of modernization, did the ideological component, racism, draw its sustenance?"[37] We can expand Saxton's framing of the issue to ask why both race and gender were central organizing principles in the capitalist labor market.

This framing of the issue is useful but still incomplete. It implies that racism was exogenous to the capitalist labor system, rather than being integral to it. Saxton's own study of race and labor in the antebellum period demonstrates that while white supremacy was a consistent principle, racial ideology was being reworked and rearticulated in conjunction with political, social, and economic developments. In line with the approach of viewing race and gender as fluid and decentered complexes, my interest is in how race-gender relations and meanings were rearticulated, contested, and transformed in the course of capitalist reorganization of the economy. Thus it is crucial to examine not only the ways in which prior race-gender hierarchies were incorporated into the capitalist labor system but also the ways in which capitalist industrialization helped create new structures and relations of race and gender. That is, just as the slave system created and maintained particular configurations of "black" and "white" manhood and womanhood,[38] so the capitalist labor regime led to new configurations of white and nonwhite manhood and womanhood.

I would argue that there were two general dynamics of capitalism that led to reconfigurations of race and gender relations and meanings. First, by transforming both production and reproduction, capitalism created a new dialectical relationship between the household and the labor market and between men's and women's work. Second, the processes of capitalist production and accumulation generated new class formations and new conflicts between them: between employers and workers, between capitalists in different sectors, and between different segments of labor—men and women, whites and nonwhites, skilled and unskilled.

Production and Reproduction

Capitalist industrialization changed the relationship between production (the creation of goods) and social reproduction (the maintenance of people), as more and more production was moved from the household to larger centralized shops, factories, and industrial establishments. This shift was quite visible by the end of the nineteenth century and almost complete by the mid-twentieth century. Thus capitalist industrialization widened the structural and conceptual separation between the "private" realm of the family and the "public" realm of industry. Households became less self-contained economic units and became more dependent on outside wages.

In capitalist production the relevant labor unit is not the household but the individual. The individual worker is employed in producing commodities (goods and services) for the market. The worker receives wages, which can then be used in the market to purchase necessities (goods and services). The household becomes an income-pooling unit rather than a production unit. What was left behind was *reproduction*, which remained organized at the household level.

A new prescribed division of labor by gender arose to carry out production and reproduction. Men were to follow production out of the household, while women were to remain responsible for reproduction at home. Some feminist theorists have argued that the capitalist labor system in fact "needed" women's labor in the home to maintain male workers, stabilize the workforce, and care for the next generation of workers.[39] This did not rule out women's participation in the labor force, for capitalists could simultaneously use women as a source of cheap labor in expanding industries. When the New England textile industry began in the first decade of the nineteenth century, the economy was still mostly agrarian and men were fully engaged in farming and independent artisanry. Mill owners actively recruited the only readily available labor force, single young white women from farm families. Similarly, the expansion of public education (a development related to political and economic changes accompanying industrialization) would not have been possible without the recruiting of women for teaching, which became feminized in the 1840s. By 1870 women made up one-fifth of the nonagricultural labor force, a percentage that rose to one-fourth by 1900 even as the number of men drawn into wage labor mushroomed.[40]

Yet, despite the large number of women working for wages, the model of male as breadwinner, female as homemaker, which arose first in the middle class, became the prevailing ideal. According to this model, the primary responsibility of male heads of households was to earn enough to support their wives and children, while the primary mission of married women was to care for the home and family members. Ideally, married women were to devote full-time to domesticity and were not to be employed outside the home. If for whatever reason they were employed, their work in the labor market was deemed to be secondary and their earnings supplementary.[41]

This model helped reconcile the conflicting demands for women's reproductive labor in the home and their productive labor in industry. It legitimated the unequal division of labor in the home and women's subordinate place in the labor market. Since women "belonged in the home" and were working only for supplementary income, it made sense that they be kept in part-time, seasonal, or irregular jobs and paid little. The ideology also gave employers great flexibility. They could use women as a "reserve army of labor," calling them up in times of shortage, such as during economic booms or wars, and letting them go during recessions or when men returned from war so that they could return to their "proper place" in the home.[42]

The male-as-breadwinner model also served as a "disciplinary" discourse that helped create masculine subjects consonant with capitalist industrialization. Being "good breadwinners" required men to be "good workers": reliable, steady, and willing to work long hours, conform to rules, and put up with dangerous conditions. Breadwinning also became a source of masculine pride and identity, the basis for claiming political equality, a decent standard of living, and the right to a family life in which wives were available to "keep house" and take care of children.[43]

The dominant culture calculated the relative value of productive versus reproductive labor differently for different groups. Motherhood and domesticity were elevated as virtues for white women. White men were seen as requiring and deserving a wife's services, and white children were viewed as valued future citizens to be nurtured and protected. In contrast, the caring that black women performed for their families was not deemed worthy of protection. Men of color were denied the kind of honorable manhood that included being served by women, and black children were not valued as future citizens. Black women were considered "useful" only for work performed outside the family, whether in production or reproduction. The older belief that people of color's labor was owed to the community, and the emerging capitalist calculation that each individual constituted an individual unit of labor, came together in the treatment of women of color. Poor black and Latina mothers were deemed to be "employable," and not requiring or deserving of charity. Women of color who were not employed were even deemed "vagrants" and put to work forcibly.[44]

Working-class families, both white and nonwhite, defended the male breadwinner/female homemaker ideal by withdrawing married women's labor from the market whenever possible. Workingmen's demands for a family wage, which began in the 1830s and 1840s, invoked republican principles of the right of workers to the fruits of their labor and traditions of workers' autonomy to determine the pace and organization of their work. These workingmen were also asserting the dignity of the (male) worker, which necessitated some independence outside of work. In opposing a purely economic or market calculation, they were asserting that not all human labor should be commodified, but rather that some—particularly women's—labor ought to be retained for the benefit of family members. The stakes were similar for ex-slaves, but there were additional complications. Freed households sought autonomy from white planters' control. They tried whenever possible to support themselves by having men engage in subsistence farming, hunting, fishing, and seasonal or occasional work and withdrawing women from field work and domestic service. The removal of black women's reproductive labor was a form of double resistance to the incorporation of the whole family into capitalist regimes of labor and to white control of family life.[45]

Class Formation and Conflict

Economic growth and concentration brought immense wealth, most of which was accumulated by the owners of industry and finance. By 1890 the richest 1 percent of Americans owned more property than the remaining 99 percent and earned more than half of the total income. Although real wages rose during this time, the gap between the incomes of skilled workmen and those of semiskilled workers grew. While the former might support their families unaided, the semiskilled household required multiple earners.[46]

Capitalist industrialization also brought about frequent and severe cycles of booms and busts. Between 1870 and 1921 the United States experienced six major economic downturns and a comparable number of less pronounced ones. With fewer opportunities for self-employment and with an influx of Irish and other immigrants, there was a larger "reserve army of labor." Unemployment emerged as a serious social problem for the first time in American history. In Massachusetts, one of the most highly industrialized states during this period, well over 30 percent of workers were unemployed at some time during the year in the depressions of the mid-1870s and the 1890s. Simultaneously, the closing of the frontier (announced by the U.S. Census Bureau in 1890) cut off a major route to self-sufficiency. For increasing numbers of Americans, wage work would be a permanent condition, not a temporary way station.[47]

Faced with these conditions, workers organized into associations and unions and engaged in mass protests and strikes. Waves of strikes occurred in 1873–74 (when railroad workers took charge of shops, uncoupled cars, tore up track, and cut telegraph wires), 1886 (when 1,433 work stoppages were recorded), and 1890–91 (when there were 1,833 and 1,717 stoppages). Labor's activism won some reforms in some states in the 1880s and 1890s with the passage of laws abolishing prison labor systems, reducing child labor, establishing factory inspection commissions, and creating bureaus of labor statistics.[48]

Capital enlisted the power of the state—the military and the courts—to put down worker protest. Corporations employed private police to beat up workers and used their political clout to have state militias and troops brought in to quell protests. A government study showed that state troopers were called out 500 times to put down labor unrest between 1875 and 1910. Employers also used legal injunctions to stop workers from striking and protesting. Courts invoked the hoary doctrine of "criminal conspiracy" in ruling that such actions interfered with the right of employers to negotiate individually with workers for the terms of contract.[49]

As northern workers organized, they sometimes succeeded in getting state legislatures to pass laws regulating hours and wages in certain industries. However, these laws were regularly struck down by state and federal courts, which invoked an extreme version of liberty of contract. For example, in 1885 a New York Superior Court issued what has been dubbed the "Freedom of Sweatshop" ruling. The court concluded that a state law prohibiting cigar making in tenements was an unreasonable abridgment of property rights. In 1886 and 1893 the Supreme Courts of Pennsylvania and Missouri invoked freedom of contract to nullify statutes prohibiting wage payment in anything except legal tender. In 1887 the U.S. Supreme Court voided a Pennsylvania statute requiring that the state's iron mill workers be paid wages at regular intervals and in cash, rather than in scrip that could only be redeemed in company stores. In a frequently cited case, *Lockner v. New York* (1905), the Court invalidated a New York state law setting maximum hours for bakers. Laws regulating labor conditions were held to be unconstitutional on the grounds that they violated the contractual freedom of workers to sell their labor for whatever periods and under whatever conditions they wished. This perverse interpretation of freedom of contract bespoke a blindness to the actual economic and material circumstances under which employers and workers "bargained." Economic coercion made possible by the greater power and resources of corporations was not deemed to compromise the freedom of choice of the workers.[50]

Organized workers, who had successfully fought for passage of reform laws, viewed freedom of contract as a sham. George McNeill, a spokesman for the Eight Hour League, testified before the Massachusetts Legislature's labor committee in 1874: "The laborer's commodity perishes every day beyond possibility of recovery. He must sell to-day's labor to-day, or never." The terms of the sale were set by employers: "An empty stomach can make no contracts." The workers "*assent* but they do not *consent*, they submit but they do not agree."[51]

Union membership grew even in the face of implacable opposition by employers. The National Labor Union of the 1860s and 1870s and the Knights of Labor of the 1870s and 1880s expressed the aspirations of workers as citizens and producers, harking back to earlier understandings of the master-worker relationship in which workers had some say about the pace and organization of work. The Knights of Labor, the largest and most prominent Gilded Age labor organization, was made up of both trade assemblies (in which the plurality of workers were from a single trade) and mixed assemblies. Membership was open to manual workers and artisans, and to small producers and wage workers. It even included blacks and women, who were formed into their own locals. Joining politics and economics in a vision of a "cooperative commonwealth," the Knights of Labor called for the nationalization of industry, the abolition of private banking, and factory reforms. Peaking in the late 1880s with a membership of three-quarters of a million, the Knights then rapidly declined in the aftermath of the failure of the mass eight-hour strikes of 1886, internal conflicts over the organization of cigar makers, the bitter clashes between police and workers in the Haymarket riot of 1886, and intensified state and police repression of strikes and union activity. The combined power of capital and the state proved too great for the Knights to overcome.[52]

The Knights were succeeded by another labor organization that emerged in the Gilded Age, the American Federation of Labor. Its founders were trade union leaders like Samuel Gompers, president of the Cigar Makers Union, who shunned the wide-ranging reforms advocated by the Knights of Labor. By the 1890s, disillusioned by dim prospects for legislative reform and by state violence against labor radicalism, the AFL turned to a pragmatic approach that abjured reform and government regulation in favor of "strong unionism"—unionized craftsmen looking to their own organizations to further their interests. This strategy effectively excluded unskilled and semiskilled workers, whose vulnerability made them prone to engage in mass strikes, which then invited government intervention. Because women and black workers were concentrated in unskilled and semiskilled jobs, they were among those excluded. Under Gompers the AFL railed against laws regulating labor as well as social and industrial reform laws, advocating instead their own version of laissez-faire labor relations. Insisting on labor's right to engage in "responsible" collective actions, including strikes and boycotts, as integral to freedom of contract, the AFL focused on campaigns to get states and courts to stop using injunctions against unions.[53]

The AFL ideal of the "manly worker" standing up to the boss, suggests Bruce Laurie, was the cousin of the republican yeoman and accorded well with Gilded Age courts' gendered understanding of free labor doctrine. Having rejected the notion that authority and control in the workplace were integral to men's independence, the courts nonetheless affirmed the principle that authority over the domestic sphere and control of the labor of wives and children were the essence of manhood. Thus the courts helped create a fictional equality among men based on their authority over women. Women's subordination to men's authority in turn meant that women lacked the capacity to direct their own labor and thus had no right to contract their own labor. On this basis courts found that state laws barring women from entering certain occupations did not violate the constitutional right to labor at one's chosen vocation.[54]

Male workers generally subscribed to the dominant ideology of female dependence, leaving it to working women themselves to challenge the idea that their gender should limit their economic freedom. As early as the 1830s a group of striking women shoe binders had declared: "Equal rights should be extended to all, . . . to the weaker sex as well as the stronger." Equal opportunity to enter the labor market was a recurring demand of nineteenth-century feminists. They understood the importance of earning to emancipating women from economic dependence and paternalistic bonds. They also recognized that many women had no choice but to support themselves and sometimes their families. The Civil War had increased the urgency of women's economic self-sufficiency by thrusting many women into the workforce and leaving many without a male provider. Most women continued to accept the domestic realm as their primary responsibility, but many did not feel that paid employment compromised their dignity. Faced with unyielding hostility to their efforts to get women's unpaid family labor recognized as "real work" that entitled them to a share of family property, late-nineteenth-century feminists were forced to change tactics by concentrating on measures that would enable women to work as equals to men in the wage-labor market.[55]

Owners of industry sought to maximize profits by paying the lowest possible wages and exerting maximum control over production processes. They were able to take advantage of existing inequalities by using groups (racialized minorities, immigrants, women, the less skilled or less educated) that could be hired more cheaply or that were less able to resist control and coercion. Yet employers sometimes had to compete with one another for certain kinds of workers. Competition with other employers for skilled workers might drive up the price of their labor. One strategy to reduce costs was to reduce reliance on human skills. Capitalists instituted mechanization and "detailed division of labor"—breaking down work processes into discrete smaller tasks that could be performed by unskilled or semiskilled workers. In addition to increasing employers' control over the work process and achieving standardized outcomes, deskilling allowed employers to save on labor costs by substituting lower-priced workers for higher-priced workers, women for men, and immigrants and workers of color for native white workers.[56]

Capitalists were not working with a passive medium, of course. Workers fought displacement, although often their hostility was directed against the groups who displaced them. Workers sought to maximize wages and to retain autonomy and control over the work process. They resisted being proletarianized in individual and collective ways, ranging from slowing down their pace to sabotage, and from making rhetorical appeals to engaging in strikes and protests. They also sought to maintain their advantage vis-à-vis other workers. Native white men, who were already in the strongest position, sought to monopolize better jobs and reduce competition by setting up barriers against other workers. Formal and informal mechanisms of exclusion were rife in the skilled trades. White workingmen and their organizations deployed cultural constructs—such as white manhood, the responsibilities of breadwinning, and citizenship—to claim their "right" to the best jobs. They used their political capital to lobby for restrictive agreements and legislation to exclude women, immigrants, and workers of color from certain jobs or industries or to prevent some groups, such as the Chinese, from entering the country at all. In turn employers used competition between groups to play off workers against one another, granting some groups symbolic and material wages to undercut collective organization.[57]

One outcome of these conflicts was segmentation in the labor market along race and gender lines. Workers with the greatest leverage—native white men—were disproportionately employed in capital-intensive and more monopolistic sectors and industries where higher labor costs could be borne. They also were overrepresented in higher-skill jobs and in supervisory positions where employers were motivated to invest in training and retention. Minorities, immigrants, and women, lacking political or other means to advance their position, were more often relegated to sectors, industries, and jobs that were labor intensive, unstable, and highly competitive (where downward pressure on wages was greatest). Since labor markets were necessarily local, the race and gender stratification of labor varied by locale, depending on the mixture of industries and the available labor pool.

Workers did at times come together across race and gender lines and across the divide between skilled and unskilled. As noted earlier, the Knights of Labor included artisans and manual workers as members and also incorporated women and blacks, albeit in separate organizations. A few early unions, such as the dockworkers, were interracial. Such efforts tended to occur in isolated pockets. Interracial coordinated strikes and protests sparked particularly virulent reactions from employers and were met by maximum force and violence.[58]

Ideology and Identity

Some theories of labor market allocation that assume that in a rational market people are assigned jobs on the basis of their human capital and are paid according to their productivity (that is, their contribution to profit). A rational market model cannot account for stratification of labor and differentials in earnings by race and gender. Alice Kessler-Harris has found that wage determination has been heavily shaped by subjective notions of what constituted an adequate wage for specific groups. A "man's wage" was sufficient to support a worker and his family at a decent standard (a so-called American standard of living) and was a badge of honor. A "woman's wage," in contrast, was calculated even by reformers at a very low level and was a mark of dishonor. Women were simply paid less for doing the same kind of work or for a given level of productivity than men were.

A "man's wage" did not apply to men of color, who were not accorded respect as heads of households. Thus, for example, black men's earnings were not assumed to cover support for a non-employed wife and children. Black women, after all, were viewed as laboring bodies. Additionally, the standard of living of blacks and other people of color was assumed to be lower than that of whites. The racial rhetoric—whether justifying lower wages for people of color or blaming people of color for driving down wages—was that blacks, Chinese, Mexicans, and other less evolved peoples could survive on next to nothing.[59]

Because the labor market was so segregated, jobs themselves took on race-gender meanings. Work associated with racialized minorities was viewed as "dirty" or "servile," and that associated with women as "unskilled" and "feminine." Epithets such as "nigger work" were attached to servantry, field labor, and cleaning. Such jobs were viewed as inappropriate for white men and shunned by them. The race-gender segmentation of jobs was in turn made to seem natural by assumptions about certain groups' affinities and capabilities that suited them for the kinds of work they did—for example, (white) women's purer morals and love of children made them ideal teachers, or Japanese men's servile attitudes made them excellent servants.[60]

Change and continuity in the idea of free labor from the antebellum period to the Progressive era can be seen in white workingmen's campaign for the family wage. The notion that the earnings of workingmen should be sufficient to support a dependent family emerged in the first half of the nineteenth century as a response to social and economic changes brought about by industrial development. In the face of eroding status and wages and increasing instability and insecurity, workingmen's demands for a family wage represented a claim both for adequate subsistence and for social justice. Workers claimed the right to live according to the dominant ideal of family based on male authority and female domesticity. Martha May notes: "One purpose of the family wage demand was to spare the workingman's wife and children the degradation of factory labor. And, equally important, it was to insure that the workingman would retain his status within the family, and his right to a family structure resembling that of the more advantaged classes."[61] During this period, advocacy for or opposition to the family wage was clearly linked to class interests. Workers saw the family wage as a means to diminish capitalist control over family life. In claiming their right to a family wage, they were challenging a purely economic calculation by raising considerations of dignity and independence. Employers and laissez-faire economists strenuously opposed the very idea, arguing that providing for nonworkers would ruin American industry and violate the spirit of free enterprise.

Except for skilled craftsmen, the family wage proved elusive. Few working-class male heads earned enough to support a household. In most cases the household economy relied on the combined efforts of husbands' wage-earning and wives' and children's subsistence and income-earning activity. Common activities for wives ranged from growing vegetables and keeping chickens and small livestock, to doing piecework at home, taking in boarders, and selling homemade or homegrown products. Children helped with industrial homework and ran errands.[62]

Nonetheless, the family wage for men remained firmly rooted as an ideal. But by the end of the nineteenth century its emphasis had shifted from a critique of capitalist ideology and a defense of family and class autonomy to the maximizing of union power and the assertion of male privilege. The campaign for a family wage—now recast as a "living wage"—was taken up by Progressive social scientists and reformers who sought to uplift the moral and physical quality of the working class. The living wage was even supported by some paternalistic industrialists, such as Henry Ford, who wanted to promote social stability. When the Progressives gained political power, they helped establish state and federal agencies to regulate and monitor public health and safety, child welfare, and labor conditions. They undertook studies to establish base living standards and household budgets in order to calculate the minimum earnings necessary to maintain a household.[63]

The ideal of a living wage assumed female dependence as a condition for men to be real men. Thus, according to May, the ideal became more closely linked to notions of gender privilege than to class autonomy. In 1907 the AFL called for a wage "sufficient to maintain (workers) and those dependent upon them in a manner consistent with their responsibilities as *husbands, fathers, men,* and *citizens.*" The focus on manhood remained the same in a 1919 statement: "The living wage is the right to be a man and to exercise freely and fully the rights of a free man." While not systematically supporting restrictions on women, the AFL did not oppose exclusion of women from its locals. Regardless of intent, the living wage and breadwinner ideals buttressed male privilege in the labor market. Men's responsibility for breadwinning (irrespective of the actual family status of particular men) was used to claim priority in access to higher-paid jobs. The corollary belief that women workers were only supplementing family income (irrespective of the actual situation of specific women) legitimated unequal wages and sex segregation of jobs.[64]

The other major direction of efforts to shore up the position of wage-earning men was to restrict women's employment through "protective legislation." Some early laws limiting hours for women workers were passed in the 1850s, but efforts to get state laws limiting the hours of working women and children accelerated in the 1880s and 1890s. Middle-class women harnessed maternalist ideology to establish their moral authority to clean up the public realm and bring relief and protection to the less fortunate. Women reformers, settlement house workers, and journalists began to focus attention on the dire situation of women workers and their families and on the dangers to their physical and moral well-being posed by working long hours under unhealthful conditions. They exposed the wretched living and working conditions of women and children engaged in sweated labor in homes, factories, and sweatshops. Female reformers and activists called for legislation to regulate the conditions of work for women and children. They were joined by male Progressives and labor leaders, some of whom hoped that protective legislation for women and children would provide an opening wedge for broader regulations covering all workers. In the decades leading up to World War I, most state legislatures passed laws that set minimum wages, limited night work, and regulated health and safety standards for women, or that barred them from certain jobs that exposed them to hazards.[65]

Protective legislation was premised on women's physical and psychological weakness rather than on their rights as workers. The same courts that had overturned broader-gauged laws protecting all workers ruled that protective legislation for women (and children) passed constitutional muster. Three years after the *Lockner* decision that had invalidated a New York law setting maximum hours for bakers, the U.S. Supreme Court in the landmark *Muller v. Oregon* case (1908) upheld an Oregon law limiting hours for women in certain occupations. In addition to agreeing with counsel Louis Brandeis's brief referring to women's physical weakness and possible harm to the health of their future children, the majority decision referred to women's lack of self-reliance and thus their inability to bargain and compete in the marketplace.[66]

The new protections were also racially selective. White women were deemed in need of protection to ensure the future of the white race. The laws were not stated in racial terms, but industries and occupations in which women of color were concentrated were exempted from coverage, usually on the grounds of economic necessity. Agricultural and domestic workers were routinely excluded. For example, in California, where many Mexican women were employed in harvesting and other agricultural activities, a protective law specifically excluded female harvesters. In 1915, in *Miller v. Wilson*, the Supreme Court upheld this law on the grounds that such laws might help "check the rapid decline in reproduction of the older American stocks."[67]

White workingmen's efforts to shore up their position also aimed to exclude men of color as competitors. In the West the focus was on Asian immigrant workers. From their earliest appearance in the United States, the Chinese had been likened to blacks as an inferior race, and one central element of white imagery of the Chinese was their "slave-like" nature. An 1878 report of the California State Senate Committee on Chinese Immigration warned of the danger posed to "American civilization" by Chinese labor: "[The Chinese] can be hired in masses; they can be managed and controlled like unthinking slaves. But our [white] laborer has an individual life, cannot be controlled as a slave by brutal masters." White workingmen's hostility to the Chinese peaked after the completion of the railroads in 1877 when a general economic recession threw thousands out of work. Labor strikes erupted in major industrial cities in the East and the Midwest. In San Francisco a demonstration against the railroads erupted into anti-Chinese mob violence. Three years later in Denver, after an extensive anti-Chinese campaign by a local newspaper, a Democratic election day parade turned into a citywide riot that ended with the gutting of Denver's Chinatown. Finally, in response to pressures from white workingmen's organizations and California political leaders, in 1882 the U.S. Congress passed the Chinese Exclusion Act, which prohibited immigration of Chinese laborers. It was the first U.S. federal law prohibiting entry by a named nationality. The Chinese Exclusion Act, as later amended, remained in force until 1943.[68]

Labor and Citizenship

Coercion continued to structure the work of men and women of color long after it became technically illegal to subject a citizen to voluntary or involuntary servitude. This was closely correlated with two factors: the character of regional economies where large numbers of workers of color were concentrated (and to which they had often been recruited), and segregation of the labor market that confined people of color to certain industries. The division between free and coercive labor regimes correlated to a significant extent with the division between more advanced capitalist industries and the less advanced preindustrial sector. Coercive labor regimes were common in large-scale commodity agriculture (sugar, cotton), extractive industries (mining), and infrastructure building and maintenance (railroad, levee, and road construction). These were labor-intensive sectors that relied on masses of laborers doing heavy physical work, where workers of color were concentrated because of sectoral and job segregation. Coercive labor regimes were more common in "backward" regions that relied on commodity agriculture and extractive industries: the South, the Southwest, and the Far West.[69]

In these sectors, land and capital were heavily concentrated in the hands of a few corporations or a few individuals who exerted almost total economic and political control over the lives of workers. In coal mining, for example, corporations not only owned and controlled the mines, they also owned the adjacent land and built camps to their own specification, including housing and facilities for workers. And they ran company stores where workers had to get their supplies. In the coal industry it was common practice to pay workers in scrip that could only be redeemed for full value at the company store. Workers were paid at the end of the month and were forced to charge fuel, food, tools, and other necessities to get by until payday. Often the whole month's pay was eaten up servicing the previous months' debts.[70]

In southern agriculture, landowners leased plots to sharecroppers who received payment only after the crop had been harvested and sold. In the meantime they received advances from the landowners to purchase necessities. Payment was based on the weight of the crop, as calculated by the landowner, a situation rife with outright cheating. By the time they settled their debts, sharecroppers were typically either barely breaking even or further in debt than when they started.[71]

Southwestern and western railroads and growers frequently employed labor contractors to recruit, transport, and oversee Chinese and Mexican labor crews. In this case it was the contractor or boss who bound the workers through debt. Impoverished workers might be induced or tricked into signing a note of debenture to pay the contractor for securing the job, transportation, and daily provisions. They would have to pay the debt over time by working on the job. Discipline and control of workers were left to the gang boss, inviting abuse.[72]

A common element of debt peonage was disruption of traditional household economies. In southwestern villages women and children had contributed to subsistence by growing food and keeping animals, but when workers and their families moved to mining camps they did not have access to land and so had to purchase food, often on credit. Cutting off workers' access to subsistence was often a deliberately calculated move. Southern landowners often stipulated that all land rented to croppers had to be devoted to cash crops (cotton). This not only reduced women and children's ability to produce food, it also led to their being forced into field work to ensure maximum yield of the cash crop. Whites employed in mining or sharecropping also were subject to debt bondage, but they were accorded some racial privileges, such as receiving the more skilled or supervisory jobs in mining or somewhat more favorable contracts in sharecropping. Coercive labor systems also affected family formation and the labor of women. Women's labor was intensified by men's employment in industries such as mining which required working in remote camps. Women who were left behind had to engage in subsistence activity, such as growing food, and had to care for children alone. In other cases, such as sharecropping, debt bondage forced women and children to do field work, or to work as domestic servants for the families of white supervisors or as laundresses or boardinghouse keepers for single male workers.[73]

These coercive labor practices can be seen as violating the intent and spirit of the Thirteenth Amendment and antipeonage laws, and therefore as deviating from the supposed American commitment to freedom. Such an interpretation might imply that these practices were inconsistent with traditional liberal ideology. However, when such practices were challenged in courts, the liberal theory of contract actually helped legitimate debt bondage. It did so by positing a theoretical equality between employer and worker that ignored the employer's economic power to affect the worker's ability to give voluntary consent. U.S. court decisions in the Gilded Age often enunciated an extreme version of liberty of contract which protected employers' rights to impose economic constraints that had the effect of preventing workers from leaving their jobs and from exercising autonomy in their "private" lives. In essence, the courts did not recognize debt bondage as a form of peonage. Ironically, the theoretical freedom of workers served to sanction practices that kept them effectively bound.

Moreover, once a worker had entered into a contract, relations were presumed to be governed by relationships prescribed by older common law and master-servant acts. These traditions assumed considerable rights on the part of employers to organize the work process and command obedience from the worker. According to Karen Orren, a "belated feudalism" continued well into the New Deal era. Up until that period, labor relations were regulated almost exclusively by the courts, which referred to common law and master-servant doctrines to determine employers' and employees' rights and obligations. Only in the 1930s did the efforts of organized labor succeed in bringing about a shift to "modern" labor relations based on collective bargaining and legislative regulation.[74]

The Obligation to Work

It was not just liberal law and belated feudalism that reinforced coercion in the labor system. Even more fundamentally, American concepts of citizenship supported the legitimacy of forced labor under certain circumstances. This is because of what some historians have identified as a central element of American citizenship, namely the obligation to work and earn. Judith Shklar has argued that, along with the ballot, "the opportunity to work and be paid an earned reward for one's labor" is the main source by which individuals gain public standing, by which she means respect and recognition as a full member of society. In her formulation, to be a citizen in good standing one must be economically independent, that is, an "earner"—a "free remunerated worker, one who is rewarded for the actual work he has done."[75] Originally, this meant being neither a slave (who works but does not earn) nor an aristocrat (who does not work); implicitly, it also meant not being a woman (whose work is owed to and owned by the male head of her family).

Conversely, as Linda Kerber points out, the obligation to work has been framed legally in negative terms as an obligation not to be (or not appear to be) "idle." Persons deemed to be able-bodied who are unemployed are seen as shirking their obligation and are vulnerable not just to social opprobrium but to societal punishment. For most of American history this obligation has been embodied in state and municipal vagrancy laws, which have defined a wide range of activities, including begging, loitering, sleeping in public, and simply having "no visible means of support," as crimes for which one could be arrested and put to forced work.[76] The continuation of vagrancy laws into the period of capitalist industrialization revealed the current of coercion running beneath the surface of labor "freedom." As with other dimensions of labor, the obligation to work has been differentially defined and enforced for men and women, whites and nonwhites.

The obligation to work and earn is seen most starkly in vagrancy laws. These types of laws originated in Elizabethan England, at a time when the labor system was based on indenture and strict rules governing master-servant relationships. Compulsory labor for those convicted of vagrancy was consistent with the semi-coercive labor system. Not surprisingly, vagrancy laws were carried over into the American colonies, along with indenture and other traditional employment practices. What may be surprising is that such laws survived the phasing out of indenture for whites in the early nineteenth century and even the prohibition of slavery and voluntary servitude later in the century. Kerber notes that the Civil War resulted in the elimination of certain kinds of work such as slavery and involuntary servitude, but that "the elimination of slavery as a form of work did not automatically eliminate an *obligation* to work."[77]

Indeed, vagrancy laws that prescribed compulsory labor were actually strengthened and enforced more vigorously after the Civil War in both the South and the North. These laws became a central component of white efforts to regain control of black labor in the South and of conservative efforts in all regions to achieve what Eric Foner called a "compulsory system of free labor."[78] As will be discussed in Chapters 4 and 5, vagrancy laws became a widely used means of compelling labor from newly emancipated blacks in the South and from Mexican immigrants in the Southwest. In the North, where a labor system based on voluntary contract between employer and employee was more advanced, imposition of vagrancy laws was a response to the increasing numbers of seasonally or temporarily unemployed wage workers visible in the streets of cities and towns. The spread of vagrancy arrests in the North raises the question of whether compulsory labor was inconsistent with a "free" wage labor system or was in fact integral to it.

In the West and the Southwest, vagrancy laws were used, as in the South, to discipline nonwhite workers. In the Southwest, these laws were part of the complex of threats that hung over Mexican workers in mining, agriculture, and cattle ranching. Neil Foley observes that in Texas, "lack of citizenship, fear of deportation or arrest for vagrancy kept Mexican immigrant workers more 'pliable.'"[79]

In the North, vagrancy laws were aimed at the growing numbers of "sturdy beggars" found in the streets of cities and towns. The increase in "beggars" reflected the precarious situation of workers, who were subject to sudden unemployment due to wildly fluctuating business cycles. Unlike the situation in the South and the Southwest, most of those charged with vagrancy in the North were white men. Amy Dru Stanley argues that northern reformers, most of whom had been firmly antislavery, were able to reconcile their simultaneous beliefs in free and compulsory labor by invoking the tenets of contract. They viewed most beggars as "idle by choice" and drew a clear distinction between working for wages and begging. The wage laborer was independent and self-supporting; he participated in the social exchange of the marketplace and obeyed its rules. The beggar was a dependent person; he "neither bought nor sold, but preyed on others." Whereas "the wage earner abided by the obligations of contract, the beggar eluded them." The reformers condemned charity and almsgiving precisely because they involved no contract: instead of *quid pro quo*, the receiver got something without having to reciprocate. In the view of reformers, such a one-way relationship was paternalistic and destructive of the receiver's dignity and independence. Compulsory labor, in contrast, would force beggars to "obey the rules of the market and enter into voluntary exchange." Thus beggars would be induced to become independent wageworkers.[80]

Labor leaders disputed the reformers' explanation of the causes of poverty and unemployment and the contrast reformers drew between the independent wage worker and the dependent beggar. Samuel Gompers spoke for many laboring men when he contended that most beggars begged not by choice but because of circumstances beyond their control. Far from being the opposite of the wage worker, the beggar's situation embodied, in an extreme way, the dependency and compulsions implicit in the wage contract. As the labor reformer Ira Steward explained, the beggar reflected the condition of a large class, "the class of people without means to employ themselves who must either sell days work or live upon charity, or starve to death." Labor leaders also pointed out the compulsion that underlay so-called voluntary wage work. Workingmen understood too well the dire need that compelled workers to consent to work; if a requirement to work was backed up by the power of the state, then even the formal right of consent was rendered void. Holding the poor in "penal servitude" violated the principles of free labor and turned citizens into slaves. Vagrancy laws were thus unjust—a throwback to bondage.[81]

In the Progressive era, the obligation to work continued to be differentially defined and enforced by race and gender. The differences were reflected in allocation of poor relief and access to other social welfare programs. For example, the architects of Mothers' Pensions assumed that many women could not earn enough to be completely independent. However, this assumption only applied to white women. When Mothers' Pensions were introduced in forty states and the territories of Alaska and Hawaii in the 1920s, benefits were allocated according to racialized criteria. Black mothers were believed to be more able to find work and were routinely denied pensions. Local administrators of New Deal programs of the 1930s, such as the Federal Emergency Relief Program, also treated women differently. Under the "employable mother" rule, black and Latina mothers were deemed "employable" as long as there was a demand for field pickers and domestics. During picking season particularly, program administrators were likely to refuse support to women of color. Relief programs thus had the dual function of keeping white mothers at home and forcing Latinas and blacks into the low-wage labor market.[82]

THE LATTER HALF of the nineteenth century saw fundamental shifts in the U.S. economy (from a small producer economy to capitalist industrialization) and expansion of civil and political citizenship (with the abolition of slavery and peonage and expanded suffrage). Ownership of one's labor and the ability to freely sell it, rather than ownership of productive property, became the basis for claiming independence. Within this definition, at least theoretically, free labor status was universalized. Despite this theoretical freedom, however, people of color and white women continued to be viewed as dependent and to find themselves subject to more intensive exploitation and restrictive controls than white men.

Why and how has the U.S. labor system maintained inequality and coercion despite a theoretically free labor system? The answers are complex. With regard to inequality and lack of mobility, one part of the answer in the case of white women was the continuing reliance on the household for reproduction and subsistence activity and women's responsibility for this labor. As a result, women continued to be defined as economically dependent on male breadwinners and their unpaid labor was considered an obligation rather than being voluntary. For men and women of color, the main structural mechanisms ensuring exploitability and lack of mobility in the labor market were occupational stratification and segregation. With regard to coercion, we have seen that it was not in fact an aberration from American principles and law. Rather, coercion was legitimated in several major ways. Contract theory as applied in the United States legitimated forms of economic coercion (such as payment in scrip) that restricted effective choice through the legal fiction of equality between employer and employee. Also, common law reflecting feudal elements gave employers almost complete authority and prescribed compliance on the part of workers. Finally, the obligation to be independent by working and earning was central to American concepts of citizenship. This obligation was codified to subject those deemed to be illegitimately idle into forced labor, with the interpretation of "illegitimate idleness" filtered through the lens of race and gender.

·4·

Blacks and Whites
in the South

FROM 1877, when federal Reconstruction ended, through the 1920s, when the system of de jure Jim Crow segregation and disfranchisement was fully realized, there was significant variation among southern states in the rigidity of political and social structures of domination and in the timing of moves and countermoves. Differences in local economies, the relative power of various white elites, the composition and deployment of black and white labor, the proportions of blacks and whites in the population, and the class makeup of communities all affected measures whites could employ to subordinate blacks as well as the opposition that blacks could mount to resist subordination. For example, in Mississippi black men were effectively disfranchised by 1875 through a combination of intimidation, gerrymandering, and fraud, while in North Carolina they continued to participate in party politics and to vote in significant numbers until legally disfranchised in 1900.[1]

Yet there were important commonalities among the former Confederate states in culture and ideology, in racial etiquette, and in the development of coercive labor arrangements, legal disfranchisement, and Jim Crow segregation. In the final analysis, the similarities in mechanisms and strategies for constraining black labor and citizenship outweighed the differences. My aim here is to delineate the general patterns while also acknowledging variation. My account emphasizes relations and contestation in the major cities of the South, which experienced significant in-migration by both whites and blacks during this period. The cities were where black men and women mounted the most significant challenges to exclusion and subordination by building institutions that expressed more communal, inclusive, and universal conceptions of citizenship and rights.

In order to appreciate what was at stake in the post-Reconstruction and Jim Crow eras, we have to understand the possibilities opened up by Reconstruction. By 1865, soon after warfare had ended, President Andrew Johnson's policy of "reconciliation" had essentially returned white Confederate rule; the newly restored state governments quickly moved to impose a regime as close to slavery as possible. The legislatures passed a series of laws, the so-called Black Codes, to control and discipline the freed blacks by restricting their movement, forcing them to work, and defining a wide variety of activities as crimes when engaged in by blacks. Faced by this wholesale negation of rights, the new radical Republican majority in Congress passed a series of Reconstruction Acts in 1867. These Acts abolished existing state regimes, established temporary military governments, and required states to write new constitutions providing for black male suffrage and ratification of the Fourteenth Amendment in order to be restored to the Union. Congress also provided for elections and voter registration under federal supervision. Black men would for the first time be allowed to participate in elections and legislative procedures.[2]

Freedpeople responded with great fervor. In Mississippi fully 96.7 percent of freedmen of eligible age registered. They formed a majority of registered voters in that state, as well as in Florida, South Carolina, Alabama, and Louisiana. Blacks were among the delegates who drafted new state constitutions that removed color bars to voting, and they were among the voters who elected legislatures that endorsed the Fourteenth and Fifteenth Amendments and returned the states to the Union. For a brief time in the 1860s and 1870s, African Americans took hold of a measure of political power, sat on juries, held elective offices, and occupied appointive positions as magistrates, bailiffs, port officials, justices of the peace, and sheriffs.[3]

These advances were due in large measure to the efforts of blacks themselves, not just of a few educated leaders, but of masses of black men, women, and children, literate and illiterate, who sought to realize their vision of freedom and full citizenship. This vision surely animated thousands of black South Carolinians who took initial steps to organize politically even before Reconstruction. Thomas Holt notes that starting in 1865 blacks in Charleston, South Carolina, and elsewhere assembled in mass meetings to vote public resolutions declaring their pro-Union sentiments. There followed a series of meetings and conventions in which attendees petitioned for the vote, selected leaders, and formed the basis for the state Republican party.[4]

A vision of citizenship and freedom also inspired three thousand freedmen and women in Richmond, Virginia, to line up outside the African Church to attend the opening of the state Republican conventions held in the summer and fall of 1867, forcing the second day's sessions to be held outdoors in Capitol Square. During the party conventions and the subsequent Virginia Constitutional Convention, which met from December 1867 to March 1868, thousands of African Americans absented themselves from their jobs to attend. In the main industry—tobacco—factories were forced to close for lack of workers. A *New York Times* reporter covering the Republican convention wrote that "the entire colored population of Richmond" was in attendance. Noting that women domestic workers made up a large portion of attendees, he reported that (white) households were forced to get their own meals or make do with cold lunch, for "not only had Sambo gone to the Convention, but Dinah was there also." Black men and women attended these political meetings not to be mere observers. They expected to take an active part and they did so, engaging in heated debates in the gallery, cheering their champions, making their concerns known to candidates, and supporting black speakers who looked up toward them while making oratorical points. Outside convention hours they gathered at mass meetings to discuss and vote on issues; votes were taken by voice or by rising, and all in attendance, men, women, and children, voted.[5]

For Elsa Barkley Brown these incidents demonstrate that "Black Richmonders were operating in two separate political arenas: an internal one and an external one. While these arenas were related, they each proceeded from different assumptions, had different purposes, and therefore operated according to different rules. Within the internal political process women were enfranchised and participated in all public forums—the parades, rallies, mass meetings and the conventions themselves." Brown adds that Richmond was typical: broad-based, gender- and class-inclusive participation in social and political affairs was common in black southern communities in the 1860s and 1870s. All people were assumed to have a stake in and therefore a voice in issues affecting the community, and decisions were to be reached only after debate and discussion among all. Indeed, the desire to accommodate large meetings inspired the First African Baptist Church in Richmond to build an auditorium that held nearly 4,000 people; it was the largest such hall in the city, and for this reason it was chosen as the site of the first state Republican convention under Reconstruction.[6]

The question of whether women should be included in the franchise in the new state constitutions was one of the issues debated by blacks prior to party conventions. The results were mixed. A mass meeting in Nansemond County, Virginia, resolved in favor of women's suffrage, while the majority at a meeting in Richmond voted against it. Significantly, however, women were among those who voted on the issue, and they continued to vote at meetings even after negative decisions on a formal franchise for women. Black delegates to state constitutional conventions were more apt to support women's suffrage—at least to take the matter seriously—than white delegates, who held the firm conviction that the very idea was absurd. During the Reconstruction era many black officials spoke out in favor of women's franchise. In South Carolina, where blacks constituted a majority of the legislature, a significant portion of black elected officials supported suffrage, including six of the eight blacks who represented the state in the U.S. Congress.[7]

In the end, all of the state constitutions qualified only men as voters. Disfranchisement in the external political arena, however, did not mean disfranchisement in the internal political arena. African American women throughout the South continued to attend, speak, and vote in internal political meetings; on occasion these meetings selected a woman to attend outside political meetings as a representative of the community. Formal disfranchisement also did not lead black women to withdraw from electoral politics. Black women in Mississippi proudly wore Republican campaign buttons during a contentious campaign in 1868, often traveling miles to acquire the buttons and displaying them at considerable peril and in defiance of their white employers. African American women in Virginia, South Carolina, Alabama, Mississippi, and elsewhere organized political societies such as Richmond's Rising

Daughters of Liberty and the United Daughters of Liberty, organized by wives of coal miners in Manchester, Virginia. According to Peter Rachleff, these organizations "were important in generating enthusiasm in campaigns, fund-raising, getting out the vote, and enforcing the black community's political consensus."[8]

In the violent atmosphere of Reconstruction politics, such involvement required great courage. White conservatives in Mississippi adopted a "shot gun plan" with the slogan "Carry the election peacefully if we can, forcibly if we must." South Carolina Red Shirts turned up at Republican meetings armed with pistols and a battle plan that declared: "Every Democrat must feel honor bound to control at least one Negro vote by intimidation, purchase, keeping him away." Louisiana's military governor reported in 1875 that since 1868, 1,200 persons, primarily black men, "had been killed or wounded on account of their political sentiments." In this climate, black women sometimes played an important and dangerous protective role. In South Carolina women were observed guarding the guns stacked behind the speaker's platform at political rallies. On election day 1876, according to a witness, "Women had sticks; no mens were to go to the polls unless their wives were right alongside of them; some had hickory sticks; some had nails—four nails driven in the shape of a cross—and dare their husbands to vote any other than the Republican ticket." In Richmond, women as well as men took off from work on election day to show up en masse at polling sites, often arriving the night before and camping out. Early arrival and massive presence were intended to forestall attempts by whites to influence black voters by intimidation and to deter poll officials from turning them away.[9]

Brown contends that African American men and women understood the vote as collective rather than individual in nature. African American women's presence demonstrated their conviction that they had a vital stake in black men's franchise. Unable to cast votes themselves, they felt that African American men's votes were theirs as well. Thus women's presence at the polls was meant not just to ensure that black men could vote but also to remind them that their votes should be cast in the interests of the entire community. Black women in South Carolina and Alabama reportedly expressed disapproval and initiated sanctions against men who violated the common good by supporting conservative Democrats. A Sea Island, South Carolina, woman reported that a Republican speaker had counseled women to refuse to marry men who voted a Democratic ticket, or, if already married, advised, "don't service to them in bed." Well into the 1890s, black women refused to let their lack of the vote mean lack of political influence. In North Carolina, where black men retained the franchise until 1900, black women continued to assert the concept of the vote as collective rather than individual. During a crucial election in 1898, as conservative Democrats sought to unseat a coalition of Republicans and Populists on a platform of white supremacy and voting reforms that would disfranchise blacks, an "Organization of Colored Ladies" in Wilmington published a broadside promising to deal harshly with "every Negro who refuses to register his name next Saturday that he may vote . . . He shall be branded a white-livered coward who would sell his liberty." Whatever the outcome, the ladies committed themselves to "teach our children to love the party of manhood's rights."[10]

As these vignettes illustrate, former slaves did not passively await the fruits of freedom, but acted affirmatively to claim them and to realize their vision of economic independence and full citizenship. Moreover, their vision did not simply mirror the dominant American philosophy of possessive individualism but was based on a more collective and inclusive notion of rights. Much recent scholarship on the immediate post-emancipation and Reconstruction periods has focused on black agency and the critical role played by freedpeople themselves in achieving a measure of political and economic progress. From the moment of emancipation blacks took initiatives to form stable families, establish economically autonomous households, build schools to educate themselves and their children, and found churches, businesses, and voluntary associations. Support and resources from the Republican-controlled federal government, together with blacks' own efforts, made possible unprecedented progress and optimism. Simultaneously, federal force put some brakes on continued white efforts to control and subordinate blacks through legal and extra-legal means.

Hierarchy and Control in the Labor System

Freed men and women understood that emancipation required some measure of economic independence. For the vast majority of former slaves who had toiled on southern plantations, independence meant ownership of the ground they farmed and the right to direct their own labor. When Freedmen's Bureau officers arrived in Mississippi, they found that nearly all of the former slaves held it as an article of faith that there would be a reapportionment of land and that they would each get a small farm. A Bureau official reported that many freedmen were loath to accept agricultural employment because they hoped to be able to "farm on their own account." Planters and federal officials tried to counter the belief, but land fever persisted. Up through the end of the 1860s there would be periodic rumors among the freedmen that land would be given to former slaves as Christmas gifts.[11]

Despite some successful experiments and programs that enabled a few thousand former slaves to acquire small homesteads on federal land, proposals to confiscate Confederate land and divide it among the freedpeople never made headway. In his study of black Reconstruction, W. E. B. Du Bois concluded that the biggest flaw of Reconstruction was the failure to bring about (or even seriously attempt) large-scale land redistribution that would have given freedpeople a chance at economic independence.[12] Thus, when federal troops were withdrawn and all the former Confederate states were returned to local control in 1877, blacks lacked a stable economic base from which to defend their rights, as white conservatives "redeemed" the South.

As former Confederates were pardoned and permitted to reclaim confiscated or occupied land, economic, if not political, control quickly fell back into the hands of former slaveholders. To be sure, some blacks succeeded in acquiring small farms by dint of hard work and sacrifice by all members of the household; black ownership increased especially in the decade between 1880 and 1890. Land available to blacks was usually in less productive areas and sold at inflated prices, so that making a living was a struggle. Even if they managed to do well as owners, their situation was fragile. Independent black farmers had to cultivate a humble manner and be careful not to appear too prosperous in order to avoid inviting jealousy and retribution from white farmers. One relatively prosperous black landowner in Mississippi told an anthropologist that his good fortune had been due to "hard work, slow saving, and staying in my place, acting humble." In some counties independent black renters and farm owners were targeted by white nightriders, who destroyed their crops and livestock and torched barns and other buildings in an effort to drive them out.[13]

The vast majority of black farmers, the proportion varying some-what from state to state, remained landless.[14] Although they were le-gally free, they lacked a material base for true independence and thus were forced to work for landowners, either for wages or as tenants.

White landowners for their part faced the problem of holding onto and controlling a newly mobile and reduced workforce. Many blacks exercised their newfound freedom by leaving their old plantations to reunite with family members, to search for better situations, or to migrate to the cities. As Herbert Gutman documented so well, freed men and women took the opportunity to legalize their unions and form conjugal households. Families sought to regulate their own affairs and live according to standards of family life that free people enjoyed. Wives and daughters of able-bodied men often withdrew from field la-bor to devote themselves to home-based production and household management. Modern and contemporary estimates agree that by 1870 the pool of black field labor had dropped between one-third and one-quarter from pre-emancipation levels.[15]

Those who remained in field labor were less docile than before as they sought to reduce their work hours to what free people were used to, establish their own work rhythms, and protect one another from ill treatment. The problem of "recalcitrant" black labor was viewed as particularly critical in the rural Cotton Belt. Plantation owners accused freed workers of "loafering around" and "lummoxing about" and re-ported that they were exasperated by workers arriving late and leaving early, taking the day off to go fishing, or malingering. The frustrations expressed by planters reflected the leverage that blacks gained from la-bor shortages. Planters were particularly incensed at the withdrawal of black women; they accused black women who declined work in the field of trying to "play the lady." They and other whites agreed that black women could not be ladies. White "ladies" were cloistered in the home, where they fulfilled their domestic and mothering duties, but black women who did so were shirking their duty to be produc-tive workers. Planters were not alone in holding racialized notions of womanhood and manhood. Freedmen's Bureau officials and northern and European visitors commented on the withdrawal of black women from field work and described black women working at home as "lazy." While they themselves undoubtedly kept their wives at home, white

double
standard

men impugned the manhood of black husbands and fathers for allowing themselves to be cowed into supporting their wives and daughters.[16]

Planters at first persisted in using work gangs, which facilitated centralized control and had been relatively successful under slavery. Gangs
could be forced to work steadily by an overseer. After the war, some
cotton growers adopted the squad system, which blacks preferred to
the gang system because the work group was self-selected and directed
by a member. Freedmen also resented arrangements that required
them to live together, often in old slave quarters, near the owner's
house.[17]

By the late 1860s the tug of war between landowners wanting a
"fixed" labor force to grow more cotton or tobacco and landless black
workers resisting old slave ways led to a shift to tenancy arrangements.
The most common form of tenancy was "going on halves," where the
planter parceled out small plots to sharecroppers and provided rations,
seed, and supplies in exchange for half the crop. Contracts were renegotiated at the end of each calendar year, after debts had been settled.
By 1880, according to Roger Ransom and Richard Sutch, only 8.9 percent of cotton cropland in their survey was cultivated as plantations;
over half was cultivated by tenants, of which 72 percent was share-
cropped. Sharecropping helped address two problems for the landowner. First, it immobilized the workforce by keeping tenants tethered
until the crop had been harvested. Second, by tying eventual profit to
the size of the crop, it impelled everyone in the household, including
women and children, to help with field work. For black farmers, sharecropping offered a measure of autonomy. They could move into a small
house or cabin some distance away from the owner's house so as to
maintain a semblance of privacy, and they could determine their own
day-to-day work arrangements.[18]

In practice, especially in the Cotton Belt, tenants were often subject
to close control. By the early twentieth century Cotton Belt plantations
were so large and tightly managed that they more closely resembled industrial establishments than conglomerations of family farms. Large
landowners often employed armed "riders" who traveled from farm to
farm monitoring tenants. These riders were authorized to inflict physical punishment on recalcitrant tenants and to order family members,

including children, into the fields. The landlord's reach extended to daily provision when he took on the role of financier and merchant, supplying seed, fertilizer, food, and clothing on credit. Propertyless black tenants had little choice but to borrow for supplies at exorbitant rates of interest—up to 25 percent—in the form of liens on the year's crop. Some landlords discouraged or flatly forbade tenants from keeping a garden or raising hogs so as to force them to be completely dependent on the commissary. Tenants were thus compelled to survive on credit and to stay until the crop was picked and sold and the debt settled. Women were compelled to do "a man's share in the field and a woman's part in the home" and children were initiated into field labor when they were four or five years old. Although some children gained a sense of their own strength from contributing to family labor, others resented their father's tyranny and the stifling of their chances to get an education or to go out to work on their own.[19]

In a good year tenants might clear a few hundred dollars; in a bad year they might wind up with almost nothing or even be in the hole. Since the accounting of debt and of the value of the crops was done by the landowner and blacks could not challenge whites without risking retribution, opportunities for cheating were rife. Various observers, from labor investigators to planters themselves, at least in private, reckoned that cheating tenants was widespread. The settling of the contract was often the occasion for the tenant family to move on in search of a better situation or a better landlord. Thus the tenant-farming life combined constant uprooting with being locked into a system that offered no way out or up.[20]

Nowhere is the connection between coercive labor systems and denial of citizenship more starkly revealed than in the various forms of legal peonage that white employers and local and state officials conspired to impose on blacks. Whites justified measures to immobilize and compel black labor by the belief that blacks were naturally lazy and inconstant and would not work unless forced to do so. Planters adjusted to the principle of free labor when it came to dismissing workers they no longer needed, but were loath to accept the right of black workers to leave employment. Between 1875 and 1890 all of the former Confederate states except Virginia and Texas adopted laws or revived so-called enticement acts that forbade employers to hire anyone employed by or under contract to another. Many states also adopted laws that imposed expensive licensing fees on labor recruiters who transported workers from one state to another. Such laws were not widely effective in stemming black mobility, however, because whites were divided on the issue. Labor-hungry employers in some regions wanted to be able to recruit workers from other areas, while those who did not employ large numbers of blacks were happy to see them migrate elsewhere.[21]

Agriculture was the major industry that maintained what contemporary writers labeled the new slavery, but it was by no means the only one. Southern railroads, lumber companies, turpentine companies, mining companies, and contractors also sought to compel black labor. Although federal statutes outlawed contract labor, southern legislatures and local governments ignored these prohibitions and enforced contract arrangements. Even after an Alabama contract labor law was declared unconstitutional in 1911, state and federal courts in Georgia continued to enforce a 1903 statute that allowed tenant farmers and lumber, railroad, and turpentine workers who attempted to quit while owing money to the employer to be charged with fraudulently procuring money and sentenced to prison or forced to work.[22] → rule bending

Debt peonage was also a product of the revival of vagrancy laws in the 1870s and 1880s throughout the South. In concert with new municipal ordinances giving wide latitude to police officers, vagrancy laws became the primary legal vehicles for compelling black labor. Under vagrancy statutes, officials could apprehend any "idler" who had no visible means of subsistence and then hire him or her out at the available wage rate, usually as a servant or common laborer. Other laws regulating minor offenses were also used to impose debt bondage. Blacks convicted of a variety of misdemeanors ranging from disorderly conduct to swearing were subject to fines as high as $25. If unable to pay, they could be bound out to work for the city or private individuals. Municipal jails and courts were thus a prime source of coerced labor for labor contractors, who paid prisoners' fines in exchange for their signatures on contracts. A black southerner described the system in a letter to W. E. B. Du Bois:

> If a colored man is arrested here and hasn't any money, whether he is guilty or not he has to pay just the same . . . A kindly appearing

man will come up and pay my fine and take me to his farm to allow
me to work it out. At the end of the month I find that I owe him
more than I did when I went there. The debt is increased year in
and year out . . . One more word about the peonage. The court
and the man you work for are always partners. One makes the fine
and the other one works you and holds you, and if you leave you
are tracked up with bloodhounds and brought back.

Although the laws did not mention race, blacks were overwhelmingly
those arrested and ordered to work. Black women and children were
not exempt, and in times of shortage of domestic servants women were
particularly likely to be targeted. Unlike their white counterparts, married black women supported by husbands were assumed to be idle if
not working for wages.[23]

Debt bondage constituted one tier of a larger system of de facto slavery, the most egregious form of which was the convict leasing system.
As early as 1868 federal authorities contracted with one Edmund Richardson of Mississippi to take overflow prisoners to work on his "farm."
He put the prisoners to work building levees, clearing swampland,
and plowing fields. Richardson became fabulously wealthy, a respected
financier, and, according to the press, the largest cotton planter in the
world, all on the basis of convict labor. The practice of leasing state and
county prisoners to private individuals and corporations accelerated in
the 1870s, as states throughout the lower South and some in the upper
South passed laws allowing prisoners to work outside of prison for railroads, levee builders, or private employers. Crime statutes were rewrit-
ten to define minor property offenses as felonies. The model was Mississippi's 1876 "Pig Law," which redefined "grand larceny" (punishable
by up to five years in state prison) to include the theft of farm animals
or other property worth more than $10. Blacks arrested under such
laws were summarily convicted without legal representation and with
the barest show of a trial. As a result, the number of black convicts
available for leasing soared. Although these laws were not formally
framed as racial laws, blacks formed the overwhelming majority of convicts in Mississippi, Alabama, Georgia, Arkansas, Texas, Florida, Tennessee, North and South Carolina, and Virginia. David Oshinsky notes
that in the 1880s a quarter of state prisoners in Mississippi were adoles-
cents or children; a roll of convicts leased to work included Mary Gay,

"a Negro, but a little over six years old," and Will Evans, eight, sentenced for stealing change.[24]

During the railroad-building boom of the 1870s and 1880s thousands of convicts, most of them black, did the dangerous work of boring tunnels and laid a major portion of the tracks through Tennessee and North Carolina. Once the railroads had expanded, other industries could develop. Southern industrialists rushed to "fill the only gaps in the national and international markets they could find: cheap iron, cheap coal, cheap lumber, turpentine, sugar, and tobacco products." In almost every one of these industries black convict labor played a role, often working alongside "free" labor. Coal mining in Alabama and Georgia used much convict labor. During the 1880s a quarter of all coal miners in the productive Birmingham district were state or county prisoners. Sentenced to hard labor at thirty to forty cents a day, prisoners had to work more than a year to pay off a fifty-dollar fine. The Florida turpentine industry, which supplied the U.S. Navy, relied heavily on forced labor performed under exhausting and dangerous conditions in desolate forests. In 1907 a journalist described a "typical" arrangement in which a turpentine operator paid a local sheriff five dollars a head to provide workers by arresting eighty "husky" men on various minor offenses over a period of three weeks. In Georgia leading politicians, including the governor, were among the largest lessees; the lessees not only used labor themselves, they subleased convicts to plantations, coal mines, sawmills, railroad corporations, and turpentine companies. By 1890 Alabama had regularized the convict-leasing system in what amounted to a state-operated slave market: black men age twelve and older were sorted into four grades at different prices for work in mines; black women, children, and "cripples" were sent to lumber camps and farms; white men remained in penitentiaries and jails; and white women and children, who were comparatively rare among convicts, were sent to special facilities. Convict leasing lasted until the late 1920s, when the last state, Alabama, abolished it.[25]

The convict-leasing system gave employers tremendous leverage over "free" workers. Free and convict workers often labored side by side. In the turpentine industry the conditions of the two groups were not very different. They were housed in compounds surrounded by barbed wire, watched over by armed guards, and forced to buy necessities from company commissaries on credit. In the coal mines convict labor was held as a sword of Damocles over free workers, who knew that if they walked out, organized, or went on strike they could easily be replaced.[26]

Racial Stratification of Urban Labor Markets

The period between 1865 and 1890 saw an increasing migration of rural blacks to southern cities to escape poverty and peonage. Although remaining predominately rooted in rural areas, by 1890 blacks constituted 30 percent of the urban population of the region and 39–59 percent of the populations of major cities such as Richmond, Atlanta, Nashville, Montgomery, and Raleigh.[27]

Work in the city offered blacks somewhat greater freedom from direct white control over their lives. Indeed, even in antebellum times, urban slaves sent out to earn wages had often arranged their own jobs. Still, their freedom of choice was constrained by the stratified labor market. The vast majority of urban black men and women were confined to low-paying, irregular, and low-status positions. In 1890, in the five cities studied by Howard Rabinowitz, two-thirds of black men were employed in unskilled labor or domestic personal service, while only 17–23 percent were in "skilled" occupations. Black workers were concentrated in "common labor" in street-work gangs, at construction sites, at wharves and docks, and occasionally in the tobacco and iron industries. Although the ranks of the unskilled were swelled by rural immigrants, even those who had been skilled artisans found themselves pushed down into unskilled jobs. Blacks were also concentrated in service jobs, working as porters, waiters, and servants. In every city blacks also had a near monopoly on some artisanal and skilled positions shunned by whites, such as draymen, livery stable operators, and barbers.[28]

Black women were even more constrained: only about 3–4 percent of those in the labor force were employed as skilled craftswomen and professionals. Most of the craftswomen were seamstresses, while the largest group of professional women was teachers. The overwhelming majority, 80–92 percent, of black women workers in southern cities were employed as laundresses or in domestic service as maids, cooks, and child nurses. Working in white households recapitulated the lack of boundaries and other dynamics of the master-slave relationship, and also left black women vulnerable to sexual advances and violence. Although forced to continue in domestic service by a lack of alternatives, black women sought some degree of autonomy by opting for day work rather than live-in service whenever possible. Day workers were less vulnerable to sexual abuse, avoided being on call at all hours, and could enjoy a private life off the job. They could also more easily avoid wearing a uniform, a badge of inferiority. Contrary to the white stereotype of the aged mammy and family retainer, most live-in maids and nurses were younger single women. Married women, especially mothers, preferred to work as laundresses, which they could do at their own homes. Laundry work was always a fallback, since before the spread of washing machines white middle-class and even working-class women relied on black washerwomen to do the physically arduous task of weekly laundry, which required pumping and boiling huge pots of water, scrubbing by hand, rinsing, and drying, followed by heating heavy irons and pressing.[29]

Beyond the skilled-unskilled divide, urban labor was characterized by finer segmentation. Among skilled male workers, black men were concentrated in a few occupations, such as barbering, plastering, and brickmaking, while being underrepresented in the higher-paying fields of carpentry, plumbing, printing, and machine operations. There was also industrial segmentation. Textile mills employed whites exclusively. Owners justified this on the grounds that blacks were temperamentally unsuited to monotonous mechanical work and lacked the required deftness, despite the variety of industrial and skilled tasks that slaves had been put to. The exclusion of blacks from textile mills was in large measure a concession to white workers, who fought to retain a monopoly over these jobs. The tobacco industry employed both blacks and whites, but in different parts of the industry and in different capacities. Cigar manufacturers employed blacks as laborers and machine operators, while cigarette manufacturers hired black women only in the dirty, heavy work of rehandling, sorting, stripping, stemming, and hanging tobacco leaves, reserving semiskilled machine jobs for white women.[30]

Job segregation facilitated differentials in working conditions and wages. The difference in living standards between whites and blacks can be gauged by the fact that many white mill and factory workers employed black women to do their wash or housework. A white tobacco operative might even employ a black co-worker, since black women to-bacco workers, whose jobs were seasonal, often worked as domestics during layoffs.[31]

Irregular and low-paying jobs forced black families to rely on mul-tiple earners. Black urban women had high rates of participation in the labor force, not only as daughters and wives in male-headed house-holds, but as single heads of households; 25–30 percent of urban households were headed by women, double the percentage in rural ar-eas. Many of these women were widows, because of frequent early deaths among black men and the tendency for widows to migrate to the city because they found it hard to support themselves in farming. In the largest southern cities, 50–70 percent of adult black women were gain-fully employed at least part of the year; young single black women were three times as likely to be employed as their white counterparts, while married black women were five times as likely to be employed as mar-ried white women.[32]

While most urban blacks were employed in unskilled labor or do-mestic and personal services, the growth of the black population in cit-ies provided new opportunities for black businesses and professionals. Most of the first generation of black business owners had little educa-tion and served a largely black clientele. They were concentrated in a few specialties, as liverymen, barbers, undertakers, grocers, and ca-terers. In the nineteenth century, with the exception of undertaking, these small businesses performed some services for whites as well as blacks. An example is barbering, over which blacks had a near mo-nopoly, catering to whites as well as blacks. In the twentieth century, however, segregation patterns dictated that white clients be served in separate shops by white barbers. In Atlanta the ten-to-one monopoly that black barbers enjoyed in 1890 shifted to a two-to-one majority for whites, and most black barbers had only black clients. Black gro-cers and merchants in particular had low rates of survival owing to low capitalization, reliance on mostly poor black clients who shopped on credit, and competition from better-financed white merchants.[33]

In addition, as black urban populations grew, so did public accom-modations and recreational facilities, restaurants, boarding and lodging houses, pool halls, saloons, and vaudeville houses and theaters. Among the largest and most successful enterprises were black insurance com-panies that grew up after 1900. These companies built on the tradition of self-insurance started by fraternal and mutual benefit associations. The growth of black higher education added black lawyers, dentists, and physicians, who were among the most prominent members of their communities. Teaching was the largest field of white-collar employment for black women, who made up the majority of the teaching staff in black schools. In 1910 there were 17,266 black women teachers in the South; they outnumbered black male teachers three to one. Although professionals, they were paid far less than white teachers and had to tide themselves over during summers working as laundresses and seamstresses.[34]

Racialized and Gendered Citizenship

The period 1890–1920 has been viewed by most historians as the nadir of black citizenship in the South, a time of increased oppression and turning back of black rights. White supremacy and second-class citizenship for blacks were imposed by a potent combination of forces at the local, state, and federal levels: the escalation of legal and extra-legal violence directed at blacks, including urban riots and thousands of lynchings; the elaboration of racist ideas and images in popular culture, media, and social science discourse; the removal of black men from the political process by disfranchisement and intimidation; and the imposition of separate and unequal conditions through Jim Crow segregation. These negations of black citizenship were facilitated by the abandonment of black civil and political rights by northern Republicans and the federal government and the voiding of the 1875 Civil Rights Act and the equal protection clauses of the Fourteenth Amendment by federal courts.

During this period the violence directed at blacks reached epidemic proportions. Leon Litwack notes that, as a conservative estimate, "between 1890 and 1917, to enforce deference and submission, some two to three black southerners were hanged, burned at the stake, or quietly murdered every week." Some 2,585 lynchings were recorded in the South from 1885 to 1903. Lynching was not a new phenomenon for terrorizing blacks, but it took on unprecedented sadism and exhibitionism in the late nineteenth and early twentieth centuries. Public lynchings became voyeuristic spectacles, sometimes involving hundreds or even thousands of spectators who were whipped into an emotional frenzy. Quick dispatch of the victim was not enough to satisfy the crowds; torture and mutilation were prolonged—in one recorded instance for seven hours. Even the death of the victims was not sufficient: their bodies might be ritualistically burned or left hanging for display, or parts might be cut off and given away as souvenirs. Although lynchings were staged as vengeance for allegedly "unspeakable crimes," blacks understood that their impetus in many cases was a show of too much independence or success. Martha Hodes has argued that the actual violations that precipitated lynchings were exercise of political rights, labor activism, economic independence, and challenging racial boundaries by talking back. Most lynching victims were black men, but black women were also targets. Mob lynching received the most attention, but Litwack points out that as many blacks were the victims of legal lynching, the preemptory conviction and public execution of black defendants, especially those accused of crimes against whites.[35]

Another form of violence that intensified in the twentieth century was the urban "riot" in which white mobs rampaged through black districts, assaulting any blacks they found and destroying their residences and businesses. The largest such collective rampages in the South occurred in Wilmington, North Carolina, in 1898; New Orleans in 1900; and Atlanta in 1906. The Wilmington massacre took place in the context of a tightly contested election and was perpetrated by a force of several hundred red-shirted whites led by a former Congressman, who marched into the black district, killed at least ten residents, injured many more, and forced hundreds to flee the city. According to Glenda Gilmore the massacre was the watershed event that marked the decline in African American fortunes in Wilmington. The slaughter of 1898, followed by disfranchisement in 1899, precipitated large-scale out-migration from Wilmington and North Carolina, especially by the most prosperous and best-educated black citizens. Between 1900 and 1910 nearly 27,827 black North Carolinians left, only 2,000 fewer than in the next decade of the Great Migration. The Atlanta riot took place in the aftermath of a racist gubernatorial campaign waged by a conservative Democrat, Hoke Smith, when newspapers filled the post-election lull with stories of alleged assaults and rapes of defenseless (white) virgins; several days of mob attacks on the black community ensued. Blacks armed themselves and fought back, and although white officials downplayed white casualties, W. E. B. Du Bois, who was on the spot, estimated that one hundred died, including some whites.[36]

As long as a significant number of black men retained the franchise, blacks retained some leverage just by being able to exact some attention and accountability in exchange for votes. The first step in neutralizing black political power, then, was to remove them from the electoral process. Black voting had already been reduced or nullified in many parts of the South by the 1870s through violence and fraud, but with Redemption (the reestablishment of conservative white rule), white Democrats added legal manipulation including gerrymandering of districts, complicated registration procedures, and secret ballots to the repertoire of mechanisms to restrict black voting. In part because of their large majorities, black men in the "black belt" states of Alabama, Mississippi, and Louisiana continued to go to the polls in significant numbers in the 1880s. In most other areas of the South, however, black voting had been effectively curtailed by the late 1880s. Nonetheless, the 1890s saw the rise of organized movements to totally eliminate the black vote, this time by amending state constitutions to institute requirements that would disqualify blacks. Michael Perman argues that this development was a third and qualitatively distinct stage in disfranchisement, designed not just to deprive blacks of the "*ability* to vote at elections" but to eliminate their "*right* to vote at registration."[37]

Proponents of disfranchisement argued that only constitutional guarantees would end temporizing with Reconstruction and restore white supremacy. Perman notes the continued preoccupation with "black domination" even after successful curtailment of black votes. To white Democrats "black domination" meant a possible swing role for black voters if political divisions among whites led competing groups, whether Republicans, dissident Democrats, or Populists, to vie for black votes. More broadly, according to Senator James Z. George of Mississippi, there was a danger to self-government posed even by the mere participation of "a race . . . which have never yet developed the slightest capacity to create, to operate, or to preserve constitutional institutions." The "great problem" needing to be overcome was the coexistence within one polity of two unequal races, artificially "made equal by the law." As in earlier discourse on citizenship, fundamental to the white supremacist argument was the notion that democratic self-government was possible only within a homogeneous polity.[38]

Mississippi pioneered successful circumvention of the Fourteenth and Fifteenth Amendments by restricting the franchise in its state constitution in 1890. Other states adopted and elaborated the so-called

Mississippi Plan, especially after the U.S. Congress in 1894 repealed the Reconstruction-era Federal Elections Law designed to protect voters, and the U.S. Supreme Court ruled in 1898 that the Mississippi provisions did not violate the U.S. Constitution. Although the plans varied in detail, their essential feature was to set up barriers, such as property and literacy requirements, then to provide "safety clauses"— loopholes such as grandfather clauses, tests of understanding, or good character clauses—to accommodate poor or illiterate whites. Whether a prospective registrant qualified under the loopholes was left to the interpretation of local registrars, thus allowing racially selective screening. South Carolina constitutionally disfranchised blacks in 1895, and in rapid order Louisiana (1898), North Carolina (1900), Alabama (1901), Virginia (1902), and Georgia (1908) followed suit. Florida, Texas, Tennessee, and Arkansas did not amend their constitutions but did adopt poll taxes and the secret ballot to restrict black votes.[39]

For those few blacks who somehow managed to clear all of the other restrictions, the final blow was the institution of the White Primary, which allowed only whites to vote in primary elections. It was adopted first by cities and then by most southern states between 1896 and 1915. The popular primary to choose party candidates, which had been introduced by Progressives as a democratizing reform, became a vehicle for racial exclusion. Since selection as the Democratic party candidate was tantamount to election in most of the one-party South, blacks were effectively removed from all parts of the electoral process. In combination, these various measures, fortified by intimidation and violence, were highly effective in driving blacks out of politics. By 1903, three years after the passage of its constitutional disfranchisement law, Mississippi's black vote was down to 8,965, or 6 percent of the eligible black population. C. Vann Woodward notes that in 1896 there were 130,334 black voters in Louisiana, but by 1904, after literacy, property, and poll taxes had been put into effect, there were only 1,342. In Georgia black registration dropped from 28.3 percent of eligible voters in 1904 to 4.3 percent in 1910.[40]

Disfranchisement of black men was only one part of the process that Joel Williamson has called the "depoliticization of the Negro." Black men lost more than the vote; they lost a host of other civil rights and protections, including the rights to hold office, to sit on juries, to have a say in how their tax dollars were allocated, and to protect themselves and their families from discrimination and ill-treatment. During Reconstruction black men gained entry into elective and appointed offices and were found as legislators, court officers, and magistrates. They gained places in jury boxes, police forces, and in various branches of government employment, where they managed to maintain a toehold for two decades. By the second decade of the new century, they had largely disappeared from these sites.[41]

Black women had never enjoyed equal rights with black men in the external political realm, but the depoliticization of black men affected them too, leaving them even more vulnerable than before. As black men were systematically erased from political life, "political institutions and representative government became simply inaccessible and unaccountable to American citizens who happened to be black." Laura Edwards points out that disfranchisement dealt black women a double defeat: "Lacking any claim to public protection through their men folk, they labored under all the constraints of womanhood and enjoyed few of the privileges."[42]

As noted in Chapter 3, separate and unequal facilities were characteristic of black-white relations in the antebellum period, in both North and South. During Reconstruction the Republicans mounted challenges to many forms of public discrimination. Yet even the radicals, who established many institutions for the benefit of freedpeople, did not attempt to provide integrated facilities. Rather, they built separate schools, orphanages, hospitals, and relief organizations specifically for blacks. Freed men and women themselves contributed to patterns of separation after the Civil War by establishing their own churches, fraternal organizations, and charitable and other voluntary associations. Thus, if customary, voluntary, and de facto separation are counted, southern society was "segregated" before the passage of Jim Crow laws. Some historians, such as Howard Rabinowitz, have argued that Jim Crow laws did not introduce a radical new order but rather continued and codified practices established during Reconstruction by Republicans who viewed "separate but equal" as progress over the complete exclusion that blacks experienced prior to Reconstruction. Other historians, notably C. Vann Woodward and George Fredrickson, have interpreted de jure segregation as representing a significant ideological and structural shift.[43]

Fredrickson notes that the term "segregation" did not come to occupy a central place in public discourse about race relations until the 1890s, when southern states began passing laws to require separate accommodations in railway cars, passenger boats, and streetcars. He views the emergence and spread of that term as indicating a fundamental structural and ideological transformation in race relations. Moreover, Jim Crow laws originated in the growing cities to which both blacks and whites were migrating, not in rural areas where black-white relations of dominance-subordination were governed by custom.[44]

Specific regulations to segregate facilities such as railway cars and urban transport came about as a result of protests by whites who objected to the implied "social equality" of sharing space. The struggle to establish residential segregation is a particularly cogent example of the changes in structure and ideology. Antebellum southern cities were characterized by close proximity between white and black residences, as white owners wanted their slaves close at hand. In postbellum cities, pockets of black residences formed, but were interspersed within white residential areas. Not until 1910, when Baltimore passed a municipal ordinance defining blocks as black or white and restricting sale, purchase, and residence to the specified race did the trend toward ghettoization pick up speed. As David Delaney has shown, the adoption of some variation of the Baltimore ordinance in cities throughout the South was the product of grassroots political activism. White citizens formed committees and with the assistance of lawyers and city officials drew lines, defined spaces, and assigned racial meanings to the lines and spaces.[45]

Obvious factors in the timing of legal disfranchisement measures and segregation laws were the political shifts and realignments taking place at the federal and regional levels. In a series of decisions starting in the 1870s the federal courts curtailed the constitutional basis for federal protection of immunities and privileges, nullified crucial parts of the Civil Rights Act in the Civil Rights Cases (1883), legitimated de jure and de facto segregation in *Plessy v. Ferguson* (1896), and allowed disfranchisement by approving Mississippi's voting plan (1898). By the 1880s the national Republican party, finding it could retain control of the federal government without southern or black votes, largely abandoned its advocacy of black rights. The Republican indifference toward blacks reflected growing northern hostility toward blacks in the era of

American imperialism. In 1898 the United States launched adventures that brought Cuba, Hawaii, and the Philippines under its jurisdiction. The nation thereby absorbed millions of "colored peoples" who would not, of course, be citizens. America's assumption of the "White Man's Burden" verified the congruence between national white racial attitudes and southern ones. As Woodward notes, "The doctrines of Anglo-Saxon superiority . . . [which] justified and rationalized American imperialism in the Philippines, Hawaii and Cuba differed in no essentials from the race theories . . . [which] justified white supremacy in the South." Ray Stannard Baker, who investigated race and labor oppression both in the South and in Hawaii, reported striking similarities between the practices and beliefs of planters in the "Old South" and those of Anglo-American planters and other elites on the Islands.[46]

This period also saw an almost complete rewriting of the history of slavery and Reconstruction by white southern scholars and writers. This revisionist history erased black resistance, striving, and accomplishments, and fabricated accounts of black depravity, incompetence, and corruption. The view of black men as happy buffoons or dangerous predators and of black women as devoted mammies or animalistic jezebels was disseminated in magazine articles, treatises, films, pictorials, and popular novels. Influenced by these depictions, white northerners and Progressives came to accept a pessimistic view of the Negro as "incapable of self-government, undeserving of the franchise, and impossible to educate beyond the rudiments."[47]

At the same time that national restraints on antiblack extremists were relaxing, regional checks were also giving way. The southern conservatives who masterminded Redemption had managed to maintain political control for two decades by mobilizing, on the one hand, anti-Negro whites around the banner of the Lost Cause and, on the other, the aspirations of freedmen around paternalistic protection and patronage. A prolonged agricultural depression in the 1880s and 1890s and the conservatives' failure to institute reforms in farm policy eroded farmers' confidence in their rule. In the 1890s southern Populists in Georgia, South Carolina, and elsewhere harnessed agrarian discontent and forged a reform program based on interracial cooperation among black and white smallholders and tenant farmers. The conservatives beat back this threat by raising the rallying cry of white supremacy and

"Negro dominance," while simultaneously using their control of the so-called black belt districts to fraudulently report huge majorities of black votes in their favor. The setback shattered the Populist party and the fragile interracial cooperation it had forged. Thereafter, white supporters of the Populists blamed corrupt black votes for their defeat. One-party rule was thus restored in the 1890s through the uniting of whites across class lines on the basis of white supremacy and negrophobia.[48]

All this discussion of white activity and politics has not addressed black agency. Fredrickson has rightly deduced that if blacks had in fact been too incompetent to pose a threat to white rule or had been naturally subservient enough to accept permanent subjugation, de jure segregation would not have been necessary. He emphasizes a factor that Woodward neglects: growing black achievement and assertiveness, which motivated whites to fashion increasingly elaborate legal constraints. The generation of blacks growing up after slavery had been raised hearing the rhetoric of equality and witnessing at least some progress. They were primed to seize the rights proclaimed by the Fourteenth and Fifteenth Amendments and were also better prepared to fight for their rights. Black literacy had climbed from just 10 percent at emancipation to over 50 percent by 1900. The share of black farmers who owned their land rose from 3–8 percent in 1880 to 25 percent by 1900.[49]

A visible middle class made up of small entrepreneurs, professionals, and educators had grown up during this same period. Having achieved modest success by hard work and sacrifice, they expected to be accorded a certain respect and access to "first-class" facilities. Their efforts to obtain this access often clashed with white efforts to maintain a color line. Rabinowitz points to increasing black assertiveness in their "insistence on voting independently, protesting unequal justice, and calling for control over their own education." At the other end of the class spectrum was the tendency for blacks to clash with urban police, particularly to prevent the arrest of other blacks. August Meier and Elliott Rudwick document the rise of retaliatory violence against police in the early twentieth century. As custom and informal controls seemed no longer effective to keep blacks "in their place," whites turned to legal measures designed to bring in the force of the state to buttress white domination. One suggestive piece of evidence of the role of black assertiveness in motivating segregation laws is that Mississippi, where whites attained the greatest domination through violence and state repression, actually had fewer such laws than other states.[50]

Delaney characterizes the system of segregation established by Jim Crow laws as a form of fanatical hyperterritoriality; he sees it as largely a spatial phenomenon and defines it as the creation of more or less durable lines and spaces, accompanied by an incremental intensification in the meaning of those lines and spaces and assignment of negative consequences for crossing lines. As Delaney has pointed out, dejurification of Jim Crow had the effect of deputizing every concerned white person—shop clerk, nurse, streetcar operator, librarian—and "allowed or compelled them to draw and police the color line as they went through their daily lives."[51]

Segregation in practice often meant exclusion in that blacks were simply barred from recreational facilities, parks, hotels, libraries, and restaurants. Sometimes it involved duplication of spaces, as in the establishment of separate schools, parks, cemeteries, YMCAs, libraries, waiting rooms, washrooms, phone booths, and elevators. At other times it meant a subdivision or compartmentalization of space, as in jails, theaters (the Jim Crow seats), and sometimes hospitals and streetcars. In subdivided spaces, boundaries were sometimes marked by fixed physical barriers, but in other cases lines were movable, as on streetcars when whites were expected to fill the seats from the front first and blacks from the back, with the dividing line varying with the distribution of riders. In white-dominated spaces, segregation meant denial of certain facilities, as in department stores where there were no dressing rooms for blacks, who had to buy clothes without trying them on. At some drugstore fountains blacks could order food but not sit at the counter to eat it. Although segregation was often spatial, it was not solely so, and had aspects of fear of "pollution," as in North Carolina and Florida laws requiring that public school textbooks be stored separately, or in the use of separate Bibles to swear in witnesses in Atlanta courts.[52]

Despite the *Plessy* formula of "Separate but Equal," separate facilities were patently unequal with the colored version invariably inferior, as in the case of black schools lacking lighting and heating or enough desks and books for pupils. Segregation not only made daily life more difficult or inconvenient for blacks but also subjected them to daily humiliation. A northern writer, visiting a building in Atlanta in 1908, observed that the main passenger elevator was marked "for whites only," while the other elevator was marked, "This car for coloured passengers, freight, express and packages." Later, while riding a streetcar, he heard a white conductor on a streetcar yell out "Heh, you nigger, get back there!" and saw a black passenger who had inadvertently taken a seat "too far forward" hastily move back.[53]

Segregation did not mean that whites were excluded from black spaces or blacks from white spaces in all circumstances. White administrators and teachers worked in black schools, white police entered black bars to enforce the law, and white jailers kept order in the black hold. Black porters worked on white and black railway cars, black elevator operators ran white elevators, and black servants and nursemaids accompanying their employers rode as passengers on white cars. In other words, as long as the lines of authority and power were clear, separation was not required. Where power was ambiguous or shared space implied equality, duplication or compartmentalization of space was imposed to make the hierarchy clear. The main point of Jim Crow segregation was not separation but hierarchy.

Not all segregation that was practiced was dictated by law: Woodward could not find any statutes prescribing separate Bibles or separate elevators. Thus gauging the extent of segregation by surveying existing laws would grossly underestimate its dimensions. This leads to the matter of racial etiquette, which was governed by an unwritten code, but like Jim Crow, was enforced by whites in daily interactions. Racial etiquette had to do with knowing one's "place," not in the spatial sense, but in the social order. The basic rule was that blacks were to display deference at every turn: "to wait in nearly any line until all whites were served; to approach a white home only by the back door; to yield the right of way to whites when walking or driving; to show respect even to poor whites they privately mocked." It was not enough to observe the letter of ritual, blacks had to show "ready acquiescence" and cheerful humility by gesture and inflection. Above all, blacks were to be agreeable in their encounters with whites, to avoid controversy, any show of anger, or any mannerism which might be interpreted as assuming equality or challenging white authority. In interracial encounters, whites withheld everyday courtesies they used with one another, such as shaking hands or raising one's hat to women. They addressed blacks by their first name or by "auntie," "uncle," "sister" but never by Mr., Miss, or Mrs. Black parents had to train their children in racial etiquette at an early age to help them survive. Some children internalized the lessons, but others only assumed it on the outside while resenting their parents'—especially their fathers'—servility toward whites.[54]

Interdependent Lives and Identities

A central question that has arisen is whether the resubordination of blacks through a combination of legal and extralegal compulsion was inevitable once external checks on white southerners were removed. It is important to keep in mind that in addition to the withdrawal of federal oversight there were other major economic, social, and political changes in the postwar South: industrialization, increased integration into the national capitalist economy, intra- and inter-regional transportation links, and urbanization. These changes ushered in a period of relative fluidity and ambiguity in race, gender, and class relations, especially in the growing cities.

Any discussion of changes and continuity in structures and ideologies of race has to reckon first with C. Vann Woodward's account in *The Strange Career of Jim Crow* (1965), which initiated a new generation of scholarship on the post-Reconstruction and Jim Crow eras. Woodward offered a fundamental refutation of the prevailing interpretation that de jure segregation was foreordained by long-held racial attitudes once northern Republican props shoring up black rights were removed. Instead, he argued, Jim Crow involved the imposition of a radical and aggressive new racial order. Woodward's thesis was based on his interpretation of the twenty-year period between the end of Reconstruction and the passage of Jim Crow laws as one of considerable fluidity in "rules" governing relations between blacks and whites, as well as permeability in race lines, exemplified by the intermixing of black and white residential areas in southern cities through the end of the century. Further, noting the variety of voices and positions on race relations during this period, he concluded that Jim Crow was not made inevitable by intractable racial attitudes, but was only one of various possible alternative paths. He points out that the first segregation law was not passed until a decade after Redemption and it was more than twenty years before states on the Eastern Seaboard adopted such laws.[55]

While there is considerable disagreement about the extent to which Jim Crow laws imposed a new aggressive racial regime or merely codified prevailing practices, there seems to be agreement among historians that there was indeed some fluidity in the color line and unevenness in the enforcement of separation between the races prior to the proliferation of Jim Crow laws. Most blacks were simply too poor to attempt to enter hotels, restaurants, and other white spaces. Those who did might be rebuffed but sometimes were not, as there were no firm rules. Blacks and whites rode side by side on streetcars, rubbed shoulders at public events, and congregated in the same parks, leading some northern observers to remark on the seeming tolerance of southern whites to the proximity of blacks.[56]

Some recent historical accounts of black and white women's experiences during Reconstruction and for the two decades afterward suggest a similar fluidity in structures and ideologies of gender. By attending political meetings, camping out at the polls, forming ceremonial militia corps to march in parades, black women appeared in public spaces and were active in ways that were considered inappropriate for "true women." Evelyn Brooks Higginbotham notes that from the start, black Baptist women assumed and sought equal partnership within the family and an equal place within the church and larger community. It was also becoming clear that black women of all classes would have to assume economic responsibility either as partners or as sole providers. They thus needed access to education. As Reconstruction-era support for black education waned, black men and women petitioned and lobbied for state-supported colored colleges and normal schools and gathered funds to establish their own private educational institutions. Significantly, black private and public institutions supported coeducation from the start, at a time when white institutions were single-sex.[57]

Although ideal southern white womanhood remained tethered to a cult of domesticity, in actuality, by the 1880s white women of all classes were pouring into public spaces, especially in the cities. White working-class women streamed into the textile mills of South Carolina, North Carolina, Georgia, and Virginia and the tobacco factories of Virginia and North Carolina. In North Carolina employment of white women in cotton mills increased from under 1,000 in 1892 to 13,973 by 1900. Women with some education entered the expanding field of teaching, which had become feminized, finding places first as students in the normal schools and then as instructors in classrooms. Meanwhile, women who did not have to work for a living were entering the public arena via club work and charitable organizations. Through such organizations as the United Daughters of the Confederacy, they participated in constructing a fictionalized antebellum past when white women supposedly had had more power, money, love, and protection.[58]

Simultaneously, generational succession was making visible changes in white manhood.[59] The men who had led the restoration of white conservative rule were former slaveholders, who retained a paternalistic attitude toward "childlike" blacks. They were confident of their superiority and ability to control blacks and looked down on poor whites for being touchy about associating with blacks. This older elite talked white supremacy and thundered against black rule, but when they regained power, they were willing to allot blacks a share of offices to secure cooperation. They distinguished between good and bad blacks and were prepared to grant favors to those they considered honorable and upright. A rising generation of newly urbanized, educated men who grew up after the Civil War saw things differently. They were critical of the older generation for losing the war and for having retarded industrialization and viewed their elders' indulgence toward blacks as inviting chaos. They favored industrialization and aimed to build a "new" South. For that to occur, white southern men would need to curb "disorder," which they associated with blacks. Less secure of their ability to control blacks, they were more overtly hostile.[60]

What was the nature of the so-called disorder that aroused such concern? One answer is that black men, as well as white and black women, were challenging social hierarchies and boundaries that tethered gender roles and white privilege. Black progress was threatening an order based on "place." White elite men seeking to reestablish a hierarchical order that placed them on top constructed a new ideology of white supremacy that rested on racialized constructions of gender and sexuality. Writers and polemicists created a narrative that reinterpreted history: it turned the history of white brutality against blacks on its head by making whites the victims of black aggression; it portrayed whiteness as under siege, threatened by social disorder and miscegenation. In this

narrative virtuous white womanhood was the central symbol and guarantor of white racial purity, while white manhood was defined in terms
of the defense and protection of imperiled white womanhood. Popular
and academic discourse in novels, textbooks, newspapers, illustrations,
and art disseminated images of black men as sexual predators and rapists lusting after white women. Black women's sexuality was depicted in
equally negative ways. As Higginbotham notes, the disjunction between the images of white and black women was much greater than
that between those of white and black men. Whereas black men represented male sexuality run rampant, black women represented the complete opposite of female sexual purity. This idea was elaborated by a
white southern woman who wrote in the *Independent:* "Negro women
evidence more nearly the popular idea of total depravity than men do
. . . I cannot imagine such a creation as a virtuous black woman."[61]

The negative representation of black women's sexuality was long-
standing; in antebellum times it helped rationalize rape, concubinage,
and other forms of sexual exploitation by white men. However, in the
earlier period the corollary, white women as uniformly virtuous, was
not assumed. Poor or otherwise disreputable white women were also
represented as sexually tainted. What was new was the creation of a
monolithic symbol of virtuous white womanhood that threw a mantle
of protection over all white women. Poor white women, for the first
time, were offered the presumption of purity, at least when it was con-
venient, to discipline blacks.[62]

White women were sometimes willing and sometimes passive
pawns. Middle-class women relished having the freedom to move
about in public but expected to retain the privileges of protected womanhood. They objected to any show of assertiveness, familiarity, or
physical proximity as disrespect that needed to be punished. As white
women expanded their activities into the public sphere, white men
sought to encapsulate them within their protection by creating the
black rapist as a threat. By stressing white women's dependency, white
men put white women and black men in their respective places.[63]

Anti-Miscegenation and the Black-White Dichotomy

Jim Crow segregation required reification of racial dualism. Thus one
of the strongest strictures was that against interracial sex. It could be

said that the color line was heavily sexualized and gendered, in that white supremacists compulsively focused on black men's uncontrolled sexuality and white women's vulnerability. The mythology of pure white womanhood required that sex between white women and black men be seen as occurring only through rape. Protecting white women from depredations by black men was the sacred duty of white men and tantamount to preserving the white race. This construction of interracial sex ignored the long history of intermixing since the seventeenth century with the arrival of the first Africans in Virginia. It also obfuscated the continuing practice of white men's exploitation of black women through concubinage, prostitution, and rape.

The result of two centuries of intermixing was the presence of a range of color and phenotype that had to be fitted into dichotomous categories. Segregation and anti-miscegenation laws presumed that individuals could be designated as belonging to one of two mutually exclusive categories, white and colored (or Negro). The question was, as Baker put it, where to draw the color line. For historical reasons, the line between white and black was drawn differently by different states and localities, on the basis of both custom and law. In the upper South, intermixing between indentured servants and African slaves began in the seventeenth century. In 1662 Virginia authorities imposed penalties on interracial unions and assigned children to the status of the mother; for another twenty years the mixed child of a slave woman was a slave, while that of a free woman was free. The racial status of mulatto descendants, however, remained uncertain, and it was not until 1785 that Virginia legally defined a Negro as anyone with a Negro parent or grandparent. This one-fourth rule was generally followed in the upper South. By 1850 there was a visible mulatto population of about 200,000 in the upper South, one-third of them free and primarily rural.[64]

In the black belt, where the number of slaves increased with the expansion of the plantation economy, most interracial sex involved white slaveholding men and slave women, following the dictum that owning slaves meant owning the sexuality and bodies of black women. Owing to the economic value of slaves, there was strong pressure to define the children of such unions as black and therefore slaves. According to James Davis, the practice of having the master's mixed children work as servants in the big house started the "genteel" tradition among mulattos. Some slaveowners gave some favor to their slave children, and some manumitted them, but others cheerfully enslaved them and even sold them to raise cash. Louisiana and South Carolina differed from the rest of the South in part because early sugar plantation owners in those states came from Barbados and Santo Domingo/Haiti respectively; both states recognized mulattos as a separate, buffer group. Not until 1865 was interracial marriage banned by statute in South Carolina, and even then racial status was based on "general reputation and acceptance"; thus some individuals with visible African features could claim white status. In Charleston and New Orleans, which had the highest concentrations, mulattos formed an intermarrying, elite class. This existed alongside the institutionalization of white men maintaining mulatto concubines.[65]

In the 1850s with antislavery criticisms of concubinage and double standards of miscegenation growing, white southern acceptance of the buffer status of mulattos diminished. Mulattos were increasingly treated as black; consequently their identities shifted from a sense of being a separate group to being "Negro." This moving of mulattos into the Negro category and erecting more stringent requirements for "whiteness" accelerated during Reconstruction. White southern distrust of Negroes and mulattos for allying with the North, and fear of miscegenation due to the shortage of white men, increased white resistance to according exemptions to lighter mulattos.[66]

Redemption brought a return to bans on interracial marriage, which had been repealed during Reconstruction. The statutes involved defining "Negro" or "colored," and the language varied, ranging from one-fourth in Virginia to one-sixteenth in North Carolina and Louisiana. States also varied in their definitions in segregation statutes, with some having different definitions in different areas of law. The overall trend was toward a "one-drop rule" as Jim Crow law spread. The shift can be clearly traced in Virginia, which lowered the one-fourth standard which had prevailed since 1785 to one-sixteenth in 1910 and finally to "any Negro blood at all" in 1930. As Jim Crow laws were passed, vigilante committees and anti-miscegenation leagues were formed in Mississippi, Louisiana, and elsewhere. White men continued to display an amazing ability to maintain contradictory ideas; white male protectors of white womanhood fought to keep the white race pure while simultaneously contributing to miscegenation by continuing to consort with black women. They were able to defend both stances through a double standard of sexuality. Perhaps Mississippi Governor Theodore Bilbo's position illustrates this mental legerdemain: he admitted that white men had "poured a broad stream of white blood into black veins," but he insisted that the white race remained "absolutely pure" because "white women have preserved the integrity of their race."[67]

It was in the *Plessy* decision that the U.S. Supreme Court affirmed the states' rights to determine racial categorization and to legislate separation on the basis of those categories. Homer Plessy, a Louisiana Creole, had included in his challenge the claim that because he was seven-eighths white his ejection from a whites-only railroad car was illegal. In upholding the Louisiana law, the majority opinion dismissed Plessy's claim that the statute deprived him of his property right, namely his reputation as a white person. The court acknowledged that there was a "difference of opinion in different states" as to "the proportion of colored blood necessary to constitute a colored person, as distinguished from a white person," but concluded that "these are questions to be determined under the laws of each State."[68]

Despite variations in legal definitions, decisions about racial assignment in fact generally followed the one-drop rule any time the question arose. This hardly resolved the continuing anxiety among whites about miscegenation; indeed, the one-drop idea raised the specter of "invisible blackness." Many white southerners came to question their own identity, racked by the fear that they might carry tainted black blood. Davis says that in the 1920s any white person who voluntarily associated with blacks or "acted" black would be suspected of being black. Among blacks a color hierarchy still operated, with lighter individuals enjoying higher status and successful black men preferring to marry lighter women. Still, ability counted and dark skin did not preclude attaining leadership and prestige. John Dittmer claims that in Georgia rigid Jim Crow segregation, opposed by the black ideal of racial pride and unity, reduced the significance of skin color among blacks; however, he also notes that light-skinned blacks remained atop the black socioeconomic pyramid.[69]

Contestation and Resistance

Because of concern with documenting the extreme oppression and exploitation of blacks and the assaults on their humanity, historians until recently have focused on the actions of whites and of white institu-tions in creating and maintaining a system of white supremacy. The re-sult has been a portrait of the Jim Crow era as one of black quiescence. Certainly the forces arrayed against black activism were daunting: de jure segregation, disfranchisement, relegation to the lowest rungs of the labor market, legal and extra legal violence to enforce racial subor-dination, and symbolic assault through racist stereotypes and carica-tures. Yet just as scholarship on black family, education, labor, and poli-tics during Reconstruction has highlighted the role of black agency in shaping these institutions, so recent studies of the black experience during the post-Reconstruction and Jim Crow eras have drawn atten-tion to black activity and self-organization as major factors provok-ing de jure segregation and disfranchisement and as laying the ground-work for the civil rights revolution of the 1960s. There were notable national campaigns, especially in the legal arena; one was the NAACP-organized challenge to municipal residential segregation ordinances, which resulted in their being declared unconstitutional by the Supreme Court in 1917.[70] However, my focus here is on local contestation. I consider three kinds of sites: separate black spaces, white-controlled public spaces, and worksites.[71]

Building Separate Spaces

In his study of black life in Norfolk, Virginia, during the period be-tween the Civil War and the civil rights movement, Earl Lewis ob-serves that African Americans were never quiescent even during the so-called nadir of black rights. They "never abided racism, 'polite' or oth-erwise, well; they boycotted, rioted, petitioned, cajoled, demonstrated and sought legal redress. During moments of introspection, some even vocalized the irony they found in accepting a policy of separate-but-equal that led to an unwanted reality of inequality." More impor-tant, they sustained themselves by nurturing family, home, and com-munity. They built churches and schools, formed benevolent and mu-tual aid associations, established literary and other cultural societies, and organized celebrations to mark important communal events and holidays, such as Emancipation Day. Lewis points out that blacks never merely reacted to white racism. Rather, they acted on their environ-ments and turned "segregation" into "congregation." "They filled the porches and windowsills, attended churches, lodges, and parades, set the rhythm, and regulated the pace. As much as possible, they transformed the city to meet their needs. Always cognizant of racism, they were never all-consumed by its presence; throughout, they remained actors in a fluid social drama."[72] Thus southern blacks were profoundly affected by segregation, but they were not rendered helpless to resist it and to develop counterstrategies.

Lewis, Robin Kelley, Brown, and others who have studied southern black communities of the late nineteenth and early twentieth centuries have argued that black cultural and social institutions reflected communal values and collective uplift that were at odds with the prevailing individualistic ideology of the dominant white classes. Indeed, the tendency for former slaves to share anything they had with poorer kin and to take in dependents was viewed by northern missionaries and Freedmen's Bureau officials as retarding their progress.[73]

If a communal orientation was a legacy of the slave experience, post-Reconstruction racial oppression and exclusion reinforced it by underscoring the extent to which the fate of individual blacks was linked to the fate of blacks as a whole. And, ironically, segregation enabled blacks to carve out social spaces within which alternative visions of society and community could thrive. In these spaces blacks built an oppositional culture, one that emphasized collectivist values, mutuality, and fellowship.

Churches were the most crucial institutions, serving a myriad of spiritual, social, and political functions. E. Franklin Frazier called the black church a "nation within a nation." Sunday services, prayer meetings, and revivals offered spiritual rejuvenation and expression of sacred values. Churches sponsored Sunday schools and numerous church associations which forged linkages among congregation members. Denominational meetings brought together men and women from throughout the South and forged ties across individual communities. Churches also published newspapers, an important source of communication. At a time when blacks were denied access to public spaces such as parks, libraries, and meeting halls, churches housed a broad range of programs and activities, such as athletic clubs, circulating libraries, and vocational classes. Churches also provided meeting space to hold conferences, political rallies, school graduations, and other large gatherings. Higginbotham describes the black church as functioning as a public discursive arena in which issues were "aired, debated and disseminated throughout the larger black community."[74]

Mutual aid and benevolent associations were perhaps the second most important community institutions. They fostered camaraderie and encouraged self-improvement. By pooling resources, associations could provide insurance, health care, medicines, and burial assistance that members could not otherwise afford. They also stood by in case of misfortune, providing charitable aid for widows, children, and disabled and ill members. The precise number of such associations cannot be determined, but according to existing commentaries there were many thousands. Peter Rachleff reports that Richmond alone had more than 400 secret societies by the early 1870s, and Sara Jane Early estimated that there were more than 5,000 women's societies with over 250,000 members throughout the South in the 1890s. Some associations were made up entirely of one sex, while others had both male and female members and officers.[75]

Kelley points to other sites such as "bars, social clubs, barbershops, beauty salons, even alleys" as semiprivate spaces for blacks to congregate, tell stories, and engage in "dissident" activities. He also suggests that "average black workers probably experienced greater participatory democracy in community and neighborhood-based institutions than in the interracial trade unions that claimed to speak for them."[76]

Policies and practices of white supremacist rule had the contradictory effects of simultaneously reinforcing the black collective orientation and fostering schisms along class and gender lines. As the race line firmed into a wall and blacks were disfranchised in the formal political arena, blacks turned even more inward to build "civic citizenship" based on black economic development and self-help. In addition to the churches and numerous fraternal and mutual aid organizations, they formed banks, insurance companies, and businesses, regional and national associations such as the National Association of Working Women, and even autonomous black towns, such as Mound Bayou in Mississippi.[77]

A collective orientation did not preclude internal divisions. By the 1880s the members of an emerging black middle class were responding to white racist ideology by acquiescing in the notion that the masses of blacks were as yet unready for citizenship, and taking on themselves the mantle of agents of black progress. According to Kevin Gaines, the black middle class and the organizations they formed adopted an ideology of "racial uplift." This ideology oscillated between two poles: one pole was grounded in liberation ideology that stressed collective

struggle, and the other was rooted in a classed ideology that emphasized bourgeois qualifications for citizenship. Over time the latter came
to dominate as middle-class black men accommodated to less inclusive
definitions of citizenship which emphasized independent manhood,
gender hierarchy, and middle-class respectability. Black political leaders urged illiterate blacks to stand back and allow literate blacks to vote
first, since they were less likely to be challenged and this would at least
ensure their vote. Established churches stopped the practice of lining
the hymn (calling out the lyrics in the songbook), which had allowed
full voice to those who could not read. At the same time, middle-class
blacks wanted to combat white racist stereotypes and caricatures of
blacks as lazy, dishonest, and sexually promiscuous by upholding standards of sobriety, hard work, and decorum. Since they were acutely
aware that in the white mind the actions of any single black person reflected on blacks as a whole, it was up to respectable middle-class blacks
to foster education, economic self-sufficiency, and respectability not
only among their own class but also among other blacks. Brown notes:
"In the changing circumstances of the late nineteenth century, working-class men and women and middle-class women were increasingly
disfranchised within the black community, just as middle-class black
men were increasingly disfranchised in the larger community."[78]

Middle-class black men's claims for political rights increasingly drew
a connection between manhood and citizenship; in this narrative, black
men's rights were essential for them to be able to act as men do—to
protect their communities, home, families, and women. Drawing on
the history of white men's sexual abuse of black women, they offered a
narrative of endangered black womanhood which needed to be protected by black men. Black men needed to assume an authoritative,
protective role in the family, and the "best" black men needed to assume leadership in the church and community. Thus black middle-
class efforts should focus on reforming common blacks, making men
sober and reliable heads of households and women respectable in de-
portment and demeanor.[79]

Within this gender- and class-inflected ideology of uplift, middle-
class black women carved out a special role for themselves to protect
and improve their poorer sisters and brothers. They formed myriad associations through churches and other institutions to provide health
and welfare services especially for women and children. Although
the ideal of black middle-class women as protectors of working-class

women resonates with the ideology of white middle-class women's political activity during this period, there were two important differences. White women's claims to moral authority were based on the notion of separate spheres for men and women and women's special responsibility for the morally pure domestic realm. Black women's notion of their charitable work was rooted in an earlier history of inclusion, not exclusion, from communal life, and assumed commonality rather than separateness in men's and women's roles. While white women's activities were aimed at getting white men to allow them a public voice as women, black women's activities were aimed at getting a voice for black men and women.[80]

Glenda Gilmore's interpretation of black middle-class women's role in the Jim Crow era is that the depoliticization of black men caused black women to emerge as "ambassadors" for the black community. They were seen as less threatening than black men and therefore could go where black men couldn't. They could organize and petition white authorities for municipal services, education, health care, and a share of relief funds as "mothers" concerned about their families' welfare without seeming to engage in forbidden political activity. At times they forged ties with white women in common causes, such as temperance and public health. Such alliances were fraught with racial politics, however, in that white women attempted to cast black women in subordinate roles as junior partners requiring white guidance, while black women knew themselves to be fully competent and entitled to an equal role.[81]

According to Evelyn Brooks Higginbotham, black women never acceded to gender inequality, but they did accept respectability and sexual discretion for women as essential to racial uplift. Black middle-class women involved in benevolent activities on behalf of their poorer brothers and sisters recognized poverty as an underlying problem and sought to relieve it by organizing services to aid families and individuals. However, they also decried the involvement of poorer blacks in drinking, dancing, prostitution, and bodily displays which they felt reinforced negative stereotypes. One of the largest women's church organizations, the Women's Convention of the National Baptist Convention, was at the forefront of moral reform. As Higginbotham describes it, "through leaflets, newspaper columns, neighborhood campaigns, lectures and door-to-door visits, an army of black Baptist women waged war against gum chewing, loud talking, gaudy colors, the nickelodeon, jazz, littered yards, and a host of improprieties." They also sought to redirect interest toward more "wholesome" activities by organizing classes and clubs. Their concern with sexual purity, child-rearing, cleanliness and order, and women's responsibility for the welfare of the family mirrored the assimilationist values of Americanization programs aimed at Mexicans in the Southwest and Southern European immigrants in the Northeast.[82]

As in these other cases, the targets of reform did not always accede to the judgments of their purported saviors. According to Tera Hunter, working-class men and women "refused to abide by the simple polarities between 'wholesome' and 'hurtful' amusements." They worked hard at having fun. Robin Kelley notes that blues clubs, dance halls, and jook joints—nightclubs devoted to music and dance—were important sites for working-class men and women "to take back their bodies, to recuperate, to be together." Dancing, long a form of black cultural expression, became a focus of conflict both between white employers and workers and between the "better class" of blacks and other blacks over the appropriate use of black bodies. Middle-class whites saw dancing as taking away energy from black men and women's exertions at wage labor, while middle-class blacks saw dancing as hindering progress toward a sober, chaste, and disciplined black working class. The free movement and display of black bodies in dancing transgressed both white and middle-class black notions of respectability. Domestics and other laborers, in contrast, viewed dance as a respite and escape from deadening routines, critical to the task of reclaiming their lives as their own. For domestic workers who wore uniforms as badges of servility and black men who wore rough work clothes, "dressing up" reflected personal style and affirmed self-worth. Hunter notes that the clothing styles favored by black women in dance halls emphasized "body parts such as buttocks," thereby subverting dominant standards of beauty. Black women were endlessly caricatured as grotesque and ugly in popular representations in the dominant culture. But in dance halls black beauty could be highlighted and celebrated.[83]

Contestation in Public Spaces

On an everyday basis, blacks could not oppose segregation of spaces or separate facilities. They did, of course, resent gross inequality of facilities, especially in commercial situations where they paid the same as whites or where they were singled out for degrading treatment. Blacks did protest paying first-class fares and being relegated to second-class trains or having respectable black women barred from ladies' cars and being forced to endure smoke, noise, and congestion in black-only cars. The most sustained resentment was generated by segregation of urban streetcars, which subjected blacks, particularly domestic workers, to daily humiliation. For several decades after Reconstruction blacks and whites had ridden side by side on urban transport. When municipalities and states started passing laws in the 1890s requiring segregation on streetcars, the new rules imposed special hardships. Blacks had to pay at the front and reenter the car from the middle; they were forced to stand even when there were seats available or to move from a row that became white when a white person claimed it. The new laws departed from the status quo and were viewed as insulting. A *Nashville Clarion* editorial described that city's new ordinance as "an effort to humiliate, degrade and stigmatize the Negro."[84]

In every state and in many cities the enforcement of the new laws precipitated boycotts. Meier and Rudwick found evidence of boycotts in twenty-five southern cities between 1900 and 1906. The boycotts were organized by elite business and professional people, including many ministers, but could not have been sustained without the participation of masses of black workers, including servants who walked or hitched rides from black hack and dray drivers rather than ride the streetcars. Boycotts were sustained for periods ranging from several weeks up to two or three years and inflicted significant financial damage on streetcar companies. Although some of the early protests in the 1890s resulted in temporary concessions, the boycotts all eventually petered out without attaining their objectives in the face of white determination to maintain white supremacy.[85]

Meier and Rudwick characterize boycotts as essentially conservative protests in that, unlike sit-ins, they avoided confrontation with white passengers or authority. The leaders were conservatives who eschewed radical rhetoric and making any reference to political rights. Nonetheless, both contemporary and recent accounts have pointed to enforcement of streetcar segregation as one of the most frequent sparks for spontaneous black resistance. One reason was that the lines demarcating black and white sections were inexact. White seating began from the front and black seating started from the back, but the dividing line shifted depending on the drivers' and white passengers' allocation of space. As the Atlantan Pauline Minniefield explained it: "It was miserable. Everybody was packed there, and all those empty seats in front. But, you see you couldn't sit in front of some old white woman or man that'd get on and sit for the heck of it right middle-way of the doggone streetcar, and you'd have to stand up." She added "Sometimes, people would say, 'I've been standing on my feet all day. Dogged if I'm going to stand up here all night.' And they'd sit down."[86]

Drivers and conductors, who were invariably white, were charged with enforcing segregation and orderliness with force if necessary, and they had police backup. Describing the practice in Atlanta during the 1920s, the social scientist Arthur Raper said: "All the conductor needed to do was blow his whistle. The policeman was just simply there to carry out the conductor's instructions." In such cases the black passenger inevitably was arrested even if only defending herself from assault by a white passenger. Mary Mebane of North Carolina recounted several instances of blacks in Durham refusing to move, and told of one incident she witnessed in which a black woman came to the defense of a fellow passenger who refused to give up his seat when ordered, shouting, "These are niggers' seats! The government plainly says these are the niggers' seats!" Mebane was embarrassed by the outburst but also proud; she noted with satisfaction that the driver backed down.[87]

In the more anonymous setting of the city, blacks were also more likely than in rural areas to defy the deference rituals of racial etiquette. Whites lamented that younger blacks lacked the obsequiousness of the "old time darkey." White newspapers regaled readers with incidents of young black men in groups physically jostling and taunting white men on the streets. When police attempted to arrest blacks in black areas, residents intervened, shouting or assaulting the officers and helping suspects escape. There was particular nervousness about younger black women failing to show proper deference. During a tense political campaign in North Carolina in 1898, several "street" incidents were reported in local papers involving white women being brushed, pushed, or poked by impudent black women. The *Chattanooga Times* editorialized about "insolent" black girls pushing not only white girls of their age but also "ladies" off the walk and prescribed the use of a horsewhip to cure them of that practice.[88]

Accounts of these kinds of confrontations provide the few glimpses of black working-class oppositional consciousness that can be found in most histories of the Jim Crow era. While there has been a great deal of scholarly attention to black leaders' political thought and to black middle-class racial uplift activity, there has been little examination of black working-class men and women as agents in their own lives, rather than as recipients and targets of middle-class black reform. In part this is because of the paucity of the usual kinds of records—manifestos, editorials, minutes, and diaries that would document black working-class activities and thought. Robin Kelley's research on working-class protest and Tera Hunter's study of black domestic workers and washerwomen in Atlanta tease out some of the covert forms of agency by reading records against the grain—to reveal what James C. Scott called "hidden transcripts"—and by identifying the political dimensions of everyday activities.[89]

Oppositional Strategies at Work

Seeking hidden transcripts is particularly important when looking at the ways blacks struggled not only for a living wage and civilized conditions of labor but also for a measure of dignity and recognition of their humanity—in short, for the marks of citizenship in its most general sense, full membership in the community. As noted previously, rural blacks sought, as their first choice, autonomy through land ownership; if forced instead to fall back on field work, they strove at least to control the rhythm and organization of their tasks. Slowdowns, absenteeism, and quitting forced many landowners to "compromise" by switching from gang labor to the quasi-autonomy of renting land or debt coercion of tenantry. Black urban and industrial workers, though technically "free" wage workers, were also subjected to close control and coercion. Confined to "nigger jobs," they had little leverage because they could be easily replaced by other blacks desperate for employment. Nonetheless, black laborers expressed their opposition in numerous ways.

Forbidden to talk or to sit near one another, black women rehandlers in tobacco factories communicated and expressed solidarity by singing together. They voiced their hope and protest: "Oh by an' by, I'm goin' to lay down this heavy load." For white visitors to the South who witnessed such scenes, black singing confirmed the myth of the carefree happy Negro. They apparently did not give too much significance to the lyrics, which were often critical of the workers' situation.[90]

Black industrial workers also engaged in classic tactics to protest unbearable working conditions and brutal workloads, including slowing down, feigning illness, being absent, pilfering goods, and sabotaging equipment. In factories such oppositional activities often involved implicit or explicit cooperation from co-workers. When black women stemmers in a tobacco factory had trouble keeping pace, black men responsible for supplying tobacco to them packed the baskets more loosely. To the extent that such strategies were used, they played into and off of white stereotypes of blacks as lazy, ignorant, shiftless, and immoral. Blacks could use the Sambo image by shuffling and scraping to evade serious punishment, but many felt honor bound to prove their worth by hard work and diligence. Kelley speculates that in some industries—those with active interracial trade unions or in jobs in which doing substandard work endangered the safety of other workers—efficiency and conscientiousness might have been the way for black workers to challenge both the job ceiling and racial stereotypes. He suggests such an ethic in the coal mines.[91]

Much that has been written about hidden resistance has focused on domestic workers. Frustrated employers complained of scrubwomen doing sloppy work, cooks scorching food and damaging kitchen utensils, and washerwomen damaging or stealing clothing. The so-called service pan—the leftover or extra food that cooks felt entitled to take—was an open secret, put up with by employers who wished to retain the services of a good cook. Pilfering, especially of food, could be seen as compensation for being underpaid and helped servants get by. Servants and washerwomen in turn complained of employers who made false accusations of damage or theft as a pretext for cheating them out of wages or payment. Still, the terms of employment remained unequal. Employers could always fire workers for theft, whereas workers cheated out of wages had no recourse.[92]

Because of the isolated character of household employment, domestic workers were generally forced to fall back on individual strategies to try to get fairer compensation and to assert their dignity, but they also cooperated and engaged in collective self-help. Black domestics, through their networks, "blacklisted" employers who were known to cheat or mistreat their employees. They also formed mutual aid and trade organizations, such as the Working Women's Society in Atlanta, the Cooks' Union, and the Colored Working Women and Laundry Women, which allowed members to pool resources and offered them an alternative to borrowing from moneylenders. Domestic service is generally viewed as one of the most difficult occupations to organize, yet three of the earliest black strikes were organized by washerwomen: in Jackson, Mississippi, in 1866; in Galveston, Texas, in 1877; and in Atlanta in 1881. The largest and most sustained of these was the Atlanta strike, where the Washing Society of Atlanta fought for a uniform rate of $1 per twelve pounds of wash. Supported by black churches and the community, 3,000 women took part at one time or another. Catching the spirit, cooks, house servants, and child nurses joined in asking for raises. Hunter argues that washerwomen were at the forefront because of their collective networks, forged at the communal water pumps where they congregated to do their work. It took the combined threat of landlords threatening rent increases, the city council threatening a $25 license fee, and the arrest and fining of strike leaders to break the strike.[93]

As this instance illustrates, racialized gender consciousness and communal solidarity were often essential elements in labor militancy and organization of black workers. For obvious reasons black men and women had an antagonistic view of white labor unions. Notwithstanding some efforts at interracial organizing, white unions most often excluded black workers altogether or imposed job ceilings on them. Employers fanned racial hostility by using blacks as strikebreakers against white workers. Black workers had little reason to stand in solidarity with white workers, from whom they frequently suffered verbal abuse, sabotage, and assaults when they worked in the same industry. When unions organized entire industries, such as lumber or coal, white workers insisted on segregated locals. Instances of successful organizing and strikes involving black workers were often in all-black jobs that whites did not want: black tobacco handlers at the turn of the century, black waterfront workers during World War I, and the washerwomen's strikes in the 1860s, 1870s, and 1880s.[94]

Education, Labor, and Citizenship

The struggle over black education is one where issues of race, gender, labor, and citizenship clearly intersected and where differences in black and white values and conceptions of these issues are highlighted. Every historical and contemporary account stresses blacks' almost sacred faith in education and their extraordinary efforts to acquire it. Black ideas about education, according to James Anderson, were formed prior to emancipation and were shaped by a communal tradition of mutual self-help and improvement. Slaveowners' strong opposition to literacy because of the danger of introducing new ideas undoubtedly underscored the value of literacy and its connection to freedom. Despite the danger of being caught, some slaves took remarkable risks to learn to read and write and to teach others. Herbert Gutman documented the existence of secret slave schools in a number of antebellum southern cities, including Savannah, Natchez, Charleston, and Richmond. Du Bois estimated that perhaps 5 percent of slaves were literate at the time of emancipation.[95]

During the war, as localities fell to Union troops, one of the first things that "contraband" blacks (slaves given refuge but not legal freedom) did was to set up schools at their own expense; instructors included both free blacks and white Yankee missionaries and schoolteachers. Although they welcomed help, freedpeople desired to direct their own education. A white American Missionary Association teacher from New England, William Channing Gannett, noted, "What they desire is assistance without control." Northern missionary and benevolent societies soon set up free schools and provided teachers and much-needed financial support, but blacks often put up the building or repaired existing facilities, furnished them, and paid tuition out of their meager resources. When John W. Alvord, the inspector of schools for the Freedmen's Bureau, traveled all over the South in late 1865, he found at least five hundred "native" schools set up and taught by blacks. Many were in remote rural areas outside the ken of the Freedmen's Bureau. Alvord found clean-scrubbed and attentive children and many adults, including mothers and elderly men and women, in attendance.[96]

In 1865–66 the Union Army and Freedmen's Bureau took over black education in their jurisdictions, organizing a system of schools funded through federal contributions and local taxes. The Bureau and northern missionary societies also helped launch more than a score of private institutions of higher learning, including Atlanta University, Central Tennessee College, St. Augustine College, and Fisk University; black philanthropic and religious organizations also established and maintained numerous small colleges. While the infusion of federal resources was critical to expanding educational opportunities, so were freedpeople's own contributions and efforts. The shortage of funds and Bureau politics meant that initiative remained with blacks themselves to maintain schools. Gutman cited widespread instances of blacks staffing schools, erecting and repairing school buildings, purchasing books, paying tuition, and feeding, boarding, and protecting teachers, often in the face of harassment and vandalism from whites. In all localities blacks paid taxes or contributed in kind. Freedmen's Bureau records showed that in early 1867 at least half of the schools in ten southern states received financial assistance from black parents, and that except in Alabama and Florida, black parents put in at least $25 for every $100 expended by the Freedmen's Bureau. In Louisiana and Kentucky blacks paid more toward expenses than the Freedmen's Bureau.[97]

Blacks not only sought education for themselves and their children, they also advocated for universal, publicly supported education. As participants in the constitutional conventions and as elected and appointed officials in the first Reconstruction governments, blacks played a central role in writing in education as a basic right into the state constitutions. As a result of black efforts, supported by Republican allies, by 1870 every southern state had provisions in its constitution for a public school system financed by state funds. Though the constitutions did not specify whether schools were to be segregated or integrated, Republican-controlled legislatures subsequently passed laws endorsing or requiring separate schools.[98]

Black ideas about universal education were unique in the South, where, with the exception of North Carolina, states had not established public school systems like those found in most of the northern states by the end of the antebellum period. Southern white attitudes toward public education continued to be shaped by dominant planters. This class saw popular education as antithetical not only to their economic interests, which lay in maintaining an ignorant and compliant labor force, but also to their stake in a social order based on "natural" hierarchy. State-funded education was seen as interfering with family authority, church authority, and a paternalistic owner-labor relationship. White small farmers, small business people, and laborers, dependent on the planter class, did not challenge the planters' ideology and remained indifferent to universal education well into the late 1880s. Du Bois was on the mark when he wrote, "Public education for all at public expense, was, in the South, a Negro idea."[99]

With Redemption and the return of the planters to political power, black educational progress was stalled. Planters as a class continued to oppose universal education generally and education for blacks specifically, especially in rural areas. If they could not completely roll back black gains, they could and did retard progress by starving black schools of funding, preventing compulsory attendance, and gutting the constitutional requirement for education.[100]

In major southern cities blacks managed to hold on to the schools built by the Freedmen's Bureau. Since the principle of separate schools was firmly established and accepted by federal law and southern Republicans alike, there was less impetus for Redeemers to try to exclude blacks from schooling altogether. By the 1880s the Freedmen's schools had been absorbed into urban school systems administered by whites and overseen by white school boards. Redeemers also moved to replace Yankee teachers with native whites. This takeover left black children getting sparse education in crowded classrooms with little in the way of books or other resources. Worst of all, they were under the tutelage of hostile teachers, often those judged incompetent to teach white pupils. Blacks began to demand black teachers for their classrooms. Despite their limited political power, they often won these important battles, largely because white school boards soon realized how much less they could pay black teachers. Black women soon came to dominate the ranks of teachers in black schools, outnumbering men three to one, and formed a large part of the student bodies in newly established black normal schools. These women became central in racial uplift efforts as black schools became important community institutions and school-related ceremonies and celebrations, such as graduations and end-of-term exhibitions, became integral parts of black community life.[101]

Despite economic hardship and scarcity of classroom space, a remarkably high percentage of urban black children enrolled in school for at least part of the year: as high as 96.5 percent in Richmond in 1890. Enrollments of school-age children in the fifteen largest southern cities in 1910 ranged from 65 percent in Charleston to 74.4 percent in Houston. Between 1890 and 1910 black literacy rates in the six largest cites rose from about 50 percent to approximately 80 percent. For the South as a whole, despite opposition in planter-dominated states, the literacy rate increased from about 40 percent in 1890 to 67 percent in 1910.[102]

In the late 1870s and early 1880s white southern attitudes toward education began to shift. A small but growing group of "forward-looking" urban industrialists and educators started advocating for mass schooling for both whites and blacks. They saw the future of the South as one of increased industrialization, and education as a "means to produce an efficient and contented labor force and as a socialization process to instill in black and white children an acceptance of the southern racial hierarchy." They shared the planters' commitment to white supremacy, supported disfranchisement, and saw blacks as a permanent subordinate caste. However, they also saw the customary feudal system of labor relations as obsolete, to be replaced by modern impersonal labor relations. They therefore advocated special education for blacks geared to their supposedly limited capabilities and their place in the new industrial order. Thus they made common cause with northern philanthropists in developing an educational system for blacks focused on industrial and vocational training rather than liberal arts.[103]

In the late 1880s and early 1890s the Farmers' Alliance and the Populists came to political prominence and took up the banner of public education. White farmers and workers were somewhat unsettled by the educational strides made by blacks. The presence of literate blacks alongside illiterate whites seemed to contradict the doctrine of white superiority. Even some planters conceded that universal education for whites might be a good thing. The result was a dramatic expansion of schooling for whites. As in the case of universal manhood suffrage, where voting rights for white men were expanded in conjunction with explicit disfranchisement of blacks and women, universal education for whites provided opportunities for whites at the expense of black education. The expansion of public schools for whites occurred through an alliance between white planters and small farmers opposed to black education. Resources were diverted to fund white schools; new taxes levied to pay for schools were collected from both blacks and whites, but the lion's share went to white schools. Several studies by educational reformers gave lie to white claims that blacks were being educated at white expense by showing that blacks paid more in taxes than they got back for their schools. The net result was gross inequality of facilities and resources such that in the 1900s nearly two-thirds of black school-age children were not enrolled because of lack of schools.[104]

The shortage of schools was particularly acute in rural areas. Only after 1914, when migration to cities and to the North threatened to depopulate the countryside of black labor, did southern states relent and allow blacks, with the aid of the Rosenwald Fund, a northern philanthropic foundation, to launch a major initiative to build common schools in rural areas; states also for the first time began to infuse public funds into building and maintaining rural schools for blacks. Between 1914 and 1932 nearly 5,000 schools enrolling 663,615 students were built. Of the $28.4 million total cost, 15 percent came from the Rosenwald Fund, 64 percent from public funds, 4 percent from whites, and 17 percent from blacks. Blacks also contributed labor and material. The common school movement typified the system of double taxation that blacks endured for the sake of education. Blacks paid taxes that went to white schools and then had to raise money to fund their own schools.[105]

Blacks also built and sustained a unique system of private colleges, augmented by poorly funded federal land grant and state-supported normal schools and colleges. Most started out educating in the elementary years and gradually added secondary and finally college-level courses. The early founders of black private colleges such as Livingston College and Atlanta University saw education as a means by which blacks would grow as citizens in a democratic order. Accordingly their long-range goal was the development of a leadership class that would organize the mass of blacks and lead them to freedom and equality. They took as their model the classical liberal arts curriculum of New England colleges.[106]

However, the exemplar of black education that was able to garner support from whites, both southern reformers and northern philanthropists, was industrial education based on the Hampton and later Tuskegee models. Chronically short of funds and heavily dependent on philanthropic support, black educational institutions were forced to shift their emphasis to industrial and vocational training and away from liberal arts and teacher education. Glenda Gilmore points out that black women were disadvantaged by the shift of support from normal schools to vocational training. Most of the available money went to pay for costlier equipment for male trades. Vocational training for black women reflected the reality of their limited occupational choices and their exclusion from most industrial jobs. Thus specialized courses for women were offered in laundry work, nursing, cooking, and dressmaking, since for black women vocational training meant training for domestic service or sewing. Additionally, black institutions were forced to respond to white concerns about separating the sexes by ending coeducational programs. Yet despite having to feature manual training in public presentations of their institutions, many private black colleges continued to offer Latin and the classics.[107]

The importance of African American efforts to establish and maintain a system of education was underscored by Du Bois toward the end of *Black Reconstruction* (1935). From the perspective of the mid-1930s Jim Crow South, he wrote: "Had it not been for the Negro school and college, the Negro would, to all intents and purposes, have been driven back to slavery. His economic foothold in land and capital was too slight in ten years of turmoil to effect any defense or stability." The counterrevolution of 1876–1877 had removed most supports. "But already through establishing public schools and private colleges, and by organizing the Negro church, the Negro had acquired enough leadership and knowledge to thwart the worst designs of the new slave drivers. They bent to the storm of beating, lynching and murder, and kept their souls in spite of public and private insult of every description; they built an inner culture which the world would recognize in spite of the fact that it is still half strangled and inarticulate."[108]

OF THE REGIONS analyzed in this book, the South was the most extreme in terms of the scope and depth of structures maintaining coercion in the labor market and the denial of civil and political citizenship. Even in this extreme case, the role of contingency and human agency is nonetheless discernible in both the maintenance and the challenging of rules and boundaries. The failure of the interracial Populist challenge to conservative white rule was one such contingency. As for human agency, de jure segregation and disfranchisement emerged as responses to black striving and achievement, rather than as inevitable outcomes of black powerlessness. For instance, Mississippi, where whites effectively suppressed blacks through violence and repression, had the fewest segregation laws. Even with supposedly explicit laws in place, maintenance of segregation required the involvement of ordinary people in the interpretation and enforcement of rules. Ambiguities and slippages in enforcement, as well as divisions among whites, created openings for blacks to challenge and subvert white rules.

The case of black-white relations in the South also demonstrates

the ways in which the construction of labor and citizenship incorporates existing race and gender principles and also transforms them. The
clear boundaries required to set up race-stratified labor and citizenship
involved the creation of mutually exclusive racial categories of black
and white out of what had earlier been more differentiated groupings.
One result was to eliminate intermediate categories and to "purify" the
white category by defining it as the absence of any blackness, such that
the trend was toward a one-drop rule in which any degree of black ancestry placed an individual in the black category. This draconian definition of whiteness in turn had repercussions for white womanhood. The
assumption of sexual purity was extended to cover all white women, regardless of class, at least when it came to patrolling black male sexuality
and assertiveness.

· 5 ·

Mexicans and Anglos
in the Southwest

THE SOUTHWEST, like the South, is a vast and heterogeneous area. One "objective" definition of the Southwest is geographic-political: the part of northern Mexico that was taken over by the United States at the conclusion of the Mexican-American War. This territory included what are now the states of California, New Mexico, Arizona, Nevada, Utah, and part of Colorado, as well as Texas, whose annexation in 1845 had helped precipitate the war. At the time of the takeover much of the area was only sparsely settled by Mexicans and was still largely under the control of various Native American groups including Navajo, Apaches, Pueblos, and Comanches. The three areas of substantial Mexican settlement prior to the takeover were coastal California, south and southeastern Texas, and the New Mexico Territory. Southern Arizona and southern Colorado had smaller settlements that grew over the next six decades through regional migration and immigration.[1]

The timing of penetration by Anglo settlers and institutions into various areas differed. Some parts of the Southwest, especially Texas and northern California, were rapidly flooded by Anglos. Drawn by offers of land by Mexican governments seeking to populate Mexico's northern frontiers, Anglo settlers dominated Texas both numerically and politically by the mid-1830s. Exact figures are lacking, but contemporary observations indicate that there were approximately 25,000 Mexicans and 122,500 Anglos in Texas in 1845.[2] Northern California, which had only small outposts of Mexican settlement, rapidly came under Anglo control in the 1840s through military occupation and an influx of Anglo fortune seekers, especially after the discovery of gold in 1848. Over 200,000 Americans and other foreigners poured into northern California between 1848 and 1850. In southern California, which had substantial Mexican settlements, Mexicans retained a majority until the 1870s, when the construction of the railroads and land speculation drew thousands of settlers from the East and Midwest. Between 1860 and 1880 Los Angeles went from being 58 percent Mexican to 19 percent, Santa Barbara from 66 percent to 16 percent, and San Diego from 28 percent to 9 percent.[3] Arizona and New Mexico did not attract substantial Anglo capital and settlers until after the Civil War, when the railroads finally reached into these areas. Mexicans remained a majority in Arizona until about 1880. When New Mexico became a state in 1912, Mexicans still made up 60 percent of the population, the only state in the Southwest where they retained a numerical advantage over Anglos well into the twentieth century.[4]

If Anglo Americans and European immigrants were on the move, so too were Mexican Americans and Mexican immigrants. From the 1850s on, Hispanic New Mexicans expanded outward from established villages to found new settlements to take advantage of open land. In the 1880s, as Anglo economic penetration accelerated, men from traditional sheepherding villages in New Mexico began migrating to earn supplemental income by taking seasonal work in the Anglo economy, principally as workers on railroads and in mines. Thousands were drawn to southern Colorado to work in the coal mines of the Colorado Fuel and Iron Company and (after World War I) into northern Colorado to work in the sugar beet fields run by the Great Western Sugar Company. These migrants turned southern and northern Colorado into major "frontiers" for Mexican-Anglo interaction.[5]

The change in locations for major Mexican-Anglo encounters was also occasioned by the enormous rise in immigration from Mexico in the first thirty years of the twentieth century. About 90 percent of an estimated 640,000 immigrants arriving before 1930 settled in the Southwest, where they were employed in cattle ranching, large-scale commercial agriculture, mining, and railroads. Texas drew between half and two-thirds of immigrants from Mexico up to 1920, while California's percentage increased to nearly a third by 1930. Arizona drew more immigrants than California prior to 1910 and attracted the third-largest number after Texas and California after 1910.[6] Because of the shifting location of encounters between Mexicans and Anglos, when discussing race-gender relations prior to 1890 I will be referring primarily to California, Texas, and New Mexico, and when discussing relations after 1890 I will include Arizona and Colorado.

QUESTIONS OF LAND and citizenship were very much in the minds of Mexican delegates meeting with American representatives in the village of Guadalupe Hidalgo on the outskirts of Mexico City in 1847 to negotiate a treaty to settle the recent war. Mexico would be forced to cede one-third of its territory, but what would be the fate of the approximately 100,000 Mexicans residing in the ceded territories? The chief American delegate, eager to conclude a treaty, agreed to a provision allowing Mexicans residing in these territories three choices: to repatriate; to continue to live in the ceded territories as Mexican citizens; or, by not electing to remain Mexican, to automatically become American citizens. The final version of the Treaty of Guadalupe Hidalgo, ratified by the U.S. and Mexican governments in 1848, promised Mexicans who stayed in the Southwest "the enjoyment of all the rights of citizens of the United States according to the principles of the Constitution."[7]

As in the case of blacks after the passage of the Fourteenth Amendment, the promise of full and inclusive citizenship was not in fact realized. As David Weber notes: "At best, Mexicans became second-class citizens. At worst, they became victims of overt racial and ethnic prejudices."[8] Indeed, the inclusive nature of the treaty was challenged the very next year at the 1849 California Constitutional Convention. The debates over suffrage centered on trying to reconcile the terms of the treaty with a section in the draft state constitution that restricted the vote to "white male citizens." Delegates for the most part agreed that blacks and Indians ought to be excluded from voting, but what of Mexicans? At issue was the question of who was white. As relative newcomers (three-quarters of them having resided in California three years or less), the Anglo delegates brought ideas about race from the regions from which they had come.[9] Throughout the debate the delegates seemed to define "white" in opposition to "black" and "Indian," leaving Mexicans in an ambiguous position.

The initial proposal was simply to insert the words "and male citizens of Mexico who shall have elected to become a citizen of the United States" after "white male citizens." However, a sticking point for many Anglo delegates was the idea that many Mexicans carried "Indian blood." One delegate proposed an amendment to insert "white" before "male citizens of Mexico." A *californio*, that is, a Californian of Mexican-Spanish descent, Noriega de la Guerra, asked for clarification, saying that if the word "white" was intended to bar "the African Race," he supported it. However, he noted that many California citizens endowed by nature with a dark skin had been allowed full rights under Mexican law. They ought not be disenfranchised. An Anglo delegate, a Mr. Botts, offered the interpretation that "color" was not the issue but "race" was. He was willing to adopt any language that excluded the inferior Indian and African races: "It was in this sense the word white was used, not objectionable for their color but for what that color indicates." In the end the delegates adopted a suffrage provision that qualified for suffrage "every white male citizen and white male citizen of Mexico who shall have elected to be a citizen of the United States."[10]

The debate revealed the still fluid conceptions of the race of Mexicans and even some awareness of the ambiguity of racial categories. In the mid-nineteenth century most Anglos made racial distinctions among Mexicans on the basis of class and appearance. They accepted the landowning elite's claims to Spanish heritage, recognizing them as a type of white person. However, Anglos rarely accepted such notions for the mass of Mexicans—small farmers, pastoralists, and workers— whom they considered variously as Indian, mestizo, or akin to blacks and thus fitting the category of "unfree" labor and not entitled to rights of American citizenship. By the early twentieth century Anglos were less apt to recognize racial distinctions among Mexicans, instead drawing the color line between themselves and Mexicans and placing all Mexicans into the category of "colored" or "partly colored" races. Ethnic Mexicans pressing for their rights had to contend with white American discourse and practices that racialized them as nonwhite and not "real Americans." Processes of racialization of Mexicans thus lay at the heart of struggles over Mexican American labor and citizenship.

THE TRANSFER OF LAND from Mexican to Anglo control was a major step in the economic, political, and social incorporation of the Southwest into the United States. As David Montejano points out, much of the controversy about how the Mexican landowners lost their land has centered on whether it occurred through illegal chicanery or through legal land transfers. In his opinion the distinction is not very meaningful since displacement involved a combination of legal and illegal means.[11]

The larger "truth" of what occurred involved a transformation of the landowning system itself. Under the Mexican system, recognition of landownership was often a matter of tradition; boundaries were inexact and established by ephemeral markers, such as cattle skulls placed at a border. Moreover, land was considered a patrimony, with ownership residing in kinship and lineage and not in individuals. Additionally, the Mexican system included communal land grants that entitled all those residing in a given area to use the land for pasturing, grazing, or farming. Such lands could not be subdivided and sold to individuals. The Anglo American land system, in contrast, was based on codified legal title. Land was individually owned and could be subdivided among heirs and sold without regard to family claims.

Anglo American law became the instrument by which Mexicans were displaced. To validate their land claims in American courts, native landowners had to pay exorbitant fees to Anglo lawyers, who often ended up with some or all of the land as payment for their services. The expense of defending their land eventually impelled many owners into debt and finally into forced sales. Other landholders lost their land through outright fraud or legal chicanery or had their land seized by the government when they were unable to pay taxes. Even direr for subsistence farmers, herders, and ranchers was the loss of public communal lands on which they grazed their animals. Anglo authorities simply did not recognize such grants; they took the lands and sold them to Anglo speculators and businessmen.[12]

The shift in landownership was part of the overall transformation of the Southwest economy and its integration into the larger U.S. capitalist economy. The building of the railroads and the rapid influx of settlers and speculators from the East, Midwest, and South ushered in dramatic changes. The pastoral economy based on cattle, sheep, and subsistence farming was put under pressure by a capitalist economy based on commercial agriculture, large-scale ranching, mining, and mercantile trade.

These changes initiated a dual process that altered the economic circumstances of small landowners and communal villagers. On the one hand, there was significant loss in their ability to sustain their family economies in the accustomed ways. On the other hand, the new economy created a demand for labor. In response to these linked circumstances, small landowners and communal villagers attempted to maintain pastoral ways of life by having men take on seasonal migratory wage work in the Anglo economy in railroad construction, mining, and agriculture. Women and children remained in the home villages or settlements and engaged in domestic production and subsistence agriculture. With small plots of land, women could still grow beans, squash, and other crops and keep goats and chickens to produce milk, cheese, and eggs. Over time men's wage work became more permanent and required longer absences as employers in some industries, such as mining, which had worksites in remote locations felt it advantageous to have a more settled labor force.[13]

The economic changes also displaced landless Mexicans who had been employed on the rancheros and haciendas as blacksmiths, carpenters, saddlemakers, and sheepshearers. As the pastoral economy shrank, displaced ranchworkers struggled to maintain their accustomed occupations by turning to seasonal migratory work as vaqueros in the declining cattle industry and as sheepshearers. Such work provided only about three to eight months of employment, so earnings had to be supplemented by other seasonal work. In California in the 1880s Mexican men began to fill some of the niches that had previously been filled by Chinese men as unskilled labor in agriculture, construction, and railroad maintenance. In Texas work for cowboys declined as fencing reduced the need for cattle handling and railroads eliminated cattle drives. Vaqueros were forced to supplement their earnings with seasonal agricultural labor or in railroad construction.[14]

For most Mexican men, then, the economic transformation meant a downward drift from independent farming, ranching, or sheepherding or from skilled and semiskilled ranch employment to unskilled wage labor. The downward movement can be traced in the changing occupational distribution of Mexican heads of households in southern California between 1860 and 1880. For example, in San Diego, 31 percent of Spanish-surnamed heads of households were farmers or ranchers in 1860; by 1880 only 1.8 percent were. Likewise, skilled artisans declined from 39.1 to 4.8 percent, while those in unskilled labor rose from 21.6 to 80.9 percent. Downward drift can also be seen in south and west Texas between 1850 and 1900. In 1850–1860 Texas Mexicans were evenly divided with about a third each among ranch-farm owners, skilled laborers, and manual laborers. By 1900 only 15.8 percent were ranch-farm owners and 12.0 percent skilled laborers, while 67.1 percent were manual laborers. By way of contrast, the share of Anglos in the ranch-farm-owning category increased from 1.8 percent in 1850 to 31.4 percent in 1900.[15]

Mexican women's economic roles also underwent change and in some cases intensification. Mexican domestic ideology still defined men as the economic heads and women as "of the house." Women mostly continued to work in or close to the home, but they were in fact co-providers. Men's wages were rarely sufficient to purchase all necessities. Mexican women raised livestock, grew vegetables, and produced clothing and other necessities long after Anglo American women turned to the market for these goods. Moreover, many women had to support themselves and dependent kin without a male earner. The hazardous conditions of men's work, which led to early death, and men's long absences or even abandonment contributed to the high incidence of female-headed households. In the 1880s, for example, more than 31 percent of Mexican American households in Los Angeles were headed by women, as were 29 percent of those in Santa Fe and 24.6 percent of those in Tucson.[16]

From necessity, women and children began to engage in paid labor, preferably in the home but sometimes outside. In urban areas women took in laundry or sewing or kept boarders. They also went out to work as maids and laundresses in private households and in commercial establishments. A few with experience in needlework became seamstresses; still others turned to prostitution. More found jobs in fruit canneries, fruit packing houses, nut picking and shelling. Some women and children followed male heads of households in migration as seasonal farm workers or joined men in lumber, mining, and railroad towns or camps where they worked as seamstresses, laundresses, cooks, boardinghouse keepers, and hotel servants.[17]

The first three decades of the twentieth century saw further development of infrastructure that accelerated the processes of incorporation and fueled explosive economic growth. A vast rail network, including branch lines, was built, tying the region to the rest of the United States and linking southwestern farms and extractive industries to national markets. Extensive irrigation projects supported by millions of dollars in federal funds under the Newlands Federal Reclamation Act turned millions of acres of arid land to cultivation.[18]

Irrigation transformed the Imperial Valley in California, the Rio Grande Valley and Winter Garden regions of Texas, and the Salt River Valley of Arizona into major agricultural areas. Between 1900 and 1909 alone, irrigated acreage in the Southwest increased from 1.6 million to 14 million acres. Two notable characteristics of southwestern agriculture were specialization in capital and labor-intensive crops (cotton, sugar beets, and fruits and vegetables) and dominance by large-scale corporate farming. By 1929 California contained 37 percent of all large-scale farms in the United States. California's 2,892 such farms made up only 2.1 percent of farms in the state, but produced 28.5 percent of the total value of agricultural output. In Colorado one company, Great Western Sugar, owned all of the sugar plants and recruited all of the labor and thus controlled all beet production.[19]

The railroads continued to be a dynamic and growing sector, as railway companies continued to extend tracks. In addition to employing huge numbers of workers for track laying and maintenance, expanding rail lines facilitated the growth of southwestern agriculture and mining. The other main industries were extractive: copper in Arizona and New Mexico, coal in Colorado, oil in Texas and California. Additionally, cattle and sheep continued to be important throughout the Southwest and lumber was significant in Texas, Arizona, and California. These primary industries spawned related industries connected with processing output: food packing and canning, meatpacking, ore smelting, and lumber milling.[20]

Hierarchy and Control in the Labor System

Lacking other sources, Texas, New Mexico, and Arizona relied heavily on Mexican labor for all of their major industries. Mexican men did the lion's share of heavy physical labor involved in laying rail lines, constructing roads and irrigation systems, and clearing brush and undergrowth to prepare land for cultivation. They were also the main workforce in Arizona and New Mexico copper mines and in Texas cattle herding. In the south Texas cotton industry, large landowners employed white tenants and black sharecroppers until the 1920s, but as black Texas tenants and sharecroppers migrated north, the landowners shifted to corporate farming methods which depended on a vast army of seasonal Mexican laborers.[21]

Similarly, California employers had looked primarily to Asia for cheap and malleable labor, but with successive restrictions imposed on Chinese (1882) and then Japanese (1907) immigration, growers increasingly turned to Mexican labor. By the late 1920s Chicanos and Mexicanos made up three-quarters of farm labor in California. Unlike Asian field workers, who were almost all single men, Mexicans often traveled and worked as family groups. Indeed, agricultural employers said they preferred Mexican labor for field work precisely because so many women and children also worked and because families were easier to control.[22]

In the copper mines of Arizona and New Mexico, the Colorado coal fields, and the Colorado sugar beet industry, employers deliberately recruited a multi-ethnic labor force. Copper and silver mines employed Anglo American, Cornish, Italian, Slav, and sometimes black workers. The coal mines employed Slavs, "Austrians," and Italians, as well as Mexicans. Colorado sugar beet fields included, in addition to Mexicans and Japanese, large numbers of ethnic Germans from Russia. These German-Russians were viewed as permanent settlers and potential citizens and were offered terms that made it easy for them to acquire small farms. One aim in diversifying the workforce was to promote division and competition among groups and to forestall workers from unifying. Nonetheless, ethnic Mexicans made up the largest component of copper, coal, and beet field workers.[23]

Overall, then, the economy of the Southwest rested on the laboring backs of ethnic Mexicans. After traveling throughout the Southwest in 1922, two officials of the U.S. Department of Labor reported that Mexicans constituted 85 percent of railroad track workers, 50 percent of cotton pickers, and 75 percent of beet, fruit, and vegetable laborers. Another estimate, for the late 1920s, is that Mexicans made up 65–85 percent of the workforce in vegetable, fruit, and truck farming, more than 50 percent in sugar beets, 60 percent of common labor in mining, and 60–90 percent of track crews on regional railroads.[24]

The growing demand for Mexican labor in the Southwest coincided with widespread deterioration in conditions for farmers and workers in Mexico under the Profirio Diaz dictatorship (1876–1910), conditions that only worsened with the outbreak of revolution in the 1910s. The loss of usual means of livelihood, falling wages, and rising food prices combined to impel large numbers of Mexicans to migrate north in search of work. Their movement was aided by labor agents who traveled around the border region recruiting agricultural and railroad workers. The size of the migrant flow can only be estimated, since the U.S. government did not monitor or record border crossings before the 1920s. One expert's figures suggest that about 50,000 immigrants arrived in the 1890s, and that the number of new arrivals more than doubled to over 120,000 from 1900 to 1910 and then doubled again to over 200,000 from 1910 to 1920. Another rough indicator of the rate of immigration can be gained from the rise in the Mexican-born population of the United States from an estimated 68,399 in 1880 to 103,339 in 1900, to 486,000 in 1920, and to 639,017 in 1930.[25]

As in the South and Hawaii, the racial and gender hierarchy in the Southwest was institutionalized by stratification of the labor market, which was segmented into separate tiers for Anglo men, Anglo women, Mexican men, and Mexican women. Managerial, supervisory, and skilled jobs were reserved for Anglo men; unskilled and manual jobs, especially "dirty" work, were allotted to Mexican men. In farming, almost all field labor was done by Mexicans, while most agricultural foremen were Anglo.[26]

A fundamental principle was that in no case should a Mexican have authority over an Anglo. Thus Mexicans could be hired to be immediate overseers of other Mexicans, but they could not supervise Anglo workers. Also, Anglos were placed in positions that offered more autonomy, while Mexicans were placed in those which were more closely controlled. Tenant farmers, for example, who owned their own implements and paid the landowner the proceeds from one-third or one-fourth of the crop, were predominately Anglo. Sharecroppers, who had only their labor and had to borrow implements and supplies from the owner, and who had to pay the owner half the proceeds from the crop plus their debts, were predominantly Mexican. Owners came to prefer the latter because they had more control over Mexican sharecroppers than over Anglo tenants.[27]

Similar patterns of stratification were found in railroads. Mexicans constituted about 75 percent of track workers employed by the six major western railroads in 1928. They were confined largely to track building and maintenance, while managerial and engineering positions were monopolized by Anglos. Skilled jobs, such as machinists and foremen, were also largely held by Anglos. However, in the 1920s in one location, El Paso, the lack of skilled Anglo workers led the railroads to train Mexican men as clerks, machinists, machinist helpers, boltmakers, and other skilled positions, and to appoint them occasionally to be foremen over other Mexicans. Stratification was also marked in the construction industry, where Mexicans were concentrated as common labor in excavation and road building, and in mining, where they were restricted to common and unskilled jobs known as "Mexican work."[28]

Separate wage scales were established for Anglo male, Anglo female, Mexican male, and Mexican female jobs. Where different categories of workers did comparable work, Anglos received higher pay than Mexicans and men were paid more than women. Numerous studies of labor conditions in the Southwest documented the separate wage scales and the payment of "Mexican wages." Arizona mines were notorious for their dual wage system. In 1908 a government investigator found Mexican miners earning $2 a day compared with $3 to $5 paid to Anglos. In coal mining, where pay depended on amount of tonnage, European (Slav and Italian) miners were given better "rooms" to work. Anglo ranchers, mine owners, and businessmen favored Mexicans for lower-level jobs precisely because they could pay them less. California growers fixed wages to ensure their profits; at first wage fixing was informal, but later growers formed associations to set industry-wide standards. Growers justified the low wages, not just in terms of their own self-interest, but also in terms of Mexicans' alleged ability to get by on less. Unlike whites, Mexicans were willing, in one farmer's words, "to live on beans and tortillas and in one or two-room shacks." Moreover, low pay ensured that they would have to work: "What a Mexican should be paid is just enough to live on, with maybe a dollar or two to spend. If he is paid any more he won't work so much or when we need him." Another farmer opined, "There's no use paying them more—they just blow it anyway and have nothing."[29]

In company towns, housing and other perquisites differed for Mexican workers and European and Anglo American workers. Copper companies set aside separate sites for Mexicans to settle and provided material for workers to construct their own housing. This contrasted with the policy of providing already-built houses for both skilled and unskilled Anglo workers. Color lines in housing and jobs and dual wage scales were supported by European and Anglo American workers. Indeed, many considered it insulting to do "Mexican work." For them, farm work carried a stigma because of its association with Mexicans. An Anglo informant told Paul Taylor in 1930 that his younger brother had chosen a filling-station job that paid $1 a day over working as a farmhand for $1.50. Another Anglo reported that many young white men preferred to be idle and hang around town rather than take on farm work.[30]

In southwestern cities and towns many Mexican men were employed as ditchdiggers, streetgraders, and day laborers. In Texas and California urban areas, Mexican men worked in a wide range of manufacturing industries, but principally as unskilled labor. Ricardo Romo found that in 1918, 70 percent of Mexican workers in Los Angeles were in unskilled blue-collar work, compared with 6 percent of Anglos. In Santa Barbara in 1930, Albert Camarillo reported, 55.6 percent of Spanish-surnamed male heads of households were in unskilled jobs, 12.7 percent in semiskilled, 8.9 percent in skilled, and 9.4 percent in white-collar, proprietorial, and professional; among Anglos, 10.8 percent were in the unskilled category, 12.7 percent in semiskilled, 21.7 percent in skilled, and 43.9 percent in white-collar, proprietorial, and professional. Mario García estimates that in El Paso in 1920, 67.5 percent of those with Spanish surnames but only 20.7 percent of those with non-Spanish surnames were either laborers, service workers, or operatives in 1920; at the upper end, 29.6 percent of those with non-Spanish surnames but only 5.3 percent of those with Spanish surnames held professional managerial jobs.[31]

Although gender ideology in both Anglo and Mexican communities prescribed domesticity for women, increasing numbers of women in both groups were forced by economic circumstances to take outside employment. When they did, there was also racial stratification in "women's work." Anglo women's work was defined and circumscribed by the dominant ideology of domesticity; their proper place was defined as the home. If they were employed outside they were restricted to female-typed jobs, such as clerical work, light manufacturing, or laundry work. Within the Anglo economy, Mexican women were not protected by the Anglo domestic code or exempted from hard physical labor or "dirty" jobs. In rural areas they were employed in field labor, picking cotton and fruit, and in packing fruits, shelling nuts, and other agricultural jobs. In urban areas they were concentrated in various branches of domestic service, in washing, cleaning, and maid services for Anglo households. Few if any Anglo women were employed in household service.

Anglo women themselves insisted on maintaining separation. Anglo garment workers in Corpus Christi compelled an employer to discharge Mexican women by refusing to work in the same room with them.[32] Within industries where both Anglo and Mexican women worked, such as commercial laundries in El Paso, Anglo women held the cleaner jobs as checkers and sorters and supervisors, while Mexicanas did the manual work of cleaning and pressing. Pay also differed dramatically; in 1919 the Texas Welfare Commission found that Mexican laundry workers averaged $6 a week compared to "American" workers' average of $16.55.[33]

Coercive Labor Practices

Like blacks in the South, Mexicans in the Southwest were subjected to coercive labor practices, with debt bondage used as a major mechanism to tie down workers. In New Mexico, formerly independent sheep owners were forced into "share sheeping" or *partido* arrangements after getting enmeshed in credit extended by Anglo merchants. During the economic downturns in the 1880s, they could no longer pay their loans. The merchants seized the sheep and then leased them back to the former owners. By 1900 one-fourth to one-half of the New Mexico sheep industry was under *partido* contracts. In cotton farming, sharecroppers had to borrow seed, supplies, and other necessities to see them through until the crops were picked; the resulting payment might not even cover the debt, which kept workers tethered to the farm. The same device was used in the mining industry, where, in remote locations, workers had no choice but to purchase necessities at the company store. By keeping wages low and prices high, employers ensured that workers remained in perpetual debt, unable to move on. Coal mines in Colorado paid workers in scrip that could be redeemed at full value only at company-owned stores. These practices held sway over all workers in mining, but disproportionately affected Mexicans because they had fewer employment options.[34]

U.S. laws against contract labor were widely flouted by employers and labor agents alike. Railroad companies procured track hands through labor agents who recruited workers not only in the region but also in Mexico. Agribusinesses also used labor contractors to deliver work crews. Contractors typically withheld 25 percent of the workers' wages until the end of the season and also deducted the cost of transportation and food. One observer reported that Texas labor speculators chained Mexicans together and guarded them to prevent them from fleeing until they were delivered to the worksite. Once at a worksite, workers would be prevented from leaving by guards until they worked off what they "owed" for transportation.[35]

In Texas local law enforcement officials colluded with farmers. Workers attempting to flee would be picked up for vagrancy and sentenced to work off their fines. Vagrancy laws also were applied at the beginning of each cotton-picking season to round up Mexicans to work in the fields. Attempts to legally constrain the mobility of Mexican workers accelerated in the 1920s as industries in the Midwest and North, suffering labor shortages because of new restrictions on European immigration, discovered Mexicans and began sending recruitment agencies to the Southwest. Thousands of Mexicans left Texas to work in sugar beet fields, railroad maintenance, and industrial jobs (steel, meatpacking) in Michigan, Illinois, and other parts of the Midwest. In an attempt to stem the tide, the Texas legislature passed the Emigrant Labor Agency Laws, which levied occupational taxes and required labor recruiters to post bonds. These measures were invalidated by the courts, but growers did not cease their efforts to curb workers' mobility. In 1934 the legislature set up an internal agency, the Texas Farm Placement Service, to regulate the movement of farm labor and to eliminate "aimless wandering." The Service stationed uniformed officers at major intersections to stop vehicles carrying workers and to direct them to farms that had requested workers.[36]

The growers constantly complained of a shortage of labor and the need to keep the borders open. Labor economists, however, found that there was actually a tremendous surplus of labor. Each grower wanted as large a group as possible to appear on short notice to pick his entire crop in a few days so as to get it to the market at peak prices; then he wanted the workers to disappear. Most important, a large surplus of workers ensured that wages were kept low. From the workers' perspective, this meant that they had to work nonstop for a few days and then endure long periods without income while awaiting another job or traveling long distances to the next site.[37]

Refuting Anglo notions of Mexican fatalism and passivity, Mexicans by the thousands responded to these restrictions by exercising their right to sell their own labor. During the 1930s, 66,000 Texas Mexicans left the state annually to find work in other states. They also shared information among themselves about employers and refused to work for those who had bad reputations. Sometimes their only recourse was flight. Carey McWilliams characterized the traffic in sugar beet workers as a virtual "underground railroad," as agents for beet growers spirited workers away at night in canvas-covered trucks on back roads to evade state agents.[38]

Racialized and Gendered Citizenship

When the Southwest was taken over by the United States a diverse group of peoples was incorporated into a nation where whiteness was an essential qualification for citizenship. Yet the Treaty of Guadalupe Hidalgo had granted "the enjoyment of all the rights of citizenship of the United States to all of the varied people recognized as citizens by the Mexican government." This basic contradiction set the stage for continued contention and contestation over the racial and citizenship status of ethnic Mexicans. In contrast to the situation of blacks in the South and Asians in the West and Hawaii, where federal and state definitions of race generally coincided, racial designation of Mexicans differed at the federal, state, and community levels. Discrepancies in policies and practices led to a certain degree of ambiguity and provided some space for maneuver.

Because of the treaty, the official federal government stance was that Mexicans were "white." The historical formula that required whiteness as a condition for citizenship in some sense dictated the reverse logic that if Mexicans were citizens, they must be white. Also, as part of its inter-American "friendship" policy, the U.S. government avoided erecting racial barriers against ethnic Mexicans, whether U.S. or Mexican nationals. Thus, until anti-Mexican sentiment reached fever pitch in the 1930s, the U.S. government did not distinguish Mexicans from whites for official purposes. The Census Bureau enumerated Mexicans as part of the white population. In federal immigration and labor statistics, Mexican immigrants were listed as "white foreign-born." In an 1897 case a federal court in Texas overturned a naturalization board's rejection of the Mexican-born plaintiff's application on the grounds that he was not white. Conceding that the plaintiff, Ricardo Rodríguez, would not be classified in anthropological terms as "white," the court nonetheless affirmed his right to be naturalized on the basis of treaties entered into at the time of incorporation. Despite the qualification, the court established the precedent that Mexicans were for naturalization purposes to be treated as "white," unlike Asian, Hawaiian, and other non-European applicants. In the 1920s the U.S. Labor Department refused a request from proponents of eugenics that it participate in a challenge to the Rodriguez decision, noting in a memo that "our Government, in its relations with the Mexican people, has uniformly recognized them as belonging to the white race."[39]

Despite the Treaty of Guadalupe Hidalgo, at least prior to the passage of the Fourteenth Amendment to the U.S. Constitution, southwestern state constitutions varied in their provisions with respect to the political citizenship of Mexican residents. The Texas constitution of 1845 extended suffrage to "free whites" and former citizens of Mexico without mentioning any racial qualification. In 1850 it extended "citizenship"—but not the vote—to detribalized and taxpaying Native Americans. In contrast, the California constitution inserted the word "white" so that suffrage was limited to "whites" and "white" citizens of Mexico. This wording set the precedent for differentiating among Mexicans, relegating some to the category of "nonwhite" on the basis that they were "Indian" or "mestizo." Since the California legislature subsequently disfranchised Indians, Mexicans designated as "Indian" could then be subject to disfranchisement, segregation, and other discriminatory treatment. Arizona followed California's model. When Arizona was separated from New Mexico in 1863, its territorial constitution limited the franchise to white men and white Mexican men. New Mexico's first territorial constitution, the Organic Act of 1850, like Texas's constitution, granted full citizenship rights to "free whites" and citizens of Mexico who became U.S. citizens as a consequence of the Treaty of Guadalupe Hidalgo. When New Mexico became a state in

1910, its constitution prohibited discrimination on the basis of race or language. Because of nuevomexicano involvement in its framing, the constitution also contained provisions recognizing Spanish in official proceedings and guaranteeing equal political and legal standing to its Mexican residents.[40]

Because of their official white status, Mexicans were not subject to anti-miscegenation laws designed to protect the purity of the white race. Statutes in the Southwest prohibiting marriages between whites and "nonwhites," that is, blacks and "Orientals," were silent on the matter of white-Mexican intermarriage. However, Mexicans were "not quite white" when it came to actual enforcement of anti-miscegenation laws. Texas officials vigorously enforced that state's statute in the case of black-Anglo marriages but not in the case of black-Mexican marriages. Mexicans thus occupied an "intermediate position," which made it acceptable for Mexican women to marry either Anglo or black men. However, much as in the case of hypodescent rules in the South, intermarried couples became part of the Mexican community and their children were considered "Mexican" rather than Anglo.[41]

In terms of everyday relationships, Anglo interpretation of Mexicans' race continued to vary, but by the 1910s it was converging toward lumping all Mexicans into the category of nonwhite or "colored." This marked a change from the nineteenth century, when Anglos often recognized color gradations among Mexicans. An old-timer in Santa Paula, California, recalled that in the 1870s the Anglo community recognized three categories, Spanish, Mexican, and Mexican Indians. Over time, as Mexicans became concentrated at the bottom of the labor market and became objects of control by a repressive labor regime, they came to be viewed by Anglos as unambiguously nonwhite. A Texas congressman noted in 1921, "We use the term Mexican to designate a race, not a citizen or subject of the nation." When queried about the race of Mexicans, a Chicago Chamber of Commerce official responded: "No, they are not regarded as colored, but they are regarded as an inferior class. Are Mexicans regarded as white? Oh, no!" In California, an Imperial Valley Labor Bureau official said in reply to the same question: "We regard them as Mexicans. I have never attempted to draw a line between white and black Mexicans."[42]

Thus, despite the federal stance and protections in at least one state's constitution, Mexicans were not recognized as American citizens and accorded the civil and political rights of citizenship. Local officials throughout the Southwest used local interpretations of law and race to differentiate between Mexicans and Anglos. As was the case with blacks in the South, political disfranchisement and de facto segregation were allowed to go on with little or no intervention from the state or federal governments.[43]

Disfranchisement

By the late nineteenth century, in California and Arizona, Mexicans who were legally American citizens lacked numbers to have much clout at the ballot box. They were also excluded from party politics; Mexican delegates were ejected from California Democratic Party conventions in the 1880s. Where they had some numerical concentration, their votes were diluted by being dispersed among gerrymandered districts. In rancher-dominated counties in Texas, Mexican voting was controlled by political machines. Political bosses reportedly offered emoluments through Mexican sub-bosses, who delivered Mexicans to the polls with instructions on how to vote. In farm-dominated counties, mechanisms used to disfranchise blacks in the South were used to limit Mexican suffrage. The poll tax, originally enacted by the legislature in 1902 to bar black voting, also prevented thousands of Mexicans from voting. In the 1870s several counties established the "White Man's Primary," in which only white electors were allowed to vote for party candidates. The practice spread to other counties, and the Texas legislature made the White Primary statewide in 1923.[44]

Some flavor of the rhetoric undergirding political exclusion can be garnered from the debate over the adoption of the White Man's Primary in Dimmit County, Texas. In addition to inveighing against letting ignorant, uneducated Mexicans have a say, proponents argued that their participation corrupted the electoral process, since their votes could easily be bought by politicians or coerced by employers. In this formulation, the multiple meanings of "dirt" in relation to Mexicans were brought to bear: ridding elections of Mexican participation would clean up politics. One writer linked electoral purity with the purity of white womanhood:

There is not a man, an American today, but will admit that all good he lays claim to, emanates from the environments of the home, from mother, sister, wife; without their influence what

would man be? Yet the laws of our state debar that woman, that
promoter of every good action on the part of man, from having
any voice whatever in the government of our state, permitting the
illiterate Mexican to say who shall and who shall not be at the head
of our government and make our laws.

This writer did not advocate extending the vote to women, but instead
called for white women to stand alongside their men to defend white
manhood: "It can be changed, but the white men and white women of
Dimmit County must rise up and demand what is *right*, demand what is
pure, and demand a *white man's election*."[45]

Exclusion from primaries discouraged Mexicans from voting in the
main election; an observer claimed that 50 percent fewer Mexicans
paid poll taxes in 1914 than in 1912. Some Anglos criticized the disfranchisement of Mexicans as undemocratic, but most Anglos believed
that Mexicans were "satisfied" and did not resent their situation. Paul
Taylor, the University of California economist who investigated labor
conditions in Dimmit County, felt there was "some measure of truth"
in the Anglo assessment, but noted that "some Mexicans are acutely
conscious of their political disabilities, particularly when these appear
to contribute to other discriminations against Mexicans."[46]

Segregation

A belief in Mexican inferiority had long undergirded Anglo responses
to Mexicans. However, as in the South, not until the twentieth century
did systematic segregation become a primary mechanism for maintaining racial hierarchy. This "modern" form of stratification was based on
impersonal and segmented relations in which contact was limited usually to a single point, the worksite. David Montejano has described
early-twentieth-century south Texas farm society as a labor-repressive
agricultural economy, in which nonmarket means—violence, segregation, and undemocratic political measures—were used to control and
contain the working population: "Viewed in this manner, many aspects of segregation can be seen as a functional extension of the need
to organize and control Mexican labor."[47] Montejano's analysis can be
applied to the Southwest as a whole, although there were some intra-
regional differences. In California and Arizona, the role of white work-

ing-class men and women, both in being "mollified" by segregation and in actively insisting on it, must be recognized. In the context of the prevailing rhetoric of "free" labor, the construction of Mexicans (and other people of color) as "unfree" workers unfit for citizenship provided white workers and small producers with contrast figures to anchor their self-identity and dignity as worker citizens.

New towns that sprang up after World War I paid careful attention to limiting Mexicans to distinct residential and business districts. Racial status was expressed in dramatic physical differences between the Anglo and Mexican sections: Anglo neighborhoods consisted of modern frame houses located on paved streets with enclosed sewers, in stark contrast to Mexican districts' corrugated tin shacks with outdoor privies located on dirt roads.[48]

Other social spaces were also organized to reinforce social distance between Anglos and Mexicans. Consequential public sites—hospitals, municipal buildings, banks, stores, and movie theaters—were Anglo territory. When Mexicans entered Anglo territory, they were confined to certain restricted times or sections. Mexican women "were only supposed to shop on the Anglo side of town on Saturdays, preferably during the early hours when Anglos were not shopping." Municipal swimming pools barred "colored" patrons except on the day before the pool was cleaned. In Anglo-run cafes, Mexicans were allowed to eat only at the counter or to use carryout, and theaters relegated Mexicans to the balcony. Many service establishments, such as restaurants, hotels, and beauty parlors, posted "whites only" signs.[49]

Thus, even though segregation of Mexicans from Anglos was technically illegal, de facto segregation was rampant. Segregation was "maintained, through the actions of government officials, the voters who supported them, agricultural, industrial, and business interests, the residents of white neighborhoods, Parent-Teacher Association members—in short, all those who constituted the self-identified white public."[50] Integral to the process of de facto segregation was the development of a coded vocabulary that defined the proper place of Mexicans and Anglos within the social order. Terms such as "citizen," "American school children," and "white taxpayer" were used interchangeably to refer to Anglos, casting Mexican Americans as "noncitizen," "non-American," and "nontaxpayer."

As in the South, the gender racial order also had to be displayed and

enacted in interpersonal relations. In south Texas Mexicans were expected to adopt "a deferential body posture and respectful voice tone,"
use "the best polite forms of speech," and "never [show] extreme anger
or aggression towards an Anglo in public." Conversely, Anglos could
use informal speech forms and "shout 'hey *cabron*' or 'hey *chingado*' (son
of a bitch) in a joking derogatory way. Anglos could slap Mexicanos on
the back, joke with them at their expense, curse them out, in short, do
all the things people usually do only among relatively familiar and
equal people." Mexicans working for Anglos were expected to come to
the back door of their employers, and if working in the house, to stay in
the kitchen or back buildings.[51]

Interdependent Lives and Identities

From the beginnings of Anglo Americans' entry into the Southwest,
their racialized and gendered constructions of Mexicans were an integral part of their expansionist ambitions and their conviction that they
were bringing a superior civilization to an untamed area. Historians
have documented the negative characterization of Mexicans by Anglo
American visitors to the Southwest during the nineteenth century. In
their letters and other writings these observers portrayed Mexican men
as "lazy, ignorant, bigoted, superstitious, cheating, thieving, gambling,
cruel, sinister, and cowardly." Some historians have argued that these
characterizations predated actual contact between Anglos and Mexicans in the Southwest, stemming from anti-Spanish, anti-Catholic sentiments of the English with later grafting on of a virulent anti-Indian
ideology (though anti-Catholicism did not appear as a major element
in later anti-Mexican rhetoric). Contact and competition in the nineteenth century led to a more elaborated racial ideology that drew on
the language and paradigms of scientific racism. The sparsely settled
expanses and crude conditions of frontier settlements came to be seen
not as characteristics of a still developing hinterland but as evidence
of the backwardness of Mexicans. Even the prosperity of the large
ranches was viewed negatively, not as the fruit of hard labor but as "ill-
gotten gains stolen from the missions, maintained by servile labor,
and augmented by too bounteous nature." The large Mexican landowners were considered indolent, ostentatious, and unproductive. In
one Anglo's eyes the californios were "a proud indolent people, riding
after herds from place to place with no apparent purpose"; to another

the local economy was a case of "Nature doing everything, man doing nothing."[52]

Whereas the elite ranchers and other landholding Mexicans were seen as typically "Spanish" in their extravagance, profligacy, and lack of interest in "progress," the mass of Mexicans were denigrated as a mongrel race, inheriting the worst of Spanish and Indian traits. The notion of racial mixing was particularly repellent. Some racial theorists argued that interbreeding led to weak offspring who embodied contradictory qualities, such as pride and self-contempt. Like the Spanish, Mexican mestizos were thought incapable of self-government; and like the Indians, they were thought incapable of making material and social progress on their own. Both notions rationalized the necessity of Anglos' taking over to bring democracy and progress to backward areas. The Mexicans in turn could not help resenting the Anglos' feeling of superiority and their "fanatical intolerance." Although not all Mexicans were contemptuous of Anglos, the common view was that "gringos" were arrogant, aggressive, unscrupulous racists.[53]

The Anglos' negative portrait of Mexicans was gendered as well as raced. Ostensibly generic, it described a feminized male subject. The feminized Mexican race was contrasted with the freedom-loving, democratic, progressive Anglo-Saxon or "American" race. Mexican men would give way because they were weak, pusillanimous, and above all lazy. Mexican women were portrayed as feminine in a different sense: they were seen as alluring and available, awaiting and welcoming Anglo-Saxon men. The sexual conquest of Mexican women as a metaphor for political conquest was often quite explicit. Popular poetry and political rhetoric talked about the extension of the Mexican race through the union of American men and Mexican women.[54]

Many narratives by Anglo American male travelers followed scathing denunciations of Mexican men by exempting Mexican women, whom they described as far superior in industry and character. Richard Henry Dana, in *Two Years before the Mast*, was struck by the "beauty" of Mexican women in California, while George Wilkins Kendall, in his account of the Texas Santa Fe expedition, was fascinated by the pleasing figures, graceful manners, and charm of the young women he encountered. Although some observers, like Dana, pronounced Mexican women to have "little virtue," most commented on the chastity of upper-class women.[55]

Indeed, many of the most prominent Anglo men both before and after the Mexican-American War married the daughters of prominent californios, tejanos, and nuevomexicanos. Tomás Almaguer argues that the prevalence of intermarriage was a concrete manifestation of the relatively favorable position of Mexicans compared with other racialized minorities. However, these marriages also reflected gender and race privilege in that they almost invariably involved Anglo men and Mexican women. The marital exchange may be considered a kind of traffic in women. Mexican oligarchs gained protection from Anglo mistreatment by forming alliances with Anglos, while the Anglo husbands solidified their position in southwestern society and established claims to land and property. Marriages between the sons of rancheros and Anglo women occurred, but they were infrequent.[56]

Because of the dearth of Anglo women in the early days of Anglo settlement, intermarriage also occurred among lower-status Anglos and Mexicanas. In Santa Ana and San Juan, California, 32 percent of European American men were married to Mexican or Native American women in 1860. In Tucson, 22 percent of all marriages in the 1870s were between Anglo males and Hispanic females. High rates of intermarriage also occurred in New Mexico. Deena Gonzalez found that 63 percent of European American men in Santa Fe were married to Mexican women in 1870.[57]

At first, when Anglos were still a small numerical minority in many areas, they were forced to accommodate and fit themselves into local society. In 1870s Santa Fe, Gonzalez notes, "the large community of Spanish-Mexicans was 'Hispanicizing' the smaller number of strangers. Up through the 1880s, Santa Feans referred to these newcomers as 'norteamericanos,' while continuing to hispanicize their first names. James became Santiago, John was translated into Juan, Susan was Susana." Many gringos learned to speak Spanish and adopted local customs. They participated in *compadrazgo* (godparenting) relations and acted as padrones toward their Mexican employees. In short, they became "Mexicanized gringos."[58] However, as Anglo settlements grew the Anglos transplanted their own cultures, which soon became dominant.

Elite Mexicans struggled to maintain their status within the new order. In New Mexico some wealthy landowners, referred to as "*ricos*," adapted well. They managed to hold on to their haciendas and even enlarge their holdings at the expense of small herders by adopting Anglo business practices such as cheating on their taxes. In California, by contrast, the remnants of the elite had little in the way of material or social capital by the end of the nineteenth century. Carey McWilliams observed that in California the "fantasy Spanish heritage" was fiercely clung to by descendants of the elite (the *gente de razon*) as a way of distinguishing themselves from the common people (the *gente corriente*) long after they had lost their land and exalted position.[59]

As their economic and political domination became more complete, Anglo Americans came to denigrate Mexican culture and to keep Mexicans at a distance. One measure of growing social distance was a decline in intermarriage. In Santa Ana and San Juan interracial marriages dropped from 32 percent of all marriages in 1860 to 7 percent by 1880. In Tucson the Anglo-Mexican intermarriage rate dropped from 23 percent in 1872–1879 to 9 percent in 1900–1910.[60] Anglo Americans also became less apt to make distinctions among Mexicans along class and nationality lines. Whereas Mexicans native to the U.S. Southwest typically distinguished themselves from Mexican immigrants from "Old Mexico" by such self-designations as tejano, California Mexican, nuevomexicano, Arizona Mexican, or Spanish, Anglos were prone to lump Mexican Americans and Mexican immigrants together as "Mexicans." By the 1920s the preferred contrasting terms in Texas were "American" and "Mexican," thus casting tejanos and immigrants from Mexico alike as non-Americans and noncitizens.[61]

In south Texas Anglo identity, particularly Anglo manhood, was defined in important ways by popular accounts of the Alamo, which glorified the valor of the small band of "American" defenders and erased the contributions of tejanos to resistance to Mexican government forces. David Weber notes that the myth of the Alamo "helped sanctify two popular articles of faith among Anglo Americans: belief in the moral superiority of Anglos and the degeneracy of Mexicans." Over eighty years after the event, an Anglo reported: "There is an inbred hatred in Texas against the Mexicans. My father and mother told us to hate the Mexicans because of the Alamo." A Mexican American said: "In the sixth grade here I studied Texas history. I had a pretty bad time because of the remarks of the children about the Alamo, the cowardice of the Mexican general at the Alamo, the many against one, the retreat of Santa Ana and his capture at San Jacinto." Another recalled that as the only Mexican in his high school he had been accepted by the

"Americans": "Then we came to the Alamo in our study of history, and then it was 'gringo' and 'greaser.' They expelled me from the baseball nine and would not sit with me anymore, and told me to drink out of my own cup."[62]

Anglos were not, of course, monolithic in their attitudes toward Mexicans or their relationships with them. For example, growers tended to have a paternalistic attitude, seeing Mexican workers as controllable if treated with a firm hand, while white laborers were more overtly hostile, viewing Mexicans as dangerous competitors because of their ability to survive on "hot tamales and green peppers," unlike white men who required "white man's food."[63]

Relations also varied intraregionally. In Texas whites' historical relations with blacks conditioned their responses to Mexicans, either through direct analogy or through contrast and comparison. Some Anglos made equivalencies between blacks and Mexicans while others made distinctions that placed Mexicans in an intermediate status between blacks and whites. In the Colorado sugar beet fields, growers often made comparisons between German-Russian and Mexican immigrants, while in rural California, relations with Chinese and Japanese laborers affected Anglos' assessments of Mexicans. In some areas, such as parts of New Mexico, where nuevomexicanos remained a majority, Anglos were more likely to recognize class differences among Mexicans and accorded some degree of political and social recognition to "higher-class" Mexican Americans. In all areas, however, working-class Mexicans, particularly immigrant laborers, were viewed as racially and culturally inferior.

Whatever their particular views on their good and bad qualities, Anglos agreed that Mexicans were satisfied with their subordinate status. They frequently complimented them for their lack of assertiveness, especially in comparison with blacks. An Anglo farmer's wife reported: "Mexicans aren't like the Negroes; they don't try to seat themselves next to you." A large onion grower in the Nueces valley opined: "They are not aggressive or belligerent. They don't bother white people." Paul Taylor, by way of summary, concluded: "Americans informed me variously that the Mexicans not only did not desire to intermarry nor live in the American quarter, but that they did not desire to be educated, nor to learn English, to attend the 'American' school, to migrate to the North, to have good houses, to earn more, to obtain social equality."[64]

That Anglos did not detect Mexicans' true feelings about their treatment is not surprising given the superficial and asymmetrical nature of their interactions. Taylor noted that in the Imperial Valley "Americans are occasionally invited to social entertainments, but the reverse is rarely true." Anglos felt entitled to enter Mexican spaces and partake of Mexican culture, for example attending local fiestas and celebrations. One Anglo landowner observed: "At the fifth of May celebration the Americans will all but push the Mexicans out of their own fiesta. They will even ask to have an American dance during which the Mexicans will keep off the floor.[65]

Anglo women, according to Taylor, were more adamant than Anglo men about not mixing with Mexicans, whom they deemed "inferior" regardless of class. "Color" thus seemed to be a particularly sensitive issue for Anglo women. In the Winter Garden district an Anglo man reported that the American Legion admitted Mexicans, but added, "They don't come to our social affairs when we have our wives who might not like to sit next to some big Mexican woman." This attitude was confirmed by an Anglo woman who said she refused to sit with Mexicans at an Eagle Pass Rotary meeting: "I did not care how high class they were, they looked black to me and I did not want to sit side of them." Taylor also found young American women in Colorado particularly emphatic in their opposition to intermarriage. Two of them told him, "We don't believe intermarriage will take place on account of color even if the Mexicans were clean and educated."[66]

Anglo women's greater opposition to interracial dating and marriage, coupled with their low rates of out-marriage compared with Anglo men, confirm the centrality of sexual purity and cleanliness to the definition of Anglo womanhood. While this notion had similarities to the cult of white womanhood in the South, it did not seem to have the same function of being invoked to terrorize Mexican men. In the Texas border region, farm wives interviewed by Taylor unanimously affirmed their feeling of safety among Mexican farmhands.[67]

Anglo women's sense of racial privilege meant they rarely felt a sense of commonality with Mexican women on the basis of shared interests as wives and mothers. For example, Mexican women took a great deal of interest in their children's education, sacrificing to pay for books and expressing concern about the quality of schooling, but their participation was not welcomed by Anglo mothers. The wife of an Anglo school principal said she felt sympathetic toward Mexican parents who were snubbed by the Anglo members of the PTA. She wanted to start a special PTA for Mexicans, but had been discouraged by Anglo parents. A principal at another school noted, "The Mexican women came to the PTA, but the Americans made it so plain that they were unwelcome that they didn't come again."[68]

The only situation in which most Anglo women felt comfortable with Mexican women was one that clearly affirmed the Anglos' superior status. As in the South and Hawaii, the most common such situation was that of employer and domestic servant. Anglo women expected not just labor but also deference from their household help. In the 1920s a farmer's wife in Texas said with some satisfaction, "A Mexican woman helps me but she knows her place and never comes into the house unless I ask her to." Another Anglo woman explained: "When they come to my house they come to the back door and when there is company they stay in the part of the house they're supposed to; they come in only for their work. They know the place for them and you don't have to tell them . . . They are good domestic servants if you train them right."[69]

FOR MEXICANS, incorporation, displacement, assimilationist pressures, and segregation placed great strains on accustomed ways of life, but these stresses also had the paradoxical effect of laying the basis for new forms of shared identity that crossed divisions of region, national origin, generation, and class. Although some elite and middle-class Mexicans continued to deny mestizo heritage and to distance themselves from common Mexicans, many others, particularly working-class Mexicans, began to articulate an identity that combined a sense of their Mexican cultural heritage with their status as Americans. Richard Griswold del Castillo found in his study of the Los Angeles barrio in the years 1850–1890 a tendency "to move from particular allegiances [as californios, tejanos, and nuevomexicanos] to a more general group solidarity."[70] This more inclusive sense of ethnicity or peoplehood emerged as a response to the shared experience of discrimination and denigration by the Anglo majority and the concentration of Mexicans in separate enclaves.

The *colonia*, the Mexican quarter, though crowded and lacking amenities of Anglo business and residential areas, nonetheless provided public gathering places, streets, stores, and churches. Small businesses and service establishments catering to a Mexican clientele were communal spaces—tamale shops, bodegas, barbershops, a few restaurants, and perhaps a branch of the post office. The local Catholic church was an important communal site; often the church had been erected with money raised by residents. "In their own enclaves," David Gutiérrez points out, "Mexican Americans continued to converse in Spanish, observed Roman Catholic rituals and celebrations, and entertained themselves in the style to which they had grown accustomed, all largely without the interference of norteamericanos."[71]

The emerging collective identity was expressed in new terminology by which Mexicans referred to themselves. Griswold del Castillo traced the emergence of the term "La Raza" to refer to Mexican people on both sides of the border to the Spanish-language press in California. He called the term the "single most important symbol of ethnic pride and identification" and noted: "There were many ways of using this term, depending on the context. '*La Raza Mexicana,*' '*La Raza Hispano-Americana,*' '*La Raza Espanola,*' and '*La Raza Latina*' were all used to convey a sense of racial, class, and national variety within the Spanish-speaking community, but in general the use of '*La Raza*' implied membership in a cultural tradition that was separate from the 'norteamericanos.'"[72]

At the same time, however, Mexicans resisted Anglo attempts to racialize them as nonwhite and to deny them rights on that basis. In 1911 the Reverend Pedro Grado ended his address to delegates at the Congreso Mexicanista in Laredo by urging Mexican laborers to unite "to strike back at the hatred of some bad sons of Uncle Sam who believe themselves better than the Mexicans because of the magic that surrounds the word white."[73] His exhortation seems to have been taken to heart, as reflected more than two decades later in the sentiments expressed to interviewers by pecan shellers in San Antonio: "Their reactions to this situation [of racial discrimination] are most clearly shown by their objection to the use of the term 'white' in such a way as to exclude Mexicans. They prefer to call whites of European extraction 'Anglo Americans' or 'Anglos.' The Mexicans are conscious of such Spanish blood as they may have, and are not ashamed of their predominately Indian blood. They jealously guard against any move that would set them apart from the self-styled 'white race.'"[74] It seems these Mexican Americans embraced a complex "both-and" identity that transcended binary oppositions. Maintaining such a stance went against the grain of the Anglo construction of "white" in opposition to "black" or "colored."

Claiming whiteness within the accepted Anglo framework, though, meant that some Mexicans distanced themselves from blacks and other "nonwhites." There is some evidence that by the 1920s and 1930s Mexican Americans had absorbed the Anglo conception of whiteness as "nonblackness," a conception they had not held earlier. Nineteenth-century Anglo observers had noted the lack of race and color consciousness among Mexicans. Before the Civil War, Mexicans helped rescue slaves by transporting them to the frontier between central Texas and the lower Rio Grande. After the Civil War, Mexican women apparently mixed freely with black troops. By the 1930s Taylor found Mexicans of all classes in Nueces County, Texas, insisting on their difference from blacks. A group of Mexican cotton-pickers whom Taylor described as "largely Indian" told him: "It does not look right to see Mexicans and Negroes together. Their color is different. They are black and we are white. It is all right for Americans and Mexicans to mix. We are both of the white race."[75]

In a situation where Mexicans were denigrated by the dominant culture, Mexican women were placed in the difficult position of being expected to maintain men's pride, demonstrate loyalty and support, and uphold standards of respectability and purity. Mexican women were exhorted by Mexican cultural institutions, including the Spanish-language press and the Catholic Church, to bow to the authority of the male heads of household and to confine their activities to the domestic sphere. Thomas Sheridan found a plethora of articles in Tucson Spanish-language newspapers between the late 1870s and 1930 defining the proper role of women as one of self-sacrifice, faithfulness, and obedience. He notes that these exhortations belied the realities of life for many women, including the significant numbers who headed their own households in Tucson and other southwestern cities.[76]

As in the case of Anglo women, color was a heightened issue for Mexican women. A young Mexican American woman, asked if color mattered, exclaimed: "I should say it does. If a person is light, they say she's not Mexican; they think if they call us 'Spanish,' it doesn't hurt you like saying 'Mexican.'" Another light-skinned tejana said she had been treated well by Anglos in high school until her darker-skinned sister joined her and she herself came to feel prejudice. She also said: "I refused two offers of marriage from Americans. My reason was that if there should be any dark children, I don't want my husband blaming me and calling them, 'my children.'" Taylor reported the heavy sale of skin-bleaching cream in stores catering to Mexicans.[77]

Another response to racialization and denial of rights, particularly among immigrants, was heightened identification with Mexico. Mexicans had the lowest rates of naturalization of all immigrant groups. Out of more than 600,000 Mexican-born residents in the United States in 1930, only 5.8 percent had become naturalized.[78] In part this identification reflected the sojourner orientation of many Mexican immigrants and their living within largely segregated Mexican communities. Additionally, their lack of interest in American citizenship reflected disillusionment with American-style discrimination and their belief that Anglo Americans would not allow them civil and political rights even if they were technically citizens. Asked why he did not want to become a citizen, a male resident of an agricultural camp in California's San Gabriel Valley responded: "I'm not interested in being a citizen because first of all it would mean nothing to anyone—I would be a citizen in name only—with no privileges or considerations. I would still be a 'dirty Mexican.'" Another protested: "Mexicans were here before the Americans. We are more American than they. Whatever there is here, besides, we built. We built the roads. We built the railroads. We built the new hospital. We built the new City Hall in Los Angeles. They are lazy. When there is work to do the Americans won't do it. They sit on the side and the Mexicans do the work! But they won't let us sit by them in the theatre."[79]

Contestation and Resistance

Mexican responses to the imposition of Anglo ideology, institutions, and economic systems varied by class, generation, and region. Responses involved a mixture of resistance and accommodation, ranging from outlawry and violence to withdrawal into community and family life, from indirect evasion to direct challenge of Anglo domination.

Violence

The most direct expression of Mexican opposition to Anglo domination, in the early years of Anglo takeover, was outlawry. Some writers have pointed to Mexican outlaws as fitting Eric Hobsbawn's model of the social bandit: "ideally a young, unmarried peasant who commits an act which the state regards as criminal, but which most of his peers regard as justifiable or heroic." Figures such as Joaquín Murieta, Tiburcio Vásquez, Juan Nepomuceno Cortina, and Juan de Dios Ortega, who were vilified by Anglos, were seen as folk heroes forced into outlawry by Anglo injustices. They were recalled in *corridos, testimonios,* and stories "as the brave ones, who refused to submit, who would break before they would bend."[80]

Sometimes violent resistance was undertaken not by an individual but by a group or community. The El Paso Salt War of 1877 was precipitated when an Anglo landowner, Charles H. Howard, attempted to monopolize previously public salt deposits on the Guadalupe Salt Lake. The Mexican community on both sides of the border rose up and took vigilante action, which eventuated in Howard's execution by the Mexican community and armed clashes with the Texas Rangers. No Mexican was ever tried for his role in the war, but the community lost when the Anglo salt monopoly succeeded in forcing people to pay for salt. The best-known instance of organized violence was that carried out by the Gorras Blancas (White Caps), a secret society formed in Santa Fe, San Miguel, and Mora counties of New Mexico to resist the fencing off of traditional communal grazing lands by Anglo landowners and railroads. During the society's peak in 1890, Gorras Blancas riders cut hundreds of miles of fences and tore up railroad tracks, apparently with the sympathy and support of the area's small farmers and ranchers. A lesser-known organization, El Guante Negro Mutualista (the Black Glove Society), operated in Eagle Pass, Texas, in the early years of the twentieth century. It reportedly extorted money from the wealthy, which it then distributed for "relief of the distressed."[81]

Building Separate Spaces

Social, cultural, and mutual aid societies were quite extensive in Mexican American communities starting in the nineteenth century. In New Mexico the most pervasive such organization was the Penitentes, which began in the late eighteenth century as a lay Catholic organization whose members practiced flagellation and other religious observances. It evolved during the nineteenth century into a mutual aid and political organization. In the Mexican period, when the national administrative apparatus rarely reached into the northern villages, the Penitentes acted as a de facto government. In the territorial period, according to José Hernández, the Penitentes emerged as "a powerful political machine in New Mexico and Colorado, defending Spanish American groups who got into trouble with the Anglo law and acting as a pressure group to secure legislation favorable to the group." The influence of the Penitentes stemmed from its large membership; one author estimated that two-thirds of Mexican men in New Mexico and Colorado belonged at one time or another.[82]

Another common type of grassroots organization was the *mutualista* or mutual benefit society, a fraternal order that operated as a social club and also provided life insurance and welfare benefits. One of the largest, La Sociedad Alianza Hispano-Americana, founded in 1894 in Tucson, had eighty-eight lodges by 1919 with over 4,000 members. There were many other benevolent and fraternal societies, and larger cities like El Paso had several such organizations. Membership was open to both U.S.-born and immigrant men, typically day laborers and semi-skilled and skilled workers. Leaders of these organizations were accorded respect regardless of their citizenship status or occupation.[83]

The mutualistas' involvement in organizing social and cultural events and celebrations of Mexican holidays has been viewed by some scholars as essentially nostalgic and regressive. David Gutiérrez, however, argues that the mutualistas' insistence on pride in Mexican culture merged into what is now called oppositional consciousness. At the very least, the community activities they organized fostered, in Griswold del Castillo's words, "the symbolic identification of La Raza as a separate cultural entity." Ethnic consciousness in turn nurtured collective action. Mutualistas were active in organizing and mobilizing support for several early Mexican labor strikes, including the Clifton-Morency copper miners' strikes in 1903 and 1915, and they continued to play a central role in labor organizing in the following two decades. In the twenties and thirties mutualistas also helped organize congresses to direct attention to violence and discrimination against ethnic Mexicans and participated in litigation to challenge discrimination.[84]

Paralleling the gender separation of spheres in the family was the gender separation of civic organizations. The Penitentes and mutualistas generally had women's auxiliaries, *auxiliadoras de la morada*, that performed female-specific duties such as nursing the sick, tending to the elderly, finding proper homes for children without parents, and attending *velorios* (wakes). Mexican women also formed their own independent mutualistas, such as the Sociedad Mutualista de Beneficiencia de Señoras y Señoritas of Corpus Christi, Texas, and the Sociedad Beneficia of Brownsville, Texas. In 1911 women attending the Primero Congreso Mexicanista, held in Laredo, voted to join forces to form La Liga Feminil Mexicanista. According to an article in *La Crónica*, they wished to "pool their talent in the struggle for recognition of individual rights for all Texas Mexicans."[85]

As in the South and Hawaii, the vernacular press played a key role in forging a sense of peoplehood and oppositional consciousness. Starting in the 1850s Spanish-language newspapers were an important source of information and views differing from those put forth by Anglo media. All major Mexican communities had one or more newspapers. Lisbeth Haas argues for the importance of the press even among those who could not read. The oral tradition meant that books, pamphlets, and newspapers "would be read aloud by a male or female family member, neighbor, or friend . . . Even in the late nineteenth century when these populations displayed sharply different literacy rates, the English-language and Spanish-language presses battled over the meaning and interpretation of events, making the written word central to the processes that shaped the new society."[86]

In the late teens through the 1930s, as Mexican labor activism accelerated, the Spanish-language press helped mobilize support for Mexican strikers. While the Anglo press mirrored employers' views and depicted Mexican workers as inefficient, violent, and manipulated by radicals, the vernacular press defended workers and emphasized their struggles for dignity. Irene Ledesma found that Spanish-language press coverage of the El Paso laundry workers' strike (1919) and the San Antonio pecan shellers' strike (1938) was enthusiastically sympathetic, if paternalistic, toward women strikers.[87]

Corridos or ballads also continued as a form of popular expression commemorating important events, such as populist uprisings and skirmishes between Anglos and Mexicans, and celebrating the lives of famous outlaws and individuals who defended their honor or rights with violence. The stories related in the corridos followed certain conventions—a hero who was *mucho hombre* and embodied all the male virtues of border culture, industriousness, skill, courage, and who acted in his own or others' defense and was eventually betrayed by a *vendido*, a Judas.[88] Corridos were also written to protest Anglo injustice; for example, the "Ballad of Aurelio Pompa" protested the execution of a Mexican man who killed his Yankee tormentors in self-defense.[89] Some, such as "El Corrido del Norte," expressed the painful ambivalence of immigrants caught in two cultures, while others, such as "El Corrido de Texas," lamented the harsh routine of field labor.[90]

Protests and Strikes

As early as the late nineteenth century, Mexican American and Mexican immigrant workers resorted to strikes to protest abuses of the contract labor system, company stores, and "Mexican" wages. By the early twentieth century, Mexican workers in agriculture, mining, railroads, and construction were compiling a substantial record of labor struggle, sometimes in concert with non-Mexican workers, but often on their own. They struck over the traditional bread-and-butter issues of wages and working conditions, but they also manifested their concern with civil rights and social justice. Among early struggles were a strike carried out jointly with Japanese field workers in Oxnard, California (1903); a strike by trackmen in Los Angeles against the Pacific Electric Railway and the Los Angeles Railway (1903); a strike by railway workers in Laredo, Texas, to protest differential wages in the railroad industry (1906); and a massive multiethnic strike against the Clifton, Morenci, and Metcalf mines in Arizona (1915).[91]

As noted previously, labor protests and strikes were widely supported by the wider Mexican community. In some cases they were even initiated by mutualistas and other community organizations. Also, significantly, labor activism brought together Mexican American and Mexican immigrant workers. Because they worked side by side and because employers made no distinction between them, ethnic Mexicans had every reason to show solidarity.

Devra Weber notes that, because they were disregarded by the American Federation of Labor, Mexican workers formed ethnic unions or allied with the more sympathetic Industrial Workers of the World, and later with affiliates of the Communist Party. In the late 1920s agricultural workers in California and Texas began to organize some of the first permanent agricultural labor organizations and to form larger labor federations that brought together urban and rural Mexican American and Mexican immigrant workers. In early 1928 more than 2,000 workers joined together to form the Confederación de Uniónes Obreras Mexicanos (CUOM). In addition to traditional trade union issues of pay and conditions, CUOM rhetoric combined advocacy of class struggle with calls for the preservation of an autonomous cultural community in the United States.[92]

Civil Rights Organizing

By the 1920s American-born Mexicans had become increasingly restive about segregation and other forms of discrimination and began to engage in more public and systematic organizing to secure their rights as citizens. Spurred by Texas Mexicans returning from military service in World War I, middle- and lower-middle-class men in several Texas cities formed new civic organizations, such as La Orden Hijos de América (The Order of the Sons of America), and La Orden Caballeros de América (The Order of the Knights of America). As is evident in their names, these organizations emphasized the American identities of their memberships, which were restricted to American citizens. While proclaiming respect for Mexico and its cultural heritage, the organizations stressed Americanism as the best route to gain respect and rights. Their goals were on the one hand to convince other Americans that they were upstanding loyal citizens and on the other to promote the interests and protect the rights of Mexican Americans.[93]

These ideas gained currency, and after a series of meetings several Texas-based organizations came together in Corpus Christi in 1929 to form the League of United Latin American Citizens (LULAC). Seeing

its membership as "a small nucleus of enlightenment" for the rest of
the Mexican community, the leadership expected members to display
the highest standard of Americanism and respectability: "to speak English, dress well, encourage education, and be polite in race relations."
The activities of individual chapters varied, but generally the political
program of LULAC was three pronged: fighting for desegregated public schools, encouraging Mexican American citizens to exercise their
franchise by organizing voter registration and poll-tax campaigns, and
undertaking legal challenges to discrimination in public accommodations and juries. Yet, by stressing integration and Americanism, the organization failed to represent the interests of a large portion of the
Mexican community, two-thirds of whom were Mexican born or had
at least one Mexican-born parent. Gutiérrez sees a central contradiction between the organization's professed principle of racial and cultural pride and its emphasis on assimilation. The contradiction was
evident when spokesmen for LULAC testified in congressional hearings in 1930 that they favored restriction of immigration as long as it
was not racially based and if it could be shown that immigrants lowered
the wages of Americans. Nonetheless, LULAC achieved many notable
successes, organizing voter drives, electing officials sympathetic to its
cause, and winning several notable legal cases that chipped away at de
jure segregation.[94]

Education

As in the South, education, the institution that prepared children for
their places in society, was a major arena in which Anglos and Mexicans
struggled over matters of labor and citizenship. Were Mexicans entitled to schooling? If so, should they go to school alongside Anglos or
in separate schools or classrooms? What kind of preparation should
schools provide?

Segregation in schooling took some time to develop. When the first
Anglo American settlers established schools in California, they allowed
Mexican students to attend. In 1855 the state legislature passed a law
prohibiting school boards from using public funds to educate nonwhite
students. In 1864 it passed another law allowing nonwhite parents to
petition to establish schools for their own children as long as monies to
fund the schools were collected from nonwhite residents. According to

Martha Menchaca, most Mexicans were considered "nonwhite" and therefore subject to these restrictions.[95]

The first schools in California specifically for Mexican children were established in the 1880s by growers interested in attracting and keeping a stable Mexican workforce. It was not until the 1910s that California school districts established systematic segregation involving tracking mechanisms and distinct curricula for Mexican children. By late 1931, according to a state report, 85 percent of school districts in California were segregated in one form or another. In Texas, as early as 1888, a "Mexican Preparatory School," begun by Olivas V. Ahoy for children who had been refused entry into the public schools, was incorporated into the El Paso public school system. Despite its name, the Preparatory School graduated few students into the public schools to attend higher grades. The first "Mexican" school in central Texas was established in 1902. Over the next three decades segregation spread to encompass the whole state. By the late 1920s 80–90 percent of Mexican and native-born californio, tejano, and nuevomexicano students were enrolled in separate "Mexican" classrooms or schools.[96]

The increase in segregation and tracking in schools in the Southwest was part of a national trend. A burgeoning "science" of intelligence and psychological testing, in tandem with racial classification schemes, was churning out a large body of "findings" about the supposed mental, emotional, and moral characteristics of different race and nationality groups. Educational reformers began to harness these findings to improve the efficiency and effectiveness of schools in fulfilling their role in shaping the social order. They argued for separating nonwhite (or non–Anglo Saxon) and other "subnormal" children so that they could be taught by educational methods tailored to their special limitations.[97] In practice, separation for those classified as "nonwhite" meant getting second-class education in underfunded schools with inferior facilities and less-qualified teachers.

Unlike the case of the South, however, segregation in the Southwest was achieved despite Mexicans' official "white" racial status. De jure segregation of blacks, Asians, and Native Americans was permitted by both federal precedents *(Plessy v. Ferguson)* and state laws, but segregation of Mexicans was not. Efforts to come up with legally allowable racial grounds for segregating Mexicans illustrate the Anglos' divergent tendencies on the one hand to racialize all Mexicans as nonwhite and on the other to recognize their heterogeneity and to differentiate them into white and nonwhite elements. As in earlier periods, class, along with physical appearance, played a role in the drawing of racial distinctions. In 1927 California school officials attempted to classify Mexicans as Indians so as to subject them to de jure segregation. The California State Attorney General issued a supporting opinion agreeing that Mexicans were in fact Indians and should therefore be segregated. However, legislation to mandate segregation did not pass because some legislators argued that some Mexicans were "Latin" or "white" and should not be classified as Indian. This line of reasoning, that Mexicans were not a single race, underpinned a Texas court's decision in a suit brought by tejanos against the Del Rio Independent School District in 1930 for unlawfully segregating "white" Mexican students. The judge agreed that half of the Mexican population in Del Rio was white and therefore that it was unjust to segregate Mexicans arbitrarily. He concluded that white Mexican students could be segregated only if they did not speak English. However, he did not require the school board to rescind its actions because it had not acted with malice.[98]

Notwithstanding these legal maneuvers, most de facto segregation of Mexicans was accomplished administratively: by locating schools in Anglo and Mexican neighborhoods, gerrymandering district lines, and busing Mexicans residing in white districts to schools in Mexican districts. Mexican parents and community organizations were well aware of the inferior education offered in "Mexican" schools. They fought segregation by petitioning school boards, lodging protests with the Mexican consulate, and bringing suit in the courts. When challenged, Anglo-dominated school boards claimed they separated students not on the basis of race but on linguistic, moral, educational, and physical grounds. They argued, for example, that Mexican children's lack of facility in English would hold back the "American" children. Yet in Texas Bohemian and German children who did not speak English were assigned to the white schools, and in California Mexican children who spoke fluent English were kept in Mexican schools. School authorities further argued that Mexican children had learning problems, lacked proper behavior, and came to school dirty and unkempt. A school superintendent in Colorado declared, "The respectable people of Weld County do not want their children to sit alongside of dirty, filthy, disease-infested Mexicans in schools." When overcrowding in the Mexican school in the mid-1920s forced school officials in Santa Paula, California, to admit Mexican students to two predominately Anglo schools, they had special showers constructed in which Mexican students were required to bathe each day before attending. Using the hygiene argument protected school boards in California districts from charges of illegal segregation because the state school board allowed administrators to bar children from attending school or to segregate them if they were "filthy" or "unhealthy."[99]

As in the South, segregation meant "separate *and* unequal." Anglos complained that they were paying taxes to support Mexican schools, but in fact taxes paid by both Mexicans and Anglos were diverted to Anglo schools. Consequently, Mexican schools were chronically underfunded and inadequately supplied and their teachers were underpaid. School officials defended the unequal situations as pedagogically and sociologically justified by Mexican students' difficulties, including mental retardation, language problems, poor hygiene and health, a failure to value education, and inherent inferiority. An overarching rationale was that Mexican Americans were not in fact permanent members of the community. Thus a southern California school board member argued against spending on "fine buildings" for Mexican children on the grounds that "the population among the Mexicans has proved so migratory that permanent buildings are not advisable."[100]

School boards were dominated by grower and business interests whose main concern was maintaining the supply of low-wage workers. School schedules were geared to the agricultural calendar. In south Texas school terms in Mexican schools ended one month earlier than in the Anglo schools so those children would be available to pick cotton. In California's Ventura County the school day for Mexican students ran from 7 A.M. to 12 noon so they could join their parents in field work for five or six hours. In northern New Mexico public education was plagued not only by lack of funds and underqualified teachers but also by short school terms.[101]

A Texas school trustee bluntly acknowledged that the schools did not intend to prepare Mexicans for a better future: "We don't need skilled or white collared Mexicans. The farmer is not interested in educating Mexicans. They know then they can get better wages and conditions." If education was to be provided for Mexican children, Anglos felt it should be geared to their inferior capacities and directed at preparing them for their limited future. Curricula for Mexican children were aimed at basic English and arithmetic, inculcation in ideals and values of American society, development of good habits such as cleanliness and punctuality, and training in vocational or domestic skills. Emphasis was put on gender-appropriate training: Mexican girls studied sewing and mending, while boys were taught "carpentry, repairing shoes, basketry, haircutting, and blacksmithing." Joe O'Campo, who went to segregated schools in Santa Ana in the 1920s and 1930s, ruefully reported that the curriculum consisted of "woodshops" and "language," and added, "prohibiting us from speaking Spanish was teaching us English."[102]

Although Anglos viewed Mexicans as not valuing education, Paul Taylor found that Mexican American parents in the Colorado sugar beet fields kept fewer school-age children in the fields than German-Russian parents did, even if it meant making less money. Often, when Mexican mothers worked in beet fields, it was to allow children to attend school. In Dimmit County, Texas, even poor and illiterate Mexican tenant farmers expressed interest in education for their children. One told Taylor: "I don't want my boy to work. I want him in the school. If they will permit Mexicans in the school this year I will send him. If I die and the children have no education it will be *muy duro* for them." Many Mexicans were critical of the unequal education provided in Mexican schools. One tejana complained about the poor equipment and lower salaries paid to teachers and continued, "They are just taking the money received for the Mexicans and spending it for the American school." Mexicans in three towns in the Winter Garden district had taken the initiative to set up private schools or classes. The Mexican community in Big Wells, Texas, provided classrooms and living quarters for a teacher. Parents paid five cents a day or twenty-five cents a week for each child attending classes. The teacher eked out a living by supplementing the tuition fees with commissions for selling medicines, toiletries, and other oddments. Parents in Asherton paid to send their children to a Catholic school rather than the free but poorly equipped and staffed public school. Both Mexicans and Anglos reported that their reasons for doing so "were quite as much or more educational than religious." As one parent put it, "The Catholic school takes better care of the children, and takes more interest in them, and the discipline is better."[103]

By the late 1920s and early 1930s more Mexican Americans were obtaining education against the odds. A high school girl reported that she was inspired by an older Mexican girl who was graduating from college: "I want to be one of the first Spanish Americans to go through college as she has done. I want to spite the Spanish American girls who make fun of me for going to school. They say that I can't get a better job anyway because the Americans won't give me a chance . . . I thinned beets this spring, but I believe it is the last time . . . The girls who don't go to school will continue to top beets for the rest of their lives."[104]

Americanization

During the Progressive era, Americanization efforts akin to those directed at European immigrants began to target Mexicans and Mexican Americans. Although many Anglos considered Mexicans inassimilable, other Anglo reformers saw them as not dissimilar to southern Europeans in their potential for Americanization. Unlike Chinese and Japanese, who they believed were truly inassimilable for racial reasons, Americanizers suggested that barriers in the case of Mexicans were cultural and linguistic and therefore mutable.

Many different groups and institutions were involved in Americanization efforts, Protestant and Catholic churches, employers, social welfare agencies, and public and parochial schools. Each group had distinct interests that shaped its approach to Americanization. For example, Protestant missionaries' aim was to "Christianize" Mexicans while simultaneously making them "true American citizens." Employers' interest was in ensuring a reliable and diligent workforce; hence they wanted men to develop "good work habits," cleanliness, sobriety, respect for authority, and industriousness. Despite these different interests, three common themes pervaded most Americanization efforts. First, Americanization programs were premised on supposed defects of Mexican culture and character that needed to be corrected. Second, they assumed that Mexicans had limited aspirations and would continue to occupy a humble place within American society. Third, the efforts were distinctly gendered: their aim was to mold Mexicans toward Anglo ideals of manhood and womanhood.

Employers sometimes got directly involved in molding the workforce. Colorado Fuel and Iron, which ran the coal fields in Southern

Colorado, created kindergartens for workers' children "to inculcate the true democratic spirit—the spirit of sympathy, of unselfishness, and of equal rights." Presumably this would assist in the main goal, which was to make "better citizens more contented with their work."[105] Protestant groups sent women missionaries to establish settlement houses and schools in urban colonias and rural villages with the aim of shaping Mexican girls into Anglo conceptions of womanhood, femininity defined primarily by domesticity.[106]

Americanization programs run by schools and voluntary organizations often focused their efforts on Mexican women and children. Their hope was that by reforming the home they would reach men and future generations. Accordingly, Americanist educators' programs for both girls and women aimed at instilling domestic skills and habits they supposedly lacked, such as preparing healthful (that is, non-Mexican) foods, practicing personal hygiene, and working hard. Such training would prepare Mexican women to run an orderly home, so that when they became mothers they would instill the same virtues in the next generation. Pearl Ellis, an Americanist working with young Chicanas in Los Angeles in the 1920s, rhapsodized that a transformation of home values would lead in the next generation to a worker who is "more dependable and less revolutionary in his tendencies." Americanist educators did not assume that Mexican women would use domestic skills only in their own homes. With domestic training, they argued, young Mexican women could go directly into the workforce and their "American" employers would not face the burden of training them. Additionally, putting women to work would be the most direct way to cure them of the Mexican's congenital laziness. Employment in an Anglo household would promote discipline, which in turn would encourage them to pass self-control on to their children.[107]

Mexican women selectively accepted what Americanizers proffered. They flocked to send their children to missionary schools, which they felt offered a better education than the public schools, and they welcomed opportunities to learn English and acquire knowledge of American customs that would help them better support their families. They were not interested in religious conversion or changing their cultures.[108]

Mexican women and men together sustained a distinct, if syncretic, culture within American society. While maintaining their ties in Mexico and staying abreast of social and political developments there, they also took pride and interest in their local communities and American society. Countering the notion of Americanness as exclusively Anglo, Mexican communities saw no contradiction in celebrating Mexican Independence Day (September 16) with parades, displaying Mexican and American flags, and giving patriotic speeches extolling both Mexican and American freedom. Such celebrations "provided alternative versions of ethnic and patriotic identities for their own group." David Gutiérrez sees the survival of Mexicans as a culturally distinct people within the United States as their most significant achievement in the face of Anglo American efforts to stigmatize them and their culture.[109]

The Coming Storm

The 1920s saw the rumblings of forces that would unleash even harsher conditions for Mexicans in the Southwest. In the years following World War I, anti-immigrant nativism reached fever pitch. Allied with the newly influential eugenics movement, nativism targeted not only Asians and other "not-white" groups but also Italians, Poles, Jews, and other southern and eastern Europeans who immigrated in massive numbers between 1890 and 1914. According to the prevailing racial theories these groups were different from and inferior to the main "American stock" that originated in northern and western Europe. The efforts of nativists culminated in the omnibus Immigration Act of 1924 that cut off immigration from Asia and set strict quotas on entry from southern and eastern Europe, Africa, and the Middle East. Despite growing anti-Mexican sentiment, agricultural interests in the Southwest and U.S. officials concerned with maintaining amicable relations with Latin America persuaded Congress to at least temporarily allow immigration from Mexico and other countries in the western hemisphere.[110]

However, with immigration from Asia and southern Europe dropping sharply, nativist anxiety came to focus more intently on the "Mexican Problem." Many of the same racialist Anglo-Saxon ideological elements that had been marshaled against southern and eastern Europeans were now targeted against Mexicans. Nativists had portrayed southern Europeans as having an "incapacity for self government" and as "racially impervious to the whole of American civilization." They were therefore "constitutionally incapable of assimilation." Similar arguments were applied to Mexicans, but additionally, Mexicans, Indians, and blacks were linked as being irredeemably inferior and depraved. Nativists charged that Mexicans were of a debased racial stock, mainly Indian with perhaps a small percentage of blood from an inferior European branch. They warned that the fecundity of Mexican women posed a demographic threat. The leading American eugenicist, Madison Grant, sounded the alarm that the high fertility of "inferior races" combined with low fertility of superior American stock constituted a form of "race suicide." Racialists also raised the specter of miscegenation, pointing out that Mexicans already were a mixed race and had no scruples against interbreeding. In 1929 the U.S. government finally acceded to racist restrictionist forces by limiting the number of visas issued to Mexicans, increasing penalties for illegal entry, and enlarging the border patrol.[111]

The situation for Mexican Americans grew even grimmer with the coming of the Great Depression. Agriculture in the Southwest was especially hard hit as farm prices and wages plummeted and hundreds of thousands of laborers were thrown out of work. In an effort to reduce welfare burdens, local officials organized mass "repatriation" drives. Welfare officials would grant temporary relief to impoverished Mexicans on the condition that they repatriate to Mexico at public expense. Los Angeles County had one of the largest and most organized such programs, transporting one trainload each month between 1931 and 1934, an estimated 13,000 in all. It has been estimated that 350,000–600,000 Mexicans, some of them born in the United States and therefore American citizens, were "returned" to Mexico in the 1930s.[112]

As the depression deepened, the poverty and emiseration of Mexicans eking out a living or thrown out of work were so marked as to shock government agents and health inspectors, who found high infant mortality rates, rampant communicable diseases, and widespread malnutrition. The fear of expulsion was such, however, that Mexicans eschewed applying for relief to which they were entitled. A U.S. Children's Bureau representative reported that "many Mexicans are afraid to accept hospital care; mothers attending the prenatal clinic refuse to accept hospital confinement."[113] The mistrust and fear that the repatriation programs sowed had far-reaching consequences for those who stayed as well as those who were transported.

Mexican workers were not completely quiescent. They responded to deteriorating conditions by stepping up labor organizing. In 1937 the Texas Agricultural Worker's Organizing Committee was absorbed into a new CIO union, the United Cannery, Agricultural, Packing and Allied Workers of America. Though it did not survive past the Depression decade, UCAPAWA broke new ground by recruiting women and immigrants, including undocumented workers, into the labor movement. Unlike virtually every other union, UCAPAWA insisted that immigrant workers had the right to work in the United States and to participate in unions.[114]

LIKE BLACKS in the South (and as we shall see in the next chapter, Japanese in Hawaii), Mexicans, American citizens as well as immigrants, were subject to coercive labor practices, and their freedom in the labor market was circumscribed by industrial and occupational segregation and hierarchy. Unlike the case of blacks in the South, however, dominant institutions at the federal, state, and local levels involved in defining racial and citizenship status varied widely in their policies. The federal policy that Mexicans were white made it difficult for state and local governments to legislate segregation and other forms of racial exclusion. Mexicans were able to use the discrepancies to challenge state and local laws that targeted them on the basis of their supposed nonwhiteness. Nevertheless, de facto segregation was rampant in many areas of the Southwest. Moreover, Anglos often made no distinction between ethnic Mexicans who were birthright citizens and those who were immigrants, treating both groups as "foreigners." The case of the Southwest illustrates the distinction between formal and substantive citizenship and the significance of everyday social practices in determining substantive citizenship.

Like blacks, who viewed citizenship as collective rather than individual, Mexicans acted on and articulated an alternative understanding of membership in the American community. Workers based their claims to belonging on their having labored in the United States. They pointed to the toil and sweat Mexicans had expended in growing food that fed Americans, reclaiming agricultural land, and building railroads and other structures that were the source of American wealth. They also expressed the inclusive notion of American culture as encompassing the varied cultures of the people who made up the nation. By their reckoning, speaking Spanish and celebrating Mexican holidays were consistent with allegiance to the United States. At this early date, Mexican Americans were beginning to advance a concept that is now called cultural citizenship—the right to maintain cultures and languages that differ from those of the majority without compromising membership in the American community or the civil, political, or social rights attached to membership. And, anticipating the current age in which individuals freely traverse national boundaries, they challenged American nationalist notions of fixed borders and boundaries delimiting nation states, moving freely within the border region and retaining ties and forming political alliances across official borders.

·6·

Japanese and Haoles
in Hawaii

HAWAII HAS OFTEN been portrayed as a racial paradise, a tolerant multicultural society in which natives and immigrants have freely intermingled. Visitors to the islands since the nineteenth century have described their fascination with the diversity of the population and the exotic beauty of the many people of mixed descent. Novelists, journalists, and academics have all contributed to the idealization of Hawaii's race relations, broadcasting glowing descriptions of Hawaii as a "racial melting pot" and trumpeting the absence of racial hostility and overt discrimination. At the same time, however, scholars and journalists have been struck by the degree to which race has served as an organizing principle in the social, political, and economic institutions of the islands. They have described an overarching racial hierarchy in which land and capital wealth, social privilege, and political control are concentrated in the hands of a small white elite, while arrayed below in a kind of political-economic pecking order are diverse nonwhite groups, including Native Hawaiians, Asians, and Pacific Islanders.[1]

These seemingly contradictory pictures of Hawaii as racially harmonious and as racially stratified both capture parts of a complex whole. This complexity makes Hawaii an especially rich source for insights into the intricacies of how race, gender, and class relations and meanings are formed and contested at the local level, even while being influenced by institutional structures and cultural forces at the national level.

190

Racial tolerance has often been viewed as a legacy of indigenous (pre–European contact) Hawaiian values of openness and generosity. The openness of Native Hawaiians to outsiders in the early post-contact period set the tone for widespread acceptance of interracial unions. Such unions occurred not just among ordinary people but also among Native Hawaiians of the *alii* (chieftain) class. The tradition of forging political and economic alliances through intermarriage had been utilized by King Kamehameha I, who unified several independent and quasi-independent entities into the Kingdom of Hawaii by 1795. Later he offered the hands of royal Hawaiian women in marriage to European and American missionaries and merchants whom he trusted and used as advisors.[2]

One measure of Hawaii's racial attitudes is that, unlike other areas of the United States with large proportions of "nonwhite" population, Hawaii never had any laws against miscegenation, nor was there any notable sentiment in favor of such legislation. The reasons for the absence of anti-miscegenation laws may be more complex than simply a culture of tolerance. Even in Hawaii, interracial unions followed certain gender patterns which contributed to a willingness by Europeans and Americans to sanction interracial marriages. Peggy Pascoe has pointed out that anti-miscegenation laws in many parts of the United States were adopted to prevent men of color from having access to white women, not to prevent white men from having access to women of color. Hence such laws were most prevalent in areas, such as the South, where men of color were seen as posing a threat to white womanhood. The imbalanced sex ratio among Asian groups in Hawaii might have created such a threat. However, the scarcity of white women and the availability of Native Hawaiian women directed Asian men toward Hawaiian women. Almost all interracial unions in Hawaii before 1940 involved Native Hawaiian, Asian, or mixed-race women. As in the Southwest, domestic unions between dominant-group women and subordinate-group men were exceedingly rare.[3]

The frequency of interracial unions meant that from the mid-nineteenth century there was a substantial and growing mixed race population in all parts of local society. By the beginning of the twentieth century part-Hawaiians made up one-fourth of the Native Hawaiian population, and by 1930 they outnumbered pure Hawaiians.[4] As part-Hawaiians further intermarried, the mixtures became increasingly complex, involving various fractions of Asian, European, Anglo American, and Native Hawaiian ancestry. The resulting heterogeneity within many extended kin networks, including some elite *haole* (European and Anglo American) families, helped forestall the kind of race- or color-based Jim Crow laws and practices that prevailed in the South and the Southwest.

The absence of blatant color barriers did not, however, mean an absence of racial hierarchy. Indeed, the growth and elaboration of race-based stratification was integral to Hawaii's development as a colonial dependent economy. Hawaii was incorporated into the world capitalist system initially as a trading center, and then as a producer of agricultural staples, particularly sugar, for the U.S. market. Although formally an independent nation before annexation by the United States in 1898, first as a kingdom (1795–1893) and briefly as a republic (1895–1898), it was in effect part of the U.S. economy from the mid-nineteenth century on.[5] The pathway to Anglo American hegemony was paved by American and European traders and New England lay missionaries who arrived in the early 1800s. They quickly established themselves economically and politically, assuming roles as advisors and agents for the Hawaiian royalty. They implanted Anglo American institutional forms in the areas of religion, government, law, language, and education. Under their influence, the Hawaiian monarchy instituted a system of private ownership of what had been communally held land.[6] Also, as in the Southwest, where in-migrating Anglo men gained control of estates through marriage to the daughters of landed Mexicanos, European and American businessmen and descendants of missionaries solidified their claims to land through marriage with Native Hawaiian women of the chieftain class.[7]

Privatization of land enabled the nascent Anglo American oligarchy to establish a plantation-based economy relying at first on Native Hawaiian labor and later on imported Asian labor. Sugar cultivation began early in the nineteenth century but did not dominate the economy until after the Civil War, when the demand for sugar caused prices to soar. A reciprocity treaty was signed in 1876, allowing Hawaiian sugar to be imported to the United States free of duty in exchange for the United States having rights to Pearl Harbor for a military and commercial base.[8] Sugar production grew by 2,000 percent over the next two decades. Planter and financial interests further consolidated their rule in 1893, when they seized control of the government and deposed Queen

Liliuokalani. They established a republic in 1895 and then engineered annexation in 1898, making Hawaii a U.S. territory and permanently exempt from all U.S. tariffs.[9]

As in the South, planters saw cheap and tractable labor as the key to profitability. Prior to 1876 Native Hawaiians were the main source of plantation labor. However, with explosion of sugar production, there were not enough Native Hawaiians to fill labor demand. The native population, by some estimates 300,000 at the time of contact, had fallen to 47,528 by 1878 and to 39,504 by 1896.[10] Moreover, Native Hawaiians could not be easily tied to wage labor because they could still live off the land and the sea. Planters briefly considered importing black labor, but discarded the idea on the grounds that, slavery having been abolished, freedmen would not be sufficiently docile. Instead they turned to male contract labor, most of it from Asia. From 1850 to 1930 over 400,000 workers were imported. The first recruits were men from China (an estimated 40,000–50,000, mostly between 1876 and 1885); after the flow from China was cut to a trickle by Hawaiian government restrictions, planters turned to Japan (around 180,000 arrivals, mostly between 1886 and 1924); and, after 1924, when immigration from Japan was cut off by U.S. law, to another U.S. colony, the Philippines (about 120,000 between 1907 and 1931). Of these Asian immigrants, only among the Japanese was there a significant number of women, 40,000 of whom arrived between 1907 and 1923. Portuguese, mostly from the Azores and Madeira, the largest non-Asian group (17,500), were recruited in two waves, from 1878 to 1887 and from 1906 to 1913. Smaller numbers of workers came from Korea, Puerto Rico, Spain, Germany, Russia, Norway, and other Pacific islands.[11]

The pattern of organization for sugar was repeated in the production of pineapple, cultivation of which began on a small scale in 1900 and which grew to become the second-largest export product by 1920. The same Anglo American corporations controlled land and financing, and much the same labor force was employed. Together, sugar and pineapple dominated the Hawaiian economy from 1876 to the mid-1930s. At the peak of the plantation economy in the 1930s, over half of the population of Hawaii was made up of sugar and pineapple workers and their dependents.[12]

Outside observers were struck by the extreme concentration of economic and political power in the hands of the local oligarchy. Eco-

nomic activity, from banking to cultivation to processing and ship-
ping, was controlled by thirty to forty corporations tied together by
interlocking directorates. Individual directors, drawn disproportionately from a handful of families descended from early missionaries, sat
on numerous boards. This network of local corporations held an iron
grip on financing, transportation, public utilities, plantations, factors,
and construction industries. Most critical to the oligarchy was control
of the land on which to grow the sugar and pineapple. By 1909 over
half of private land was owned by haole corporations; of the remainder,
one-third was controlled by individual haoles; one-third by the haole
directors of the Bishop Estate, a giant land trust; and the last third by
individual Native Hawaiians, part-Hawaiians, and Asians.[13]

With land and capital heavily concentrated, Hawaii offered few opportunities for small producers. Consequently, Hawaii never experienced a major influx of agrarian white settlers. The absence of a white
"yeomanry" simplified the race and class structure. Aside from the se-
verely reduced Native Hawaiian population, the main division was between a small white planter and business elite and a large group of imported Asian laborers. The relative paucity of white small producers
and laborers precluded the kind of "race warfare" that raged between
white and Asian workers in California.[14]

Relations between haoles and Japanese in Hawaii provide a localized
example of the contestation over labor and citizenship in the United
States in the period 1870–1930. In the beginning of the period the Japanese consisted of male workers concentrated in field work, seen as and
seeing themselves as temporary residents, and lacking a stake in or
membership in the society. By the end of the period the Japanese were
permanent settlers, made up of families, and at nearly 38 percent of the
population the largest racial ethnic group in Hawaii. A substantial generation born in Hawaii and therefore entitled to U.S. citizenship, the
"nisei," had reached adulthood; many had moved out of plantation labor and into trades, small businesses, and urban employment. The
haoles still held political and economic control, but the Japanese had
achieved considerable educational and occupational mobility.

This relationship unfolded within a larger context of shifting multicultural relations, but the conflict and contestation between haole and
Japanese was the most prominent in this crucial sixty-year period. Because of their numbers, the Japanese were seen as genuine competitors

and threats to haole domination. Also, compared with other groups, haoles and Japanese had low rates of out-marriage, thus retaining more or less distinct communities and identities. Other groups, particularly Native Hawaiians, were active in struggles over resources and status, but the Japanese (as the predominant workforce) and the haoles (as the predominant owner/manager class) positioned themselves in particularly oppositional ways. Japanese and haole representations of self and other, "us" and "them," were interdependently constructed, as was the case with whites and blacks in the South and Anglos and Mexicans in the Southwest. Haoles defined themselves as "Americans" or "we" in contrast to the Japanese as "other" or "foreign"; they constructed Japanese as "not-American" or "un-American." Japanese were forced to confront haoles as the dominant other; through their organizations and vernacular press, Japanese in Hawaii countered haole representations, sometimes rearticulating dominant concepts and values to assert their identities as simultaneously "Japanese" *and* "American."

Hierarchy and Control in the Labor System

In setting up the labor system, planters designed an elaborately stratified structure to maintain white privilege and facilitate control over work and workers. White privilege was manifested in two principles: that Europeans and Americans should not have to work as equals or subordinates of non-Europeans/Americans; and that skill and authority were the purview of "higher races." Accordingly, planters recruited mainland whites and Europeans to fill managerial and skilled positions rather than promoting "Oriental" assistants. Surveys found that management positions were filled by white Americans, English, Germans, and Scots, and skilled and supervisory positions by Europeans (such as Germans and Norwegians). The largest category, unskilled laborers, was made up overwhelmingly of Chinese, Japanese, and later Filipinos, with smaller numbers of Puerto Ricans, Koreans, and others. Planters' control over this mass of lower-level field workers was mediated by the employment of "middlemen minorities" in field-supervisory positions. Thus jobs as field foremen *(luna)* as well as middle-level semiskilled positions were given to Native Hawaiians and Portuguese. This practice shielded elite haoles from the dirty work of disciplining workers; it deflected field workers' hostility onto other groups; and it kept field workers in the fields by cutting off avenues of mobility. A 1902 survey of 55 plantations showed that Japanese and Chinese made up 83 percent of the plantation workforce but held only 18 percent of the superintendencies. In contrast, "Portuguese" and "Other Caucasians" made up 6.3 percent and 2.4 percent of the workforce respectively but held 24 percent and 44 percent of the superintendencies. This basic structure was still in place in 1915, when another survey showed that 89 percent of the mill engineers and 83 percent of the overseers were of European descent.[15]

Wages were similarly stratified, with separate pay scales that ensured that Anglo Americans and northern Europeans received higher pay for equivalent work. The above-mentioned 1902 survey revealed that "American" blacksmiths averaged $3.82 a day, "Scotch" $4.33 a day, Portuguese $2.61, Native Hawaiian, $2.12, and Japanese $1.63. On these same plantations, "American" carpenters received $4.38 a day, Portuguese $1.98, Chinese $1.56, Native Hawaiians $1.49, and Japanese $1.17. White American overseers received 57 percent more than Portuguese overseers and 100 percent more than Japanese overseers. The wage differentials continued in 1915, with American overseers earning 73 percent and 107 percent more than Portuguese and Japanese overseers.[16]

Recruiting practices and perquisites also differed. Asian workers were treated strictly as laborers, not as settlers and potential citizens. At first the policy for Asian workers favored single men—sojourners free of family ties. In the words of a U.S. official, the sugar interests sought "cheap, not too intelligent, docile unmarried men."[17] Wages could be kept low and housing costs and perquisites minimized if men were not supporting families. Indeed, early plantation camps afforded Asian and Native Hawaiian male workers only the most primitive shelter, usually hastily constructed shacks and barracks. Lacking adequate sanitation, workers' housing harbored rats and insects, which set off periodic epidemics of typhoid and bubonic plague. Plantation owners rationalized the conditions by citing the Oriental's low standard of living and primitive notions of hygiene.[18]

In contrast, Portuguese, Germans, and other Europeans were from the outset recruited as family groups or couples, in order to encourage them to become permanent settlers. European men were treated as family heads and potential citizens. Unlike Asian immigrant workers,

Spanish, Portuguese, and Russians had their passage paid and were accorded better housing, plots of land to homestead, and free medical care. Plantation owners acknowledged a higher standard of living for European workers.[19]

Only when faced with continuing labor shortages after 1905 did planters rethink the policy of favoring single men for the Japanese workforce. The absence of attachments that made single male workers cheap and malleable also made them mobile. By the first decade of the twentieth century plantation owners concluded that women stabilized the workforce. They began to provide cottages for families, often with small subsistence plots to grow food. Motivated by these incentives and the opening provided by the 1907–08 Gentleman's Agreement, which cut off immigration of laborers from Japan but allowed entry to spouses, Japanese men begin sending for brides. Between 1907 and 1923 over 40,000 Japanese women immigrated to Hawaii. Women constituted only 19.2 percent of the Japanese population aged twenty and older in 1900; by 1920 they were up to 38.3 percent and by 1930 to 42.9 percent.[20]

Although plantation owners now encouraged family formation, they did not adjust men's wages to meet the greater consumption needs of families. For example, in 1910 the estimated cost of food alone for two adults was $12–$14 per month, while the lowest-paid male workers received only $18 per month. Wives had to make up the income gap by engaging in subsistence farming and wage-earning activities. While Hawaiian, Portuguese, German, Norwegian, and a few Chinese women were drawn into mill operations, Japanese women were pulled into field labor. There they were concentrated in the backbreaking jobs of hoeing weeds and stripping dry leaves off the cane stalks. They were also employed in so-called men's jobs of cane cutting and cane loading. Women field workers typically worked a sixty-hour week (six ten-hour days), the same as the men; they earned about two-thirds of the pay of Japanese male field workers, who in turn earned less than Portuguese or Native Hawaiian male workers.[21]

The planters developed elaborate racial theories to justify the stratification of labor. Racial-ethnic stereotyping was rampant as planters and managers debated labor problems and the advantages and disadvantages of employing one group or another. Stereotypes made racial or ethnic stratification of occupations seem natural by portraying specific groups as suited to particular types of work by their physical, moral, or psychological attributes. A 1902 U.S. Labor Department report on the "present plantation labor supply" presented extensive descriptions of the supposed characteristics of major ethnic groups. The report recognized the non-haole status of the Portuguese, noting that they "form a class apart": "This is probably because the 'white man' has always been a sort of aristocrat in the islands, and a large body of immigrants who live in ordinary plantation quarters and work with hoes could hardly aspire to that rank in public estimation." Nonetheless, in the authors' opinion, the Portuguese were the most "hopeful" element of the population, as they rapidly Americanized, made good citizens, were "industrious and frugal," and raised enormous families of "bright, sturdy children—the most desirable crop of all in a country like Hawaii." Planters described them as more individualistic than either the Chinese or the Japanese. Apt to disagree with fellow workers, they were not inclined to strike against the employer.[22]

Native Hawaiians were described as desirable as teamsters, plowmen, ranch hands, wharf men, and porters because of their superior strength. They were said to be good workers and "almost perfectly honest" unless corrupted by city influences. However, they lacked industrial discipline and were "indisposed" to occupations of a monotonous character. They were thus ideally suited to jobs involving irregular employment, such as wharf men and porters.[23]

For unskilled labor, most managers felt that an ideal labor force would be equally divided between Chinese and Japanese. The report notes: "The two people in spite of their kinship, have marked dissimilarities. The Chinaman is usually the more steady and reliable but the less energetic laborer of the two, and is preferred for irrigation and cane cutting. The Japanese has greater physical strength, and is the better man for loading or for general roustabout work in the mill." This report was made only two years after a series of strikes following the Organic Act which had made Hawaii a U.S. Territory. Planters' attitudes toward Japanese had soured, while those toward Chinese (whose immigration was halted when Hawaii was annexed) had mellowed. The planters reported: "In matters of business honor, the Chinaman is considered vastly more reliable. He seldom deserts a contract, even though he lose heavily, while a Japanese will walk off and leave a manager in the lurch if he fails to get what he considers a profitable bargain." The Chinese were praised for being more constant in domestic relations and raising their children in strict accord with their ethical ideals. The report is particularly critical of Japanese "private morals," citing the practice of picture marriages. It describes the wives as having been "practically purchased by friends or agents." Consequently wives "promptly desert the men if they do not meet with their approval. Much looseness in the sex relations results."[24]

By 1926 Stanley Porteus, an Australian who was a professor of psychology and director of the Psychology and Psychopathology Clinic at the University of Hawaii, was translating racial stereotypes into the then-popular science of "race and temperament." On the basis of his observations and psychological tests, he concluded that while the temperaments of Native Hawaiians and Chinese harmonized with those of the ruling whites, "between white and Japanese there was an inevitable clash of temperaments. The latter was too adaptable and too ready to seize and turn the white man's own weapons against him." Summing up, he wrote: "The outstanding traits of Japanese character as these have been brought to attention during their stay in the Islands, we may say that collectively they are intensely race-conscious, ready to combine for any purposes of group advancement, aggressive and rather untrustworthy when self-interest is in question. Individually they are extremely adaptable, ambitious and persistent and emotionally self controlled."[25]

Prior to annexation by the United States, most plantations relied on a quasi-slave system based on penal contracts. Under the Master Servant Act of 1850 employers could "bind" workers for fixed terms of up to ten years, with penal provisions allowing for fines, imprisonment, and doubling of the length of the contract for desertion or absence from work. The original act declared a contract void upon the death of the employer and banned inheritance of servants, thus avoiding one key feature of chattel slavery. However, transfer of contracts was common.

Starting in 1864 an agency of the Kingdom, the Hawaii Bureau of Immigration, took charge of recruiting workers, making contracts with them, and assigning them to plantations upon arrival. Many Asians signing "labor contracts' did not understand that they were selling themselves into quasi-slavery; the shock of discovering their true status led many contract laborers to resist abusive treatment and thus to incur imprisonment or physical punishment. Planters found ways to evade the prohibition of sale or transfer of labor contracts by forming companies to hire contract workers. A court ruled in 1876 that contracts could be written with a company and that a change of partners did not invalidate a contract. Moreover, throughout the contract period, employers were allowed to unilaterally assess fines and penalties. Workers' only recourse was desertion or refusal to serve, which brought down the forces of the law against them. In 1877 the Hawaii Supreme Court further hemmed in workers by ruling that matters regulated by the Master Servant Act were civil and not criminal matters. Workers were left with no recourse, since they lacked legal representation to bring suit in civil court. Workers under penal contracts were also subjected to types of physical abuse, such as whipping, used by white slaveholders in the South.[26]

Edward Beechert notes that throughout the 1880s and 1890s, despite some amendments designed to increase protections for workers, for example by limiting time served to the length of the contract, overall there was a further drift toward peonage: "The legal situation as it developed in Hawaii before annexation placed the workers in a category *outside* the law. For those under a penal contract, there was only the flimsy reed of appeal to the provisions against physical abuse, failure to pay wages, or transfer of contracts."[27]

Annexation by the United States meant that Hawaii law was replaced by U.S. law and jurisprudence barring penal contracts and upholding "liberty of contract." Planters in Hawaii thus faced similar problems as landowners of the South in maintaining coercion within an ostensibly free labor system. Without the existence of penal contracts, Chinese and Japanese workers could no longer be legally bound. Nonetheless, many planters continued to impose the old harsh methods of discipline. They granted overseers considerable leeway to chastise workers, and some overseers still made use of the black snake whip.

Workers responded to miserable living conditions and harsh treatment by desertion, malingering, and other forms of individual resistance, as well as by organized protest. In response, planters employed police to ferret out deserters and used a passbook system to prevent workers from moving from one plantation to another. Even after penal contracts ended, planters claimed that workers were incapable of governing themselves and attempted to regulate all aspects of their lives from diet to waking hours. In Miriam Sharma's words: "People who wished to enter the plantation needed passes. This was supposed to protect the 'gullible' and 'childlike' workers from confidence men, extortionists, and others of their ilk." Elaborate lists of rules established fines for infractions ranging from insubordination to drunkenness. Suspecting workers of malingering, overseers denied ill workers permission to take time off. Owners attempted to overcome forms of resistance such as self-pacing, soldiering, malingering, and absenteeism by keeping regular wages low and offering substantial year-end bonuses for those who averaged more than twenty days of work a month. They deducted payments for housing, food, and supplies purchased at the company store, and even dues for community center membership.[28]

Perhaps the most common response of workers was to leave plantation work as quickly as possible. They moved to town or city, fled to the mainland, or returned to their homelands. Turnover was a continuous problem. Over the years planters tried numerous methods to bind workers to their jobs and to motivate them to work longer hours.

After 1900 many planters sought to keep workers on the plantation by bettering conditions. They improved housing and recreational facilities and expanded perquisites such as hospital and medical benefits. The 1902 U.S. Labor Department report stated that workers were comfortably housed and well treated and that sanitary conditions were uniformly good, with regular cleanup and pickup of trash. Most plantations had special facilities for laundry, bathing, and cooking. Workers were encouraged to improve their quarters. Managers furnished them with plants and flowers for yards and awarded prizes for the most attractive quarters. Still, paternalism, not equality, was the goal; owners preferred to dispense charity rather than allow workers' autonomy.[29]

Many workers chafed at the overarching control by plantation management and preferred to forgo the amenities and convenience of plantation housing in order to live more independently. A manager expressed his perplexity that many of the workers "insisted on moving down into the squalid town, paying money for their house, buying their own fuel and walking an unnecessarily long distance to work in the morning."[30]

To further discourage movement to nonplantation jobs, in 1903 the planter-controlled territorial legislature passed a law banning the employment of Japanese in public works jobs on the grounds that their labor was needed on the plantations. Less formally, business firms in Honolulu were implored not to hire Japanese. Such measures had a limited effect as turnover accelerated. One unintended consequence of annexation was to open up Hawaii as a source of labor for the mainland. Labor agents soon arrived to lure workers to fill jobs in agriculture and railroads at wages that plantations could not or would not match. Over 1,000 Japanese workers left Hawaii for the mainland in 1902. By 1904 the number of annual departures was 6,000 and by 1905 more than 10,000. To stem the mass exodus planters sought to impose penalties on outside labor agents, but there was only so much they could do to restrict freedom of movement. They would not succeed in getting the federal government to cut off migration of Japanese from Hawaii to the mainland until 1907. Hawaii officials also continued to look for replacements for Japanese labor. Their representatives in Washington lobbied unsuccessfully for a special exemption to the Chinese Exclusion Act to allow planters to recruit workers from China.[31]

In response to workers' mobility, plantation owners increasingly moved from a straight wage system toward various forms of subcontracting and tenancy. One type of short-term arrangement was similar to a piece-rate system: workers were offered short-term contracts in which they were paid for accomplishing a given task, such as irrigating a field or cutting a field of cane, rather than for time worked. Under one type of long-term contract a group of workers under a headman was allotted acreage and given seed, cane, water, fertilizer, and tools. The group performed all the tasks needed to bring the field to harvest and were paid at the end. In another type of long-term contract owners made tenancy agreements with heads of households similar to southern sharecropping arrangements. By 1929 half of all plantation workers were employed as short- or long-term contractors.[32]

Like sharecropping in the South, subcontracting was adopted in response to perceived recalcitrance and withholding of labor by "free" workers. As in the South, contracts were designed to tie workers down while reducing any risks on the part of the landowner. Beechert observed, "The contracts, although elaborate in detail, were principally one-sided instruments." They contained clauses that allowed for rewriting the terms if the price of sugar fell or rose, and many contained provisions that required contractors to perform additional work desired by the employer. In a revised "uniform cultivation contract" drafted by the sugar producers in 1922, the contractor was required to give two months' notice to cancel the contract while plantation owners could cancel at will. Like tenant farmers in the South, contract workers in Hawaii seldom realized much of a profit after settling their debts. Beechert found that for the period 1915–1917 Japanese day workers could earn a maximum of $36.32 a month including bonuses, while cultivating and cutting contractors could receive $38.23 for a slightly shorter work month. However, "the vicissitudes of agriculture—a drought, pests, such as the leafhopper, or too much rain—might reduce his harvest to a point below the amount advanced for living expenses and fertilizer."[33]

Racialized and Gendered Citizenship

For much of the late nineteenth and early twentieth centuries the usefulness of Chinese and Japanese labor for the planter class was closely tied to their exclusion from citizenship. Their noncitizen status helped mitigate one potential problem for the planters: how to ensure an abundant supply of labor and at the same time retain their political dominance despite their small numbers. During the contract-labor period Asian men were taxed but were not allowed to vote. The 1887 Hawaii Constitution set substantial property requirements for voting and restricted suffrage to "male residents of Hawaiian, American, or European birth or descent." When the planters and the haole elite seized control of the government in 1893, they wrote a new constitution that continued to disfranchise Asian workers (as well as many Native Hawaiians): it required that a voter be a citizen by birth or naturalization *and* be able to speak, read, write, and explain the constitution in English.[34]

Disfranchisement for Asians continued after annexation. Unlike Mexicans following the Treaty of Guadalupe Hidalgo and blacks after the Fourteenth Amendment, who were at least technically accorded national citizenship, Asian immigrants were formally excluded. The applicable law was the 1790 Naturalization Act as amended in 1870, which limited the right to become a naturalized citizen to "white persons" and persons of African nativity or descent. In key cases involving Asian applicants, the U.S. courts created a separate legal status for Asian immigrants as "aliens ineligible for citizenship." Thus not only were most plantation workers not citizens, their special status as "ineligible for citizenship" differentiated them from other noncitizens. They could be singled out for discriminatory treatment and deprived of protections accorded noncitizens who were eligible for naturalization. In California and Oregon "aliens ineligible for citizenship" were barred from owning agricultural land. In Hawaii the Hawaii Sugar Planters Association (HSPA) adopted a resolution in 1904 stating that skilled jobs should be limited to "citizens" and those "eligible for citizenship."[35]

Ineligibility for citizenship underlined the position of Asians as temporary workers, not permanent settlers. As noted earlier, in contrast to policies aimed at encouraging Europeans to settle as families, initial policies toward Asians were aimed at recruiting single males and discouraging the entry of women. Because of the scarcity of Japanese women, the population remained extremely gender imbalanced well into the 1930s, and the growth of an American-born generation entitled to citizenship by birthright, and therefore eligible for suffrage, was considerably delayed. As late as 1905, more than twenty years after the Japanese started immigrating, not a single Japanese resident of Hawaii was registered to vote. In 1910, when the Japanese population was 79,675, only 0.2 percent of the adult Japanese population had been born in Hawaii and therefore were citizens. At this time, Japanese constituted 41.5 percent of the population—the largest ethnic group in Hawaii—but were a minuscule 0.4 percent of adult citizens and 0.1 percent of registered voters.[36]

Citizenship status and race were so closely intertwined that planters and officials often used the contrasting terms "citizen labor" and "noncitizen labor" interchangeably with "white" and "nonwhite" ("Oriental" or "Asiatic"). The reports of labor officials refer frequently to the problem of "noncitizen labor" rather than referring to race or nationality. As noted, in 1904 the HSPA barred Japanese from skilled positions not by making reference to race but by referring to citizenship status. Seven years later, perhaps owing to an increasing influence of mainland racial discourse, the HSPA adopted a resolution that recommended restricting semiskilled and skilled jobs to Native Hawaiians and "whites."[37]

According to the U.S. Labor Department report of 1902, planters believed that the Japanese would not be desirable citizens because of their "inherited reverence for authority" (presumably Japanese authority). Not only was their allegiance suspect, they lacked the independence necessary for true American citizenship. While granting that the Japanese were clean and tidy and apt to adopt "the superficial tokens of Caucasian civilization" (such as wearing European clothing and carrying a watch), the report continued, "His white employers consider him mercurial, superficial and untrustworthy in business matters." Japanese were seen as good imitators; thus their adoption of Western cultural ideals betokened only surface change.[38]

Territorial status opened Hawaii to greater scrutiny, both from mainland critics and from Republicans in control of the national government. One observer, the Progressive journalist Ray Stannard Baker, who investigated economic conditions in Hawaii in 1911, was moved to compare the position of the Anglo American elite to that of the white planter class in the "Old South." According to Baker, domination in both situations was based on control of the most fertile land, the machinery of production, and the labor supply: "Control is made easier in Hawaii, as it was in the old South, by the presence of a very large population of non-voting workmen . . . Fully three quarters of the population of Hawaii have no more to say about the government under which they are living than the old slaves."[39]

Annexation also heightened concerns on the mainland about maintaining both white supremacy and the semblance of political democracy. Visiting officials raised worries about the sheer number of "non-whites" in the population and the absence of a substantial class of "white yeomen" who could be allies of the tiny planter and business elite. By 1901, when the Japanese made up nearly 40 percent of the population, a mainland official was fretting about the consequences of Japanese becoming permanent settlers and their incorporation as citizens. He conceded that the Japanese adopted "occidental habits" but added that they were "intensely alien in their sympathies, religion and customs." Regarding the sharp increase in Hawaii-born Japanese, he noted the embarrassment that would be created "should this oriental population ultimately get control of the local government, by means of institutions established by Americans, and employ their racial solidarity to maintain themselves in power in the Territory." Since the Caucasian population was unlikely to increase through voluntary immigration, he urged special legislation to allow planters to import European field hands and families through civil contracts without penal provisions.[40]

In his 1905 report on Hawaii, the Commissioner of Labor blamed some segments of the planter class for stifling the growth of a white yeomanry. He said the planters' "democratic impulses were blunted by long years of being feudal lords" and suggested that what was good for the planters' profits might be bad for a democratic civic community. For the planters, the problem was one of securing a sufficient and stable labor force. For citizens of the Territory and people of the United States, the problem was one of "securing a working population with the civic capacity necessary to an upbuilding of a self-governing American commonwealth." He expressed concern over the harm done to democratic self-government by the presence of a large "Oriental labor population excluded from citizenship by law and apparently indifferent to citizenship as a matter of fact." Echoing prevailing Republican sentiments, he noted that such a situation bred no community of thought, feeling, or sympathy. Assimilation into American ideals "cannot be expected in a community in which only a very small percentage of the population are even descendants of people who have known representative government and have long had traditions of free institutions." He recommended efforts to increase the population of small producers and citizen residents. Such residents should not be "soft-handed" and should be suited for the physical hardships of Hawaii. Portuguese from the Azores, Spaniards, Italians from Sicily, and even Finns were suggested as candidates. The Commissioner added hopefully: "The fair-haired Portuguese of the Azores, whose descendants are now growing up in the Territory, are said to have been originally of Saxon stock."[41]

In response to these concerns about the lack of a significant "citizen population," the territorial government created a Board of Immigration in 1905 to recruit immigrants from Spain and Portugal, subsidizing their passage with subscriptions from the Planters' Association and then with a special income tax. Later the Hawaii Board of Immigration paid for passage of thousands of Russians from Siberia. These recruitment programs were intended only in part to fill labor needs. They were designed primarily to increase the white population. As the U.S. Labor Commissioner reported, "the fear of an oriental electorate had much to do with the adoption of this policy."[42]

Despite the inducements of wages one-third higher than those paid to Asians and land on which to homestead, most of these potential "white citizens"—with the exception of a significant number of Portuguese—left as soon as they saved enough money to flee. In 1911 a mainland journalist observed Portuguese and Russian families "living in utmost squalor and misery in Honolulu waiting for the men of the family who had gone to California to earn enough money to send for them." The Hawaii Board of Immigration also employed recruitment agents in California and New York City, but attempts to attract immigrants from the mainland proved "fruitless."[43]

Interdependent Lives and Identities

The plantation has been called the central "race making experience" by Andrew Lind, a dean of race-relations scholars of Hawaii. It was race making in two senses. First, it forged culturally and linguistically disparate immigrants into larger "nationality" groups. Laborers from the main islands of Japan (so-called Naichi) and from Okinawa, who considered themselves to be ethnically distinct, were lumped together as "Japanese." Workers recruited through Canton as culturally and linguistically diverse as the Hakka and the Punti became "Chinese." Lind notes, "A comparable growth in nationalistic or what is called racial unity, as a consequence of the planters having dealt with their workers as if they were culturally and linguistically alike, occurred among the more sharply differentiated Tagalogs, Visayans, and Ilocanos recruited from the Philippines."[44] Thus new ethnic identities were encouraged by the practice of assigning workers to ethnically homogenous housing compounds and work groups.

Second, and most significantly, the plantation system created the racial-class category of haole to which all others were counterpoised. The word "haole" in the Hawaiian language originally denoted "stranger," that is, someone without family and therefore without ties to the land. It referred to status as an outsider and did not designate race. A black sailor and a white missionary, for example, were both haoles. The term took on a more specific meaning as English and Anglo Americans acquired positions of prestige and influence in the government, starting in the reign of King Kamehameha I and accelerating thereafter. The European/American came to represent the "stranger" or haole, in contrast to the Native Hawaiian. The consolidation of haole as a racial category occurred with the development of the plantation and the need for the small proprietorial and managerial class to distinguish itself from workers. According to Lind, this class's influence "appeared to depend in some instances on their ability to keep the workers at a distance through the barriers of race. Hence even groups which in the strict biological interpretation of race were akin to the promoting groups, such as the Germans, Norwegians, Poles, Russians, and Spanish, who came to Hawaii as laborers, were designated as separate racial groups while on the plantation, and it was not until they moved into the less class conscious atmosphere of the city, or the plantation developed to its later stage, that they were able to become associated with the haole community."[45] Thus the term "haole" came to have a specific class as well as racial meaning in contrast to an ethnically diverse laboring class.

Within the stratified plantation system, the racial-class category of haole was constructed and preserved through a contrast schema that drew a sharp distinction between haoles and non-haoles. Social distance, materially and symbolically, was central to this distinction. With regard to the distance in material circumstances, Lawrence Fuchs observes, "By 1910, many managers were making $1,000 a month in addition to extensive perquisites, a fantastic sum in Hawaii, where the field hands were getting less than seventy-five cents a day." The huge disparity in earnings enabled the managerial class to enjoy an opulent colonial lifestyle unknown on the mainland. Letters and diaries of nineteenth- and early-twentieth-century visitors to Hawaii are replete with references to "the open handed hospitality of [haole] residents, which was dispensed by the ever-present maids and houseboys."[46] The plethora of servants in the households of plantation owners, managers, and supervisors was a natural outgrowth of the race- and class-structured plantation system.

Employment of household staff to maintain gardens and grounds, run stables, prepare and serve meals, clean, run errands, and care for infants and children was necessary to the standard of living appropriate to haole status. The employment of servants was also symbolically important as a marker of social distance between haoles and others. Mainland and European whites recruited to fill managerial and skilled positions on plantations were encouraged to consider themselves members of the privileged class. These newcomers became haoles by adopting the accouterments and rituals of haole status, and the employment of domestic servants was one important sign. Mainlanders who came from modest backgrounds were initially startled by their newfound status. A public school teacher who arrived from the mainland to teach in a plantation school found that she was to be housed in a cottage with four other mainland teachers. The principal had engaged a maid, and each teacher was to pay her four dollars a month. "A maid! None of us had ever had a maid. We were all used to doing our own work . . . Our principal was quite insistent. Everyone on the plantation had a maid. It was therefore, the thing to do."[47]

Houseboys, gardeners, stable hands, cooks, and maids could be drawn from the very groups that supplied field laborers. While the general patterns of dominant and subordinate group relations in domestic service did not differ from those in the Southwest and the South, one peculiarity of Hawaii was the scarcity of subordinate-group women. Unlike the situation in the rest of the country, the majority of domestic servants in Hawaii were men until well into the twentieth century. In the late nineteenth century Chinese men predominated among household servants; by the beginning of the twentieth century Japanese men had succeeded the Chinese. Only with the arrival of Japanese women in substantial numbers after 1907 did domestic service gradually become feminized. It was not until the late 1920s that women finally outnumbered men in household service.[48]

Managers were made to feel like monarchs, for there were few checks on their power. As Fuchs puts it:

> The manager was king. He lived in a superb house, usually on the highest hill in the area. His court consisted of other haoles—assistant managers, section *lunas*, bookkeepers, and engineers . . . His every word was followed with excitement by the plantation community and even in the small villages beyond. He might speak graciously at the sixth or eighth-grade commencement of the village school and give out prizes on behalf of the plantation; he might ungraciously fire and punish employees according to his whims. It was up to him whether gambling and drinking would be sanctioned or prostitutes permitted to visit the camps. It was his decision whether movies would be shown or primitive recreational facilities be built. His word determined whether workers could leave camp for weekends in Hilo or Honolulu.[49]

Despite their luxurious style of life, women from missionary families can be said to have lost power relative to men in the transition to a plantation economy. In the earlier period men and women were considered partners in missionary work, concentrating on instructing Native Hawaiians of their own sex. According to Joyce Lebra, who collected oral histories, an elite haole woman "would enjoy the perquisites of the colonial life-style . . . But she had no direct or immediate role in the political and economic mechanisms that sustained her privilege." While haole men ran the plantations and businesses of Hawaii along paternalistic lines, their wives, much like their elite sisters in the South and the Southwest, were expected to play a complementary "maternalistic" role managing the household and engaging in charitable activities.[50]

As to life before marriage, in stark contrast to daughters of Japanese plantation workers, who often had to start working at an early age, young unmarried haole daughters were conspicuously unengaged in any gainful pursuits. As explained by Margaret Catton, a prominent haole social worker:

> In that era it was the exception, rather than the rule, for island [haole] girls to go to college, and unless they needed money, they did not take jobs. It was a period, too, when domestic help was both plentiful and cheap, and girls of the leisure class had little responsibility in the way of household duties. Until they married, girls graced their parents' homes and drove their mothers by horse and carriage to market or to make formal calls. They gave parties—riding, swimming, tennis, and dancing. Taking their sewing, embroidery or crocheting, the young ladies of Honolulu would spend an afternoon or day with one another. They had picnics, card parties, and tea parties.

Catton adds, "Girls of that time, brought up with a sense of noblesse oblige, also gave many hours in volunteer service to church or community."[51]

FOR WORKERS, clustering according to haole-perceived race/ethnic category encouraged the formation and maintenance of old and new ethnic identities among the diverse plantation workforce. Planters housed workers in ethnically specific housing compounds and assigned them to ethnically homogeneous work gangs. This grouping made it possible for some workers to sustain native languages, prepare food in native style, and modify living quarters into some semblance of homes they had left, and as mentioned previously, submerged groups such as Okinawans into broader ethnic categories.

For Japanese workers, a Japanese-style bath—an *ofuro*—for nightly bathing was the most basic necessity. As they became more settled the Japanese began to build community institutions, forming sumo and sports clubs, sponsoring entertainers, and establishing Buddhist temples and Japanese-language schools. Some planters contributed funds to help build temples and foreign-language schools, even though these institutions might seem contrary to Americanism, because they were seen as pacifying the workers. Although planters resisted the imposition of taxes to pay for public schools, they viewed donations to ethnic institutions as consistent with their roles as benevolent patrons.[52]

Ethnic clustering and donations to community institutions were not just for the workers' comfort, however. Plantation managers also wanted to encourage separation among groups and play them off against one another. Concerned that reliance on any one group gave it too much leverage, managers continually sought to "diversify" the workforce. A labor commissioner report of 1902 details a number of such attempts and concludes, "Hardly a locality in the world exists where there is a surplus of unskilled labor that has not been visited and investigated by Hawaiian labor agents."[53]

Despite planters' efforts to play groups off against one another, and workers' own efforts to build distinct cultural communities, the shared experience of plantation life forged a sense of commonality among workers. Whatever their cultural differences, all were subordinate to the haole. Plantation workers developed a local culture that drew on their various traditions and on the daily practices of plantation life, including a distinct local cuisine that drew on techniques and foods from all groups, often adapted to make use of available foodstuffs. They developed a common dialect, derived from the pidgin English used by overseers and traders to deal with Asian traders and workers. This local dialect had a distinctive syntax, intonation, and accent, with words borrowed from all of the languages of the plantation camp. Use of this "local" dialect marked off plantation workers from the haoles, who spoke standard English. John Reinecke commented that the "sharpest racial and social line drawn between haoles and non-haoles is thus to a considerable extent reinforced by the linguistic line between them." For local youth "it is considered snobbish and presumptuous to speak without the Island intonation, accentuation, and other peculiarities. This is being a 'black haole.'"[54]

The lives of "local" women, including the Japanese, contrasted sharply with those of haole women. Especially within Japanese American families, economic provision was an expected aspect of wives' duties. Edna Oshiro reported that ten days after her mother arrived in 1922 she "went to work in the sugar cane fields. She did all kinds of work, including *hanawai* (irrigation of the fields), cutting grass (commonly referred to as *hoe hana*), planting cane slips, flume cane (sending cane to the mill in the water flumes), and *pula* (cutting cane slips) . . . despite the hard work, Mother kept right on working until a month before her first child was born in August, 1924. In November, 1925 a second daughter was born. But Mother did not stay home for long. When the baby was four months old, Mother went back to work for six months, because of some family reverses."[55] Oshiro does not mention whether her mother took her infants to the fields, but contemporary observers saw mothers carrying infants on their backs in the fields. A mainland journalist described working mothers making tents of cloth and placing their babies in them on the ground, where they attracted swarms of flies.[56] Despite the fact that they worked the same hours as men, women remained responsible for childcare and housework, which had to be fit around their work schedules.

Mothers who did not work in the fields often earned income by providing domestic services to bachelor workers: taking them in as boarders, cooking their meals, and laundering and ironing their clothes. There were ethnic differences in the economic role of mothers. In Japanese families, mothers were more likely to work to enable children to attend school, while among the Portuguese, children were more likely to be employed to enable mothers to stay at home. A 1901 survey of 225 families of various nationalities found that among the Japanese "the wife was almost without exception engaged in work outside the home," but that in all other nationality groups, including the Portuguese and Native Hawaiians, wives were for the most part "engaged solely in home duties." However, the data table shows that while 51 out of 62 of the Japanese families reported "income from wives," a large proportion of the European and Native Hawaiian families reported income from "boarders and other sources." The authors of the report ignore the fact that keeping boarders requires considerable labor—cleaning, washing, and cooking—which almost certainly was performed by wives. We may infer that many European and Native Hawaiian women reported as "engaged solely in home duties" were actually contributing to family income through their labor. Inclusion of these women would lead to the conclusion that a substantial proportion of wives in all worker groups were bringing in income.[57]

The degree to which Japanese women were engaged in field labor is nonetheless striking. By 1910, out of 43,917 Japanese field workers, 24,093 were women and children. Of all female field workers, Japanese women constituted 80 percent. Japanese women were clearly not thought to be subject to physical limitations due to sex. Haoles apparently included Asian women in their notion that some races were inherently suited to labor that would have broken most white men. Officials of the U.S. Department of Labor responsible for monitoring labor in Hawaii reported extensive employment of women and children, but did not advocate special protections for them.[58] In any case, federal laws regulating hours and working conditions for women in most industries specifically exempted agriculture and domestic service.

Domestic service continued to be an important area of employment for immigrant Japanese and their daughters both on the plantation and in town. Because it was one of the few situations in which dominant and subordinate groups interacted in the private sphere of the household, it allows us to look at the way race/gender identities and meanings were created and contested in daily interactions. The availability of women for domestic service was ensured by the feudal system of dependence and paternalism which gave owners and managers considerable sway over workers and their families. Lind observes:

It has been a usual practice for a department head or a member of the managerial staff of the plantation to indicate to members of his work group that his household is in need of domestic help and to expect them to provide a wife or daughter to fill the need. Under the conditions that have prevailed in the past, the worker has felt obligated to make a member of his own family available for such service if required, since his own position and advancement depend upon keeping the good-will of his boss. Not infrequently, girls have been prevented from pursuing a high school or college education because someone on the supervisory staff has needed a servant and it has seemed inadvisable for the family to disregard the claim.[59]

Even when they moved to town from the plantation, Japanese women found that the most readily available jobs were positions as maids, nursemaids, laundresses, cooks, and housekeepers. Many Japanese high school students spared their families from having to support them by working as live-in "school girls" (servants). Students from other islands who wanted to attend high school or college on Oahu had to come to Honolulu and take domestic positions as babysitters, housekeepers, and maids to pay for their room and board.

Relations between mistresses and female employees retained the feudal character of plantation relations. The servant was intimately involved in the household, and her status was tied to the status of the family she served. In many cases workers reported feelings of affection for the employing family, particularly for children. Some mistresses reciprocated by showing an interest in the schoolgirl's studies and friends. The more usual pattern was one of asymmetry. The servant saw all the intimate details of daily life and the employers' faults and foibles and sometimes petty meanness. In contrast, employers knew little about (and often did not care to know about) the servant's personal life, which existed only as a vague aspect outside the boundaries of their concerns.[60]

Some haole women felt entitled to the services of Asian women, who presumably existed to serve them. They viewed quitting a job as a form of betrayal. An interviewer reported that a Japanese woman and her mother were working as full-time maids for a haole woman who kept piling on more and more work until the daughter became distressed at her mother's being so overworked. When her complaint about this went unheeded for some weeks, the two women decided to quit. The mistress became infuriated at this announcement, shouting: "You Japs speak of loyalty, you make me sick! None of you can be depended upon! I knew this was going to happen when the 'sneaking' mama-san [another Japanese maid] next door first started visiting you."[61]

Despite haole women's beliefs about the natural subservience of Japanese girls and women, nisei schoolgirls reported feeling resentment at being treated like servants. One student wrote about this in detail: "Never in my life did I have such a 'cooped-up' feeling; as if I were bound to something. My independent spirit seemed to gradually [be] taking wings, and I felt as though my individuality was propped on top of those wings." Another domestic worker reported: "The foremost thing that hit me was an inferiority complex . . . I felt this unpleasant feeling when guests came to the house where I was working in. I was nothing but a housemaid, not to be seen or heard. I felt as if the sons, who were younger than I am, of these two families looked down at me."[62]

Contestation and Resistance

Haole efforts at control of workers were in some sense responses to resistance from those being controlled. Planters frequently complained that the Japanese were "difficult" to deal with compared to Chinese, Native Hawaiians, and Portuguese. Though their characterizations of the Japanese were colored by their own interests, we can still look at haole complaints as evidence of Japanese resistance, especially smaller-scale cases of face-to-face and hidden resistance that would otherwise be difficult to document. Many themes that recur over and over in various documents and reports are encapsulated in the following uncited report quoted by Porteus:

> "From the outset," says Coman in her review of the labour situation, "they were difficult to deal with, proving to be restless and self-assertive to a degree hitherto unknown in the canefields of Hawaii. They were moreover remarkably clannish, clubbing together for the championship of their common interests in a way that was distinctly embarrassing. They showed no disposition to marry Hawaiians and while readily adopting American dress and ways, cherished allegiance to their native land with peculiar tenacity. They found their way into skilled trades even more rapidly than the Chinese."[63]

Thus, from the perspective of the haole, the Japanese were being difficult when they did not accept their subordinate place and when they attempted to "better themselves," as well as when they persisted in maintaining a distinct cultural community and did not marry out and when they stood up for their rights and fought back, whether individually or collectively.

Despite the planters' view of the Japanese as clannish, within the Japanese community itself, class, ethnic, and political schisms fostered a certain amount of tension and conflict. As Eileen Tamura points out, the Japanese came from a hierarchical society. Those with more education and from "better families" tended to look down on others. There was also division between Japanese from the home islands (the Naichi) and those from Okinawa, which had been a separate entity until annexed by Japan in 1879. Okinawans, who made up about 14 percent of the immigrant population, had their own language and a distinct culture. Their differences made them targets of Naichi discrimination.[64] Okinawans recall being taunted by Naichi children, who called them unclean and pig eaters. Naichi parents forbade their sons and daughters to marry Okinawans, while Okinawan parents warned their children that if they married Naichi they would be subject to degradation by their in-laws.[65]

Building Separate Spaces

The building of formal and informal organizations and institutions was important as a defense against the cultural oppression experienced by the Japanese. Ethnic associations connected immigrants with their home country and with one another and offered a more expansive identity and more respect than could be gotten at work. Through leadership in an organization, donation to a community fund, or contribution of labor to a building project, ordinary workers could gain status and recognition. Tamura describes the plethora of "spaces" the issei (those of the immigrant generation) built and the nisei (the Hawaii-born children of immigrants) continued:

> [They] organized Buddhist and prefectural associations, held bon dances to honor their ancestors, celebrated the emperor's birthday with sumo wrestling matches, and welcomed the new year in the Japanese way. As among Japanese on the mainland, a strong sense of group solidarity enabled Hawaii's issei to look to their

ethnic community for social and economic support. One example of this was the practice of tanomoshi, or rotating credit associations adapted in Japan from the Chinese hui. Like the Chinese hui, and the Filipino hulugan, the tanomoshi helped immigrants finance expenses they could not otherwise afford, and its effectiveness depended on trust, honor and community solidarity.[66]

One major formal institution was the Buddhist temple, a central site of community life. Despite opposition from Christians, plantation managers initially supported the building of temples. According to the U.S. Labor Commissioner's report for 1902, managers believed "the moral and social influence of the priests among the laborers to be good." The first temple was established in 1889, and by 1909 there were 33 temples of the two main sects, Hongwanji and Jodo Mission. Buddhism continued to attract adherents; by 1937 there were 107 temples representing 12 sects and enrolling some 39,719 registrants.[67] The issei generation also established Shintoism, the ancient religion of Japan, building shrines throughout the islands. While there were converts to Christianity, they remained a tiny minority, perhaps 2–3 percent of the Japanese in Hawaii through the 1920s.[68]

As anti-Japanese sentiment waxed in the wake of a 1909 strike and as the size of the American-born generation grew, Buddhist leaders began adapting Buddhism toward more American forms by emulating Christian churches. Temples installed pews and organs and held Sunday services, which included sermons and the singing of *gathas*, religious songs patterned after Christian hymns. Temples also conducted Sunday schools and sponsored Young Women's and Young Men's Buddhist Associations, patterned after the YWCA and YMCA. The YWBA and YMBA (later merged into the Young Buddhist Association or YBA) sponsored lectures, classes in arts and crafts and martial arts, oratorical contests, and social events. They were important training grounds for nisei leadership and provided forums for discussion of social and political issues. Island-wide and inter-island conferences helped forge ties among nisei in different plantation communities.[69]

A second major community institution was the Japanese-language school. The early issei pioneers expected to eventually return to Japan and wanted their children to be prepared for life there. The first such school was established in 1892 on Maui, and by 1900 there were 10 schools enrolling 1,500 students. A decade later 140 schools were teaching over 7,000 students. Some schools were sponsored by Christian churches and Buddhist temples, others by parents. As with the temples, plantation managers considered the schools a stabilizing influence and supported them with free land and financial help. Funding was provided by student tuition and by donations from members of the community. By 1920 close to 20,000 students, 98 percent of all Japanese children attending public schools, were enrolled in Japanese-language schools. The percentage dipped in the 1920s as a result of attacks by Americanists, but rebounded in the 1930s. As the orientation of the Japanese shifted to being permanent settlers, the schools were no longer viewed as preparing children for living in Japan but as helping retain Japanese culture in Hawaii. Schools were central sites for marking Japanese holidays. Until the 1920s children were kept home from public schools on those days and entire families gathered to celebrate holidays at the schools.[70]

A third important institution was the Japanese-language press. When they arrived in Hawaii, issei men had an average of four to six years of schooling and women two to five years. They were functionally literate and valued learning regardless of their occupational status. They read and kept afloat an amazing number of newspapers. Between 1900 and 1941 a total of eighty-six Japanese-language publications appeared, nineteen of which survived ten years or more. At the midpoint, in 1920, there were thirteen newspapers and journals. Like other immigrant publications, the Japanese-language press kept the community informed about events in the homeland and preserved a sense of connection there; however, it also helped acculturate immigrants by "informing them of American ways, interpreting events around them, and encouraging integration in the larger community." Although taking varied, often conflicting positions on issues, the press encouraged community discussion by editorializing about working and living conditions on the plantations. During World War I the newspapers unanimously endorsed the Liberty Bond campaign and urged the nisei to give up dual citizenship, and after the war the major papers, led by the *Nippu Jiji*, began publishing English-language sections to reach a wider audience.[71]

Workplace Resistance

Plantation laborers, whether Chinese, Japanese, Native Hawaiian, Puerto Rican, Portuguese, or Filipino and whether male or female, were far from docile. Under the brutal and relentless conditions, Japanese laborers, like other plantation workers, sometimes resorted to violence, especially against overseers. Chinzen Kinzo reports being stopped just in time from delivering a fatal karate chop to a luna who had whipped him. In 1900 striking Japanese workers wielded hoes to fight lunas trying to evict them. Setting fire to sugar mills or cane fields was another form of revenge, one that was particularly potent because of the cost exacted.[72]

The more common forms of resistance, however, were indirect, aimed at slowing down work and evading the constant surveillance of the lunas. Managers and overseers complained about the slowness of workers, their taking of frequent breaks, smoking, and gossiping. Workers became experts in deception. Jack Hall, a haole luna, recorded in his diary his frustration at trying to supervise women workers on a Kohala plantation:

> Hoeing was more pleasant and would have been all right except for the fact that the gangs on this work were largely composed of Japanese wahines [women] and it always seemed impossible to keep them together, especially if the fields were not level. The consequence was that the damsels were usually scattered all over the place and as many as possible were out of sight in the gulches or dips in the field where they could not be seen, where they would calmly sit and smoke their little metal pipes until the luna appeared on the skyline, when they would be busy as bees.[73]

Malingering was another classic strategy, as workers feigned illness or invented a death in the family or some other problem to get excused from work. Ronald Takaki notes that some Japanese laborers resorted to drinking shoyu (soy sauce) to raise their temperatures.[74]

Like their counterparts on plantations in the South who sang while working, issei workers composed folk songs (called *hole hole bushi*) while toiling in the fields. *Hole hole*, from the Hawaiian for "peeling," refers to stripping cane, a job done primarily by women, and *bushi* is Japanese for "tune." Hole hole bushi expressed the workers' sorrow and pain, while lyrics also allowed workers to comment critically on the plantation system and the lunas.

> Wonderful Hawaii, or so I heard.
> One look and it seems like Hell.
> The manager's the Devil and
> His lunas are demons.[75]

> The only reason I'm doing
> This tough and painful hole hole work
> Is for the sake of my wife and children
> Who live back home.

> Those who curry favor and spur us to work
> For mere extra ten cents
> Better be bitten by a dog
> And killed.

> Two contract periods
> Have gone by
> Those who do not return
> Will end up as fertilizer
> For the cane.[76]

Women's hole hole bushi were especially apt to comment on their exploitation and double day:

> My husband cuts the cane
> I do the hole hole
> By sweat and tears
> We get by.[77]

> It's starting to pour
> There goes my laundry
> My baby is crying
> And the rice just burned.[78]

> Why settle for 35 cents
> Doing *hole hole* all day,
> When I can make a dollar
> Sleeping with that *pake*.[79]

Perhaps the most common form of resistance was "voting with one's feet." During the era of contract labor, many workers fled before the end of the contract period. Planters employed agents to track down and bring back "deserters" and instituted passbooks that any worker found away from the plantation would have to show. Once the contract era ended, Japanese workers could move to the city or migrate to the mainland. Between 1898 and 1907 an estimated thirty to forty thousand issei—one out of every five—departed for the mainland. The flow was stemmed in 1907, when President Theodore Roosevelt, at the behest of anti-Japanese forces in California, issued an executive order barring entry to the mainland United States by Japanese workers from Hawaii, Mexico, and Canada.[80]

Protests and Strikes

When given the opportunity, Japanese workers demonstrated a willingness to confront employers to register their grievances. The very first group from Japan, who were recruited by labor agents in 1868, began lodging complaints with the Hawaii Bureau of Immigration within a month of their arrival. Of the 149 emigrants, 40 returned to Japan before the end of their contracts, 39 of whom signed a complaint charging the planters with violation of contracts and cruelty. This early experiment was deemed a failure and immigration was not resumed until the mid-1880s under agreements secured by Robert Walker Irwin, Hawaiian consul general and immigration agent in Japan. Irwin arranged for the importation of some 29,000 workers between 1885 and 1904. The first group of 676 men, women, and children arrived in 1885, and again there were "incidents" that had to be mediated by a Japanese "inspector" of labor employed by Irwin. In 1886, 50 of 92 workers on Koloa plantation were jailed for refusing to work, and in 1890, 170 workers on Heeia plantation rebelled against the lunas.[81] Between 1890 and 1899 the major Hawaiian newspapers reported 30 "disturbances" by Japanese workers, including marches and strikes, and many more incidents must have gone unreported.[82]

Japanese workers expressed their pent-up frustration and hopes for the future by engaging in demonstrations for several days when Hawaii became a U.S. territory in June 1900. Workers understood well that annexation meant the end of the hated contract-labor system. At a mass march in Honolulu demonstrators carried a banner declaring, "We are a Free People." All plantation activity was brought to a halt. U.S. officials chose to interpret these actions not as real strikes, "as no real demands were made by the laborers regarding their employment. It was merely a pause, during which the laborers seemed to expect some sort of readjustment in their relations with employers." In fact, there had been three major strikes—at Pioneer Mill, Olowalu plantation, and Spreckelsville plantation (all on Maui), in the months before the Organic Act took effect. In each of these strikes workers made specific demands for higher payment for accident victims, shorter workdays, and higher wages. In the remaining six months of 1900, Japanese field hands and cane workers engaged in at least 18 further strikes, the largest of which involved 1,350 strikers.[83]

The walkouts in celebration of annexation signaled growing worker militancy, as protest began to take more organized forms. Six major strikes, each involving more than a thousand workers, occurred between July 1904 and January 1906. The involvement of women in these protests is seen in some of the demands. In a December 1904 strike on the Waialua plantation, one of the demands was "that the white overseer of the women's gang be discharged upon the ground that he favored the pretty girls in assigning work."[84]

The first cross-plantation strike was an island-wide action by Japanese workers on Oahu in 1909. This strike differed from previous more limited actions in that it was spearheaded by an educated elite and supported by an inter-island network of voluntary organizations, newspapers, temples, and business associations. In stating their demands, leaders of the new movement (the Higher Wages Association) displayed a full command of Americanist labor movement discourse. Leaders called for "full fledged" manhood and the workers' right to a "just reward for their labor." In a letter to the Hawaii Sugar Planters Association, they demanded a rise in wages from $18.00 to $22.50 per month, the amount paid to Portuguese and Puerto Rican workers. Declaring that "the Japanese here are not coolies," the HWA proclaimed the Japanese the "equal of any man before the law" and thus deserving "the same consideration as any other labor." Echoing the larger labor movement, the HWA called for a "living wage" to maintain families and dependents in "a decent respectable manner."[85]

Instead of agreeing to negotiate, planters conducted a propaganda campaign through the press. As positions hardened, Japanese workers on Kauai, Maui, and Hawaii as well as business and social organizations pledged support for the HWA. In May, when workers from individual plantations presented their own petitions and were rebuffed, the strikes began, eventually encompassing all of the major plantations on Oahu and involving some seven thousand workers.

Planters quickly mounted a counteroffensive. The HSPA trustees signed a compact to share the cost of any losses from strikes on individual plantations. Plantation owners began mass evictions from plantation housing, using police to turn workers out. More than five thousand adults found shelter in Honolulu in vacant buildings, theaters, or private homes or camped out in A'ala Park. Mass outdoor kitchens were set up to feed thousands of evictees. Yasutaro Soga recalled: "The city of Honolulu was like a battlefield . . . Women volunteers turned out in full force and helped in caring for [the strikers]." Planters hired Chinese, Portuguese, Native Hawaiian, and Korean workers to replace the Japanese, paying more than twice the rate the HWA had asked for. They also had strike leaders arrested and jailed on conspiracy charges. The strikers held out for four months but were finally exhausted by the prolonged encampment and the separation from their leaders. In early August representatives of the HWA met and voted to end the strike.[86]

Four months later the planters quietly raised the wage rate and abolished wage differentials by nationality. Observers of Hawaiian labor history conclude that the results of the strike were both discouraging and exhilarating for the workers: it accelerated both the move of Japanese out of plantation labor and simultaneously the movement up into more skilled and white-collar positions for those who stayed on the plantation. It also helped politicize and further Americanize the participants.[87]

A second major island-wide strike, in 1920, united Japanese and Filipino workers. Sparked by inflation and the worsening standard of living in the aftermath of World War I, it took place in the context of rising trade unionism by longshoremen, fishermen, telephone operators, and ironworkers and molders. Unlike the 1909 strike, which had been led by educated professionals and the vernacular press, the 1920 strike was instigated by leaders indigenous to the plantations. The Japanese Federation of Labor brought together worker associations from each of the plantations. The Federation grew out of the organizing activities of the Young Men's Buddhist Associations, whose membership consisted of young men from plantations. Filipino workers were organized under a separate union, the Filipino Federation of Labor.[88]

Overall, 8,300 workers representing 77 percent of the plantation labor force on Oahu went on strike. As in the 1909 strike, women were active and visible, not just as supporters, but as strikers. In addition to higher wages, an eight-hour day for field workers and ten for millhands, overtime pay, old age insurance, and a greater share of the crop price for tenant growers, the union demanded an eight-week paid maternity leave for women.[89]

Two weeks after the start of the strike, planters evicted all strikers and their families, some 12,020 adults and children. The union quickly set up tent cities, rented buildings, and opened kitchens. The mass encampment occurred in the midst of a raging influenza epidemic that eventually killed an estimated 55 Japanese and 95 Filipinos. Planters again employed scabs of varying ethnicity and carried out a vigorous anti-Japanese campaign in the press. Despite pressure from the planters, Governor Curtis Iaukea, a Native Hawaiian, stoutly refused to call out any troops. In April, responding to the anti-Japanese propaganda orchestrated by the planters, the Japanese Federation of Labor voted to change its name to the Hawaii Laborers' Association and applied for membership in the American Federation of Labor. The union mobilized support throughout the Islands, collecting and disbursing a strike fund of $600,000 and raising another $300,000 of in-kind donations. Still, it could not hold out indefinitely, and on July 1 the leaders finally capitulated. Afterward the owners quietly raised wages by 50 percent, began paying bonuses on a monthly rather than yearly basis, and expanded recreational and welfare benefits. However, strike leaders were blacklisted and participants denied promotion to higher jobs. One outcome of the strike, then, was to spur the exodus of more politicized workers out of plantation labor.[90]

Education and Americanization

By the mid-1920s, with immigration from most of Asia cut off and the U.S. Congress contemplating measures to stem immigration from the Philippines, the planters had to rely more heavily on native-born, and therefore citizen, labor of Asian descent. In 1927, for the first time, the number of native-born youth was sufficient to meet the needs for agricultural labor. Confronted with these shifting demographics, planters had to rethink their strategies for securing and maintaining labor. The realization that there was a rising generation of Hawaii-born Japanese who were citizens by birthright also changed the dominant discourse on race. During most of the nineteenth century and into the 1910s, the haole elite had subscribed to a belief in the natural inferiority of the Oriental. This belief justified their rule and also excused such practices as flogging and the enforcement and sale of labor contracts. By the 1920s, as haoles observed Japanese "invad[ing] the social and political life of the islands," some haoles began to worry that, far from being inferior, the Japanese had a greater capacity for hard work and study than Caucasians. Some haoles advocated restricting the mobility of Orientals to curb this unfair "racial superiority." A significant minority, led by descendants of missionaries, saw the problem as one of culture and sought to "uplift" the Oriental population by "haolifying" or "Americanizing" it.[91]

The shift in emphasis from controlling noncitizen immigrant labor to Americanizing the nisei generation marked the transition from categorical exclusion to stratified citizenship. The nisei could not be denied citizenship, but perhaps they could be molded to occupy a permanent subordinate position. They were already rapidly acculturating on their own, although not in the ways that the haoles wished, by joining labor unions, engaging in strikes, pursuing education, starting businesses, and entering the professions. In Fuchs's view, the Americanizers did not agree precisely on what Americanization meant, but at the least it meant "attending Christian churches, playing American sports, and eating apple pie; there was nearly complete accord that it did not mean labor unions, political action, and criticism of the social order of the Islands." According to Tamura, some haoles talked about inculcating the ideals of democracy and representative government and freedom, but such views were in the minority: "What Americanizers really wanted was for the nisei to give undivided loyalty to the United States and discard all vestiges of Japanese culture. They also insisted that the nisei read, write and speak Standard English, become Christians, obey the law, and be good plantation workers."[92] Accordingly, Americanization efforts were three-pronged: first, wiping out all vestiges of foreign and nondominant local culture; second, inculcating American culture and values; and third, constraining nisei ambitions and keeping the nisei in agricultural labor.

Efforts to eliminate alien influences focused on "cutting off fresh supplies of Asiatic immigrants," suppressing foreign languages, and discouraging forms of nonstandard English. Haole planters who had earlier supported the building of Buddhist temples and foreign-language schools now viewed them as subversive. Indeed, schools and temples had become sites for organizing resistance. During the 1920 island-wide sugar workers' strike, Japanese-language schools and the vernacular press came under attack by the major Honolulu newspapers, the *Star-Bulletin* and the *Advertiser.* The *Star-Bulletin* accused the "priests of Asiatic Paganism," made up of foreign-language teachers, editors of Japanese newspapers, and Buddhist priests, of seeking to gain control of Hawaii's industry. It declared that Hawaii must remain "in the hands of Anglo-Saxons whose brains and means have made the Territory what it is."[93] Tellingly, Filipinos, who were equally active in the strike but not seen as a major political threat, were not subject to this kind of racist attack.

Soon after the strike was broken, the territorial legislature passed laws to hobble foreign-language schools by requiring tests of teachers' knowledge of American culture, forbidding the enrollment of children before they had completed three years in an American school, limiting the hours of instruction to six per week, and directing that the courses and texts be selected by public school officials. It also passed legislation requiring Japanese-language newspapers to publish translations of all articles, a requirement which would have bankrupted the vernacular press. The restrictions on language schools exacerbated divisions within the Japanese community between those who favored accommodation and those who supported a more militant position. In the end, a group of Japanese challenged the restrictions in court, and the laws were found to be unconstitutional by the U.S. Supreme Court in 1927.[94]

On another front, there were concerted attacks on the local dialect. Pressure was exerted on the schools to discourage the speaking of Hawaiian Creole (pidgin). Separate "English Standard" schools were established in the 1920s as a response to haole objections to their children being educated in schools with Asian majorities. Entrance to English Standard schools was based on examination in English skills. Ostensibly their purpose was to encourage Americanization, but their actual result was segregated schooling. Virtually all "Caucasians" in the public schools were enrolled in the English Standard schools, while only a small number of Japanese were able to gain entrance into them. The *Hawaii Hochi* newspaper attacked the segregated system, calling the school board a "Jim Crow" board.[95]

Related to the establishment of English Standard Schools were efforts to inculcate American culture, values, and lifestyles. Although these efforts were influenced by Americanization programs on the mainland, there were two significant differences. First was a difference in the timing and duration of Americanizing fever. On the mainland, Americanization efforts targeting eastern and southern Europeans had begun in the 1910s, peaked in the mid-teens, and died out by the mid-1920s when immigration from these regions slowed to a trickle. While the Southwest received federal support for Americanization of Mexicans, Hawaii was not included in federal programs. Americanization efforts in Hawaii were locally organized; they began later, starting in the early 1920s and continuing until World War II. As on the mainland, the timing of Americanization efforts in Hawaii was related to anxieties about perceived threats to the dominant cultural system. In Hawaii the threat loomed in the 1920s as the nisei generation grew to adulthood and was projected to become a plurality in the electorate.[96]

A second difference was in the targets of Americanization. Mainland programs, including efforts in the Southwest, targeted women in their roles as mothers, but Japanese women were not the focus in Hawaii, possibly because they were seen as inassimilable aliens. Instead, efforts were directed at the Hawaii-born children through the public schools. Curricula were fashioned to focus on American history, civics, and literature, as well as music, drawing, and vocational work. Science and mathematics were not stressed because they did not inculcate patriotism. A nisei teacher in rural Oahu recalled: "We always had patriotic programs. In the morning the whole school assembled and we used to have the pledge to the flag and we used to sing patriotic songs—everyday."[97]

The focus on Americanization through schools was consistent with the missionary heritage of a substantial portion of the haole elite, who supported education for the masses as a form of racial uplift. According to Fuchs, the haole plantation oligarchy did not favor public education but did not actively attempt to prevent its development. Too busy to get involved, they left it to "do-gooders," often women descendants of missionaries, to run school committees. These haole women, like their mainland counterparts, engaged in charitable and educational efforts. For example, Mrs. Baldwin, the wife of the "Lord of Maui," established the Baldwin House, which ran a kindergarten, a library, night school classes, a high school, and a language program. She also helped organize the Maui Aid Association, which set up "American Citizenship Evening Schools."[98]

Also aiding the growth of public education was the local elite's sensitivity to mainland views of Hawaii as backward. They were eager to prove that Hawaii was civilized and truly American. Thus, when a U.S. Department of Education survey of the Hawaii schools in 1920 called for extensive reforms, local officials quickly acted to carry out the recommendations. They increased liberal arts education, following the precepts of the then-influential progressive education movement of John Dewey. Mainland educators were recruited to administer and teach in the public schools, and many fine schools, including the first public high school, McKinley in Honolulu, provided liberal arts education to the children of immigrants.[99]

Despite these strides, public schools remained seriously underfunded. Haoles and others who could afford the fees sent their children to private schools. For the entire period prior to 1941, Hawaii had the highest proportion of children enrolled in private school of any U.S. state or territory. Since the haole elite did not make use of public schools, they were loath to support them with their taxes. Also, as the nisei eagerly pursued education, including high school and college, some segments of the planter group began to declare that too much education would spoil them for plantation labor. These planters lobbied to limit education beyond the eighth grade. In 1928 the Department of Public Instruction, responding to criticisms by plantation industry leaders, ruled that beginning in 1930, 20 percent of junior high school graduates would be denied entry into high school. The effect, much to the chagrin of the planters and the dismay of public school educators, was to swell private secondary enrollments. Haole planters and property owners also complained about paying the lion's share of taxes for educating "Orientals," whose parents did not for the most part own property. During the 1920s proposals to charge tuition for high school were advocated by the Hawaii Chamber of Commerce, representatives of the Planters Association, and even a former president of the University of Hawaii. In 1933 the State Education Board did institute a $10 tuition for attending public high school, a considerable sum for poor families.[100]

Some haole educators and business leaders expressed concern that the nisei were overly ambitious when it came to education and aspiring to white-collar and professional employment. In a parallel with the conflict between Booker T. Washington and W. E. B. Du Bois over black education and aspirations, the Reverend Takie Okumura, a Congregationalist minister, and Fred Kinzaburo Makino, a newspaper publisher, clashed over Japanese educational aspirations. In 1921, in the aftermath of the bitter sugar strike and in the midst of the assault on the Japanese schools, Okumura, backed by sugar plantation interests, began a six-year campaign to Americanize the issei and nisei. He admonished the Japanese to "go more than halfway" to dispel suspicions and improve their relations with the haoles. He organized meetings of plantation workers to urge them to "adopt American ways, become Christians, remain on the plantation, and encourage their children to do likewise." While urging nisei to be 100 percent American, Okumura advised them to hold on to the Japanese values of duty, responsibility, and loyalty, which he saw as compatible with Americanization. He also opposed legal challenges to the territorial restrictions on foreign-language schools. Starting in 1927 Okumura organized a series of New American Conferences, at which haoles and Japanese businessmen and leaders spoke to nisei men and women delegates of community organizations about issues related to Americanization. The general tenor of the messages can be gauged by the address delivered at the first conference by David Crawford, president of the University of Hawaii (and older brother of the territorial superintendent of schools). He opined that "too many young people of Japanese and Chinese ancestry consider agriculture beneath them—they want white collar jobs," when it was "obvious" that they "must go into agricultural industry—sugar, pineapple, coffee and general farming." Three years later he admonished the delegates, "do not count too much on education to do too much for you, do not take it too seriously."[101]

Okumura's main critic was Makino, who had vigorously taken up the cause of the Japanese in their struggles against discrimination and labor exploitation. Among other actions, he had helped lead the sugar strike of 1909, headed the legal challenge to the territorial laws aimed at destroying the Japanese-language schools, and editorialized in his newspaper against injustice and discrimination against the Japanese. Makino agreed that the Japanese should retain aspects of Japanese culture while adopting American values, but stressed the importance of justice and fair play. Subscribing to the dominant discourse of white manliness, Makino noted: "Americans bow to no master and cringe to no superior. They are straight shooters and are very apt to say exactly what they think, because they are not afraid of anyone." He urged the nisei not to be obsequious: "When the young Japanese are able to look their white brother squarely in the eye and tell them to 'get out of the way,' they will find out whether there is any race discrimination that can hinder them or keep them from success." In a later critique of the New American Conferences, Makino said the conferences were attempts at "mental grooming" of the nisei through speeches in which "selected 'pap'" fell from the "lips of big shots" to plant the "right views."[102]

While the debate was roiling the Japanese community, haole public officials were taking action to allay the concerns of haole educators and businessmen who felt that too many nisei students were pursuing liberal studies. Using newly available federal funds, the Department of Public Instruction expanded vocational training programs aimed at instilling respect for the dignity of manual labor. Auto mechanics, machine shop, carpentry, and electrical work were offered for boys, and dressmaking, cafeteria and restaurant service, and lauhala weaving for girls. "Homemaking" programs for girls were actually intended to train them as maids, "the rationale," as one official put it, "being that many students worked as maids while attending school and would continue to do so after graduation." The greatest emphasis was on vocational agriculture. In one program boys over fourteen attended classes for half the day and spent the other half in the sugar fields. In the another program high school boys studied coffee production, poultry and hog raising, and gardening.[103]

Nisei responses to these agricultural education programs paralleled the reactions of Mexican American girls to domestic work training programs in the Southwest: although the programs were offered in some twenty schools, they were under-enrolled. The nisei disputed the notion that their futures lay in plantation labor. From their perspective, issei parents had put up with plantation work so their children could live a better life. Moreover, nisei students were already familiar with manual labor. Many of them had done field work while going to school and wanted no part of it. A young nisei woman enrolled in normal school said about her experience of field work: "I shed my tears secretly. I thought if I only had the chance, I'll never come back to the fields."[104]

Portents of Things to Come

Young nisei understood all too well the lack of opportunities in plantation labor and aspired to enter skilled crafts and white-collar employment, despite admonitions by haole leaders that such aspirations were unrealistic. The number of Japanese employed in the plantation sector fell from a peak of 31,029 in 1902 to 16,992 in 1922 and to 9,395 by 1932. They also moved up the occupational ladder: Japanese classified as laborers fell from 33,871 in 1916 to 12,754 in 1930.[105]

As the American-born children of immigrants reached adulthood, they added to the citizen population. By 1930, 16 percent of adult Japanese were citizens. The haole oligarchy did not cede control of the political realm without a struggle. The haole-controlled Republican party tried to curb Japanese voting by making registration difficult. Nisei registrants had to "prove" their citizenship by furnishing sworn statements from midwives or other witnesses that they had been born in the Islands. The haole-controlled legislature sought to curtail Japanese political activity by passing a bill requiring any material on politics written in a foreign language to be translated and submitted with the names, residences, and businesses of the authors to the attorney general for approval.[106]

Haoles persisted in their belief that the Japanese, despite Americanization, did not act independently. Just as Mexican workers in the Southwest were accused of being in the thrall of bosses, Japanese laborers in Hawaii were suspected of being controlled by others—in this case the government of Japan. Testifying before members of a U.S. Senate Committee on Immigration in 1920, Hawaii Governor Charles J. McCarthy speculated that Hawaiian-born Japanese were not registering to vote on instruction from the Japanese government. He noted that a thousand Japanese were eligible and surmised that if the policy of the Japanese government changed "and they were all instructed to register and vote, we might be swamped."[107]

Japanese in Hawaii pressed the case for inclusion by demonstrating their civic virtue and displayed their Americanization by fighting for their rights. They subscribed heavily to World War I bonds, published broadsides asserting their patriotism, and lobbied officials. They also engaged in walkouts and strikes, hired lawyers to challenge discriminatory legislation, took officials to court for violating their rights, and lobbied to gain the ears of influential mainlanders. Senator William H. King of Utah, at the U.S. Senate hearing of the Committee on Immigration, told of his fact-finding visit to Hawaii two years previously. He said he had visited homes and found that Japanese women were devoted to their homes and children and kept their households in good condition. He reported that Japanese in good standing complained that not enough attention was given to their Americanization, "but rather there was an effort made to isolate them and to make them feel that they were not welcome as American citizens, and they begged me to use what influence I might have—of course I have none there, not being a resident—to induce the people of Hawaii to extend to them in their schools and in their businesses and other relations a more generous welcome, to the end that they might—those who were Americans who were entitled to American citizenship—they might feel they were a part and trifle of this American Republic."[108]

In the meantime the nisei were becoming aware of the importance of suffrage. As early as 1915 some Japanese leaders were decrying the lack of an electoral voice and urging those eligible to vote to do so. They saw voting as a mark of first-class citizenship and first-class citizenship as the only way to gain respect. In an article entitled "Get Your Right to Vote" in the Japanese-language *Maui Shimbun*, the writer opined: "Treatment by authorities and ordinary individuals differs greatly on whether one has the right to vote or not . . . people with the right to vote are respected among *gaijin* . . . Sometimes even white people who look down on Japanese treat those with the right to vote as first class citizens and try not to treat them shamefully." Makino and other leaders organized a movement, which they publicized in Makino's newspaper, *Hawaii Hochi*, to assist nisei to have their citizenship certified. In an editorial headlined "Citizenship! Citizenship! Reporting to Those Obtaining Citizenship," the writer warned that the territorial government was "posturing" to stop accepting applications, and declared: "The movement to gain citizenship is a pressing task and we cannot let our guard down for even one day. We must rally those of us who have the right to citizenship and walk together toward our goal through legal means."[109]

As the nisei generation grew to maturity in the 1920s and 1930s, the number of nisei registered voters rose dramatically. In 1920 only 658 of the 26,335 registered voters in Hawaii were nisei. One factor exacerbating the low numbers was that only 57 women were registered, a much smaller proportion than in other ethnic groups. Nonetheless, by 1930 nisei made up 7,017 out of a total of 52,149 registered voters, and by 1936 they made up about a quarter of the registered electorate, the largest voting bloc in Hawaii.[110]

By the end of the 1930s the fears of the haole elite were being realized. It was clear that U.S. citizens of Asian descent would make up the majority of the labor force and citizenry of Hawaii in the future. The U.S. Labor Commissioner reported that citizen labor on plantations had risen from 12 percent in 1930 to 45 percent in 1939. Overall, four-fifths of the population were citizens. The Commissioner warned that conditions that had been "acceptable" to illiterate alien labor would not be so to citizen labor. His 1939 report noted some improvement in material conditions, in wage levels, housing, recreation, medical care, and mechanization. Less satisfactory was the continuation of paternalistic policies and arbitrary methods of determining wages and benefits. Such practices made workers too dependent on the goodwill of managers. In sum, the Commissioner reported: "The complete dependence of employees upon the plantation in respect to every aspect of the life of the working community makes them less independent than farm laborers on the mainland."[111] Not until the decline of the sugar and plantation economy after World War II would the assumed "dependence" of Japanese and other Asians be shattered and the majority Asian population come to dominate politics.

IN HAWAII, despite the frequent blurring of racial boundaries and the absence of widespread legalized segregation, race was a central organizing principle in the labor system and other social institutions. As in the South and the Southwest, the labor market was stratified by race and gender, and workers were subject to coercive and abusive controls common to colonial labor regimes. There was also considerable spatial and social separation between haoles and Asians, and patterns of interaction underscored racial difference and social hierarchy. Racializing discourse was also rampant as planters constructed elaborate portraits of each group's "racial temperaments" and gender "characteristics."

In terms of citizenship status, we have seen that blacks in the South were excluded as anti-citizens (enemies of the social compact) and Mexicans in the Southwest were excluded on grounds of nationality (including those born on the U.S. side of the border). The excuse used against the Japanese in Hawaii was based on supposed lack of allegiance. The Japanese were not merely "aliens," like other immigrant groups, they were "aliens ineligible for citizenship," incapable of voluntary allegiance to the United States. Ordinary signs of assimilation, such as the adoption of Western dress, were seen as superficial; inside these clothes the Japanese were seen as forever alien. Even second-generation Japanese born in Hawaii were suspected of acting under the direction of the Japanese government.

For the Japanese in Hawaii, as for blacks and Mexicans, education was a central arena of struggle. Planters' resistance to publicly funded education for children of immigrant plantation workers retarded the development of public education beyond the elementary years. During the 1920s the white elite shifted its efforts toward Americanization programs, which involved the closing down of Japanese-language schools, the teaching of patriotic Americanism in public schools, and the expansion of vocational education designed to track Japanese boys into agriculture and girls into domestic work. Like blacks and Mexican Americans, Japanese in Hawaii strove to acquire education despite the barriers. Community activists disputed the notion that maintaining their language and culture was incompatible with Americanism. In this belief they were conjoined with blacks and Mexicans, and indeed other nonwhite Americans, in arguing for a pluralistic nation in which being a true American did not require "whiteness."

· 7 ·

Understanding
American Inequality

IN THE UNITED STATES, race and gender have been simultaneously organizing principles and products of citizenship and labor. That is, labor and citizenship have been permeated by gender and race, but at the same time labor and citizenship have helped create race and gender relations, meanings, and identities. The racialization and engendering of citizenship and labor have taken place not just through formal law and policy but also through localized practices, as men and women in their daily lives have enforced and challenged rules and boundaries that maintain distinctions. Labor and citizenship and gender and race are thus historically and regionally varied formations, the outcome of struggle between those attempting to maintain power and privilege and those resisting exclusion and subordination.

From the early republic to the 1930s, as discussed in Chapters 2 and 3, changes in the gender and race construction of labor and citizenship occurred in concert with major economic, social, and political transformations, including movements for democratization and workers' rights. Citizenship shifted from a restrictive definition of membership that categorically excluded major classes of people, including nonwhites, women, and those without property, to one that was ostensibly inclusive but assigned differential rights and obligations to different categories of people. Labor, meanwhile, changed from a system that consisted of a range of statuses between freedom and slavery to one in which free (wage) and unfree (slave) labor were polarized and racialized, and then to one in which free labor was universalized, but in which coercion, especially coercion directed at people of color, was still widely practiced and legitimated. These shifts illustrate both the persistence and the plasticity of race and gender inequalities in citizenship and labor.

The detailed examinations, in Chapters 4–6, of contestation over labor and citizenship between dominant and subordinate groups in the South, the Southwest, and Hawaii documented the importance of local conditions and local actors in shaping substantive citizenship and labor stratification. A comparative look at the three regions reveals connections between these local processes and national ones, as well as commonalities in the racialization and engendering of labor and citizenship, that point to underlying patterns of race and gender formation and thus advance our understanding of American social relations and inequality.

National and Local Connections

Although the United States is recognized as a single entity, with a federal legal, administrative, and judicial apparatus and a national economy, culture, and identity, there has always been considerable regional diversity. Regions such as the South, the Southwest, and Hawaii have had distinct histories of incorporation and development and have contained different mixes of people, cultures, and traditions. Additionally, within the federal system, considerable autonomy has been reserved to the states. Indeed, the concept of national citizenship as distinct from state citizenship took some time to develop, and even then was not uniformly recognized and implemented. The Reconstruction amendments for the first time inserted the concept of national citizenship into the U.S. Constitution. However, after Reconstruction ended, federal courts once again asserted the primacy of states' rights; their rulings in a variety of cases limited national citizenship rights enunciated in the Fourteenth Amendment. During the period from the early republic to the 1930s, national social and cultural integration was accelerating with the development of an interconnected capitalist economy. At the same time, there remained considerable isolation of localities, which therefore retained distinct cultures and traditions. The mixture of integration and isolation raises interesting questions regarding connections between national and local levels as well as between localities.

One area of connection between national and local was the flow of ideas about race and relations among groups. The closing decades of the nineteenth century and the first decade of the twentieth century marked the high point of American imperialism as U.S. military incursions brought the Philippines, Cuba, Hawaii, and Puerto Rico into the American orbit as colonial dependencies or U.S. territories. Established patterns of race relations in internal colonies shaped responses to peoples in external colonies. Simultaneously, encounters with "dark people" in external colonies shaped notions of whiteness and manliness that reverberated in internal colonies. As noted in Chapter 4, justifications for the takeover of the Philippines, Cuba, and Hawaii drew on racial thinking that differed little from southern white ideology. Both were premised on the need for whites to guide and control childlike (but dangerous) others who lacked the capacity to govern themselves or progress on their own. Because of their long history of managing blacks, white southerners became the supposed experts in the managing of "dark people." After 1890 there seems to have been only minor northern opposition to white southern methods of dealing with "their" blacks. All three branches of the federal government adopted a hands-off approach that allowed white southerners free rein to deny civil rights to African Americans and to control and exploit black labor.

The connections went in the other direction as well, from local to national. Local elites turned to national-level political structures and actors to garner support for their political and economic agendas. The southern elite, through a one-party system, accumulated enormous power at both regional and national levels. Southern Democrats in Congress were reelected term after term, accumulating seniority and gaining chairmanships of key Senate and House committees. In addition to securing legislation benefiting their region's agricultural interests, southern congressmen helped erect almost impenetrable barriers to national citizenship rights for southern blacks under the banner of "states' rights." White southern Democrats also monopolized federal judgeships in their region, thus ensuring the interpretation and enforcement of law to buttress white supremacy.

The ruling elites in the Southwest and Hawaii also directed efforts at the national government to further their interests. Southwestern growers wielded their political influence to prevent federal restrictions on immigration by Mexican laborers. Thus when the Immigration Act of 1924 was passed, restricting entry from Asia, Africa, and eastern and southern Europe, immigrants from Mexico and other parts of Latin America were exempted. Later, in the 1940s, southwestern agricultural interests persuaded Congress to establish a guest worker program that allowed growers to bring in workers from Mexico on short-term contracts in contravention of the intent of anti-peonage laws. This special program was promulgated at a time when immigration from other regions remained tightly restricted. The Hawaii Sugar Planters Association maintained a permanent representative in Washington to lobby Congress and the executive branch. The plantation owners could also work through the official Hawaii Territorial Representative to Congress, who was responsive to planter interests. (But, when Hawaiian planter interests conflicted with more powerful mainland interests, they usually gave way: in 1910 the sugar planters lobbied for a special exemption to the Chinese Exclusion Act so that they could recruit Chinese laborers to Hawaii to weaken the position of the increasingly militant Japanese workers, but their efforts were stymied by California's anti-Asian forces determined to maintain the restriction.)

Connections among elites in the three regions undoubtedly existed, though these are harder to document. One can catch glimpses of planters and landowners in one region being aware of the thinking of their counterparts in other regions. When Hawaiian sugar planters were dramatically expanding production in the 1870s and 1880s, they considered importing emancipated southern black labor. However, they were alert to reports that planters in the South were finding freed people no longer sufficiently docile and controllable. This consideration was one element in their decision to turn to Asian immigrant labor. We also know that individuals must have traveled between regions—carrying ideas back and forth. One such person was the economist Dr. Victor S. Clark, a member of the Hawaii Territorial Board, who conducted research for the U.S. Bureau of Labor Statistics and later for the Brookings Institution. He investigated labor conditions in various regions and wrote or contributed to reports that analyzed in great detail the supposed "characteristics" of workers of various ethnicities in Hawaii, the Southwest, and Puerto Rico.[1]

In comparison with more powerful whites, subordinated groups had few resources and connections to influence federal law and policy. They had to be resourceful to take advantage of any opportunities that arose. Hawaii was a popular location for inspection visits by federal officials, who were wined and dined by planters, local officials, and businessmen. On at least one occasion Japanese organizations in Hawaii were able to reach an important visitor from the mainland, Senator William H. King of Utah, a member of the Senate Committee on Immigration. They invited him to visit some plantation communities. As a result of his observations, King testified during Senate hearings in 1920 that the Japanese in Hawaii led model family lives and deserved full access to education and other rights of citizens.[2] Japanese immigrants also had the option of asking the Japanese consul to intervene with Territorial officials to address violations of rights. The relatively prestigious position of Japan (in contrast to the weak position of China) meant that U.S. officials paid some heed to Japanese consular requests. Similarly, Mexicans who remained citizens of Mexico were able to take some of their grievances to the Mexican consul assigned to their locality. However, for both Japanese and Mexicans this approach underlined their supposed non-American status: instead of framing their grievances in terms of rights due to all Americans, they cast themselves as subjects of a foreign nation.

Disfranchised and shut out of national politics, southern blacks were forced to rely largely on their own resources to establish ties across states and regions. In the 1910s and 1920s they were able to establish relationships with foundations and philanthropic organizations outside the South. Some of these private entities provided northern money and support that enabled blacks to build housing and schools during the Jim Crow period. Additionally, some federal agencies continued to monitor the economic and social conditions of groups residing in the South, the Southwest, and Hawaii. The U.S. Labor Bureau investigated and exposed conditions in agriculture, mining, and factory work in these regions. While not acting as a brake on exploitation or denial of suffrage, the Bureau gathered information that could be used by activist groups to press for reforms.

Patterns of Domination

Labor

For those who controlled economic resources, the primary function of subordinate groups—whether black, Mexican, or Japanese—was to provide a cheap and malleable source of labor. Under a "free labor" system, workers were deemed to have a choice in their conditions of work because they could leave a job at any time. Yet, as noted in Chapter 2, underlying this ostensible freedom was a more fundamental lack of choice about whether or not to work at all. Because of the unequal distribution of productive property, the majority of people did not own land or other means of self-subsistence. They therefore had no choice but to sell their labor to earn what they needed to live. In this respect men and women of color did not differ from propertyless white men— but they faced more formidable barriers to accumulating resources and acquiring or keeping sufficient property to be independent. For example, Mexicans residing in the Southwest when the region was taken over by the United States were systematically stripped of landownership and access to communal lands that were vital to subsistence. They were thus forced to turn to seasonal wage labor. The land system in Hawaii concentrated huge tracts in a few hands and left almost none available for immigrants to acquire. Freed slaves in the South were almost never allotted land after emancipation, and subsequently found it virtually impossible to acquire productive land.

Once in the labor market, the choices of blacks, Mexicans, and Japanese were circumscribed by industrial and occupational segregation and tracking mechanisms that cut off avenues to a large part of the labor market. Within the local labor markets of the South, the Southwest, and Hawaii, men of color were restricted to so-called unskilled dirty work in agriculture, construction, and mining, and women of color were restricted to field work, food packing, and domestic service. In this light, color lines in employment can be seen as mechanisms to force people of color to remain in low-paid service and agricultural employment that they would have left if better jobs had been available. Vocational schooling to fit blacks, Mexicans, and Japanese to the labor needs of white landowners, especially when combined with denial of access to broader liberal arts education, can also be viewed as restricting meaningful choice.

The coercive aspects of labor market structures were buttressed by community customs and law. First, there was selective application and enforcement of feudal elements entrenched in employment practices and law. At least until the New Deal era, courts continued to interpret employer-employee relations according to the template of master-servant acts that gave employers almost complete authority and discretion. Employers could effectively bind workers by such mechanisms as debt bondage, postponing payment until the end of a contract period, and paying in scrip, without incurring any legal liability. These mechanisms were prevalent in agriculture, mining, and other sectors that heavily employed workers of color. Second, there was selective application and enforcement of the "obligation to work," which had a long tradition in common law and in American concepts of citizenship. This obligation was differentially defined and enforced so that men and women of color were primarily the targets of forced labor.

As we saw in Chapters 4–6, the obligation to work was structured and enforced by means ranging from personal to impersonal, indirect to direct, and informal to highly formal and codified. At the most personalized level, the obligation to work was imposed by white employers in face-to-face relations with workers dependent on them for survival. An example was the custom of Hawaii planters of "requesting" the services of wives and daughters of plantation workers as maids and domestics. In a similar vein, white southern employers sometimes assumed that the daughters of their domestic employees would also come to work for the family. Workers and their families found it hard to refuse such requests for fear of losing the goodwill of their employer or even their jobs.

A more direct mechanism used to enforce the obligation to work was the application of race-differentiated criteria for determining eligibility for public welfare. Local officials administering state programs for Mothers' Pensions and the federally funded Aid to Dependent Children disqualified black and Mexican women on the grounds that they were "employable mothers," forcing them to accept field work or domestic service.[3] These officials sometimes explicitly stated the assumption that black and Latina women should not be allowed to avoid working for whites. At the most blatant end of the spectrum of coercion was the use of vagrancy laws in the South and the Southwest to round up blacks and Mexicans and to force them into field and mining labor to "pay off" their fines, as well as the leasing of convict labor to private employers. For people of color, then, the local labor market and the local legal system operated in tandem to enforce the requirement to work—not to work on their own account so as to be economically self-sufficient, but to provide labor for the benefit of the dominant group.

Citizenship

The three regional chapters demonstrated the importance of local conditions and local actors in effectuating substantive citizenship. Under the Jim Crow system, all whites in the South were deputized to interpret and enforce segregation laws, while police and courts used their formal authority to back up white civilians. Thus white drivers and passengers policed the division of white and colored sections on public transport, with police getting involved primarily when there were altercations. In the Southwest, theater owners, store clerks, swimming pool attendants, and others interpreted the race of Mexican patrons to decide whether or not to allow them access to public facilities. Simultaneously, white planters in Hawaii sorted workers into sundry ethnic categories when assigning them to work groups. Some of these categories, such as "Filipino" and "Japanese," combined heterogeneous groups that did not share a language or a cultural identity. But these racializing moves were resisted by their targets: in the South blacks organized city-wide streetcar boycotts to protest segregated seating, and individual black passengers sometimes defied conductors' orders to move or give up a seat. Mexicans petitioned officials to stop having their children travel long distances to segregated schools and also protested being barred from public facilities. Okinawans resisted incorporation into being "Japanese" by maintaining their own organizations and cultural practices. As in these examples, race and gender were constantly being reinscribed and challenged through men's and women's actions in everyday life.

National-level legal and political institutions and discourses established some parameters within which negotiation could take place. The federal Constitution, congressional legislation, executive orders and directives, and federal court rulings created certain categories of people—"whites," "aliens ineligible for citizenship," "free workers"—and defined their rights and obligations. The meaning of these terms, however, required interpretation in specific circumstances. For example, the meaning of "white" in naturalization law had to be interpreted by regional officials in relation to specific applicants for naturalization. Decisions were based on varying criteria, leading to inconsistent outcomes. There were individual cases of Chinese or Japanese immigrants being granted naturalized citizenship. The interpretation of the race of Asian Indians was particularly variable. During the Progressive era the prevailing racial classification system identified three "great races": Caucasoid (to which Europeans belonged), Mongoloid, and Negroid. Caucasoid was generally equated with white, but it included some nationalities that were not popularly considered white, such as Asian Indians. Officials who relied on "scientific knowledge" were likely to allow naturalization of an Indian applicant, while other judges who fell back on "common knowledge" were likely to rule an Indian applicant ineligible.[4]

One of the clearest examples of the gap between formal law and informal custom and between federal law and local practice was in determining the race and rights of Mexicans in the Southwest. Three distinct levels were involved. Federal government policy was based on the 1848 Treaty of Guadalupe Hidalgo, which had granted U.S. citizenship rights to all Mexicans residing in territories taken over by the United States. Federal agencies and officials maintained the position that Mexicans (both in the United States and in Mexico) were white and thus eligible for naturalization and for other rights that were reserved for whites. Southwestern states varied in their constitutional provisions and laws regarding who was eligible for jury duty, suffrage, and other rights. While some states limited suffrage to white men without any further additions or clarifications, Texas franchised white men and "former citizens of Mexico," and California had more restrictive language that covered white men and "white male citizens of Mexico." Finally, at the community level, Anglo individuals and institutions interpreted the race of Mexicans in varying ways, but usually not as white. Sometimes they considered all Mexicans "colored," and sometimes they differentiated among them on the basis of class and appearance, recognizing light-skinned middle-class Mexicans as "Spanish" and casting darker-skinned or indigenous-appearing individuals as mestizos or Indians and subjecting them to segregation or exclusion on the basis of their supposed nonwhiteness. Yet such local practices as excluding Mexicans from municipal swimming pools or assigning them to separate schools could be negotiated. Where Mexicans had sufficient political leverage, they could sometimes induce Anglos to moderate racist policies.

As noted in Chapter 2, it is useful to distinguish among several facets of citizenship in order to identify different types of exclusion. Let us consider three aspects of membership: standing, nationality, and allegiance. For much of the nineteenth century and part of the twentieth, white women were considered members of the nation but were denied *standing* (recognition as full adults capable of exercising choice and responsibility). Instead they were treated as dependents of men. Thus when they married their nationality and allegiance were assumed to follow those of their husbands. Limitations on their civil, political, and social rights also flowed from their lack of standing.

Blacks in the South continued to be viewed and treated not just as noncitizens but as "anti-citizens" lacking standing and allegiance. On the one hand, white southerners tended to consider any degree of black political power illegitimate and dangerous to white democracy. Southern Democrats effectively harnessed this fear to maintain one-party rule. On other hand, many white southerners also viewed black powerlessness as a threat: the idea that the wealthy could use blacks to drive down the price of labor and to negate white votes fed the unwillingness of poor and working-class whites to make common cause with poor and working-class blacks.

Mexicans, for their part, were excluded, at least in local practice, primarily from American *nationality*. Anglos in the Southwest failed to distinguish between Mexicans born in the United States and Mexican immigrants, treating both as equally foreign. Anglos reserved the term "American" for themselves while referring to ethnic Mexicans as "Mexican." Accordingly, Mexicans were viewed as not entitled to the usual rights of civil protection, political participation, and social welfare that were owed to American citizens. The majority of the Mexican Americans who were "repatriated" to Mexico at public expense during economic downturns in the 1920s and 1930s were actually U.S.-born children of immigrants. Subsequently they found it difficult to prove their U.S. citizenship.

Japanese in Hawaii were excluded both from American *nationality* and from supposed *allegiance* to the United States. Whether they were immigrants or members of the second generation, they were suspected of acting not independently but as subjects of Japan. Signs of assimilation, such as the wearing of Western clothing, were viewed as purely superficial overlays that did not signal any change in their essential "Japaneseness." The move to close down Japanese-language schools in the 1920s and the incarceration of hundreds of community leaders as "enemy aliens" at the start of World War II were logical outcomes of the lack of acceptance of Japanese as Americans by allegiance.[5]

Social Interaction

In all three regions race and gender hierarchies were enacted and sometimes challenged in interpersonal interaction. Subordinate groups were expected to affirm the superiority of the dominant group through rituals of deference. Rules of etiquette required members of subordinate groups to address members of dominant groups with honorific titles, maintain an acceptable physical distance, give way on sidewalks and in other public places, enter white homes through the back door, and generally appear to be accommodating and agreeable. In turn, dominant-group members enacted dominance, treating those serving them as invisible, performing acts of benevolence and charity such as donating discarded furnishings or leftover food, and acting as patrons for fetes and celebrations.

Assertiveness by the subordinate group was viewed as a threat to white authority. Accordingly, open displays of defiance or noncompliance might be occasions for punishment. In the South any show of independence or pride on the part of blacks, whether male or female, could trigger murderous violence. Prosperous and successful blacks learned to hide their achievements and affluence for fear of inviting retribution from whites. Displays of deference served to reassure whites of their power. Black, Mexican, and Japanese children learned to conceal their feelings from whites, to broach matters obliquely, and to give way when necessary.

Perhaps this is why landowners and managers in all three regions generally seemed satisfied with their own employees. They spoke of their black, Mexican, or Japanese workers as appropriately respectful and nonthreatening, even while characterizing the general mass of blacks, Mexicans, or Japanese as immoral, dishonest, or even violent. Hawaiian planters may have complained that Japanese men were too ambitious, assertive, and easily offended, but not that they were dangerous to haole men or women. In Texas growers and ranchers invariably described their own Mexican workers as respectful and family oriented, though careless in their work and somewhat spendthrift. Notwithstanding the widespread popular depictions of Mexican men as bandits, murderers, and rapists, Anglo ranchers and their wives testified that Anglo women felt safe among Mexican ranch hands.

As feudal relationships gave way to "modern" race relations in more urban settings after the turn of the century, residential and other forms of spatial segregation became more important in maintaining hierarchy. Whites began to use the dangers of dirt, disease, and pollution, which they associated with dark skin, to justify segregation. Yet, to maintain their privileged lifestyles, whites depended on blacks, Mexicans, and Japanese to work in their homes and perform all manner of personal services involving close contact. Even while not allowing blacks to sit next to them in public accommodations, whites in the South employed blacks to cook their food, iron their clothes, nurse them when they were sick, and care for their children. The contradiction between notions of pollution that justified petty segregation and the close proximity of black servants may have been behind the tuberculosis hysteria that struck Atlanta in the 1910s, when whites became terrified that black laundresses and domestics were introducing disease into their households.[6]

Over time, blacks who grew up after emancipation, second-generation Japanese, and U.S.-born Mexicans became less deferent. As whites saw subordinate groups being more assertive and independent, some began to wax nostalgic about an earlier time when these others "knew their place." Haole planters in Hawaii contending with Japanese labor militancy looked back fondly to the days when the supposedly less ambitious and more tractable Chinese had been the predominant labor force. As a prominent social scientist explained, unlike the ambitious Japanese, who tended to act in concert, "the Chinese because of their individualistic viewpoint and the peculiarities of their temperament, exerted little influence as a group in the Territory."[7] Planters had apparently forgotten that the Chinese in their time had sometimes attacked their overseers, run away, or caused other problems. Employers in the Southwest expressed greater satisfaction with "old time Mexicans" than with American-born Mexicans, who were more "tenacious in their rights." Victor Clark found that Colorado beet growers preferred "laborers from 'old Mexico' to Spanish-speaking laborers from New Mexico because of their greater steadiness and reliability."[8] About the South, David Katzman notes, "As time passed Southerners began to romanticize the days of slavery and to recall only the faithfulness,

loyalty, and competence of the slave and slave-bred servant." A southern white woman said in 1904: "By the time I was fourteen years of age,
the first set of free-born Negroes were getting old enough to interpret life for themselves, and without the well-disciplined experiences of
their parents, who had not only been slaves, but had passed through the
very drastic training of the Ku Klux Klan after the war."⁹ Her words
jarringly remind us that behind the myth of an ideal southern past was
the long history of white repression and violence aimed at teaching
blacks to "know their place." Still to come at the time of this statement
were the Hollywood epic *Birth of a Nation,* the resurgence of the Ku
Klux Klan, and the tide of terrorism, violence, and lynching in the
1910s, 1920s, and 1930s.

Racialization and Boundaries

Clear racial boundaries were necessary to preserve racial stratification.
Interracial unions resulting in "mixed" children threatened boundaries
by confusing mutually exclusive, dichotomous categories. Anti-miscegenation statutes prohibiting marriage (and sometimes cohabitation)
between whites and various "others" were common in most states (with
the exception of those in New England) up to the mid-twentieth century. White fear of miscegenation was particularly pronounced in the
South, where the system of Jim Crow segregation necessitated the
elimination of an intermediate "mixed" group. Anxiety about light-
skinned blacks "passing" and of "hidden blackness" called for strict
measures to prevent interracial liaisons.

Despite mechanisms to erect boundaries, white/haole/Anglo men
retained access to women of color in all regions, contributing to continued intermixture. Intermarriage across racial lines generally took
the form of men in the dominant group marrying women in the subordinate group. Prior to full incorporation into the U.S. economy and
polity and the establishment of an elaborate system of racial stratification in Hawaii and the Southwest, such intermixing took place even at
the elite level. Newly arrived Anglo men married the daughters of
landowning californios, tejanos, and nuevomexicanos. Similarly, haole
adventurers married the daughters of Hawaiian royalty. These were in
the nature of dynastic marriages through which white men formed
strategic alliances and gained access to land. These marriages created a

temporary mixed elite which became increasingly whitened in subsequent generations, as members of this group tended to marry within their own class. In the South the sexual exploitation of slave women by white slaveholders is well known. The keeping of black and mulatto concubines by wealthy slaveowners created a significant community of somewhat more privileged mulattos, especially in Louisiana and South Carolina. The practice of concubinage continued in these two states even into the Jim Crow period, though interracial unions became more restricted in the South.

Anti-miscegenation laws prohibiting intermarriage or cohabitation between whites and nonwhites came into play primarily when there was a perceived threat of men of color having access to white women. In Hawaii, where intermarriages almost exclusively involved haole men and non-haole women, there is no record of an anti-miscegenation law even being proposed. Where there were such laws, they were differentially enforced. Although laws against unions between whites and Indians or mestizos existed in many areas of the Southwest, they were not enforced in the case of white men and Native American or mestizo women. They were, however, sometimes used after the fact to deny inheritances to Native American or mestizo wives when relatives of the Anglo husband disputed his will.

In the Jim Crow South, black and white dichotomous categories were maintained in spite of considerable intermixture through legal formulas that definitively assigned individuals to one category or another. These formulas differed from state to state. Initially these ranged from one-quarter black ancestry to smaller fractions, but eventually they converged toward a "one-drop rule." The contradictions and ambiguities in the racial status of Mexicans resulted in inconsistent application of anti-miscegenation laws and of racial classification. In California Anglo school officials classified many Mexicans as Indians or mestizos and accordingly assigned them to separate segregated schools; they considered other Mexicans to be white (presumably of Spanish heritage) and therefore entitled to attend white schools. For those of mixed Anglo-Mexican background, "passing" was correspondingly easier than for blacks, and racial-ethnic membership was more dependent on personal choice.

Despite these differences, in all three regions the category "white" was defined as the absence of nonwhiteness. Given the relatively free access of white men to women of color, the maintenance of whiteness depended on the "purity" of white women. The ideal white woman was chaste and monogamous. At the same time, the prevailing cultural understanding of women as either virgins or whores created suspicion and ambivalence toward white female sexuality. Hence white women supposedly needed to be guarded from possible depredation and from any implications of "looseness" on their part. The maintenance of racial boundaries thus entailed close controls over white women.

Openings for Agency

Although national and local economic structure, laws, and ideology all operated together to contain and control people of color, domination was neither monolithic nor complete. The meshing of national and local economic structures, laws, and ideologies was like a tightly woven net that nonetheless had interstices and points of slippage that allowed for challenge and contestation. Resistance created small tears or breaks in the net, which in turn stimulated repairs by the dominant group to try to regain control. Major economic and social transformations (such as the abolition of slavery, the spread of large-scale commercial agriculture, and territorial annexation) led to massive rending of the net. In these cases, structures and discourses of control had to undergo thorough revision.

One major point of slippage at the local level was division within the dominant group. Whites in the three regions were usually united in their support of white male domination, but different segments of the white elite had divergent economic, social, and political interests. This meant that different segments sometimes favored different approaches to dealing with subordinate groups. In the post-Reconstruction South a rift developed between the traditional planter class, which had "redeemed" the South for white rule, and a rising professional and business class that looked to an industrialized future. The latter saw control of "disorder" as the key to building an industrial society. The traditional planters were firmly convinced of their own superiority and black inferiority. When they were in power, they felt sufficiently secure to allocate a small share of political jobs and other indulgences to "good" blacks. The members of the professional business elite were less secure, perhaps because they were encountering greater assertiveness from urban blacks. With the rise in influence of the new class at the turn of the century, anxiety about possible disorder and loss of control over blacks contributed to the creation and spread of Jim Crow segregation.

In post-annexation Hawaii there were differences within the haole elite in orientation toward the education and Americanization of laboring classes. Some members of the planter elite, especially those with large holdings on the outer islands (including European managers who intended to return to their home countries) viewed laborers more purely as factors in production and were not concerned about developing a democratic citizenry. They opposed any taxation for education of laborers' children and efforts to develop them into "citizen labor." Other members of the elite, especially those descended from missionaries, carrying on business in Honolulu, and retaining connections to New England via education at Yale or Wesleyan, were more imbued with republican and Protestant missionary ideals. They were also more sensitive about the mainland image of Hawaii as backward and uncivilized. A significant portion of this group supported the expansion of public education, which helped raise the aspirations of children of Japanese immigrants and accelerated their move out of plantation employment.

In the Southwest divisions among Anglos fell along industry lines, with railroads, mining, cattle ranching, and growers representing distinct interests. In south Texas hostility between cattle ranchers and growers festered because of conflicts over fencing and encroachment on grazing land. Cattle ranching was the earlier industry, and owners of large ranches had a paternalistic relationship with Mexicans. Anglo ranchers did not oppose Mexican suffrage as long as they felt the Mexicans' votes were controllable and would be cast in favor of ranchers' interests. Where ranchers had the balance of power, Mexicans continued to vote in county elections. Growers, in contrast, particularly smaller ones, were primarily interested in seasonal Mexican labor that would not remain in the area. They were hostile to voting by Mexicans, charging that ranchers were dictating workers' votes. They argued that the participation of Mexicans corrupted elections.

Another line of divergence was between smaller Anglo farmers and large agribusiness interests, who took opposing sides on Mexican immigration. While both sides considered Mexicans inassimilable, Anglos associated with agribusinesses, railroads, and other businesses dependent on agriculture argued that Mexican laborers were essential to the Southwest's economy and opposed immigration restrictions. Their view was that Mexicans were temporary sojourners, "natural homers" who would return to Mexico. Besides, they wanted an excess of laborers so that masses could be hired at peak harvest times and wages could be kept low. Small farmers, retailers, and other groups, meanwhile, saw the flood of low-wage Mexican labor as threatening their economic survival by giving large agribusinesses an unfair advantage. Restrictionist rhetoric, which brought together small farm interests, unionists, and eugenicists, was laced with pseudo-scientific concepts and alarums. Both restrictionists and anti-restrictionists were racist, but they expressed different racisms. One side viewed Mexicans as a means to an end, an exploitable group that was useful for labor; the other saw Mexicans as a dangerous economic, biological, and cultural threat.[10] A much smaller group of Anglos, mostly reformers and missionaries, held paternalistic and maternalistic notions about Mexicans. This group expressed a limited appreciation for some of the cultural values and contributions of Mexicans—generally citing their artistic and musical talents—and supported education and Americanization for Mexican children.

Racialized Gender

In all three regions domination involved the construction and maintenance of oppositional concepts of white and racial manhood and womanhood. Because they were relationally constructed, white and racial manhood and womanhood need to be examined together.

As noted in Chapter 2, white manhood has been equated with citizenship and economic independence since the early republic. The status and qualities of white men were seen as necessary for political governing and for directing others' labor. White masculinity increasingly became associated with the conquest and "civilizing" of non-European peoples in the age of U.S. expansionism. The glorification of the white man's burden reached a zenith in the early twentieth century as the United States expanded its sphere of influence to include areas of the Caribbean, South and Central America, and the Pacific.

Legally and by common understanding, free white manhood also entailed command not only of one's self but of women and children, including ownership and control of their labor. The conception of white manhood was thus linked to a complementary conception of white womanhood in terms of marital service, motherhood, and economic dependence. With the growth of capitalist industrialization and the shift of men from family farming and craft production to wage work, breadwinning came to define white manhood. The complementary definition of white womanhood came to be that of homemaking.

Within the dominant gender conventions of the period, white men and women were assumed to have very different natures. According to racist interpretations of evolutionary theory, a wide differentiation between males and females was associated with more advanced levels of development of a species. Hence the supposed physical and emotional delicacy of white women was viewed as a sign of the highly evolved state of the white race.

Layered upon these cultural conceptions were region-specific constructions of racialized gender. White men and women, because of their different natures and places in society, were assigned different roles in the racial regime. Within a dual racial system, white men of the elite and the middle class were charged with control of the public realm of the economy and politics. As heads of households, they were responsible for keeping "others" in their place and protecting white women and children from these others. The cult of domesticity idealized women as moral keepers of the home. Their sexual purity needed to be preserved to ensure the future of the white race. The need for protection meant that women needed to be confined to the domestic sphere or to separate women's spaces.

During the late nineteenth and early twentieth centuries, however, white middle-class women in all regions were challenging these restrictions by becoming involved in reform movements and charitable and welfare organizations to uplift and bring relief to the less fortunate. These efforts have been interpreted by some critics as dovetailing with and reinforcing the larger systems of exploitation and inequality controlled by the men of their class. In this view, by mitigating some of the misery, women's charity work helped defuse pressure that would have built up against the existing system. Further, their efforts were not aimed at giving the poor the means to become independent; instead they encouraged dependence and conformity to dominant-culture prescriptions.

DOMINANT CONCEPTIONS of racial manhood and womanhood were complex and contradictory, but certain themes were specific to each region. Southern white conceptions of black men centered in their supposed animalistic nature, emotionality, lack of higher intelligence, and unrestrained sexuality. Lazy and prone to crime, they required a strong controlling white hand. Contradictorily, they were depicted as either shiftless and slow-witted buffoons or dangerous rapists. A duality also characterized white images of black women as sexual temptresses (Jezebel) or self-sacrificing domestics (Mammy). Black women were simultaneously defeminized as overly aggressive and hypersexualized as actively promiscuous. In contrast to the high degree of physical, intellectual, and emotional differentiation assumed to exist between white men and women, "lesser" races, especially blacks, were assumed to manifest less sexual dimorphism.

In Hawaii haoles involved in the plantation system had elaborate notions of the characteristics of each of the major ethnic groups. They viewed Japanese men, somewhat incongruously, as assertive and touchy but also clannish, as personally ambitious but lacking individualism and independence and thus not fit for citizenship. Some social reformers argued that crowded and poor living conditions encouraged "sexual looseness" among the Japanese. However, this was seen as primarily an internal community problem. Japanese male sexuality was not viewed as dangerous for white women. Perhaps because most women of the immigrant generation were married and mothers and did field work, Japanese women did not seem to figure in the haole imagination as sexually available and alluring as Native Hawaiian women did. Japanese women were desexualized as work drones and producers of children.

Anglo conceptions of Mexican men were also largely negative. One common image, popularized in the media, was that of the Mexican bandit, treacherous, amoral, and bloodthirsty, who robbed innocent whites. More common as Mexicans came to be associated with agricultural field work was the image of the peon, dirty, uneducated, superstitious, and lazy. In contrast to the industrious, forward-looking, rational American man, the Mexican was deemed to lack the independence of republican citizens. Mexican women were hyperfeminized, either as alluring dark-haired beauties (Mexican spitfire) or as traditional, homebound, overly fertile domestic drudges. At least in the early twentieth century, the popular image of ethnic Mexican women was the closest of the three groups to dominant ideals of appropriate womanhood.

Because whiteness was constructed in relation to varying contrast figures, it did not have quite the same meaning from region to region. Whiteness in the South was defined rather starkly in opposition. to blackness. The mobilization of poor, middle-class, and elite whites around the doctrine of white supremacy undercut the possibility of mounting effective challenges to a system that exploited both poor whites and blacks and benefited the white elite. Concentration of land and the lack of a diversified economy left both blacks and a large portion of the white population landless and impoverished.

In Hawaii "haole" was originally a Native Hawaiian word that referred to any non-Hawaiian; subsequently it came to have a narrower meaning of European and Anglo American and was adopted by all groups on the islands. Haoleness was defined in relation to various others. Native Hawaiians were the initial contrast group; later, as immigrants arrived, a conglomeration of groups, including Native Hawaiians and Asians, became the contrast for haoleness. The Japanese became major contrast figures as they became numerous and as haoles became inflected with "Americanness" in the Progressive era. Absent a significant group of white independent farmers or proletarians, "haole" was a class as well as a racial designation, an amalgam of "Anglo-European" and "owner-managerial class." Thus, as noted in Chapter 6, the Portuguese were not considered haoles as long as they remained in plantation labor.

In the Southwest "Anglo" was initially a Mexican designation, just as haole was initially a Native Hawaiian concept. The term "Anglo" was thus counterpoised with "Mexican" and had cultural connotations that included speaking English and being Protestant. "Anglo" overlapped and coexisted with "white." When used by Anglos, "white" meant "not colored," and thus it was defined in relation not only to Mexicans but also to blacks and Native Americans. As the old landowning "Spanish," "nuevomexicano," and "californio" elites lost their land holdings and as Mexicans became overwhelmingly associated with agricultural labor, "Anglo," "white," and "Mexican" came to have clear class inflections.

Even so, as noted in Chapter 5, Paul Taylor found Mexican American field workers in the early 1930s challenging Anglo notions of whiteness by claiming themselves to be white like the Anglos in contrast to blacks. However, Tomás Almaguer recalls that, twenty years later, "to be Mexican in the Southern California agricultural world that I grew up in meant that one was unambiguously *not* white."[11]

The denigration of manhood for men of color contributed to tension between men and women in racialized communities. The black community had a long tradition of relatively egalitarian relations, with women participating actively in political discussions, girls being educated alongside boys in coeducational institutions, and the sharing of family breadwinning. Pressure to fit dominant-culture norms of family and gender meant that women should be less visible and assume supportive secondary roles. While black women continued to be active, they often had to do so in ways that placed black men in positions of public spokesmen. Women often felt they should not challenge male authority or expose certain issues, such as domestic violence, which might reinforce white racist conceptions.

In contrast to the relatively egalitarian black tradition, the Japanese in Hawaii inherited a tradition of gender hierarchy and segregation. Much of village life in Japan was organized by gender, with separate parallel organizations for men and women in every area of life from village work brigades to political organizations to kin relations. The Hawaii labor system that drafted women into waged field labor broke down traditional separation despite the sexual segregation of work gangs. Mexican gender conventions also prescribed distinct male and female spheres. The concept of *machismo* stressed men's responsibility for taking care of and protecting wives and children. From the Anglo perspective, Mexican men were being indulgent and therefore unmanly when they spent their hard-earned money on dressing their wives and children well while wearing worn-out clothing themselves.

Patterns of Contestation

Variation in local conditions and in forms of oppression led to somewhat different kinds of contestation by people of color in the three regions, although underlying parallels and commonalities were striking. Given that much resistance had to take place hidden from white eyes and in disguised forms, the uncovering of contestation requires careful examination.

Micropolitics of Resistance

Looking at formal political realms and collective activities reveals only a small portion of actual resistance and contestation. When groups are shut out of formal political processes, and moreover are prevented by violence and other means from expressing their opposition in open and organized ways, they have to resist in less direct ways and in sites hidden from dominant-culture surveillance. This is even more true of subordinate-group women, who may be excluded from public roles even though they may do much of the behind-the-scenes work of mobilizing. During Reconstruction black women were disfranchised but participated in debates about political issues within the community and thereby influenced black men's votes. In Hawaii Japanese women were visible as strikers but were most active in classic female support activities such as working in outdoor kitchens to prepare food for strikers and evicted families.

Uncovering hidden resistance is also important to correct the bias in dominant-group-centered as well as in male-centered narratives. Because written history relies heavily on textual sources, public spokesmen and polemicists whose words are recorded appear as central actors, whereas those who do behind-the-scenes organizing remain faceless and voiceless. Karen Brodkin Sacks has shown that, in union organizing at the Duke University Medical Center in the 1970s, black women used their kin and community ties to organize meetings at which men were put forward to speak.[12] In such instances, without Sacks's participant observation, women's oppositional activities would have been left undocumented. Furthermore, written sources are often overly weighted toward the view of superordinates. If, in fact, much resistance is hidden from the master's eyes, the oppressed may appear acquiescent and unresisting. For example, if we take Anglo ranch owners' accounts at face value, their Mexican workers' respectful forms of address to employers may be interpreted as acquiescence to subordination rather than as an expression of their sense of personal dignity and propriety. This bias toward the superordinates' perspective can be partially countered by reading between the lines to uncover hidden transcripts of resistance; scholars of African American southern history have led the way in doing this to reveal the micropolitics of resistance. This approach has been used only sporadically for Hawaii and the Southwest, but I have tried to read planters' complaints in Hawaii and growers' complaints in the Southwest for evidence of resistance and cultural assertion. Thus "disreputable" activities cited by the dominant groups to discredit people of color, such as malingering, fighting, banditry, stealing, fleeing, slowing down, feigning illness, or playing the clown, can be read as oppositional practices.

Building Community

Community building by racialized groups required overcoming their internal divisions. Mechanisms of domination such as Americanization, segregation, interpersonal etiquette, and the drawing of color lines in the labor market appear to have exacerbated class and other divisions within subordinate groups even while fostering unity in opposition to these injustices. Color consciousness seems to have been a source of division in all three regions. Lighter-skinned New Mexicans designated themselves as "Spanish," rejecting identification with darker-skinned mestizos and Indians. Japanese in Hawaii expressed prejudice against "dark" groups and also favored fair skin among their own group. Women field workers wore long sleeves and elaborate cover-up bonnets even in the stifling heat to avoid becoming too tanned. In the South black class status was linked to light skin color and straight hair.

Class divisions were encouraged by racist notions about the backwardness and depraved sexuality of people of color. Many members of the black middle class subscribed to strict norms of respectability. They condemned working-class forms of recreation and expression and engaged in "racial uplift" to reform the lower classes. Descendants of landowning californio families socialized among their own kind and hobnobbed with influential Anglos. *Ricos* in New Mexico and southern Colorado lived apart on their remote ranches and remained aloof from village life, eschewing local fetes, markets, and other activities. Some educated Japanese Christians agreed with Americanists that plantation workers needed to be Christianized and should accommodate to the established order by remaining in plantation labor.

Americanization campaigns and denial of rights to noncitizens fostered divisions between immigrants and those born in the United States. After World War I, U.S.-born Mexican Americans formed a variety of organizations open only to American citizens. The organizers believed their best chance of fighting discrimination was to stress their Americanness. This stance, and the exclusion of noncitizens, meant that these organizations abandoned the interests of hundreds of thousands of ethnic Mexicans. The position taken by these groups regarding U.S. immigration policy toward Mexico was pragmatic and equivocal; they voiced some concern that the Mexican American struggle for equal rights was being held back by the negative attitudes of white Americans toward Mexican immigrants. At least one major organization, the League of United Latin American Citizens, came out with qualified support for immigration restrictions.

Countering these fragmenting forces was the unifying effect of being "lumped together" by residential ghettoization, color lines in employment, and discrimination in schooling and public services. Unity in action did not follow automatically from a shared fate, however. It had to be painstakingly achieved. The bases for concerted action were the webs of connections that blacks, Mexicans, and Japanese wove by establishing community institutions such as vernacular newspapers, churches, schools, mutual aid associations, fraternal and sororal organizations, business associations, sports leagues, and cultural societies. Blacks formed a variety of sororal and fraternal organizations. Mexicans in the Southwest formed *mutualistas* that brought together immigrant and American-born members, semiskilled and unskilled workers. Japanese in Hawaii formed rotating credit associations and prefectural associations.

As Benedict Anderson has argued, the vernacular press historically has been a critical force in the forging of an "imagined community."[13] Southwestern Spanish-language newspapers first spread the term "La Raza" to refer to a community that included both U.S.- and Mexican-born American citizens, immigrants, and transnationals. Black and Japanese newspapers played similar roles in creating a sense of peoplehood across geographic spans and class lines. The middle class also connected to working-class and poor members of the community through involvement in welfare and health projects. For example, black business and professional women in Atlanta organized to provide health care for washerwomen and servants stricken by tuberculosis. In both

the 1909 and 1920 island-wide strikes, Japanese business and professional associations provided crucial financial help and organized shel-
ters and kitchens for workers evicted from plantation housing. The
lines between culture and politics, between individual self-help and
mass organization were breached regularly. Mutualistas kept cultural
traditions alive by arranging celebrations of Mexican holidays, but they
also organized some of the first labor unions among Mexican agricultural workers in the Southwest. The Young Men's Buddhist Associations of Hawaii were ostensibly religious and social groups, but they
also organized discussions of labor issues and provided the initial leadership for the 1920 strike of sugar plantation workers.

Sometimes the need for unity led to the silencing of some voices and
the marginalization of some elements of the communities. Men and
middle-class members were more likely to be thrust into leadership positions, while women and lower-status men were forced to step back
and allow others to assume "manly" tasks. For women especially, putting forth grievances might be seen as divisive and disloyal. Working-
class and less reputable elements of a minority community might be
subject to censure or even shunning for violating norms of respectability and bringing shame on the community.

Education and Americanization

Education was a major area where contestation over labor and citizenship intersected. Whites who viewed racialized minorities strictly as
factors in labor were either opposed to or indifferent about education for workers and their children, refusing to allocate resources for
this purpose. Those who had an interest in maintaining a controllable
labor force actively opposed enforcement of compulsory school attendance for workers' children. Blacks, Mexicans, and Japanese, however,
understood the importance of education for occupational mobility and
rights. All three groups fought for access to schooling, and when public funding was denied or inadequate they put their scarce and hard-
earned resources into building and maintaining their own schools.

By the 1910s and 1920s some whites in all three regions were conceding the desirability of education for racialized minorities, but they
had specific ideas about what kind of education was appropriate. The
greatest white support was for schooling to prepare workers' children

for a subordinate place in society. Thus education for blacks, Mexicans, and Japanese emphasized vocational training in manual and agricultural pursuits for boys and domestic arts for girls. Whites also favored education designed to address the cultural deficiencies of nonwhite people by inculcating the whites' ideas of American values and habits. More clearly than in Americanization programs aimed at European ethnic groups in eastern cities, similar programs in the South, the Southwest, and Hawaii assumed that race and gender inequality would continue. These programs had a dual thrust: on the one hand, undermining cultural influences that might be sources of resistance; on the other hand, maintaining a permanent working class by training people for appropriately humble positions in the local labor market.

Americanization programs thus sought to undermine "foreign" or "traditional" values and practices (strong extended kin ties, communalism, alternative systems of knowledge, internal leadership) and to replace them with "American" culture and practices (individuality, competition, science, established authority). But while assimilation into the mainstream was the stated ideal, cultural assimilation was not intended to lead to structural assimilation, which would have brought mobility in the labor market and full substantive citizenship. In all three regions the assumption of Americanization programs was that participants would be incorporated into American society as a long-term, most likely permanent, subordinate group. Throughout the 1920s and 1930s white racial liberals who believed in the eventual assimilability of blacks—including social scientists and executives of foundations which supported black education—assumed that southern blacks were so backward that complete assimilation would take many generations.[14] In the meantime they supported vocational training and education that would direct black men into agricultural and mechanical pursuits and black women into domestic service and homemaking. Similarly, Americanization and vocational education programs in the Southwest and Hawaii were aimed at preparing Mexican and Japanese boys for agriculture and girls for domestic positions. Also, some middle-class elements in minority communities favored accommodation to the dominant group by youth, who should be responsible, work hard, and curb unrealistic ambitions. However, others in the middle class articulated strong cultural pride and called for an immediate end to discrimination.

Blacks, Mexicans, and Japanese alike were selective in their reception of Americanization and moral education. They accepted some parts of what was offered and rejected others. They did not necessarily internalize the moral messages that went along with literacy. Nor did they always accept inferior schooling. Parents in New Mexico villages sent their children long distances to attend Protestant-run schools to obtain better education than offered by the public schools at less expense than the cost of Catholic boarding schools. Neither they nor their children converted to Protestantism in great numbers despite the missionaries' stated aim of breaking Mexicans from "priestly bondage and superstition." Mexican women in Los Angeles attended classes to learn English and acquire job skills but did not accept Americanist admonitions to change their dietary, healing, and other cultural practices. Black educational administrators in the South acceded to the requirement of white liberal foundations to expand vocational education but did not stop offering liberal arts classes in their institutions. Japanese youth in Hawaii absorbed haole speakers' messages about the importance of "Americanizing" but not their admonitions to "go back to the soil."

In response to Americanization programs that touted the superiority of Anglo American culture, activists in all three regions began to defend their traditions and to articulate what recent scholars have termed cultural citizenship—the right to maintain distinct cultures and institutions without giving up full membership in the American community. Ironically, while Americanizers attempted to inculcate their own version of Americanism, Mexicans, Japanese, and blacks demonstrated a keen understanding of fundamental American ideals. Perhaps because they were denied recognition and inclusion, they were among the most eloquent articulators of American concepts of justice and freedom. Moreover, they worked within the dominant discourse while challenging it. Activists in the Japanese community in Hawaii invoked the American language of rights to rally the community to mount a legal challenge to restrictions on Japanese-language schools. Even traditionalists argued that the values inculcated in Japanese schools were congruent with Americanization; if anything, such values as duty and perseverance made them better and more loyal Americans. Mexican field workers cited American ideals of hard work and noted that Mexicans had done the work of building roads, buildings, and other infrastructures of the United States. Activists claimed the right to value the cultural heritage of Spanish-speaking people and called for the equal recognition of Spanish and English languages. Blacks simultaneously sought to claim full rights as American citizens and to maintain distinct cultural traditions that emphasized communal and egalitarian values. These values frequently were at odds with the individualistic and competitive norms of the dominant culture and were critical for the survival of black peoplehood.

Roots and Branches

Tracing the material and ideological roots of labor and citizenship has revealed the extent to which race and gender have been central organizing principles in the political and economic institutions of American society and integral to the ideals and assumptions underlying American democracy. Race and gender inequality are deeply rooted, pervasive, and complexly interwoven. But pointing to the breadth and depth of race-gender inequality should not lead to the conclusion that race-gender hierarchy is inevitable and therefore impossible to eliminate. Rather, this analysis is meant to direct attention to the multiple levels at which efforts for change are needed—large-scale institutions and structures, local labor markets, and everyday practices.

Ironically, the very tenets of republican and democratic ideology, which proclaim universal equality while simultaneously assuming exclusion and hierarchy, have helped obscure the existence of institutionalized systems of inequality. To the extent that Americans believe in independence and free choice, they deny interdependence and are blind to institutional constraints on choice. There is thus an overwhelming tendency to view racism and sexism as products of individual beliefs and attitudes. According to such a view, if individual bias and prejudice can be eliminated, racism and sexism will no longer divide the society and hobble efforts to achieve social justice. Since Americans in the twenty-first century are less likely than ever before to express overtly negative views of minorities and women, one likely conclusion is that sexism and racism are disappearing.

Unfortunately, such conclusions ignore the fact that various forms of coercion that African Americans, Mexican Americans, and Japanese Americans were subjected to in the period 1870–1930 are still clearly operative in the contemporary United States. Sometimes they are directed at the same groups and sometimes at new groups.

The cruel sweatshops of New York and Los Angeles, filled with Chinese and Southeast Asian immigrant women, mirror the hardships of plantation labor in the earlier period. Mexican and Mexican American agricultural workers are still subjected to inhuman labor conditions: poisoned by pesticides, threatened with deportation if they should protest, and often denied access to schooling and health care. The labor force remains sex-segregated such that women are still concentrated in predominantly female occupations; simultaneously, women continue to be burdened by a disproportionate share of unpaid reproductive labor, including care of children, the disabled, and the elderly. And, as was dramatically shown in the national presidential election of 2000, blacks are still systematically disfranchised and denied full access to voting in violation of the Voting Rights Act of 1965. Perhaps most dramatic has been the massive criminalization and imprisonment of blacks through the war on drugs, selective policing, and judicial discrimination. As a result of felony convictions, nearly one and a half million black men currently have lost their voting rights, often permanently.[15]

Efforts to roll back hard-won rights also continue. Proposals by some members of Congress to end birthright citizenship for children of undocumented immigrants would nullify a key provision of the Fourteenth Amendment. Other proposals to deny welfare and voting rights to naturalized citizens resemble earlier efforts to create second-class citizenship for "others," who reside in and contribute their labor to the community but are not included in "We the People." All of these examples bespeak the continued centrality of citizenship and labor as sites both for maintaining and for challenging race and gender inequality in American society.

Notes

Index

Notes

Introduction

1. William H. Sewell Jr., "A Theory of Structure: Duality, Agency, and Transformation," *American Journal of Sociology* 98 (July 1992), 1–29.

2. Nancy Leys Stepan, "Race and Gender: The Role of Analogy in Science," in David Theo Goldberg, ed., *Anatomy of Racism* (Minneapolis: University of Minnesota Press, 1990), 40.

1. Integrating Race and Gender

1. The concept of structure I use is consistent with William H. Sewell Jr.'s definition of structure as "composed simultaneously of schemas, which are virtual, and of resources, which are real." Sewell, "A Theory of Structure: Duality, Agency, and Transformation," *American Journal of Sociology* 98 (July 1992), 13.

2. As the title of Gloria T. Hull, Patricia Bell Scott, and Barbara Smith's edited collection on African American women puts it, *All the Women Are White, All the Blacks Are Men, But Some of Us Are Brave* (Old Westbury, N.Y.: Feminist Press, 1982).

3. See, e.g., Bonnie Thornton Dill, "The Means to Put My Children Through: Childrearing Goals and Strategies among Black Female Domestic Servants," in La Frances Rogers Rose, ed., *The Black Woman* (Beverly Hills: Sage, 1980), 107–124; Cheryl Townsend Gilkes, "'Together and in Harness': Women's Traditions in the Sanctified Church," *Signs* 10, no. 4 (1985), 678–699; Vicki Ruiz, *Cannery Women, Cannery Lives: Mexican Women, Unionization and the California Food Processing Industry, 1939–1950* (Albuquerque: University of New Mexico Press, 1987); Patricia Zavella, *Women's Work and Chicano Families: Cannery Workers of the Santa Clara Valley* (Ithaca: Cornell University Press, 1987); Lucie Cheng, "Free, Indentured, Enslaved: Chinese Prostitutes in Nineteenth Century America," in

Lucie Cheng and Edna Bonacich, eds., *Labor Immigration under Capitalism: Asian Immigrant Workers in the United States before World War II* (Berkeley: University of California Press, 1984), 402–434; Evelyn Nakano Glenn, *Issei, Nisei, War Bride: Three Generations of Japanese American Women in Domestic Service* (Philadelphia: Temple University Press, 1986).

4. Kimberle Crenshaw, "Demarginalizing the Intersection of Race and Sex: A Black Feminist Critique of Anti-discrimination Doctrine, Feminist Theory and Anti-racist Politics," *University of Chicago Legal Forum* 139 (1989); Kimberle Crenshaw, "Whose Story Is It Anyway? Feminist and Anti-racist Appropriations of Anita Hill," in Toni Morrison, ed., *Racing Justice, Engendering Power* (New York: Pantheon, 1992), 402–440; Angela Harris, "Race and Essentialism in Feminist Legal Theory," *Stanford Law Review* 42 (1990), 581–616; Patricia Hill Collins, *Black Feminist Thought* (New York: Allen and Unwin, 1990); Evelyn Nakano Glenn, "From Servitude to Service Work: Historical Continuities in the Racial Division of Women's Work," *Signs* 18, no. 1 (1992), 1–43.

5. Some preliminary attempts have been illuminating; see Candace West and Sara Fenstermaker, "Doing Difference," *Gender and Society* 9, no. 1 (1995), 8–37; Edna Bonacich, "Race, Class and Gender: A Tentative Theoretical Exploration," paper presented to Honors Colloquium, University of Rhode Island, 1994; Karen Brodkin Sacks, "Toward a Unified Theory of Class, Race and Gender," *American Ethnologist* 16, no. 3 (1989), 534–550.

6. Tessie Liu, "Teaching Differences among Women from a Historical Perspective: Rethinking Race and Gender as Social Categories," *Women's Studies International Forum* 14, no. 4 (1991); Evelyn Brooks Higginbotham, "African-American Women's History and the Meta-Language of Race," *Signs* 17, no. 2 (1992), 251–274; Amy Kaminsky, "Gender, Race, *Raza*," *Feminist Studies* 20, no. 1 (1994), 3–32; Ann Stoler, "Carnal Knowledge and Imperial Power: Gender, Race and Morality in Colonial Asia," in Joan Scott, ed., *Feminism and History* (New York: Oxford University Press, 1996), 209–266.

7. Gayle Rubin, "The Traffic in Women: Notes on the Political Economy of Sex," in Rayna R. Reiter, ed., *Toward an Anthropology of Women* (New York: Monthly Review Press, 1975), 159.

8. Joan W. Scott, "Gender: A Useful Category of Historical Analysis," *American Historical Review* 91 (Dec. 1986), 1053–1075; R. W. Connell, *Gender and Power* (Stanford: Stanford University Press, 1989); Barbara Laslett and Johanna Brenner, "Gender and Social Reproduction: Historical Perspectives," *Annual Review of Sociology* (1989), 381–404.

9. Joan Acker, "Hierarchies, Jobs, and Bodies: A Theory of Gendered Organizations," *Gender and Society* 4 (1990), 139–158; Judith Lorber, *The Paradoxes of Gender* (New Haven: Yale University Press, 1994).

10. Barrie Thorne, *Gender Play: Girls and Boys in School* (New Brunswick: Rutgers University Press, 1993); Candace West and Don Zimmerman, "Doing Gender," *Gender and Society* 1 (1987), 125–151.

11. Judith Butler, *Gender Trouble: Feminism and the Subversion of Identity* (New York: Routledge, 1990); Judith Butler, *Bodies That Matter: On the Discursive Limits of "Sex"* (New York: Routledge, 1994); Lorber, *Paradoxes of Gender.*

12. Barbara J. Fields, "Ideology and Race in American History," in J. Morgan Kousser and James M. MacPherson, eds., *Region, Race and Reconstruction: Essays in*

Honor of C. Vann Woodward (New York: Oxford University Press, 1982), 144–146; Peggy Pascoe, "Race, Gender, and Intercultural Relations: The Case of Interracial Marriage," *Frontiers* 12, no. 1 (1991), 5.

13. Fields, "Ideology and Race," 145; Barbara J. Fields, "Slavery, Race and Ideology in the United States of America," *New Left Review* 181 (1990), 107; James F. Davis, *Who Is Black? One Nation's Definition* (College Park: Pennsylvania State University Press, 1991), 99–109; Virginia Dominguez, *White by Definition: Social Classification in Creole Louisiana* (New Brunswick: Rutgers University Press, 1986), 149–181.

14. David Roediger, *The Wages of Whiteness: Race and the Making of the American Working Class* (London: Verso, 1991); Roediger, *Towards the Abolition of Whiteness* (London: Verso, 1994); Karen Brodkin Sacks, "How Did Jews Become White Folks?" in Steven Gregory and Roger Sanjek, eds., *Race* (New Brunswick: Rutgers University Press, 1994), 78–102; Tomás Almaguer, *Racial Fault Lines: The Historical Origins of White Supremacy in California* (Berkeley: University of California Press, 1994); Noel Ignatiev, *How the Irish Became White* (New York: Routledge, 1995); Matthew Frye Jacobson, *Whiteness of a Different Color: European Immigrants and the Alchemy of Race* (Cambridge, Mass.: Harvard University Press, 1998).

15. Cheryl I. Harris, "Whiteness as Property," *Harvard Law Review* 106, no. 8 (June 1993), 1707–1791.

16. Yen Espiritu, *Asian American Panethnicity: Bridging Institutions and Identities* (Philadelphia: Temple University Press, 1992). See articles in *Amerasia Journal*, 22, no. 2 (1996), esp. Leny Mendoza Strobel, "Born-Again Filipino: Filipino American Identity and Asian Panethnicity," 31–54, and Nazli Kibria, "'Not Asian, Black or White? Reflections on South Asian American Racial Identity," 77–88. Aihwa Ong, "Cultural Citizenship as Subject Making: Immigrants Negotiate Racial and Cultural Boundaries in the United States," *Current Anthropology* 37, no. 1 (1996), 751.

17. Michael Omi and Howard Winant, *Racial Formation in America*, 2d ed. (New York: Routledge, 1994), 13, 55, 63.

18. Ibid., 77–91; Carole Pateman, "The Patriarchal Welfare State," in Amy Gutmann, ed., *Democracy and the Welfare State* (Princeton: Princeton University Press, 1988), 231–278.

19. Richard Dyer, "White," *Screen* 29, no. 4 (Autumn 1988), 45–46.

20. Phyllis Marynick Palmer, *Domesticity and Dirt* (Philadelphia: Temple University Press, 1989); Peggy Pascoe, *Relations of Rescue* (New York: Oxford University Press, 1990); Vron Ware, *Beyond the Pale: White Women, Racism and History* (London: Verso, 1992).

21. Michelle Barrett, "The Concept of 'Difference,'" *Feminist Review* no. 26 (July 1987), 29–41.

22. Fields, "Slavery, Race and Ideology," 101, 110, 117.

23. Sonya Rose, "Class Formation and the Quintessential Worker," in John R. Hall, ed., *Reworking Class* (Ithaca: Cornell University Press, 1997), 147–148. Roediger, *Wages of Whiteness*, 68; Alexander Saxton, *The Rise and Fall of the White Republic: Class Politics and Mass Culture in Nineteenth-Century America* (London: Verso, 1990), 296.

24. Lillian Breslow Rubin, *Families on the Fault Line* (New York: Harper-Collins, 1994), 38–43, 206.

25. Scott, "Gender," 1067; Connell, *Gender and Power,* 99; Omi and Winant, *Racial Formation,* 55, 71.

26. Antonio Gramsci, *Selections from the Prison Notebooks* (New York: International Publishers, 1971). Michel Foucault, *Power/Knowledge: Selected Interviews and Other Writings, 1972–1977* (New York: Pantheon, 1980); Michel Foucault, *The History of Sexuality,* trans. Robert Hurley, vol. 1 (New York: Vintage, 1990).

2. Citizenship: Universalism and Exclusion

1. Reginald Horsman, *Race and Manifest Destiny* (Cambridge, Mass.: Harvard University Press, 1981), 300–301.

2. Rogers M. Smith, "'One United People': Second-Class Female Citizenship and the American Quest for Community," *Yale Journal of Law and the Humanities* 1 (1989), 244.

3. Stuart Hall and David Held, "Citizens and Citizenship," in Hall and Held, eds., *New Times: The Changing Face of Politics in the 1990s* (London: Lawrence and Wishart, 1989), 175.

4. T. H. Marshall, "Citizenship and Social Class," in *Class, Citizenship and Social Development* (New York: Doubleday, 1964), 78.

5. Benedict Anderson, *Imagined Communities,* rev. ed. (London: Verso, 1991), 19–22; James H. Kettner, *The Development of American Citizenship, 1608–1870* (Chapel Hill: University of North Carolina Press, 1978), 3.

6. Hall and Held, "Citizens and Citizenship," 175.

7. J. G. A. Pocock, "The Ideal of Citizenship since Classical Times," in Ronald Beiner, ed., *Theorizing Citizenship* (Albany: State University of New York Press, 1995), 30–32, 34–36.

8. Carole Pateman, *The Sexual Contract* (Stanford: Stanford University Press, 1988); Susan Moller Okin, *Women in Western Political Thought* (Princeton: Princeton University Press, 1979); Iris Marion Young, "Polity and Group Difference: A Critique of the Ideal of Universal Citizenship," in Beiner, ed., *Theorizing Citizenship,* 175–208; Carole Pateman, *The Disorder of Women* (Cambridge: Polity, 1989), 4; Uday S. Mehta, "Liberal Strategies of Exclusion," *Politics and Society* 18 (Dec. 1990), 436–437.

9. Joan R. Gunderson, "Independence, Citizenship, and the American Revolution," *Signs* 13, no. 1 (1987), 60; Nancy Fraser and Linda Gordon, "A Genealogy of Dependency: Tracing a Keyword of the U.S. Welfare State," *Signs* 19 (Dec. 1994), 313.

10. Kettner, *American Citizenship,* 18–19, 174–175; Gunderson, "Independence," 62.

11. David Roediger, *The Wages of Whiteness: Race and the Making of the American Working Class* (London: Verso, 1991), 28–29; Winthrop Jordan, *White over Black: American Attitudes toward the Negro, 1550–1812* (Chapel Hill: University of North Carolina Press, 1968), 291–292; Judith N. Shklar, *American Citizenship: The Quest for Inclusion* (Cambridge, Mass.: Harvard University Press, 1991), 39–42.

12. Linda K. Kerber, *No Constitutional Right to Be Ladies: Women and the Obligations of Citizenship* (New York: Hill and Wang, 1998), 11; Rogers M. Smith, *Civic Ideals: Conflicting Visions of Citizenship in U.S. History* (New Haven: Yale University Press, 1997), 112.

13. Chilton Williamson, *American Suffrage: From Property to Democracy, 1760–1860* (Princeton: Princeton University Press, 1960), 104; Philip Foner, *History of Black Americans*, vol. 1: *From Africa to the Emergence of the Cotton Kingdom* (Westport, Conn.: Greenwood Press, 1975), 517–518.

14. Gunderson, "Independence," 66.

15. Kettner, *American Citizenship*, 301, 288–300.

16. Benjamin Ringer, *"We the People" and Others: Duality and America's Treatment of Its Racial Minorities* (New York: Tavistock, 1983), 127–148.

17. Kerber, *No Constitutional Right*, 41–44.

18. Ian F. Haney López, *White by Law: The Legal Construction of Race* (New York: New York University Press, 1996), 128–129.

19. Shklar, *American Citizenship*, 3.

20. Ibid., 37.

21. Williamson, *American Suffrage*, 218–219; Smith, *Civic Ideals*, 170.

22. Shklar, *American Citizenship*, 81–82; George M. Fredrickson, *Black Liberation: A Comparative History of Black Ideologies in the United States and South Africa* (New York: Oxford University Press, 1995), 17.

23. Roediger, *Wages of Whiteness*, 54.

24. Michael Omi and Howard Winant, *Racial Formation in America*, 2d ed. (New York: Routledge, 1994), 65.

25. Fraser and Gordon, "Genealogy of Dependency," 315–316; Sonya O. Rose, "'Gender at Work': Sex, Class and Industrial Capitalism," *History Workshop* 21 (Spring 1986), 124–125.

26. William E. Forbath, "Caste, Class, and Second-Class Citizenship," *Michigan Law Review* 98 (Oct. 1999), 20.

27. Class did not completely disappear as an axis. By the middle of the nineteenth century, as industrialization and mass immigration brought about genuine proletarianization, there were attempts to repeal universal manhood suffrage and to introduce property and educational requirements. These efforts failed because workers and the politicians they elected to office refused to acquiesce in their disfranchisement. Instead, restrictions on participation were achieved by complicated registration procedures and the secret ballot which required voters to read. Fredrickson, *Black Liberation*, 17.

28. Shklar, *American Citizenship*, 48–49.

29. Williamson, *American Suffrage*, 96–98; Smith, *Civic Ideals*, 105–106, 143.

30. Smith, *Civic Ideals*, 172; Leon F. Litwack, *North of Slavery: The Negro in the Free States, 1790–1860* (Chicago: University of Chicago Press, 1961), 83–86; Williamson, *American Suffrage*, 96; Eric Foner, *The Story of American Freedom* (New York: Norton, 1998), 58.

31. Marshall, "Citizenship and Social Class," 96; Nancy Fraser and Linda Gordon, "Contract versus Charity: Why Is There No Social Citizenship in the United States?" *Socialist Review* 22, no. 2 (July 1993), 47.

32. Shklar, *American Citizenship*, 100–101.

33. Benjamin Quarles, *The Negro in the American Revolution* (Chapel Hill: University of North Carolina Press, 1961), 26–31, 52–67; Foner, *Black Americans*, vol. 1, 324–344; Ira Berlin, *Slaves without Masters: The Free Negro in the Ante-Bellum South* (New York: Pantheon, 1974), 16–20.

34. Berlin, *Slaves without Masters*, 29–35, 91; Foner, *Black Americans*, vol. 1,

517; Litwack, *North of Slavery*, 13, 9–11, 14; Peter S. Onuff, *Statehood and the Union: A History of the Northwest Ordinance* (Bloomington: Indiana University Press, 1987), 70–74, 111–116.

35. Roediger, *Wages of Whiteness*, 57.

36. Kettner, *American Citizenship*, 312–314; Litwack, *North of Slavery*, 35–39; Peter Schuck and Rogers M. Smith, *Citizenship without Consent: The Illegal Alien in the American Polity* (New Haven: Yale University Press, 1985), 66–68.

37. Smith, *Civic Ideals*, 178–179; Berlin, *Slaves without Masters*, 48–50, 89–107, 316–340; Foner, *Black Americans*, vol. 1, 453–455, 508–515, 521–523; John Hope Franklin and Loren Schweninger, *Runaway Slaves: Rebels on the Plantation* (New York: Oxford University Press, 1999), 11–15.

38. Litwack, *North of Slavery*, 70, 263, 154, 162, 91, 97.

39. Ibid., 248–252.

40. Smith, *Civic Ideals*, 253; Litwack, *North of Slavery*, 250–252; Eric Foner, *Free Soil, Free Labor, Free Men: The Ideology of the Republican Party before the Civil War* (New York: Oxford University Press, 1995), 134–136.

41. Smith, *Civic Ideals*, 176.

42. Ringer, *"We the People,"* 104–107; Litwack, *North of Slavery*, 60–61.

43. Eric Foner, *Reconstruction: America's Unfinished Revolution, 1863–1877* (New York: Harper and Row, 1988), 51.

44. Allan Spear, "Origins of the Urban Ghetto, 1870–1915," in Nathan I. Huggins, Martin Kilson, and Daniel M. Fox, eds., *Key Issues in the Afro-American Experience* (New York: Harcourt Brace Jovanovich, 1971), 158–159; Paul R. Spickard, *Mixed Blood: Intermarriage and Ethnic Identity in Twentieth-Century America* (Madison: University of Wisconsin Press, 1989), 374.

45. Spear, "Urban Ghetto," 159; David Delaney, *Race, Place, and the Law, 1836–1948* (Austin: University of Texas Press, 1998), 125–147, 149–180; Douglas S. Massey and Nancy A. Denton, *American Apartheid: Segregation and the Making of the Underclass* (Cambridge, Mass.: Harvard University Press, 1993), 30–35; Melvin L. Oliver and Thomas M. Shapiro, *Black Wealth, White Wealth: A New Perspective on Racial Inequality* (New York: Routledge, 1996), 33–52; William J. Wilson, *The Declining Significance of Race: Blacks and Changing American Institutions*, 2d ed. (Chicago: University of Chicago Press, 1980), 79–80; Howard N. Rabinowitz, *Race Relations in the Urban South, 1865–1890* (New York: Oxford University Press, 1978), 196.

46. Ringer, *"We The People,"* 218–224.

47. In Corrigan v. Buckley, 1926: Ringer, "We the People," 258; Delaney, *Race, Place, and Law*, 154–156.

48. Desmond King, "The Segregated State? Black Americans and the Federal Government," *Democratization* 2 (1995/6), 66, 71; Desmond King, *Separate and Unequal: Black Americans and the U.S. Federal Government* (New York: Oxford University Press, 1995), 28–30, 72–171, 4; Oliver and Shapiro, *Black Wealth*, 17, 18, 38–39, 41–42; Gwendolyn Mink, *The Wages of Whiteness: Inequality in the Welfare State, 1917–1942* (Ithaca: Cornell University Press, 1995), 49–50.

49. Fredrickson, *Black Liberation*, 104–114; King, *Separate and Unequal*, 10; Robin D. G. Kelley, "'We Are Not What We Seem': Rethinking Black Working-class Opposition in the Jim Crow South," *Journal of American History* 80 (June 1993), 77–78; Spear, "Urban Ghetto," 159–160, 165–166.

50. August Meier and Elliott Rudwick, "Early Boycotts of Segregated Schools: The Case of Springfield Ohio, 1922–23," in Meier and Rudwick, eds., *Along the Color Line: Explorations in the Black Experience* (Urbana: University of Illinois Press, 1976), 290; Litwack, *North of Slavery*, 142–151.

51. George C. Wright, *Life behind a Veil: Blacks in Louisville, Kentucky, 1865–1930* (Baton Rouge: Louisiana State University Press, 1985), 65–70; Rabinowitz, *Race Relations in the Urban South*, 171–179.

52. Kerber, *No Constitutional Right*, 146; Lawrence J. Friedman, *Inventors of the Promised Land* (New York: Knopf, 1975), 119.

53. Kerber, *No Constitutional Right*, 146–147.

54. Alexis de Tocqueville, *Democracy in America*, ed. J. P. Mayer, trans. George Lawrence (New York: Perennial Library, 1988), 600–603; Mary P. Ryan, *Cradle of the Middle Class: The Family in Oneida County, New York, 1790–1865* (Cambridge: Cambridge University Press, 1981), 179–181; Carl Degler, *At Odds: Women and the Family in America from the Revolution to the Present* (New York: Oxford University Press, 1980), 332–333; Mary Beth Norton, *Liberty's Daughters: The Revolutionary Experience of American Women, 1750–1800*, with a new preface (Ithaca: Cornell University Press, 1996), 242–250, 272–287.

55. Elizabeth Bowles Warbasse, *The Changing Legal Rights of Married Women, 1800–1861* (New York: Garland, 1987), 287–291; Richard H. Chused, "Married Women's Property Law: 1800–1850," *Georgetown Law Journal* 71 (June 1983), 1398–1426.

56. Paula Baker, "The Domestication of Politics: Women and American Political Society, 1780–1920," *American Historical Review* 89, no. 3 (June 1984), 625–632; Ellen Carol DuBois, *Feminism and Suffrage: The Emergence of an Independent Women's Movement in America, 1848–1869*, with a new preface (Ithaca: Cornell University Press, 1999), 22; Janet Zollinger Giele, *Two Paths to Women's Equality: Temperance, Suffrage, and the Origins of Modern Feminism* (New York: Twayne, 1995), 54.

57. Eleanor Flexner, *Century of Struggle: The Woman's Rights Movement in the United States*, rev. ed. (Cambridge, Mass.: Harvard University Press, 1982), 45–50, 71–77; Giele, *Two Paths*, 56–58; Ellen Carol DuBois, *Woman Suffrage and Women's Rights* (New York: New York University Press, 1998), 85.

58. DuBois, *Woman Suffrage*, 88; Kathryn Kish Sklar, *Catharine Beecher: A Study in American Domesticity* (New Haven: Yale University Press, 1973), 132, 158–164.

59. DuBois, *Woman Suffrage*, 94, 116; DuBois, *Feminism and Suffrage*, 190–202; Flexner, *Century of Struggle*, 154–156.

60. DuBois, *Woman Suffrage*, 117.

61. Jo Freeman, "The Revolution for Women in Law and Public Policy," in *Women: A Feminist Perspective*, 4th ed. (Mountain View, Calif.: Mayfield, 1995), 371, citing *Bradwell v. Illinois* 83 U.S. (16 Wall.) 130, 141–42 (J. Bradley, concurring).

62. DuBois, *Woman Suffrage*, 129–131.

63. Smith, *Civic Ideals*, 388, 389; Flexner, *Century of Struggle*, 228.

64. Giele, *Two Paths*, 63, 79, 94, 96, 99, 101, 105–106, 111; Smith, *Civic Ideals*, 387.

65. Smith, *Civic Ideals*, 387–388.

66. Ibid., 390.

67. Flexner, *Century of Struggle*, 208–221; Kathryn Kish Sklar, "Two Political Cultures in the Progressive Era: The National Consumers' League and the American Association for Labor Legislation," in Linda Kerber, Alice Kessler-Harris, and Kathryn Kish Sklar, eds., *U.S. History as Women's History: New Feminist Essays* (Chapel Hill: University of North Carolina Press, 1995), 43–51; Alice Kessler-Harris, *Out to Work: A History of Wage-Earning Women in the United States* (New York: Oxford University Press, 1982), 166, 171, 205.

68. Flexner, *Century of Struggle*, 223, 225, 316–318; Elna C. Green, *Southern Strategies: Southern Women and the Woman Suffrage Question* (Chapel Hill: University of North Carolina Press, 1997), 10; on the differential value of black and white babies leading to different policies toward unmarried white and black mothers, see Rickie Sollinger, *Wake Up Little Susie: Single Pregnancy and Race in the Pre–Roe v. Wade Era* (New York: Routledge, 1992).

69. Freeman, "Revolution for Women," 372.

70. Smith, *Civic Ideals*, 17.

71. Gunnar Myrdal, *The American Dilemma: The Negro Problem and Modern Democracy* (New York: Harper, 1944) 2 v., 1–25, 1021–1022, xix.

72. James B. McKee, *Sociology and the Race Problem: The Failure of a Perspective* (Urbana: University of Illinois Press, 1993), 2, 6–9.

73. Michael Burawoy, personal communication; Anthony Giddens, "T. H. Marshall, the State, and Democracy," in Martin Bulmer and Anthony M. Rees, eds., *Citizenship Today: The Contemporary Relevance of T. H. Marshall* (London: UCL Press, 1996), 66.

74. Angela P. Harris, "Foreword: The Jurisprudence of Reconstruction," *California Law Review* 82 (July 1994), 744.

75. Ringer, "*We the People*," 8.

76. Smith, *Civic Ideals*, 6, 35–39.

77. James C. Scott, *Domination and the Arts of Resistance: Hidden Transcripts* (New Haven: Yale University Press, 1990), 183–201.

78. See Charles McClain, *In Search of Equality: The Chinese Struggle against Discrimination in Nineteenth-Century America* (Berkeley: University of California Press, 1994); Lucy E. Salyer, *Laws Harsh as Tigers: Chinese Immigrants and the Shaping of Modern Immigration Law* (Chapel Hill: University of North Carolina Press, 1995); Guadalupe San Miguel, "*Let All of Them Take Heed*": *Mexican Americans and the Campaign for Educational Equality in Texas, 1910–1981* (Austin: University of Texas Press, 1987).

79. Marshall, "Citizenship and Social Class," 107.

80. Renato Rosaldo, "Cultural Citizenship in San José, California," *PoLAR* 17 (Nov. 1994), 57.

3. Labor: Freedom and Coercion

1. See Keith McClelland, "Rational and Respectable Men: Gender, the Working Class, and Citizenship in Britain, 1850–1867," in Laura L. Frader and Sonya O. Rose, eds., *Gender and Class in Modern Europe* (Ithaca: Cornell University Press, 1996), 287.

2. Eric Foner, *Free Soil, Free Labor, Free Men: The Ideology of the Republican*

Party before the Civil War (New York: Oxford University Press, 1995), 12–13; David Roediger, *The Wages of Whiteness: Race and the Making of the American Working Class* (London: Verso, 1991), 21; Judith Shklar, *American Citizenship: The Quest for Inclusion* (Cambridge, Mass.: Harvard University Press, 1991), 64.

3. Shklar, *American Citizenship*, 68–69.

4. Foner, *Free Soil*, 13–14.

5. Shklar, *American Citizenship*, 68, 66–67; William E. Forbath, "The Ambiguities of Free Labor: Labor and the Law in the Gilded Age," *Wisconsin Law Review*, 1985, no. 4, 774–775; Foner, *Free Soil*, 15–16.

6. Roediger, *Wages of Whiteness*, 25; Robert J. Steinfeld, *The Invention of Free Labor: The Employment Relation in English and American Law and Culture, 1350–1870* (Chapel Hill: University of North Carolina Press, 1991), 41–54. The term "servant" in these statutes, and often in the vernacular, referred to a wide variety of workers employed by another, not just household help.

7. Bernard Bailyn, with the assistance of Barbara DeWolfe, *Voyagers to the West: A Passage in the Peopling of America on the Eve of the American Revolution* (New York: Knopf, 1986), 166, 172–174; Steinfeld, *Invention of Free Labor*, 171–172.

8. Bailyn, *Voyagers to the West*, 296–353.

9. Roediger, *Wages of Whiteness*, 54, 49; Steinfeld, *Invention of Free Labor*, 127.

10. Roediger, *Wages of Whiteness*, 57; Robert J. Steinfeld, "The Philadelphia Cordwainers' Case of 1806: The Struggle over Alternative Legal Constructions of a Free Market in Labor," in Christopher L. Tomlins and Andrew J. King, eds., *Labor Law in America: Historical and Critical Essays* (Baltimore: Johns Hopkins University Press, 1992), 37.

11. Arthur F. McEvoy, "Freedom of Contract, Labor, and the Administrative State," in Harry N. Schreiber, ed., *The State and Freedom of Contract* (Stanford: Stanford University Press), 203.

12. Roediger, *Wages of Whiteness*, 46; Steinfeld, *Invention of Free Labor*, 154.

13. Steinfeld, *Invention of Free Labor*, 143–146.

14. McEvoy, "Freedom of Contract," 203; Steinfeld, *Invention of Free Labor*, 157.

15. Bruce Laurie, *Artisans into Workers: Labor in Nineteenth Century America* (New York: Hill and Wang, 1989), 64.

16. Laurie, *Artisans into Workers*, 79–84; Roediger, *Wages of Whiteness*, 66–74.

17. Eric Foner, *The Story of American Freedom* (New York: Norton, 1998), 65–68.

18. Foner, *Free Soil*, 15, 30; Forbath, "Ambiguities of Free Labor," 769, 774–775, 779–780; Steinfeld, *Invention of Free Labor*, 124–125.

19. Foner, *Free Soil*, 23–24, 30; David Montgomery, *Beyond Equality: Labor and the Radical Republicans, 1862–1872* (New York: Knopf, 1967), 30.

20. Foner, *Story of American Freedom*, 85, 86–88; Forbath, "Ambiguities of Free Labor," 784; David Roediger, "Race, Labor and Gender," in Stanley L. Engerman, ed., *Terms of Labor: Slavery, Serfdom and Free Labor* (Stanford: Stanford University Press, 1999), 186.

21. Foner, *Free Soil*, 40–51, 68–69.

22. Shklar, *American Citizenship*, 79; Foner, *Free Soil*, 58–61.

23. McEvoy, "Freedom of Contract," 203.

24. Philip S. Foner, ed., *Life and Writings of Frederick Douglass* (New York: In-

ternational Publishers, 1955), vol. 4, 271–272; Reva Siegel, "Home as Work: The First Women's Rights Claims Concerning Wives' Household Labor, 1850–1880," *Yale Law Journal* 103 (March 1994), 1076–1079.

25. Foner, *Free Soil*, 66–67; Roediger, "Race, Labor and Gender," 170–179.

26. Robert F. Heizer and Alan F. Almquist, *The Other Californians: Prejudice and Discrimination under Spain, Mexico and the United States to 1920* (Berkeley: University of California Press, 1971), 47; James J. Rawls, *Indians of California: The Changing Image* (Norman: University of Oklahoma Press, 1984), 91.

27. Steinfeld, *Invention of Free Labor*, 179–184.

28. Elmer C. Sandemeyer, *The Anti-Chinese Movement in California* (Urbana: University of Illinois Press, 1939), 25–29; Gunther Barth, *Bitter Strength: A History of the Chinese in the United States* (Cambridge, Mass.: Harvard University Press, 1964), 57; Lucy E. Salyer, *Laws Harsh as Tigers: Chinese Immigrants and the Shaping of Modern Immigration Law* (Chapel Hill: University of North Carolina Press, 1995), 10.

29. Jeanne Boydston, "To Earn Her Daily Bread: Housework and Ante-bellum Working-Class Subsistence," in Vicki L. Ruiz and Ellen Carol DuBois, eds., *Unequal Sisters: A Multicultural Reader in Women's History*, 3d ed. (New York: Routledge, 2000), 84–85; Jeanne Boydston, *Home and Work: Housework, Wages, and the Ideology of Labor in the Early Republic* (New York: Oxford University Press, 1990), 89, 93–94; Eileen Boris, *Home to Work: Motherhood and the Politics of Industrial Homework in the United States* (New York: Cambridge University Press, 1994); Joan M. Jensen, *Loosening the Bonds: Mid-Atlantic Farm Women, 1750–1850* (New Haven: Yale University Press, 1986), 134–136; Joan Jensen, "Cloth, Butter, and Boarders: Household Production for the Market," *Review of Radical Political Economy*, 12 (Summer 1980), 15–18; James Oliver Horton, "Freedom's Yoke: Gender Conventions among Ante-bellum Free Blacks," *Feminist Studies* 51 (1986), 60–66; see Carole Turbin, "Beyond Conventional Wisdom: Women's Wage Work, Household Economic Contribution, and Labor Activism in a Mid-Nineteenth Century Working Class Community," in Carole Groneman and Mary Beth Norton, eds., *"To Toil the Livelong Day": America's Women at Work, 1780–1980* (Ithaca: Cornell University Press, 1987).

30. Glenn Matthews, *"Just a Housewife": The Rise and Fall of Domesticity in America* (New York: Oxford University Press, 1987), 11–17; Ruth Schwarz Cowan, *More Work for Mother: The Ironies of Household Technology from the Open Hearth to the Microwave Oven* (New York: Basic Books, 1983), 63–68. See Boydston, *Home and Work*, 132–133, and Jensen, "Cloth, Butter, and Boarders," 18–20, for calculations of the relative economic contribution of women's labor to family income.

31. Reva B. Siegel, "The Modernization of Marital Law: Adjudicating Wives' Rights to Earnings, 1860–1930," *Georgetown Journal of Law* 82, no. 7 (Sept. 1994), 2130, 2174–2181; Mary Blewitt, *Men, Women and Work: Class, Gender, and Protest in the New England Shoe Industry, 1780–1910* (Urbana: University of Illinois Press, 1988), 45.

32. Nancy F. Cott, *The Bonds of Womanhood: "Woman's Sphere" in New England, 1780–1835* (New Haven: Yale University Press, 1977), 63–100; Carl N. Degler, *At Odds: Women and the Family in America from the Revolution to the Present* (New York: Oxford University Press, 1980), 26–51; Alice Kessler-Harris, *Out to Work: A History of Wage-Earning Women in the United States* (New York: Oxford University Press, 1982), 49–50.

33. Siegel, "Home as Work," 1112–1146; Richard H. Chused, "Married Women's Property Law, 1800–1850," *Georgetown Journal of Law* 71 (June 1983), 1359–1425; Elizabeth Bowles Warbasse, *The Changing Legal Rights of Married Women, 1800–1861* (New York: Garland, 1987), 137–247.

34. Harry N. Scheiber, Harold G. Vatter, and Harold Underwood Faulkner, *American Economic History* (New York: Harper and Row, 1976), 221–227; Joshua Freeman et al., *Who Built America? Working People and the Nation's Economy, Politics, Culture and Society,* vol. 2: *From the Gilded Age to the Present* (New York: Pantheon, 1992), 7–19; Alfred D. Chandler Jr., *The Visible Hand: The Managerial Revolution in American Business* (Cambridge, Mass.: Harvard University Press, 1977), 124–125, 148–159, 287–314.

35. Laurie, *Artisans into Workers,* 116–121. On immigrant labor, see Montgomery, *Beyond Equality,* 35–37; Scheiber et al., *American Economic History,* 240–243; Richard A. Easterlin, David Ward, William S. Bernard, and Reed Ueda, *Immigration: Dimensions of Ethnicity* (Cambridge, Mass.: Harvard University Press, 1982), 21–26; John Higham, *Send These to Me: Immigrants in Urban America* (Baltimore: Johns Hopkins University Press, 1984), 23.

36. Harry L. Braverman, *Labor and Monopoly Capital: The Degradation of Work in the Twentieth Century* (New York: Monthly Review Press, 1975), esp. 59–69, 257–269; Dan Clawson, *Bureaucracy and the Labor Process: The Transformation of U.S. Industry, 1860–1920* (New York: Monthly Review Press, 1980), esp. 167–201.

37. Alexander Saxton, *The Rise and Fall of the White Republic: Class Politics and Mass Culture in Nineteenth-Century America* (London: Verso, 1990), 16.

38. Barbara J. Fields, "Ideology and Race in American History," in J. Morgan Kousser and James M. MacPherson, eds., *Region, Race and Reconstruction: Essays in Honor of C. Vann Woodward* (New York: Oxford University Press, 1982), 143–177.

39. For various formulations, see Margaret Benston, "The Political Economy of Women's Liberation," *Monthly Review* 21 (Sept. 1969), 13–27; Wally Secombe, "The Housewife and Her Labour under Capitalism," *New Left Review* 83 (Jan.–Feb. 1974), 3–24; Batya Weinbaum and Amy Bridges, "The Other Side of the Paycheck," in Zillah R. Eisenstein, ed., *Capitalist Patriarchy and the Case for Socialist Feminism* (New York: Monthly Review Press, 1979); Michele Barrett, *Women's Oppression Today: Problems in Marxist Feminist Thought* (London: Verso, 1980); Natalie Sokoloff, *Between Money and Love: The Dialectics of Women's Home and Market Work* (New York: Praeger, 1980).

40. Edith Abbott, *Women in Industry: A Study in American Economic History* (1910; New York: Arno, 1969), 109–147; Gerda Lerner, "The Lady and the Mill Girl: Changes in the Status of Women in the Age of Jackson, 1800–1840," in Nancy F. Cott and Elizabeth H. Pleck, eds., *A Heritage of Her Own: Toward a New Social History of American Womanhood* (New York: Simon and Schuster, 1979), 189; Thomas Woody, *A History of Women's Education in the United States* (New York: Science Press, 1929), vol. 1, 460–518; Joseph A. Hill, *Women in Gainful Occupations, 1870–1920,* Census Monographs IX (Washington: Government Printing Office, 1929), 54, table 39.

41. Kessler-Harris, *Out to Work,* 49–54.

42. Heidi Hartmann, "Capitalism, Patriarchy, and Job Segregation by Sex," *Signs* 1, no. 1 (1976), 159–167.

43. For connections between family breadwinning and masculinity, see Ava Baron, "An 'Other' Side of Gender Antagonism at Work: Men, Boys, and the

Remasculinization of Printers' Work, 1830–1920," in Baron, ed., *Work Engendered: Toward a New History of American Labor* (Ithaca: Cornell University Press, 1991), 67–68; Mary Blewitt, "Manhood and the Market: The Politics of Gender and Class among the Textile Workers in Fall River, Massachusetts, 1870–1880," in Baron, ed., *Work Engendered*, 92–113.

44. Gwendolyn Mink, *The Wages of Motherhood: Inequality in the Welfare State, 1917–1942* (Ithaca: Cornell University Press, 1995), 49–52; Linda K. Kerber, *No Constitutional Right to Be Ladies: Women and the Obligations of Citizenship* (New York: Hill and Wang, 1998), 47–80.

45. Martha May, "Bread before Roses: American Working Men, Labor Unions and the Family Wage," in Ruth Milkman, ed., *Women, Work and Protests: A Century of U.S. Women's Labor History* (Boston: Routledge and Kegan Paul, 1985), 3–6; Leon F. Litwack, *Been in the Storm So Long: The Aftermath of Slavery* (New York: Knopf, 1979), 244–246; Herbert G. Gutman, *The Black Family in Slavery and Freedom, 1750–1925* (New York: Pantheon, 1976), 167–168; Eric Foner, *Reconstruction: America's Unfinished Revolution, 1863–1877* (New York: Harper and Row, 1988), 84–87, 103–105, 108.

46. Foner, *Story of American Freedom*, 117; Laurie, *Artisans into Workers*, 128; David Montgomery, *The Fall of the House of Labor: The Workplace, the State, and American Labor Activism, 1865–1925* (New York: Cambridge University Press, 1987), 138–140; Elizabeth H. Pleck, "A Mother's Wages: Income Earning among Married Black and Italian Women, 1896–1911," in Cott and Pleck, eds., *A Heritage of Her Own*, 343–366.

47. Alexander Keyssar, *Out of Work: The First Century of Unemployment in Massachusetts* (New York: Cambridge University Press, 1986), 14, 47, 52; Foner, *Story of American Freedom*, 117.

48. David Montgomery, *Workers' Control in America: Studies in the History of Work, Technology, and Labor Strategies* (New York: Cambridge University Press, 1979), 20. Florence Peterson, *Strikes in the United States, 1880–1936*, U.S. Bureau of Labor Statistics, Bulletin no. 651 (Washington: Government Printing Office, 1938), 29, documented that 38,303 strikes and lockouts involving 9,529,434 workers took place between 1881 and 1905. Also see Freeman et al., *Who Built America*, 123; Kim Voss, *The Making of American Exceptionalism: The Knights of Labor and Class Formation in the Nineteenth Century* (Ithaca: Cornell University Press, 1993), 125–126.

49. Laurie, *Artisans into Workers*, 136; William E. Forbath, *Law and the Shaping of the American Labor Movement* (Cambridge, Mass.: Harvard University Press, 1991), 59–79.

50. Forbath, "Ambiguities of Free Labor," 795–800; McEvoy, "Freedom of Contract," 211–223.

51. Montgomery, *Beyond Equality*, 252; Steinfeld, *Invention of Free Labor*, 186–187.

52. Montgomery, *Beyond Equality*, 176–185; Voss, *American Exceptionalism*, 72–89.

53. Laurie, *Artisans into Workers*, 176–211; Freeman et al., *Who Built America*, 184–187; David Brian Robertson, *Capital, Labor and State: The Battle for American Labor Markets from the Civil War to the New Deal* (Lanham, Md.: Rowman and Littlefield, 2000), 66–67, 76; Forbath, *Law and American Labor Movement*, 130–141.

54. Rogers M. Smith, "'One United People': Second-Class Female Citizen-

ship and the American Quest for Community," *Yale Journal of Law and the Humanities*, 1 (1989), 260.

55. Blewitt, *Men, Women and Work*, 36–39, 123–140; Foner, *Story of American Freedom*, 80; Kessler-Harris, *Out to Work*, 77; Siegel, "Home as Work," 1189–1198.

56. Braverman, *Labor and Monopoly Capital*, 169–182; David M. Gordon, Richard Edwards, and Michael Reich, *Segmented Work, Divided Workers: The Historical Transformation of Labor in the United States* (Cambridge: Cambridge University Press, 1982), 112–121, 204–208, 141–142.

57. Kessler-Harris, *Out to Work*, 153–156; Rudolph M. Lapp, *Blacks in Gold Rush California* (New Haven: Yale University Press, 1977), 24; Mario Barrera, *Race and Class in the Southwest: A Theory of Racial Inequality* (Notre Dame: University of Notre Dame Press, 1979), 50–51; Edna Bonacich, "Asian Labor in the Development of California and Hawaii," in Lucie Cheng and Edna Bonacich, eds., *Labor Immigration under Capitalism: Asian Workers in the United States before World War II* (Berkeley: University of California Press, 1984), 174–175.

58. For example, black and white dockworkers in New Orleans had a long history of sharing jobs and biracial unionism. See Eric Arnesen, *Waterfront Workers in New Orleans: Race, Class and Politics, 1863–1923* (New York: Oxford University Press, 1991). The United Mine Workers of America was an interracial union from its earliest days. The most notorious instance of employers' violence against interracial strikes was the Ludlow massacre of 1914, in which armed militia fired machine guns at strikers and set fire to their tents, killing 14 including 11 children. Freedman et al., *Who Built America*, 197–198.

59. Alice Kessler-Harris, *A Woman's Wage: Historical Meanings and Social Consequences* (Lexington: University Press of Kentucky, 1990), 3, 8–9; California State Senate, *Special Committee on Chinese Immigration: Its Social, Moral, and Political Effect: Report to the California State Senate of Its Special Committee on Chinese Immigration* (Sacramento: State Printing Office, 1878), 47–49.

60. Montgomery, *Fall of the House of Labor*, 242–243; Joanne Preston, "Gender and the Formation of a Woman's Profession: The Case of Public School Teaching," in Dana Dunn, ed., *Workplace/Women's Place: An Anthology* (Los Angeles: Roxbury Press, 1997), 329–331; David M. Katzman, *Seven Days a Week: Women and Domestic Service in Industrializing America* (New York: Oxford University Press, 1978), 221.

61. May, "Bread before Roses," 5.

62. Kessler-Harris, *Woman's Wage*, 10–11. See Robert W. Smuts, *Women and Work in America* (New York: Schocken, 1971), 11–12, for descriptions of town and urban families keeping livestock and growing vegetables in the coal mining regions of Pennsylvania and even in Queens, Brooklyn, and uptown Manhattan in the 1890s. See Kessler-Harris, *Out to Work*, 123–124, on the widespread use of children's labor, and Boris, *Home to Work*, 9–14, on industrial homework.

63. Nancy Fraser and Linda Gordon, "A Genealogy of Dependency: Tracing a Keyword in the U.S. Welfare State," *Signs* 19, no. 2 (1994), 318.

64. Kessler-Harris, *Woman's Wage*, 3–10, 36–39; May, "Bread before Roses," 8, 9; Boydston, *Home and Work*, 47–55.

65. Kessler-Harris, *Out to Work*, 184, 186, 188, 205–210; Barbara M. Wertheimer, *We Were There: The Story of Working Women in America* (New York: Pantheon, 1977), 212–224.

66. Kessler-Harris, *Out to Work*, 183–187; Smith, "One United People," 271–272.

67. Smith, "One United People," 273.

68. Tomás Almaguer, *Racial Fault Lines: The Historical Origins of White Supremacy in California* (Berkeley: University of California Press, 1994), 174, 6, 180; Saxton, *Rise and Fall of the White Republic*, 297, 299.

69. Bob Blauner, *Racial Oppression in America* (New York: Harper and Row, 1972), 63–64; Evelyn Nakano Glenn, "Racial Ethnic Women's Work: The Intersection of Race, Gender, and Class Oppression," *Review of Radical Political Economy* 17, no. 3 (Fall 1985), 89–91.

70. Sarah Deutsch, *No Separate Refuge: Culture, Class, and Gender on an Anglo-Hispanic Frontier in the American Southwest, 1880–1940* (New York: Oxford University Press, 1987), 88–93; Barrera, *Race and Class in the Southwest*, 41.

71. William Cohen, *At Freedom's Edge: Black Mobility and the Southern White Quest for Racial Control, 1861–1915* (Baton Rouge: Louisiana State University Press, 1991), 19–22.

72. Albert Camarillo, *Chicanos in a Changing Society: From Mexican Pueblos to American Barrios in Santa Barbara and Southern California, 1848–1930* (Cambridge, Mass.: Harvard University Press, 1979), 213–214.

73. Neil R. McMillen, *Dark Journey: Black Mississippians in the Age of Jim Crow* (Urbana: University of Illinois Press, 1990), 133; Deutsch, *No Separate Refuge*, 92; Jacqueline Jones, *Labor of Love, Labor of Sorrow: Black Women, Work, and the Family from Slavery to the Present* (New York: Basic Books, 1985), 87–91.

74. Karen Orren, *Belated Feudalism: Labor, the Law, and Liberal Development in the United States* (New York: Cambridge University Press, 1991), 15–19, 211–215.

75. Shklar, *American Citizenship*, 64.

76. Kerber, *No Constitutional Right*, 51–52.

77. Ibid., 55.

78. Ibid., 58; Foner, *Reconstruction*, 56.

79. Neil Foley, *The White Scourge: Mexicans, Blacks, and Poor Whites in Texas Cotton Culture* (Berkeley: University of California Press, 1997), 37.

80. Amy Dru Stanley, "Beggars Can't Be Choosers: Compulsion and Contract in Post-bellum America," in Christopher L. Tomlins and Andrew J. King, eds., *Labor Law in America: Historical and Critical Essays* (Baltimore: Johns Hopkins University Press, 1992), 143–144.

81. Stanley, "Beggars Can't Be Choosers," 133–134.

82. Joanne Goodwin, "'Employable Mothers' and 'Suitable Work': A Re-evaluation of Welfare and Wage-earning for Women in the Twentieth-Century United States," *Journal of Social History* 29, no. 2 (1995), 257–258; Mink, *Wages of Motherhood*, 50–51.

4. Blacks and Whites in the South

1. Neil R. McMillen, *Dark Journey: Black Mississippians in the Age of Jim Crow* (Urbana: University of Illinois Press, 1989), 39; Glenda Elizabeth Gilmore, *Gender and Jim Crow: Women and the Politics of White Supremacy in North Carolina, 1896–1920* (Chapel Hill: University of North Carolina Press, 1996), 123.

2. Eric Foner, *Reconstruction: America's Unfinished Revolution, 1863–1877* (New York: Harper and Row, 1988), 176–280.

3. Leon F. Litwack, *Been in the Storm So Long: The Aftermath of Slavery* (New York: Knopf, 1979), 546; W. E. B. Du Bois, *Black Reconstruction* (New York: Russel and Russel, 1935), 371; Thomas Holt, *Black over White: Negro Political Leadership in South Carolina during Reconstruction* (Urbana: University of Illinois Press, 1977), 35; McMillen, *Dark Journey*, 36.

4. Holt, *Black over White*, 11–12.

5. Litwack, *Been in the Storm*, 548; Elsa Barkley Brown, "To Catch the Vision of Freedom: Reconstructing Southern Black Women's Political History, 1865–1880," in Ann D. Gordon, ed., *African American Women and the Vote, 1837–1965* (Amherst: University of Massachusetts Press, 1997), 73.

6. Elsa Barkley Brown, "Negotiating and Transforming the Public Sphere: African American Political Life in the Transition from Slavery to Freedom," *Public Culture* 7 (1994), 120, 110.

7. Brown, "To Catch the Vision," 79, 76–77; Brown, "Negotiating and Transforming," 121.

8. Brown, "To Catch the Vision," 80n41, 81; Peter J. Rachleff, *Black Labor in the South: Richmond, Virginia, 1865–1890* (Philadelphia: Temple University Press, 1984) 32.

9. Dorothy Sterling, ed., *We Are Your Sisters: Black Women in the Nineteenth Century* (New York: Norton, 1984), 370–371; Holt, *Black over White*, 35; Brown, "Negotiating and Transforming," 122–124.

10. Brown, "Negotiating and Transforming," 123–124; Holt, *Black over White*, 35; Brown, "To Catch the Vision," 82–83; Sterling, *We Are Your Sisters*, 370; Gilmore, *Gender and Jim Crow*, 107.

11. Litwack, *Been in the Storm*, 400; McMillen, *Dark Journey*, 112.

12. The Southern Homestead Act of 1866 made 80-acre homesteads on federal land in Florida, Alabama, Mississippi, Louisiana, and Arkansas available to freedpeople. However, funds for stock, tools, and subsistence were not allocated. In the six years of the program only 4,000 black farmers gained homesteads, mostly in Florida; only a third of them managed to hold on to the land as of 1870. See William Cohen, *At Freedom's Edge: Black Mobility and the Southern White Quest for Racial Control, 1861–1915* (Baton Rouge: Louisiana State University Press, 1991), 53; Du Bois, *Black Reconstruction*, 611.

13. McMillen, *Dark Journey*, 119, 120; Hortense Powdermaker, *After Freedom: A Cultural Study in the Deep South* (New York: Viking, 1939), 106.

14. In Mississippi, surveys of land ownership showed a consistent pattern between 1900 and 1940 that 85 percent of black farm operators did not own land. See McMillen, *Dark Journey*, 113.

15. See Herbert G. Gutman, *The Black Family in Slavery and Freedom, 1750–1925* (New York: Pantheon, 1976), 363–431; Jacqueline Jones, *Labor of Love, Labor of Sorrow: Black Women, Work, and the Family from Slavery to the Present* (New York: Basic Books, 1985), 48.

16. Cohen, *At Freedom's Edge*, 16; Jones, *Labor of Love*, 58–59.

17. Foner, *Reconstruction*, 173; Jones, *Labor of Love*, 60–61.

18. Foner, *Reconstruction*, 173–174; Cohen, *At Freedom's Edge*, 21, 20; Roger L. Ransom and Richard Sutch, *One Kind of Freedom: The Economic Consequences of Emancipation* (Cambridge: Cambridge University Press, 1977), 87–88, 68–70; Jones, *Labor of Love*, 61.

19. Ray Stannard Baker, *Following the Color Line: American Negro Citizenship in*

the Progressive Era (1908; New York: Harper and Row, 1964), 76; Jones, *Labor of Love*, 82–83; McMillen, *Dark Journey*, 133; Theodore Rosengarten, *All God's Dangers: The Life of Nate Shaw* (New York: Knopf, 1975), 26.

20. McMillen, *Dark Journey*, 133; Cohen, *At Freedom's Edge*, 18, quotes an Alabaman who admits there was "a good deal of cheating" in his area.

21. Cohen, *At Freedom's Edge*, 282, 230–232.

22. John Dittmer, *Black Georgia in the Progressive Era, 1900–1920* (Urbana: University of Illinois Press, 1977), 76–77; see also Pete Daniels, *The Shadow of Slavery: Peonage in the South, 1901–1969* (Urbana: University of Illinois Press, 1972), 23–39.

23. William C. Cohen, "Negro Involuntary Servitude in the South, 1865–1940: A Preliminary Analysis," *Journal of Southern History* 42, no. 1 (Feb. 1976), 47–51; Herbert Aptheker, ed., *A Documentary History of the Negro People in the United States*, vol. 3 (New York: Citadel Press, 1993), 31–32; Dittmer, *Black Georgia*, 87–88; Tera W. Hunter, "Domination and Resistance: The Politics of Wage Household Labor in New South Atlanta," *Labor History* 34 (Spring/Summer 1993), 257–258; Walter F. White, "'Work or Fight' in the South," in Aptheker, ed. *Documentary History*, 238–239.

24. David Oshinsky, *"Worse than Slavery": Parchman Farm and the Ordeal of Jim Crow Justice* (New York: Free Press, 1996), 35–36, 47–48; Cohen, *Freedom's Edge*, 225–226.

25. Oshinsky, *"Worse than Slavery,"* 57–58, 60, 63–64, 70–71, 76, 79–80, 56; Dittmer, *Black Georgia*, 83.

26. Oshinksy, *"Worse than Slavery,"* 81–82.

27. Jones, *Labor of Love*, 112; Harold N. Rabinowitz, *Race Relations in the Urban South, 1865–1890* (New York: Oxford University Press, 1978), 19.

28. Rabinowitz, *Race Relations*, 62–66; Joseph Hill and John Commings, *Negro Population 1790–1915*, U.S. Bureau of the Census (Washington: Government Printing Office, 1918), 508–510.

29. Jones, *Labor of Love*, 143, 128. Tera W. Hunter, *To 'Joy My Freedom: Southern Black Women's Lives and Labors after the Civil War* (Cambridge, Mass.: Harvard University Press, 1997), 56–57.

30. Rabinowitz, *Race Relations*, 68, 66; Jones, *Labor of Love*, 136, 148; Emma L. Shields, *Negro Women in Industry*, Bulletin of the Women's Bureau, no. 29, U.S. Department of Labor (Washington: Government Printing Office, 1922), 37.

31. Delores Janiewski, "Sisters under Their Skin: Southern Working Women, 1880–1950," in Joanne V. Hawks and Sheila L. Skemp, eds., *Sex, Race and the Role of Women in the South* (Jackson: University of Mississippi Press, 1983), 29.

32. Jones, *Labor of Love*, 113.

33. Rabinowitz, *Race Relations*, 84, 90; Dittmer, *Black Georgia*, 37–38, 40–41; McMillen, *Dark Journey*, 190–194.

34. Dittmer, *Black Georgia*, 41, 45–46, 35–37; Jones, *Labor of Love*, 144.

35. Leon F. Litwack, *Trouble in Mind: Black Southerners in the Age of Jim Crow* (New York: Knopf, 1998), 284, 297, 285, 298; Dittmer, *Black Georgia*, 131; Martha Hodes, "The Sexualization of Reconstruction Politics: White Women and Black Men in the South after the Civil War," in John C. Fout and Maura Shaw Tantillo, eds., *American Sexual Politics: Sex, Gender and Race since the Civil War* (Chicago: University of Chicago Press, 1993), 63.

36. Litwack, *Trouble in Mind*, 312–319, 406–410; Gilmore, *Gender and Jim Crow*, 111–113, 131; Dittmer, *Black Georgia*, 123–131.

37. Cohen, *At Freedom's Edge*, 206; Michael Perman, *Struggle for Mastery: Disfranchisement in the South, 1888–1908* (Chapel Hill: University of North Carolina Press, 2001), 10–17, 15.

38. Perman, *Struggle for Mastery*, 22–28, 22.

39. McMillen, *Dark Journey*, 41–42, 45; Perman, *Struggle for Mastery*, 29–30; Cohen, *At Freedom's Edge*, 209.

40. Perman, *Struggle for Mastery*, 300–313; C. Vann Woodward, *The Strange Career of Jim Crow*, 3rd rev. ed. (New York: Oxford University Press, 1974), 85; Dittmer, *Black Georgia*, 103.

41. Joel Williamson, *A Rage for Order: Black-White Relations in the American South since Emancipation* (New York: Oxford University Press, 1986), 171.

42. Evelyn Brooks Higginbotham, *Righteous Discontent: The Women's Movement in the Black Baptist Church, 1880–1920* (Cambridge, Mass.: Harvard University Press, 1993), 4; Laura Edwards, *Gendered Strife and Confusion: The Political Culture of Reconstruction* (Urbana: University of Illinois Press, 1997), 23.

43. Rabinowitz, *Race Relations*; Woodward, *Strange Career*; George M. Fredrickson, *Black Liberation: A Comparative History of Black Ideologies in the United States and South Africa* (New York: Oxford University Press, 1995).

44. Fredrickson, *Black Liberation*, 96.

45. David Delaney, *Race, Place, and the Law, 1836–1948* (Austin: University of Texas Press, 1998), 107–108.

46. Woodward, *Strange Career*, 72–73; Baker, *Following the Color Line*, 32.

47. Higginbotham, *Righteous Discontent*, 189–190; Woodward, *Strange Career*, 95.

48. Woodward, *Strange Career*, 77–81.

49. Fredrickson, *Black Liberation*, 99.

50. Rabinowitz, *Race Relations*, 336; August Meier and Elliott Rudwick, "Negro Retaliatory Violence in the Twentieth Century," *New Politics* 5 (1966), 41–51; McMillen, *Dark Journey*, 9.

51. Delaney, *Race, Place, and Law*, 101.

52. Ibid., 96–97, 101; Baker, *Color Line*, 31; Bertram Wilbur Doyle, *The Etiquette of Race Relations in the South: A Study in Social Control* (Chicago: University of Chicago Press, 1937), 146–147; Rabinowitz, *Race Relations*, 182–187; Woodward, *Strange Career*, 102.

53. Baker, *Color Line*, 29, 33.

54. Delaney, *Race, Place, and Law*, 97; Woodward, *Strange Career*, 102; McMillen, *Dark Journey*, 24; Doyle, *Etiquette of Race Relations*, 143; Rosengarten, *All God's Dangers*, 48; see also James Farmer, *Lay Bare the Heart: An Autobiography of the Civil Rights Movement* (New York: Arbor House, 1985), 63–65.

55. Woodward, *Strange Career*, 31–65, 97.

56. Ibid., 33–34.

57. Higginbotham, *Righteous Discontent*, 12–13, 23–24; Gilmore, *Gender and Jim Crow*, 36–37.

58. Janiewski, "Sisters under Their Skin," 20, 23–27; Gilmore, *Gender and Jim Crow*, 95.

59. I do not imply that there were only two models of white masculinity.

Gilmore points out that there were a number of different "models" of masculinity which varied by location and class. However, I am focusing on two important "hegemonic" models among those most in a position to shape southern race/gender relations.

60. Gilmore, *Gender and Jim Crow*, 62–63, 66–67.

61. George M. Fredrickson, *The Black Image in the White Mind: The Debate on Afro-American Character and Destiny, 1817–1914* (New York: Harper and Row, 1971), 276–282; Gilmore, *Gender and Jim Crow*, 72; Higginbotham, *Righteous Discontent*, 190.

62. Victoria E. Bynum, *Unruly Women: The Politics of Social and Sexual Control in the Old South* (Chapel Hill: University of North Carolina Press, 1992), 109–110; Gilmore, *Gender and Jim Crow*, 72.

63. Gilmore, *Gender and Jim Crow*, 95–96.

64. F. James Davis, *Who Is Black? One Nation's Definition* (University Park: Pennsylvania State University Press, 1991), 33, 34; Paul R. Spickard, *Mixed Blood: Intermarriage and Ethnic Identity in Twentieth-Century America* (Madison: University of Wisconsin Press, 1989), 247.

65. Davis, *Who Is Black*, 38, 59, 35–37.

66. Ibid., 40–41, 45–46.

67. Ibid., 55; Joel Williamson, *New People: Miscegenation and Mulattos in the United States* (New York: Free Press, 1980), 97, 138.

68. *Plessy v. Ferguson*, 163 U.S. 537 (1896), 549, 552.

69. Williamson, *New People*, 103–105; Davis, *Who Is Black*, 56; McMillen, *Dark Journey*, 20; Dittmer, *Black Georgia*, 61–62.

70. Delaney, *Race, Place, and Law*, 125–147.

71. I borrow these categories from Robin Kelley's seminal work on black working-class resistance during the 1930s and 1940s. I am including in my account middle-class black activity and gender conflicts within these sites. Robin D. G. Kelley, "'We Are Not What We Seem': Rethinking Black Working-Class Opposition in the Jim Crow South," *Journal of American History* 80 (June 1993), 75–112.

72. Earl Lewis, *In Their Own Interests: Race, Class, and Power in Twentieth-Century Norfolk, Virginia* (Berkeley: University of California Press, 1991), 3, 91–92.

73. Jones, *Labor of Love*, 65–66.

74. E. Franklin Frazier, *The Negro Church in America* (New York: Schocken, 1964), ch. 3; Higginbotham, *Righteous Discontent*, 7.

75. Peter J. Rachleff, *Black Labor in the South: Richmond, Virginia, 1865–1890* (Philadelphia: Temple University Press, 1984), 25–27; Sara Jane Early, "The Organized Effort of the Colored Women of the South to Improve Their Condition," in Ellen NicKenzie Lawson, ed., *The Three Sarahs: Documents of Antebellum Black College Women* (New York: E. Mellen Press, 1984), 718–724.

76. Kelley, "We Are Not What We Seem," 79, 83.

77. Gilmore, *Gender and Jim Crow*, 109; McMillen, *Dark Journey*, 180–184, 186–190.

78. Kevin Gaines, *Uplifting the Race: Black Leadership, Politics, and Culture in the Twentieth Century* (Chapel Hill: University of North Carolina Press, 1996), 1–2; Brown, "Negotiating and Transforming," 135, 139.

79. Brown, "Negotiating and Transforming," 139; Gilmore, *Gender and Jim Crow*, 62–63; 75–76.

80. See Elsa Barkley Brown, "Womanist Consciousness: Maggie Lena Walker and the Independent Order of Saint Luke," *Signs* 14 (Spring 1989), 610–633; Brown, "Vision of Freedom," 85–86.

81. Gilmore, *Gender and Jim Crow*, 147, 150–153, 170–172.

82. Higginbotham, *Righteous Discontent*, 195, 199, 202–203.

83. Hunter, *To 'Joy My Freedom*, 166, 182; Kelley, "We Are Not What We Seem," 84.

84. McMillen, *Dark Journey*, 293; Hunter, *To 'Joy My Freedom*, 99; August Meier and Elliott Rudwick, "The Boycott Movement against Jim Crow Streetcars in the South, 1900–1906," *Journal of American History* 55 (March 1969), 761.

85. Meier and Rudwick, "Boycott Movement," 758–759, 761, 774–775.

86. Cliff Kuhn, Harlon E. Joye, and E. Bernard West, eds., *Living Atlanta: An Oral History of the City, 1914–1948* (Athens: University of Georgia Press, 1990), 80.

87. Meier and Rudwick, "Boycott Movement," 770–771; Kuhn, *Living Atlanta*, 80; Delores E. Janiewski, *Sisterhood Denied: Race, Gender, and Class in a New South Community* (Philadelphia: Temple University Press, 1985), 141.

88. Harold N. Rabinowitz, "The Conflict between Blacks and the Police in the Urban South, 1865–1900," *Historian* 39 (Nov. 1976), 70–71; Meier and Rudwick, "Negro Retaliatory Violence," 44–45; Gilmore, *Gender and Jim Crow*, 102–103; Jones, *Labor of Love*, 149.

89. Kelley, "We Are Not What We Seem"; Hunter, *To 'Joy My Freedom*; James C. Scott, *Domination and the Arts of Resistance: Hidden Transcripts* (New Haven: Yale University Press, 1990).

90. Emma Shields, "Fifty Years in the Tobacco Industry," *Southern Workman* 51 (Sept. 1922), 420; Nannie M. Tilley, *The Bright-Tobacco Industry, 1860–1929* (Chapel Hill: University of North Carolina Press, 1948), 318–319. In this book are lyrics from one refrain heard in 1895: "Befo' I'd work for Simpkins, J., / I'd walk all night an' sleep all day: / Walk all night tu keep f'om sleeping, / An' sleep all day tu keep f'om eatin'."

91. Kelley, "We Are Not What We Seem," 90, 95.

92. David M. Katzman, *Seven Days a Week: Women and Domestic Service in Industrializing America* (New York: Oxford University Press, 1978), 197–198; Hunter, *To 'Joy My Freedom*, 133–134; Anonymous, "I Live a Treadmill Life," in Gerda Lerner, ed., *Black Women in White America: A Documentary History* (New York: Pantheon, 1972), 229.

93. Hunter, *To 'Joy My Freedom*, 135, 74, 88–97.

94. Jones, *Labor of Love*, 148; Eric Arnesen, *Waterfront Workers of New Orleans: Race, Class, and Politics, 1863–1923* (New York: Oxford University Press, 1991), 230–232; Lewis, *In Their Own Interests*, 47–58.

95. James D. Anderson, *The Education of Blacks in the South, 1860–1935* (Chapel Hill: University of North Carolina Press, 1988), 5, 282; Rabinowitz, *Race Relations*, 156; Herbert G. Gutman, "Schools for Freedom: The Post-Emancipation Origins of Afro-American Education," in *Power and Culture: Essays on the American Working Class* (New York: Pantheon, 1987), 261–262; Du Bois, *Black Reconstruction*, 638.

96. Anderson, *Education of Blacks*, 5; Gutman, "Schools for Freedom," 270.

97. Anderson, *Education of Blacks*, 9–14, 239–240; Rabinowitz, *Race Relations*, 157, 162–163; Gutman, "Schools for Freedom," 293–297.

98. Rabinowitz, *Race Relations,* 164–165; Anderson, *Education of Blacks,* 19.

99. Rabinowitz, *Race Relations,* 164; Anderson, *Education of* Blacks, 2, 25–26; Du Bois, *Black Reconstruction,* 638.

100. Anderson, *Education of Blacks,* 101, 150.

101. Rabinowitz, *Race Relations,* 167, 172–176; Jones, *Labor of Love,* 144.

102. Rabinowitz, *Race Relations,* 179; U.S. Bureau of the Census, *Thirteenth Census of the United States,* Negro Population (Washington: Government Printing Office, 1913), table 31, 434; table 9, 409.

103. Anderson, *Education of Blacks,* 27, 31–32.

104. Ibid., 81, 150, 154–156.

105. Ibid. (percentages calculated from table 5.2, 155), 183, 238, 244–245.

106. Ibid., 238, 244–245.

107. Gilmore, *Gender and Jim Crow,* 138–141.

108. Du Bois, *Black Reconstruction,* 667.

5. Mexicans and Anglos in the Southwest

1. See David J. Weber, ed., *Foreigners in Their Native Land: Historical Roots of Mexican Americans* (Albuquerque: University of New Mexico Press, 1973), 140.

2. David G. Gutiérrez, *Walls and Mirrors: Mexican Americans, Mexican Immigrants, and the Politics of Ethnicity* (Berkeley: University of California Press, 1996), 21; David Montejano, *Anglos and Mexicans in the Making of Texas, 1836–1986* (Austin: University of Texas Press, 1987), 31.

3. Calculated from Albert Camarillo, *Chicanos in a Changing Society* (Cambridge, Mass.: Harvard University Press, 1979), table 10, 116–117.

4. Andrés E. Jiménez Montoya, "Political Domination in the Labor Market: Racial Division in the Arizona Copper Industry," Working Paper, Institute for the Study of Social Change, University of California, 1977, 14–16; Mario Barrera, *Race and Class in the Southwest: A Theory of Racial Inequality* (Notre Dame: University of Notre Dame Press, 1979), 8–10; Robert J. Rosenbaum, *Mexicano Resistance in the Southwest: "The Sacred Right of Self Preservation"* (Austin: University of Texas Press, 1981), 26; Weber, *Foreigners,* 144–150.

5. Sarah Deutsch, *No Separate Refuge: Culture, Class, and Gender on an Anglo-Hispanic Frontier in the American Southwest, 1880–1940* (New York: Oxford University Press, 1987), 9, 32–34.

6. Barrera, *Race and Class,* 66, 81; José Hernández Alvarez, "A Demographic Profile of the Mexican Immigration to the United States, 1910–1950," in Renato Rosaldo, Robert A. Calvert, and Gustav L. Seligmann, eds., *Chicano: The Evolution of a People* (Minneapolis: Winston Press, 1973), 37–38; Victor S. Clark, *Mexican Labor in the United States,* U.S. Bureau of Labor, Department of Commerce and Labor, Bulletin no. 78 (Washington: Government Printing Office, 1908), 477, 486.

7. Gutiérrez, *Walls and Mirrors,* 13–18; Weber, *Foreigners,* 140–144, 162–168; Richard Griswold del Castillo, *The Treaty of Guadalupe Hidalgo: A Legacy of Conflict* (Norman: University of Oklahoma Press, 1990), 190, appendix A.

8. Weber, *Foreigners,* 143.

9. A total of 47 delegates attended. Of the 11 with Mexican surnames, 9 had lived in California their whole lives. Of 38 delegates with Anglo surnames, 29 had lived in California for three years or less and 9 for less than a year; the majority of

Anglo delegates listed a state in the Northeast as their last previous residence. Computed from data in Robert F. Heizer and Alan F. Almquist, *The Other Californians: Prejudice and Discrimination under Spain, Mexico, and the United States* (Berkeley: University of California Press, 1971), 226–228.

10. Ibid., 98, 102, 115.

11. David Montejano, *Anglos and Mexicans in the Making of Texas, 1836–1986* (Austin: University of Texas Press, 1987), 51–53.

12. Weber, *Foreigners*, 154–160; Leonard Pitt, *The Decline of the Californios: A Social History of the Spanish-Speaking Californians, 1846–1890* (Berkeley: University of California Press, 1970), 250, 251–252; Camarillo, *Chicanos in a Changing Society*, 115–116; Deutsch, *No Separate Refuge*, 20.

13. Deutsch, *No Separate Refuge*, 31–55.

14. Lisbeth Haas, *Conquests and Historical Identities in California, 1769–1936* (Berkeley: University of California Press, 1995), 70–71; Camarillo, *Chicanos in a Changing Society*, 82–83; Montejano, *Anglos and Mexicans*, 90.

15. Camarillo, *Chicanos in a Changing Society*, tables 11 and 13, 128, 133; Arnoldo de León, *The Tejano Community, 1836–1900* (Albuquerque: University of New Mexico Press, 1982), 63.

16. Gilbert G. González, "Women, Work and Community in the Mexican Colonias of the Southern California Citrus Belt," in Manuel G. Gonzales and Cynthia M. Gonzales, eds., *En Aquel Entonces: Readings in Mexican-American History* (Bloomington: Indiana University Press, 2000), 151–152; Richard Griswold del Castillo, *The Los Angeles Barrio, 1850–1890* (Berkeley: University of California Press, 1979), 65; Deena Gonzalez, "The Widowed Women of Santa Fe: Assessments on the Lives of an Unmarried Population, 1850–1880," in Arlene Scadron, ed., *Widows and Widowhood in the American Southwest, 1848–1939* (Urbana: University of Illinois Press, 1988), 72; Thomas E. Sheridan, *Los Tucsonenses: The Mexican Community in Tucson, 1854–1941* (Tucson: University of Arizona Press, 1986), 143.

17. Camarillo, *Chicanos in a Changing Society*, 135–137; Pitt, *Decline of Californios*, 256; Gutiérrez, *Walls and Mirrors*, 265.

18. Carey McWilliams, *North from Mexico: The Spanish-Speaking People of the United States* (Philadelphia: Lippincott, 1949), 175.

19. The U.S. Department of Commerce and Agriculture defined "large-scale" as any farm producing $30,000 or more in crops annually. Mark Reisler, *By the Sweat of Their Brow: Mexican Immigrant Labor in the United States, 1900–1940* (Westport, Conn.: Greenwood Press, 1976), 79; Paul S. Taylor, "Mexican Labor in the United States: Valley of the South Platte Colorado," *University of California Publications in Economics* 6, no. 2 (June 12, 1929), 115.

20. Barrera, *Race and Class*, 61–62.

21. Carey McWilliams, *Ill Fares the Land: Migrants and Migratory Labor in the United States* (New York: Barnes and Noble Books, 1941; rpt. 1967), 231–232; Texas State Employment Service, *Origins and Problems of Texas Migratory Farm Laborers* (Austin, 1940), 70.

22. Gutiérrez, *Walls and Mirrors*, 43–45; Dennis Nodin Valdés, "Settlers, Sojourners, and Proletarians: Social Formation in the Great Plains Sugar Beet Industry, 1890–1940," in Gonzales and Gonzales, eds., *En Aquel Entonces*, 120.

23. Clark, *Mexican Labor*, 486; Deutsch, *No Separate Refuge*, 94–95; Valdés, "Settlers, Sojourners," 118; Taylor, "South Platte," 103–108.

24. Reisler, *Sweat of Their Brow,* 57; Gutiérrez, *Walls and Mirrors,* 45.

25. For a succinct account of economic and social changes in Mexico fostering migration during this period, see George J. Sánchez, *Becoming Mexican American: Ethnicity, Culture and Identity in Chicano Los Angeles, 1900–1945* (New York: Oxford University Press, 1993), 17–37. Figures for 1880, 1900, 1910, and 1920 from *Mexicans in California, Report of Governor C. C. Young's Mexican Fact-Finding Committee* (San Francisco: State Building, Oct. 1930), 29, 31. Figures for 1930 computed from Leo Grebler, *Mexican Immigration to the United States,* Mexican American Study Project Advance Report no. 2 (Los Angeles: UCLA Graduate School of Business Administration, 1966), 54, 102.

26. Paul S. Taylor, *An American-Mexican Frontier: Nueces County, Texas* (1934; New York: Russel and Russel, 1971), 103; Taylor, "South Platte," 119, 123.

27. Taylor, "South Platte," 131–132; Montejano, *Anglos and Mexicans,* 170–171.

28. *Mexicans in California,* 71; Clark, *Mexican Labor,* 477; Mario García, *Desert Immigrants: The Mexicans of El Paso, 1880–1920* (New Haven: Yale University Press, 1981), 66–68; Jiménez Montoya, "Political Domination," 24.

29. Clark, *Mexican Labor,* 488, 486; Reisler, *Sweat of Their Brow,* 80–81; Paul S. Taylor, "Mexican Labor in the United States: Dimmit County, Winter Garden District, South Texas," *University of California Publications in Economics* 6, no. 5 (1930), 340, 444, 446.

30. Jiménez Montoya, "Political Domination," 24; Taylor, "Dimmit County," 341.

31. Barrera, *Race and Class,* 46; Ricardo Romo, "Mexican Workers in the City: East Los Angeles, 1915–1930" (Ph.D. diss., University of California, Los Angeles, 1975), 140; Camarillo, *Chicanos in a Changing Society,* 173, 180; García, *Desert Immigrants,* 86.

32. Emilio Zamora, *The World of the Mexican Worker in Texas* (College Station: Texas A&M Press, 1993), 40.

33. Mario García, "The Chicana in American History: The Mexican Women of El Paso, 1880–1920: A Case Study," *Pacific Historical Review* 49 (May 1980), 335.

34. Deutsch, *No Separate Refuge,* 22–23, 91; Neil Foley, *The White Scourge: Mexicans, Blacks and Poor Whites in Texas Cotton Culture* (Berkeley: University of California Press, 1997), 127; Barrera, *Race and Class,* 41.

35. Reisler, *Sweat of Their Brow,* 10, 82.

36. Montejano, *Anglos and Mexicans,* 204, 207–213.

37. Reisler, *Sweat of Their Brow,* 81–82.

38. Montejano, *Anglos and Mexicans,* 217–219; McWilliams, *Ill Fares the Land,* 275.

39. Ian F. Haney López, *White by Law: The Legal Construction of Race* (New York: New York University Press, 1996), 61–62; Reisler, *Sweat of Their Brow,* 136.

40. Taylor, *American-Mexican Frontier,* 231; Heizer and Almquist, *Other Californians,* 115–117; Tomás Almaguer, *Racial Fault Lines: The Historical Origins of White Supremacy in California* (Berkeley: University of California Press, 1994), 132–133; Weber, *Foreigners,* 145–146, 215–216, 247–248.

41. Paul R. Spickard, *Mixed Blood: Intermarriage and Ethnic Identity in Twentieth-Century America* (Madison: University of Wisconsin Press, 1989), 374–375; Reisler, *Sweat of Their Brow,* 135; Foley, *White Scourge,* 208; Taylor, "Dimmit County," 392; Sheridan, *Los Tucsonenses,* 147–149.

42. Martha Menchaca, *The Mexican Outsiders: A Community History of Marginalization and Discrimination in California* (Austin: University of Texas Press, 1995), 15; Reisler, *Sweat of Their Brow*, 134.

43. Weber, *Foreigners*, 143–150; Pitt, *Decline of Californios*, 43–45; Heizer and Almquist, *Other Californians*, 226–228; Martha Menchaca, "Chicano Indianism: A Historical Account of Racial Repression in the United States," *American Ethnologist* 20, no. 3 (1993), 587–591; José Amaro Hernández, *Mutual Aid for Survival: The Case of the Mexican American* (Malabar, Fla.: Kreiger, 1983), 23.

44. Taylor, "Dimmit County," 398–410; Montejano, *Anglos and Mexicans*, 143–145.

45. Taylor, "Dimmit County," 398–404, 401.

46. Ibid., 407.

47. Montejano, *Anglos and Mexicans*, 160.

48. Menchaca, *Mexican Outsiders*, 25–27; Montejano, *Anglos and Mexicans*, 79–80; Haas, *Conquests*, 180–184; see also Paul S. Taylor, "Mexican Labor in the United States: Imperial Valley," *University of California Publications in Economics* 6 (1930), 1–94, and Taylor, "Dimmit County," "South Platte," and *American-Mexican Frontier.*

49. Montejano, *Anglos and Mexicans*, 168; Taylor, "Dimmit County," 407; Foley, *White Scourge*, 42–44; Haas, *Conquests*, 185.

50. Haas, *Conquests*, 106.

51. Douglas E. Foley, with Clarice Mota, Donald E. Post, and Ignacio Lozano, *From Peones to Politicos: Class and Ethnicity in a South Texas Town, 1900–1987*, rev. ed. (Austin: University of Texas Press, 1988), 43–44.

52. Weber, *Foreigners*, 59–60; David J. Weber, "'Scarce More than Apes': Historical Roots of Anglo-American Stereotypes of Mexicans in the Border Region," in Weber, *The Mexican Frontier, 1821–1846: The American Southwest under Mexico* (Albuquerque: University of New Mexico Press, 1982), 153; Raymund A. Paredes, "The Origins of Anti-Mexican Sentiment in the United States," in Ricardo Romo and Raymund Paredes, eds., *New Directions in Chicano Scholarship*, Chicano Studies Monograph Series (La Jolla: University of California, San Diego, 1978); Pitt, *Decline of Californios*, 15–16.

53. Almaguer, *Racial Fault Lines*, 55; Reginald Horsman, *Race and Manifest Destiny: The Origins of American Racial Anglo Saxonism* (Cambridge, Mass.: Harvard University Press, 1981), 211–212; Weber, *Foreigners*, 60–61; Arnoldo de León, *They Called Them Greasers: Anglo Attitudes toward Mexicans in Texas, 1821–1900* (Austin: University of Texas Press, 1983), 5–9; see also José de Onís, *The United States as Seen by Spanish American Writers, 1776–1890*, 2d ed. (New York: Gordian Press, 1975).

54. Horsman, *Race and Manifest Destiny*, 233; Almaguer, *Racial Fault Lines*, 60–62; de León, *They Called Them Greasers*, 9–10.

55. Horsman, *Race and Manifest Destiny*, 234.

56. Darlis Miller, "Cross-Cultural Marriages in the Southwest: The New Mexico Experience," *New Mexico Review* 57 (1982), 335–359; Jane Dysart, "Mexican Women in San Antonio: The Assimilation Process," *Western Historical Quarterly* 7 (1976), 365–375; Almaguer, *Racial Fault Lines*, 58–59.

57. On intermarriage rates see Ricardo Romo, "The Urbanization of Southwestern Chicanos in the Early Twentieth Century," in Romo and Paredes, eds., *New Directions in Chicano Scholarship*, 199. See also Pitt, *Decline of Californios*, 267–

268; Haas, *Conquests*, 74; Deena Gonzalez, *Refusing the Favor: The Spanish-Mexican Women of Santa Fe, 1820–1880* (New York: Oxford University Press, 1999), 73, 113–114; figures for Tucson calculated from table 8.4 in Sheridan, *Los Tucsonenses*, 149.

58. Gonzalez, *Refusing the Favor*, 113; Montejano, *Anglos and Mexicans*, 34–35, 37; Sheridan, *Los Tucsonenses*, 146–149.

59. Deutsch, *No Separate Refuge*, 28–29; McWilliams, *North from Mexico*, 37.

60. Haas, *Conquests*, 74; Gonzalez, *Refusing the Favor*, 73, 113–114; Sheridan, *Los Tucsonenses*, 149.

61. Taylor, "South Platte," 212.

62. David Weber, *Myth and the History of the American Southwest* (Albuquerque: University of New Mexico Press, 1988), 150; Taylor, *American-Mexican Frontier*, 272–273.

63. Taylor, *American-Mexican Frontier*, 314.

64. Ibid., 254, 261; Taylor, "Dimmit County," 448.

65. Taylor, "Imperial Valley," 92; Taylor, "Dimmit County," 447.

66. Taylor, "Dimmit County," 423, 442; Taylor, "South Platte," 230, 234.

67. Taylor, "Dimmit County," 442.

68. Clark, *Mexican Labor*, 508; Taylor, "South Platte," 220.

69. Taylor, "Dimmit County," 443, 442.

70. Griswold del Castillo, *Los Angeles Barrio*, 133.

71. Camarillo, *Chicanos in a Changing Society*, 147; Haas, *Conquest*, 201–208; Gutiérrez, *Walls and Mirrors*, 34.

72. Pitt, *Decline of Californios*, 267; Griswold del Castillo, *Los Angeles Barrio*, 133–34.

73. Weber, *Foreigners*, 250.

74. Selden C. Menefee and Orin C. Cassmore, "The Pecan Shellers of San Antonio: The Problem of Underpaid and Unemployed Mexican Labor," Works Project Administration, 1940, rpt. in *Mexican Labor in the United States* (New York: Arno Press, 1974), 51.

75. Foley, *White Scourge*, 25; Taylor, *American-Mexican Frontier*, 266, 314.

76. Sheridan, *Los Tucsonenses*, 141–142.

77. Taylor, *American-Mexican Frontier*, 256; Taylor, "South Platte," 229–230; Taylor, "Imperial Valley, 93.

78. Reisler, *Sweat of Their Brow*, 111 and table 3, 270.

79. Gutiérrez, *Walls and Mirrors*, 89, 90.

80. Weber, *Foreigners*, 205–207; Rosenbaum, *Mexicano Resistance*, 53–61, quote 61.

81. Weber, *Foreigners*, 208; Rosenbaum, *Mexicano Resistance*, 111–124; Hernández, *Mutual Aid*, 67.

82. Hernández, *Mutual Aid*, 15–29; Rosenbaum, *Mexicano Resistance*, 17.

83. García, *Desert Immigrants*, 223–228; Taylor, *American-Mexican Frontier*, 173–175; Griswold del Castillo, *Los Angeles Barrio*, 138; Romo, "East Los Angeles," 149; Camarillo, *Chicanos in a Changing Society*, 151–154; Manuel Gamio, *Mexican Immigration to the United States* (Chicago: University of Chicago Press, 1930), 136; Zamora, *World of the Mexican Worker*, 93.

84. Gutiérrez, *Walls and Mirrors*, 98–99; Griswold del Castillo, *Los Angeles Barrio*, 138; Hernández, *Mutual Aid*, 36, 45–59.

85. Hernández, *Mutual Aid,* 16, 65, 72.

86. Haas, *Conquests,* 119. Some of the newspapers whose records have survived are *El Clamor Público,* Los Angeles; *La Crónica,* Laredo, Texas; *La Prensa,* San Antonio; *La Mutualista,* Texas; *El Horizonte,* Texas; *El Labrador,* Las Cruces, New Mexico; *El Observador Frontierizo,* Texas 1886; *La Opinión,* Los Angeles 1920s; *La Voz de la Pueblo,* Las Vegas, New Mexico; and *La Patria,* El Paso.

87. Irene Ledesma, "Texas Newspapers and Chicana Workers' Activism," *Western Historical Quarterly* 26 (Autumn 1995), 315–316, 320–321.

88. Américo Paredes, *"With a Pistol in His Hand:" A Border Ballad and Its Hero* (Austin: University of Texas Press, 1956); Américo Paredes, *A Texas-Mexican Cancionereo: Folksongs of the Lower Border* (Urbana: University of Illinois Press, 1976); James Reed, *The Border Ballads* (London: Athlone Press, 1973); Gamio, *Mexican Immigration.*

89. Some translated lyrics are as follows: "And the Yankee people sentenced him. / 'The death penalty,' they all demanded, / And the lawyer did not object. / Twenty thousand signatures of compatriots / Asked for his pardon from the governor / All the newspapers asked for it too, / And even Obregón sent a message. / All was useless; the societies, / All united, asked his pardon." Hernández, *Mutual Aid,* 47.

90. Gutiérrez, *Walls and Mirrors,* 67–68; Montejano, *Anglos and Mexicans,* 218.

91. Juan Gómez-Quiñones, "The First Steps: Chicano Labor Conflict and Organizing: 1900–20," *Atzlan* (Spring 1972), 24–25, 26–27, 31; Emilio Zamora, "Chicano Socialist Labor Activity in Texas, 1900–1920," *Atzlan* (Summer 1975), 223–224. See also Zamora, *World of the Mexican Worker.*

92. Devra Weber, *Dark Sweat White Gold; California Farm Workers, Cotton, and the New Deal* (Berkeley: University of California Press, 1994), 85; Devra Weber, "The Organization of Mexicano Agricultural Workers, the Imperial Valley and Los Angeles, 1928–1934: An Oral History Approach," *Atzlan* (Fall 1972), 313; Victor Nelson Cisneros, "La Clase Trabajadora en Tejas, 1920–1940," *Atzlan* (Summer 1975), 234; Gutiérrez, *Walls and Mirrors,* 103–105.

93. Gutiérrez, *Walls and Mirrors,* 75.

94. Montejano, *Anglos and Mexicans,* 232; Gutiérrez, *Walls and Mirrors,* 77–78, 85–86, 93.

95. Menchaca, *Mexican Outsiders,* 60–64.

96. Ibid., 64; Gilbert G. González, "Segregation of Mexican Children in a Southern California City: The Legacy of Expansionism and the American Southwest," *Western Historical Quarterly* 16, no. 1 (Jan. 1985), 57; García, *Desert Immigrants,* 110–111; Haas, *Conquests,* 190.

97. Haas, *Conquests,* 189–190.

98. Menchaca, *Mexican Outsiders,* 73; Martha Menchaca, "Chicano Indianism: A Historical Account of Racial Repression in the United States," *American Ethnologist* 20, no. 3 (1993), 598. See also Jorge Rangel and Carlos Alcala, "De Jure Segregation of Chicanos in Texas Schools," *Harvard Civil Rights–Civil Liberties Law Review* 7 (March 1972), 307–391.

99. Hernández, *Mutual Aid,* 70–71; Menchaca, *Mexican Outsiders,* 68–69, 67; Taylor, "South Platte," 232.

100. See, e.g., Taylor, "Dimmit County," 377, on diversion of school funds; Haas, *Conquests,* 192.

101. Hernández, *Mutual Aid,* 71; Gilbert G. González, *Chicano Education in the Era of Segregation* (Philadelphia: Balch Institute Press, 1990), 95; Haas, *Conquests,* 39.

102. Taylor, "Dimmit County," 437; Haas, *Conquests,* 194, 190.

103. Taylor, "Dimmit County," 383–384, 385–386.

104. Taylor, "South Platte," 205.

105. Deutsch, *No Separate Refuge,* 95–96; see also Sánchez, *Becoming Mexican American,* 97.

106. Vicki L. Ruiz, "Dead Ends or Gold Mines? Using Missionary Records in Mexican American Women's History," in Elizabeth Jameson and Susan Armitage, eds., *Writing the Range: Race, Class and Culture in the Women's West* (Norman: University of Oklahoma Press, 1997), 357–358; Deutsch, *No Separate Refuge,* 63–65.

107. García, *Desert Immigrants,* 212–219; Pearl Idelia Ellis, *Americanization through Homemaking* (Los Angeles: Wetzel Publishing, 1929), 31; George J. Sanchez, "'Go after the Women': Americanization and the Mexican Immigrant Woman, 1915–1929," in Vicki L. Ruiz and Ellen Carol DuBois, eds., *Unequal Sisters: A Multicultural Reader in Women's History,* 2d ed. (New York: Routledge, 1994), 293. For involvement of states and municipalities in Americanization programs, see Gilbert G. González, "The Americanization of Mexican Women and Their Families during the Era of De Jure School Segregation, 1900–1950," in Sucheng Chan, ed., *Social and Gender Boundaries in the U.S.* (Lewiston, N.Y.: E. Mellen Press, 1989), 67–71.

108. Sánchez, "Go after the Women," 294; Deutsch, *No Separate Refuge,* 180.

109. Haas, *Conquests,* 188; Gutiérrez, *Walls and Mirrors,* 37.

110. Mathew Frye Jacobson, *Whiteness of a Different Color: European Immigrants and the Alchemy of Race* (Cambridge, Mass.: Harvard University Press, 1998), 79–85, 151–181; Reisler, *Sweat of Their Brow,* 68; Gutiérrez, *Walls and Mirrors,* 52.

111. John Higham, *Strangers in the Land: Patterns of American Nativism, 1860–1925* (New York: Atheneum, 1973), 140, 156–157; Reisler, *Sweat of Their Brow,* 215.

112. Gutiérrez, *Walls and Mirrors,* 72; Reisler, *Sweat of Their Brow,* 232.

113. Agnes K. Hanna, "Social Services on the Mexican Border," *National Conference of Social Work Proceedings* (1935), 700–701.

114. Cisneros, "La Clase Trabajadora," 249–250; Gutiérrez, *Walls and Mirrors,* 110.

6. Japanese and Haoles in Hawaii

1. See Glen Grant and Dennis Ogawa, "Living Proof: Is Hawaii the Answer?" *Annals of the American Academy of Political and Social Sciences* 530 (Nov. 1993), 137–154; Jonathan Okamura, "The Illusion of Paradise: Multiculturalism in Hawaii," manuscript, n.d.; Jonathan Okamura, "Aloha Kanaka Me Ke Aloha 'Aina: Local Culture and Society in Hawaii," *Amerasia* 7, no. 2 (1980), 119–137. Some observers have found rampant ethnic stereotyping, albeit often expressed in humorous form and including one's own group. See, e.g., Jitsuichi Masuoka, "Race Attitudes of the Japanese People in Hawaii: A Study in Social Distance" (Master's Thesis, University of Hawaii, 1931).

2. Romanzo Adams, "Race Relations in Hawaii: A Summary Statement," *So-*

cial Process in Hawaii 2 (1936), 56–60; Romanzo Adams, *Interracial Marriage in Hawaii* (New York: Macmillan, 1937), 47–48.

3. Peggy Pascoe, "Race, Gender, and Intercultural Relations: The Case of Interracial Marriage," *Frontiers* 12, no. 1 (1991), 5–18; Adams, *Interracial Marriage*, 49–54.

4. Andrew W. Lind, *Hawaii's People*, 4th ed. (Honolulu: University Press of Hawaii, 1980), table 3, 34. There is substantial contention over who should be called "Hawaiian." The term has at various times been used to describe any person who is primarily (usually 50 percent) descended from the people who lived in the Hawaiian Islands prior to contact by Captain Cook in 1778; any person who can trace any ancestor to the pre-contact period; any person born in the Hawaiian Islands at any time regardless of current residence; or any current citizen of the state of Hawaii. (Issues of "Hawaiianness" were dealt with by the U.S. Supreme Court in *Rice v. Cayetano*, decided in March 2000.) In this book I describe persons who consider themselves or most likely would have considered themselves to be descended from pre-contact Hawaiians as "Native Hawaiians."

5. Hawaii was a territory until 1959, when it became the forty-ninth state. See Gavan Daws, *Shoal of Time: A History of the Hawaiian Islands* (Honolulu: University of Hawaii Press, 1968), 264–320.

6. In the Great Mahele of 1848 King Kamehameha III divested the crown of its feudal entitlement and divided up the islands' 4 million acres: two-fifths was allotted to some 250 *alii* (chiefs), while most of the remainder was divided between crown land (the private property of the king) and public land to be controlled by the legislature and its agents. Less than 30,000 acres was set aside for the common people. Over the next decades two-thirds of the public land and much of the land held by the crown and the chiefs was sold or leased to European and American individuals and corporations. The Great Mahele represented the triumph of a European and American conception of land as a commodity, whereas Hawaiians viewed land as part of the sacred domain. See Robert H. Horwitz, "Hawaii's Lands and the Changing Regime," *Social Process in Hawaii* 26 (1963), 67; Lawrence Fuchs, *Hawaii Pono: A Social History* (New York: Harcourt, Brace and World, 1961), 15–16.

7. Fuchs, *Hawaii Pono*, 38, reports that as many as 30 early white residents married *alii* women.

8. Edward D. Beechert, *Working in Hawaii: A Labor History* (Honolulu: University of Hawaii Press, 1985), 79–80, 122.

9. Ibid.; Daws, *Shoal of Time*, 270–292.

10. These figures include part-Hawaiians. Lind, *Hawaii's People*, 20 and table 3, 34. Estimates of the population at the time of contact range from 100,000 to well over a million. See, e.g., David E. Stannard, *Before the Horror: The Population of Hawaii on the Eve of Contact* (Honolulu: Social Science Research Institute, University of Hawaii, 1989).

11. Statistics on Chinese are from Eleanor Nordyke, *The Peopling of Hawaii* (Honolulu: East West Center/University of Hawaii Press, 1977), 27, 37–38, 4; on Japanese and Filipinos from Eileen H. Tamura, *Americanization, Acculturation and Ethnic Identity: The Nisei Generation in Hawaii* (Urbana: University of Illinois Press, 1994), 27, 5; on Portuguese from Lind, *Hawaii's People*, 32, 35, 36. A group's actual population at any time was less than half of the total who immigrated because of return migration and remigration to the mainland United States.

12. Andrew Lind, *Hawaii: The Last of the Magic Isles* (London: Oxford University Press, 1969), 22.

13. Fuchs, *Hawaii Pono*, 251–253.

14. Edna Bonacich, "Asian Labor in the Development of California and Hawaii," in Lucie Cheng and Edna Bonacich, eds., *Labor Immigration under Capitalism: Asian Workers in the United States before World War II* (Berkeley: University of California Press, 1984), 130–186, 179–182.

15. U.S. Commissioner of Labor, *Report of the Commissioner of Labor on Hawaii, 1902* (Washington: Government Printing Office, 1903), calculated from tables on 84–85; U.S. Bureau of Labor Statistics, *Labor Conditions in Hawaii: Fifth Annual Report of the Commissioner of Labor Statistics on Labor Conditions in the Territory of Hawaii, 1915* (Washington: Government Printing Office, 1916), calculated from table B, 120–153, 132, 135–136, 143. Virtually all of the white/European field workers were Portuguese or Spanish.

16. U.S. Commissioner of Labor, *Report, 1902*, 152–155, 170–171; U.S. Bureau of Labor Statistics, *Report, 1915*, 143.

17. U.S. Bureau of Labor Statistics, *Report, 1915*, 40.

18. Ibid., 40, 33–35.

19. U.S. Bureau of Labor Statistics, *Fourth Report of the Commissioner of Labor on Hawaii, 1910* (Washington: Government Printing Office), 52–58; U.S. Bureau of Labor Statistics, *Report, 1915*, 35–37.

20. Calculated from Nordyke, *Peopling of Hawaii*, table 4b.3, 144–145.

21. U.S. Bureau of Labor Statistics, *Report, 1910*, 21 and table 6, 227; U.S. Bureau of Labor Statistics, *Report, 1915*, table A, 96.

22. U.S. Commissioner of Labor, *Report, 1902*, 23.

23. Ibid., 23–24.

24. Ibid., 35, 37. Picture marriages were ones in which overseas male migrants who could not afford to return home used go-betweens in Japan to select prospective mates and arrange for the exchange of photographs. The marriage was legally registered in Japan without the groom being present, after which the bride would leave to join the husband in Hawaii.

25. Stanley D. Porteus and Marjorie E. Babcock, *Temperament and Race* (Boston: Richard G. Badger, 1926), 49, 52.

26. Fuchs, *Hawaii Pono*, 19; Beechert, *Working in Hawaii*, 42–57.

27. Beechert, *Working in Hawaii*, 56.

28. Miriam Sharma, "Labor Migration and Class Formation among the Filipinos in Hawaii, 1906–1946," in Cheng and Bonacich, eds., *Labor Immigration*, 588.

29. U.S. Commissioner of Labor, *Report, 1902*, 55–56.

30. Ibid., 211.

31. Fuchs, *Hawaii Pono*, 209; Ray Stannard Baker, "Wonderful Hawaii, Part 2: The Land and the Landless," *American Magazine* 73 (Dec. 1911), 211.

32. C. J. Henderson, "Labor: An Undercurrent of Hawaiian Social History," *Social Process in Hawaii* 15 (1951), 44–55.

33. Beechert, *Working in Hawaii*, 138–139; Andrew Lind, *An Island Community: Ecological Succession in Hawaii* (Chicago: University of Chicago Press, 1938), 230–231.

34. Daws, *Shoal of Time*, 240–252, 281.

35. Ian F. Haney López, *White by Law: The Legal Construction of Race* (New

York: New York University Press, 1996), 44; Ronald Takaki, *Pau Hana: Plantation Life and Labor in Hawaii, 1835–1920* (Honolulu: University of Hawaii Press, 1983), 76.

36. Data from Lind, *Hawaii's People*, table 3, 34, table 17, 99, table 18, 100, and table 19, 102.

37. Takaki, *Pau Hana*, 76.

38. U.S. Commissioner of Labor, *Report, 1902*, 23.

39. Ray Stannard Baker, "Wonderful Hawaii," *American Magazine* 73 (Nov. 1911), 32.

40. U.S. Commissioner of Labor, *Report, 1902*, 119.

41. U.S. Bureau of Labor Statistics, *Third Report of the Commissioner of Labor on Hawaii, 1905* (Washington: Government Printing Office, 1906), 19, 57, 79.

42. U.S. Commissioner of Labor, *Report, 1902*, 42–46; U.S. Bureau of Labor Statistics, *Report, 1915*, 10.

43. Ray Stannard Baker, "Human Nature in Hawaii," *American Magazine* 73, no. 3 (Jan. 1912). 330. See also U.S. Bureau of Labor Statistics, *Report, 1910*, 53–58, 99, 61.

44. Henry Toyama and Kiyoshi Ikeda, "The Okinawan-Naichi Relationship," *Social Process in Hawaii* 14 (1950), 51, 54–55; Lind, *Hawaii*, 44.

45. Lind, *Hawaii*, 45–56.

46. Andrew W. Lind, "The Changing Position of Domestic Service in Hawaii," *Social Process in Hawaii* 15 (1951), 73.

47. Ibid., 78.

48. Ibid., 74.

49. Fuchs, *Hawaii Pono*, 62.

50. Joyce Chapman Lebra, *Women's Voices in Hawaii* (Niwot: University Press of Colorado, 1991), 76; Margaret M. L. Catton, *Social Service in Hawaii* (Palo Alto: Pacific Books, 1959), 9–13, 15–21, 33–41, 63–77, 163–165.

51. Catton, *Social Service in Hawaii*, 30–31.

52. U.S. Commissioner of Labor, *Report, 1902*, 36–37.

53. Ibid., 22.

54. John Reinecke, "The Competition of Languages in Hawaii," *Social Process in Hawaii* 2 (1936), 7–10, 9. The use of the term "local" to refer to a certain race-class segment of the population seems to have appeared in the 1930s. At the most general level, "local" designated those born and raised in Hawaii or residing long enough to be steeped in the distinctive lifestyle of the Islands. Beneath this meaning, however, lie several other registers, whose significance varies by context and period. Eric Yamamoto, citing Lind, notes that the term "local" first was used in reports of the Massie Trial of 1931 to distinguish the island-bred alleged rapists (two Native Hawaiians, two Japanese, and a Chinese-Hawaiian) from their white military accusers. In this usage the emphasis was on differentiating locals from "outsiders." However, there was also a racial register, in that locals were nonwhites, while Massie and the military officers in charge of the case were whites. In the latter sense, "local" is counterpoised against "haole." Thus, in the eyes of many "locals," haoles born and bred in the islands are "kamaaina," a term that distinguishes them from mainland haoles, but they are not "local." Finally, there is a class register to the term "local," which may or may not exclude all haoles. According to Jonathan Okamura, "locals" see themselves as embodying certain values and character traits

that include being "easygoing, friendly, open, trusting, humble, generous, loyal to family and friends, and indifferent to achieved status distinctions." These traits are viewed as consonant with idealized Native Hawaiian culture and as discordant with haole or American values and ideals of individualism, competition, achievement, and contractual relations. Yamamoto, "From Japanese to Local: Community Change and the Redefinition of Sansei Identity in Hawaii" (Undergraduate thesis, Sociology Department, University of Hawaii, 1974), 105; Okamura, "Aloha Kanaka Me Ke Aloha 'Aina,'" 127–128.

55. Edna Oshiro, "The Americanization of My Mother," *Social Process in Hawaii* 18 (1954), 30.

56. Baker, "Human Nature in Hawaii," 334.

57. Takaki, *Pau Hana*, 78–80; U.S. Commissioner of Labor, *Report of the Commissioner of Labor on Hawaii, 1901* (Washington: Government Printing Office, 1902), 101, tables V and VI, 141–253.

58. U.S. Bureau of Labor Statistics, *Report, 1915*, table B; U.S. Bureau of Labor Statistics, *Report, 1910*, 48–50.

59. Lind, "Changing Position of Domestic Servants," 77.

60. Ibid.

61. Document MA hl 27m, 2, Romanzo Adams Papers, Department of Sociology, University of Hawaii–Manoa.

62. Document MA 15 I, 4–5, Romanzo Adams Papers; Document MA 18-I 3, Romanzo Adams Papers.

63. Porteus and Babcock, *Temperament and Race*, 46. The idealization of the Chinese and Native Hawaiians as less assertive and more agreeable was nostalgic nonsense; when these groups were the main labor force, they also resisted control, ran away, and engaged in violence, arson, and strikes, prompting bitter complaints from managers and overseers. See Takaki, *Pau Hana*, 127–152.

64. Henry Toyama and Kiyoshi Ikeda have characterized the relationship between the Naichi and the Okinawans as analogous to that between the British and the Irish, with feelings of superiority on one side and defensiveness on the other. This analogy has some aptness because of a colonial relationship between Japan and Okinawa. Okinawan culture had been influenced by cultures from the south such as from Taiwan and the Philippines, and its language, though belonging to the same family as Japanese, had become separated sometime before the sixth century A.D. After annexation and conversion into a prefecture, Okinawans were subject to government policies aimed at assimilating them into the dominant Japanese culture and language. In Hawaii, Okinawans were set apart not only by culture and language but also by their arrival after the Naichi had already established themselves. See Toyama and Ikeda, "Okinawan-Naichi Relationship," 51, 54–55; and the following articles, all in Ethnic Studies Oral History Project, *Uchinanchu: A History of Okinawans in Hawaii* (Honolulu, 1981): Mitsugu Sakihara, "History of Okinawa," 7–10; Tomonori Ishikawa, "A Study of the Historical Geography of Early Okinawan Immigrants to the Hawaiian Islands," 82; Mitsugu Sakihara, "Okinawans in Hawaii: An Overview of the Past 80 Years," 110–112.

65. Dorothy Ochiai Hazama and Jane Okamoto Komeji, *Okage Sama De: The Japanese in Hawaii, 1885–1985* (Honolulu: Bess Press, 1986), 71–76.

66. Tamura, *Americanization*, 27.

67. Ibid., 15, 17, 208.

68. U.S. Commissioner of Labor, *Report, 1902,* 37; Louise H. Hunter, *Buddhism in Hawaii: Its Impact on a Yankee Community* (Honolulu: University of Hawaii Press, 1971), 71–73; Tamura, *Americanization,* 15, 17, 208; U.S. Bureau of Labor Statistics, *Report, 1910,* 72.

69. Tamura, *Americanization,* 205; Beechert, *Working in Hawaii,* 197.

70. Tamura, *Americanization,* 146–147.

71. Ibid., 205, 146, 71–72.

72. Takaki, *Pau Hana,* 127–129.

73. Ibid., 130–131.

74. Ibid., 131.

75. Franklin S. Oda and Harry Minoru Urata, "Hole Hole Bushi: Songs of Hawaii's Japanese Immigrants," *Mana* (Hawaii ed.) 6, no. 1 (1981), 72.

76. Yukio Uyehara, "The Horehore-Bushi: A Type of Japanese Folksong Developed and Sung among the Early Immigrants in Hawaii," *Social Process in Hawaii* 28 (1980–81), 115, 116.

77. Ibid., 114.

78. Gary Y. Okihiro, *Cane Fires: The Anti-Japanese Movement in Hawaii, 1865–1945* (Philadelphia: Temple University Press, 1991), 32.

79. Odo and Urata, "Hole Hole Bushi," 74. *Pake* is the local term for Chinese.

80. Tamura, *Americanization,* 19–20.

81. Masaji Marumoto, "First Year Immigrants to Hawaii and Eugene Van Reed," in Hilary Conroy and T. Scott Miyakawa, eds., *East across the Pacific: Historical and Sociological Studies of Japanese Immigration and Assimilation* (Santa Barbara: ABC Clio, 1972), 33; Hilary Conroy, "The Japanese Frontier in Hawaii, 1868–1898," *University of California Publications in History* 46 (1953), 30, 65; Okihiro, *Cane Fires,* 22, 23–26; Ernest Katsumi Wakukawa, *A History of the Japanese People in Hawaii* (Honolulu: Toyo Shoin, 1938), 28, 39.

82. Fuchs, *Hawaii Pono,* 113–114.

83. Takaki, *Pau Hana,* 148–149; U.S. Commissioner of Labor, *Report, 1901,* 17, 112–115, table 7, 254–257.

84. U.S. Bureau of Labor Statistics, *Report, 1905,* 140; Beechert, *Working in Hawaii,* 163–169.

85. Takaki, *Pau Hana,* 154; U.S. Bureau of Labor Statistics, *Report, 1910,* 64, 65–75.

86. Quoted in Takaki, *Pau Hana,* 160; Okihiro, *Cane Fires,* 51–53.

87. Okihiro, *Cane Fires,* 55–57.

88. Beechert, *Working in Hawaii,* 196–197, 199–201; Okihiro, *Cane Fires,* 68.

89. Okihiro, *Cane Fires,* 71; Beechert, *Working in Hawaii,* 199.

90. Beechert, *Working in Hawaii,* 204–208; Okihiro, *Cane Fires,* 80; Fuchs, *Hawaii Pono,* 225.

91. Beechert, *Working in Hawaii,* 240–242; Fuchs, *Hawaii Pono,* 51.

92. Fuchs, *Hawaii Pono,* 50; Tamura, *Americanization,* 59.

93. U.S. Bureau of Labor Statistics, *Report, 1915,* 41; Fuchs, *Hawaii Pono,* 219.

94. Tamura, *Americanization,* 147–150, 73–74.

95. Ibid., 112. Tamura (113) notes that until World War II "Caucasians" constituted half of all students in the English Standard schools but only 2.5 percent in non-Standard schools. Japanese made up 3–8.5 percent of the students in English Standard and 55 percent in non-Standard public schools. Native Hawaiian, Portu-

guese, and Chinese students were more equally represented in proportion to their numbers in the public schools.

96. John Higham, *Strangers in the Land: Patterns of American Nativism, 1860–1925*, 2d ed. (New Brunswick: Rutgers University Press, 1994), 234–261; John F. McClymer, "Gender and the 'American Way of Life': Women in the Americanization Movement," *Journal of American Ethnic History* 10 (Spring 1991), 3–20; Gayle Gullett, "Women Progressives and the Politics of Americanization in California, 1915–1920," *Pacific Historical Review* 64 (Feb. 1995), 71–74. The Hawaii delegate to the U.S. House of Representatives, a native Hawaiian, complained that Hawaii was not included in federal funding of Americanization programs. U.S. Congress, Senate Subcommittee on Immigration, *Japanese in Hawaii* (Washington: Government Printing Office, 1920), 42.

97. Tamura, *Americanization*, 60.

98. Fuchs, *Hawaii Pono*, 266, 269–270.

99. Ibid., 271–288.

100. Fuchs, *Hawaii Pono*, 291; Tamura, *Americanization*, 133–135.

101. Tamura, *Americanization*, 62; Okihiro, *Cane Fires*, 142, 144.

102. Tamura, *Americanization*, 63, 64.

103. Ibid., 135–137.

104. Ibid., 137–139, 140.

105. Lind, *Hawaii's People*, 82, 99.

106. Ibid., 99; Fuchs, *Hawaii Pono*, 177.

107. U.S. Congress, *Japanese in Hawaii*, 9–10.

108. Ibid., 10.

109. *Maui Shimbun* (newspaper) "Get Your Right to Vote," Feb. 9, 1915, trans. Wesley Ueunten; *Hawaii Hochi* (newspaper), "Citizenship! Citizenship! Reporting to Those Obtaining Citizenship," June 11, 1915, trans. Wesley Ueunten.

110. Romanzo Adams, *The Peoples of Hawaii* (Honolulu: American Council, Institute of Pacific Relations, 1933), 18; Fuchs, *Hawaii Pono*, 135. The ratio of female to male voters remained low.

111. U.S. Bureau of Labor Statistics, *Labor in the Territory of Hawaii, 1939* (Washington: Government Printing Office, 1940), 79.

7. Understanding American Inequality

1. In the transmittal letter for his report *Labor Conditions in Hawaii, 1905*, U.S. Commissioner of Labor Charles P. Neill acknowledges "Dr. Victor S. Clark, who collected the material therefor and assisted largely in the preparation of the text" (6). Clark was the sole author of *Mexican Labor in the United States*, Department of Commerce and Labor Bulletin no. 78 (Washington: Government Printing Office, 1908). He also wrote *Porto Rico and Its Problems* (Washington: Brookings Institution, 1930).

2. U.S. Congress, Senate, Hearing before a Subcommittee of the Committee on Immigration, 66th Cong., 2d sess., *Japanese in Hawaii* (Washington: Government Printing Office, 1920), 9–10.

3. Susan Gooden, "Local Discretion and Welfare Policy: The Case of Virginia (1911–1970)," paper presented at the Meetings of the Social Science History Association, Washington, 1997, 3–4.

4. Ian F. Haney López, *White by Law: The Legal Construction of Race* (New York: New York University Press, 1996), appendix A, table 2, 204–206.

5. Gary Y. Okihiro, *Cane Fires: The Anti-Japanese Movement in Hawaii, 1865–1945* (Philadelphia: Temple University Press, 1991), 207–224.

6. Tera W. Hunter, *To 'Joy My Freedom: Southern Black Women's Lives and Labors after the Civil War* (Cambridge, Mass.: Harvard University Press, 1997), 187–218.

7. Stanley D. Porteus and Marjorie E. Babcock, *Temperament and Race* (Boston: Richard G. Badger, 1926), 49.

8. Clark, *Mexican Labor*, 484.

9. David M. Katzman, *Seven Days a Week: Women and Domestic Service in Industrializing America* (New York: Oxford University Press, 1978), 192–193.

10. David Montejano, *Anglos and Mexicans in the Making of Texas, 1836–1986* (Austin: University of Texas Press, 1987), 186.

11. Tomás Almaguer, *Racial Fault Lines: The Historical Origins of White Supremacy in California* (Berkeley: University of California Press, 1994), 212.

12. Karen Brodkin Sacks, *Caring by the Hour: Women, Work and Organizing at Duke Medical Center* (Urbana: University of Illinois Press, 1988), 138–141.

13. Benedict Anderson, *Imagined Community: Reflections on the Origin and Spread of Nationalism*, rev. ed. (London: Verso, 1991), 67–82.

14. James B. McKee, *Sociology and the Race Question: The Failure of a Perspective* (Urbana: University of Illinois Press, 1993), 96–97.

15. Jamie Fellner and Marc Mauer, *Losing the Vote: The Impact of Felony Disfranchisement Laws in the United States* (New York: Human Rights Watch, 1998), overview and summary.

Index